VISUAL QUICKSTART GUIDE

Photoshop 4

FOR WINDOWS

Elaine Weinmann
Peter Lourekas

 **Peachpit Press**

Visual QuickStart Guide
Photoshop 4 for Windows
Elaine Weinmann and Peter Lourekas

Peachpit Press
2414 Sixth Street
Berkeley, CA 94710
510/548-4393
510/548-5991 (fax)

Find us on the World Wide Web at: http://www.peachpit.com
Peachpit Press is a division of Addison Wesley Longman

Cover design: The Visual Group
Interior design: Elaine Weinmann
Production: Elaine Weinmann and Peter Lourekas
Illustrations: Elaine Weinmann and Peter Lourekas, except as noted

Colophon
This book was created with QuarkXPress 3.3 on a Macintosh
Quadra 650 and Power Macintosh 8500. The fonts used were
Sabon and Futura from Adobe Systems Inc. and Anna and Gillies
Gothic from Image Club Graphics, Inc.

ISBN 0-201-68842-5
9 8 7 6 5 4 3 2 1

Printed and bound in the United States of America

In memory of Bert Weinmann
(1924-1996)
Loving, vivacious, and courageous spirit

Introduction

Photoshop 4.0 is not an earth-shaking upgrade, but, nevertheless, all the instructions needed revision and every dialog box and palette required reshooting for this edition (such is the life of computer book authors!). Also included in this new edition are scads of new keyboard shortcuts and a sprinkling of new features. Our favorite new feature is adjustment layers, which you can use to try out various color or tonal adjustments to underlying layers without having to make them permanent. We use adjustment layers so often, we honestly can't imagine Photoshop-ing without them.

And, to our great astonishment, we actually deleted or shortened some pages from the previous edition because many procedures have been streamlined and no longer require cumbersome work-arounds. When you create text in 4.0, for example, it automatically appears on its own layer—no more fiddling around with floating selections. It's as if the folks at Adobe spied on Photoshop power users and said, "Hmm, if we redesign this feature to work this way, people won't have to bother doing such-and-such, and they'll be much happier." Version 4.0 tries to do more with less. The streamlining process allowed us to sneak in oodles of new tips and suggestions, and new—and larger—illustrations (we couldn't resist). This book also includes a whole new and expanded color section, with imagery by real pros.

We've always encouraged our readers to be creative and to experiment with whatever application they're working in. We've resisted bogging down beginning Photoshoppers in the technical aspects of the program, especially since there are already so many humongous tomes in the marketplace that can be used as reference guides. These days, however, not only do you have to come up with a stunning visual concept and execute it with finesse—on a deadline—you must also navigate the image through other software applications and then shepherd it through the shark-infested waters of color separation, or get it onto the Web and make it look remotely like the dazzling image you started with (sound familiar?). So we've included more techy stuff in this edition, topics like getting Photoshop images onto the Web, and producing color separations. But this book is still light and thin enough to be called a Visual QuickStart Guide, stuff into a mini backpack, and leaf through without having to take your other hand off the mouse.

Whether you're a student learning Photoshop for the first time, or a seasoned freelance artist who uses our books as a "cheat sheet," you're certain to find something in this volume that will help you. Because what hasn't changed is our boil-it-down-to-the-essentials, haiku writing style and the fact that we think illustrations really do tell much of the story—certainly when it comes to computer graphics. In fact, this new and improved edition contains more than a thousand images! Dive in.

TABLE OF CONTENTS

Chapter 4: **Navigate**

Table of Contents

Table of Contents

Table of Contents

Table of Contents

THE BASICS 1

Hardware you'll need to run Photoshop

Photoshop will run on an Intel 80386 or higher PC processor; Windows95, Windows NT, or DOS 5.0 or later for Windows 3.1x; a hard drive with at least 20 megabytes of available space after loading Photoshop's 20 megabytes of data; and at least 16 megabytes of RAM (random access memory) allocated to the application. You'll also need a CD-ROM drive to install the software (though a floppy drive version can be ordered). Photoshop will run faster on a Pentium with 32 megabytes of RAM and a large hard drive with at least 50 megabytes of available space. For optimal speed, we recommend a 200 megahertz Intel processor, 32 megabytes or more of RAM, and a large, fast access hard drive (one to four gigabyte, 9-11 millisecond random seek time). For even better performance, add the new Intel MMX chipset. For those who need very fast processing, Photoshop 4.0 supports multi-processors on the Windows NT platform.

Photoshop requires a lot of RAM: about four times the size of the file! The number of layers, channels, and pixels in an image also impact on the amount of RAM required for processing and the amount of storage space an image occupies. To improve Photoshop's performance speed, try installing more RAM.

Color monitors display 8-bit, 16-bit, or 24-bit color, depending on the video card or Video RAM. With an 8-bit card, 256 colors are available for on-screen color mixing. With a 24-bit card, 16.7 million colors are available. A 24-bit card provides optimal display, because every color can be represented exactly. All Photoshop pictures are saved as 24-bit, regardless of the monitor's resolution.

Hardware

LOUREKAS / WEINMANN

File size units

Byte	=	8 bits of digital information *(approx. one black or white pixel, or one character)*
Kilobyte (KB)	=	1,024 bytes
Megabyte (MB)	=	1,024 kilobytes
Gigabyte (GB)	=	1,024 megabytes

You'll probably also need to purchase a removable storage device—such as an Iomega Zip or Jaz drive, an EZFlyer Syquest drive, or an optical drive—to back up files and to transport files to and from your print shop or other output service.

Memory allocation

To learn how much RAM you have available to allocate to Photoshop, launch Photoshop and any other applications that you want to run at the same time, click on the Start button in the Taskbar, choose Settings, then click on Control Panel. In the Control Panel window, double-click the System icon and click on the Performance tab to find the percentage of free system resources. The total amount of RAM is also indicated 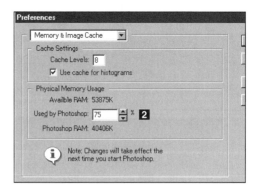.

You should allocate as much RAM as possible to Photoshop. To do this, in Photoshop, choose File menu > Preferences, then click on Memory & Image Cache 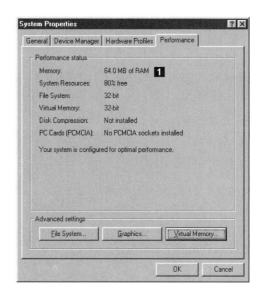. The default percentage of RAM used by Photoshop is 75%. The Available RAM and Photoshop RAM are also indicated. To adjust the percentage of RAM to be used by Photoshop, click on the spinners or enter a percentage. Any changes you make will take effect when you re-launch Photoshop.

When Photoshop requires more RAM for processing than is assigned to it in the Memory & Image Cache dialog box, it uses available hard drive space that has been allocated as the scratch disk (see page 232), a technique known as using virtual memory. The amount of RAM assigned to Photoshop cannot be greater than the amount of available hard drive space, because Photoshop writes the entire contents of its RAM segment whenever it can. Processing is much faster in actual RAM than in virtual memory.

Purge

Use the Edit > **Purge** commands periodically to regain RAM used for the Clipboard or the Undo, Define Pattern, or Take Snapshot command. The Purge commands can't be undone.

Memory Allocation

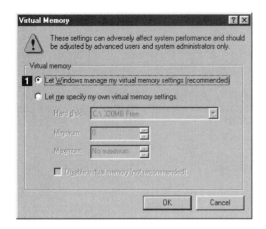

Virtual memory

In most cases, you should let Windows manage your virtual memory settings. If you decide, for some reason, that you want to specify your own virtual memory settings, you should not disable the virtual memory option in the Performance tab of the System Properies in the Control Panel. If you are using a PC with only 16MB of total RAM (which means you're really short on RAM), turn on the "Let Windows manage my virtual memory settings (recommended)" button **1**. Using virtual memory, Windows writes to its designated scratch disk drive when it runs out of RAM.

Accelerators

Application accelerators can speed up certain Photoshop functions, like RGB-to-CMYK conversions, Gaussian Blur filter, Sharpen filter, etc.). Third-party accelerators, in order to achieve Photoshop-like results when performing a filter function, use their own processes to alter pixels, not Photoshop's algorithms. If you opt to purchase a third-party product, choose one that bears the Adobe Charged logo. These accelerators will make some Photoshop functions run faster on older Pentium machines. The latest Intel MMX chipset is sufficiently powerful that the advantages of adding this type of accelerator are minimal.

With sufficient Video RAM installed on a graphics card (4 MB or more), a new Intel chipset will perform fast screen redraw. The faster the screen redraw, the faster you'll be able to work in Photoshop.

Scratch disk info

Choose **Scratch Sizes** (press the arrowhead at the bottom of an image window) to see how much RAM is currently used by all open Photoshop files (the left number) **2**, and how much RAM has been allocated to Photoshop (the right number) **3**. When the left number is greater than the right number, the scratch disk is being used. Choose **Efficiency** from the same drop-down menu to see what percentage of RAM is being used. A percentage below 100 also indicates the scratch disk is being used.

The Photoshop screen

5 Application close box

4 Application maximize button

1 Application Control menu box

2 Menu bar

3 Application minimize button

Document Control menu box

6 Title bar/display size/target layer name

Document minimize button

Document close box

7 Rulers

The image window.

8 Layers/Channels/Paths group.

11 Window border, window corner

9 Toolbox

10 Sizes bar: displays Document Sizes, Scratch Sizes, Efficiency, or Timing information.

Document Sizes
✓ Scratch Sizes
Efficiency
Timing

Press on the Sizes bar to display a page preview: A thumbnail of the image relative to the paper size, including custom printing marks, if chosen).

8 Brushes/Options group.

Hold down Alt and press and hold on the Sizes bar to display the image's dimensions, number of channels, mode, and resolution.

8 Color/Swatches group.

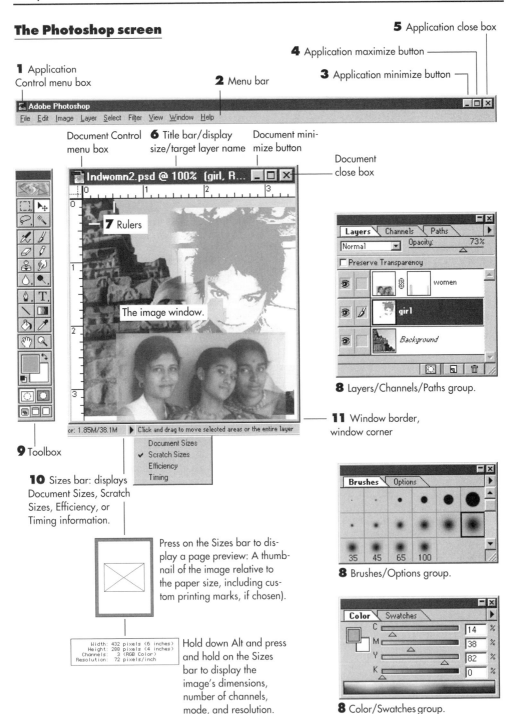

Key to the Photoshop screen

1 *Application (or Document) Control menu box*
The Application Control menu box commands are Restore, Move, Size, Minimize, Maximize, and Close. The Document Control menu box commands are Restore, Move, Size, Minimize, Maximize, Close, and Next.

2 *Menu bar*
Press any menu heading to access dialog boxes, submenus, and commands.

3 *Application (or Document) minimize button*
Click the Application Minimize button to shrink the document to an icon in the Taskbar. Click the icon on the Taskbar to restore the application window to its previous size.

Click the Document Minimize button to shrink the document to an icon at the bottom left corner of the application window. Click the icon to restore the document window to its previous size.

4 *Application (or Document) maximize/restore button*
Click the Application or Document Restore button to restore a window to its previous size. When a window is at the restored size, the Restore button turns into the Maximize button. Click the Maximize button to enlarge the window.

5 *Close box*
To close an image or a palette, click its close box.

6 *Title bar/display size/target layer name*
The image's title, color mode, and display size, and the name of the current target layer.

7 *Rulers*
Choose Show Rulers from the View menu to display rulers. The position of the cursor is indicated by a mark on each ruler. Choose ruler units in the Units & Rulers Preferences dialog box (see page 230).

8 *Palettes*
There are ten moveable palettes. Some palettes are grouped together: Layers/Channels/Paths, Brushes/Options, and Color/Swatches. Click a tab (palette name) to bring that palette to the front of its group. The other palettes are displayed individually.

9 *Toolbox*
Press Tab to hide the Toolbox and all open palettes. Press Tab again to display the Toolbox and all previously displayed palettes.

10 *Sizes bar*
When Document Sizes is chosen from the Sizes bar pop-up menu, the Sizes bar displays the file storage size when all layers are flattened and any alpha channels are removed (the first amount) and the file storage size when the layers are separate (the second amount).

When Scratch Sizes is chosen, the bar displays the amount of storage space Photoshop is using for all currently open pictures and the amount of RAM currently available to Photoshop. When the first amount is greater than the second amount, Photoshop is using virtual memory on the scratch disk.

When Efficiency is chosen, the bar indicates the percentage of RAM being used. A percentage below 100 indicates the scratch disk is being used.

11 *Window border, Window corner*
Press and drag a horizontal or vertical border or a corner to resize the window.

The Toolbox

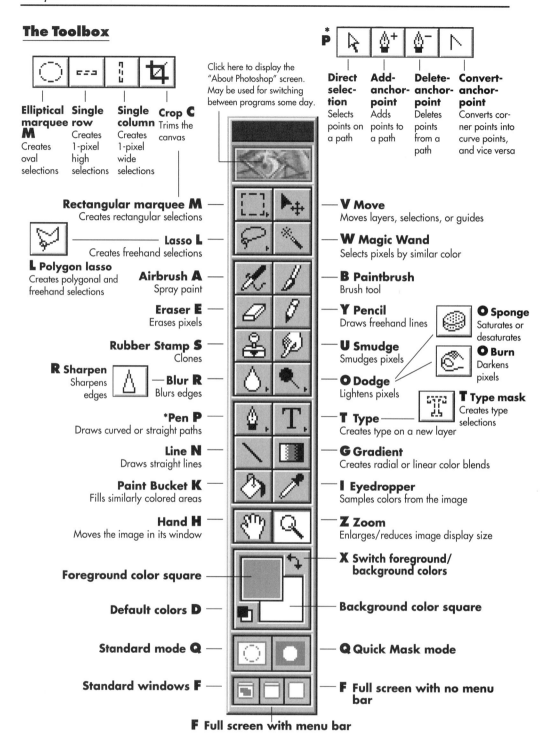

Elliptical marquee M
Creates oval selections

Single row
Creates 1-pixel high selections

Single column
Creates 1-pixel wide selections

Crop C
Trims the canvas

Click here to display the "About Photoshop" screen. May be used for switching between programs some day.

Direct selection
Selects points on a path

Add-anchor-point
Adds points to a path

Delete-anchor-point
Deletes points from a path

Convert-anchor-point
Converts corner points into curve points, and vice versa

Rectangular marquee M — Creates rectangular selections

V Move
Moves layers, selections, or guides

Lasso L — Creates freehand selections

W Magic Wand
Selects pixels by similar color

L Polygon lasso
Creates polygonal and freehand selections

Airbrush A — Spray paint

B Paintbrush
Brush tool

Eraser E — Erases pixels

Y Pencil
Draws freehand lines

O Sponge
Saturates or desaturates

Rubber Stamp S — Clones

U Smudge
Smudges pixels

O Burn
Darkens pixels

R Sharpen
Sharpens edges

Blur R — Blurs edges

O Dodge
Lightens pixels

T Type mask
Creates type selections

*Pen P — Draws curved or straight paths

T Type
Creates type on a new layer

Line N — Draws straight lines

G Gradient
Creates radial or linear color blends

Paint Bucket K — Fills similarly colored areas

I Eyedropper
Samples colors from the image

Hand H — Moves the image in its window

Z Zoom
Enlarges/reduces image display size

Foreground color square —

X Switch foreground/ background colors

Default colors D —

Background color square

Standard mode Q —

Q Quick Mask mode

Standard windows F —

F Full screen with no menu bar

F Full screen with menu bar

On-screen help

To learn a tool name or shortcut or a palette option in Photoshop 4.0 or later, simply rest the pointer—without clicking or pressing the mouse button—on the tool or palette icon you're interested in **1**. (Check the Show Tool Tips box in the File menu > Preferences > General dialog box to access this feature.)

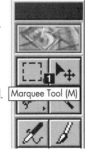

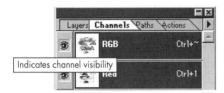

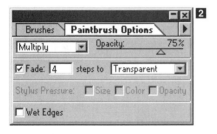

Context menus-try this!

To choose from an on screen context menu, right-click on a Layers, Channels, or Paths palette thumbnail or name or other area of a palette **3**. Or choose a tool, then right-click with the pointer over the image window to access options for that tool **4**.

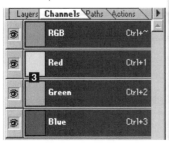

How to use the Toolbox

Press Tab to hide or show the Toolbox and all open palettes. Press Shift-Tab to hide/show all palettes except the Toolbox. Drag the top of the Toolbox to move it around.

To choose a tool whose icon is currently visible, click once on its icon. Press and drag to choose a hidden tool from a pull-out menu. Or choose tools using the shortcuts listed on the previous page. If you forget a tool's shortcut, just leave the cursor over the tool for a moment, and context sensitive help will remind you! **1** Keep pressing the same shortcut key to "cycle through" hidden, related tools, or Option-click the currently visible tool.

Choose attributes for a tool—like a blending mode or opacity percentage—from its Options palette **2**. If the Brushes palette is in front of the Options palette, double-click the tool to bring the Options palette to the front, or press Enter if the tool is already highlighted. You can also customize some tools using the Brushes, Swatches, and Color palettes. From the Brushes palette, you can choose a predefined brush tip or you can create your own brush tip. For example, you can make an Airbrush tool tip soft and transparent, or a Paintbrush stroke round and opaque.

To restore a tool's default settings, click the tool, then choose Reset Tool from the Options palette command menu. Choose Reset All Tools from the Options palette command menu to restore the default settings for all the tools.

To choose whether tool cursors look like their Toolbox icons or a crosshair, see page 228.

Mini-glossary

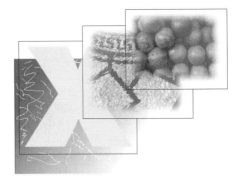

Target layer and layer transparency

The currently highlighted layer on the Layers palette, and the only layer that can be edited. An image can have just a Background (no layers) or it can be multi-layered. Layers can be restacked and moved, and are transparent where there are no pixels, so you can see through a whole stack of them. The advantage of working with multiple layers is that you can assign image components to separate layers and edit them individually without changing the other layers.

Layers are like clear acetate sheets: opaque where there is imagery and transparent where there is no imagery.

Adjustment layer

Unlike a standard layer, modifications made to an adjustment layer don't alter actual pixels until it is merged with the layers below it, so adjustment layers can be used for experimenting with color or tonal adjustments. Only layers below the adjustment layer are affected.

The Layers palette for a four-layer image. "water" is the target (currently active) layer.

Pixels (picture elements)

The dots used to display a bitmapped image on a rectangular grid on a computer screen.

Individual pixels are discernible in this image, which is shown at 500% view.

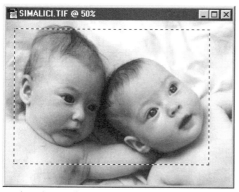

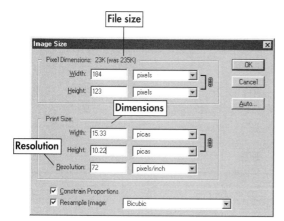

A selected area of an image.

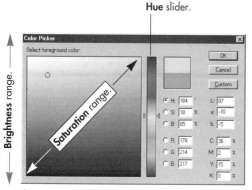

Photoshop's **Color Picker**.

Selection

An area of an image that is isolated so it can be modified while the rest of the image is protected. A moving marquee marks the boundary of a selection. If you move a non-floating selection, the cutout area that's left behind will be filled automatically with the current Background color if the selection is on the Background, or with transparency if the selection is on a layer.

Floating selection

A floating selection is created when a selection is Control-Alt-dragged or transformed, and, while it is still selected, it floats above and can be altered without affecting, the underlying pixels in the target layer. Once it is deselected (defloated), floating selection pixels are merged with the pixels in the layer directly below it.

Resolution

Image resolution is the number of pixels contained in an image, and is measured in pixels per inch. The monitor's resolution is also measured in pixels per inch. Output devices also have their own resolution, which is measured in dots per inch.

File size

The file size of an image, which is measured in bytes, kilobytes, megabytes, or gigabytes.

Dimensions

The width and height of an image.

Brightness

The lightness (luminance) of a color.

Hue

The wavelength of light that gives a color its name—such as red or blue—irrespective of its brightness and saturation.

Saturation

The purity of a color. The more gray a color contains, the lower is its saturation.

(See Appendix B: Glossary for more definitions.)

Mini-Glossary

The menus

File menu

File menu commands are used to create, open, place, close, save, scan, import, export, or print an image, set preferences, and exit Photoshop.

Edit menu

Edit menu commands include Undo, which undoes the last modification made, the Clipboard commands Cut and Copy, and the Paste commands. The Fill, Stroke, and Define Pattern commands are also executed via the Edit menu. The Purge commands free up memory used by the Undo, Clipboard, Snapshot, or Pattern buffer.

Image menu

An image can be converted to any of eight black-and-white or color modes via the Mode submenu. The invaluable Adjust commands modify an image's color, saturation, brightness, or contrast. The Image Size command modifies an image's file size, dimensions, or resolution. The Canvas Size dialog box is used to add or subtract from an image's editable canvas area.

Layer menu

Layer menu commands add, duplicate, delete, modify, add masks to, group, transform, merge, and flatten layers. Many of these commands can also be accessed via the Layers palette command menu.

The Menus

Select menu

The "All" Select menu command selects an entire layer. The None command deselects all selections. Other Select menu commands enlarge, contract, smooth, or feather selection edges, and save selections to and from channels. The Color Range command creates selections based on color.

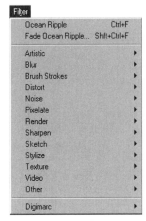

Filter menu

Filters, which perform a wide range of image editing functions, are organized in pop-up menu groups. The Fade command lessens the effect of the last applied filter or Adjust command. The Digimarc filter embeds a copyright watermark in an image.

View menu

View menu commands control new view creation, display sizes, and the display of rulers, guides, and grids. The Gamut Warning highlights colors that won't print on a four-color press. Choose CMYK Preview to see how your image looks in CMYK color without actually changing its mode.

Window menu

Window menu commands display or hide the palettes. Open images are also listed and can be activated via the Window menu.

Help menu

Help menu commands provide access to on-screen support. Choose How to Use Help to learn about the Help commands. Plug-in information can also be accessed from this menu. If you are connected to the World Wide Web, you can access the Adobe Photoshop Home Page from this menu. If an image has a URL as part of its file information, you can click on Open Image URL to open the Web site from which the image was obtained.

The Menus

11

The palettes

How to use the palettes

There are ten moveable palettes that are used for image editing. To save screen space, some of the palettes are joined into groups: **Color/Swatches, Brushes/Options,** and **Layers/Channels/Paths.** The other palettes are **Navigator, Actions,** and **Info.**

You can **separate** a palette from its group by dragging its tab (palette name) **1**–**2**. You can **add** a palette to any group by dragging the tab over the group. When you release the mouse it will be the frontmost palette in the group. The Layers/Channels/Paths group window can be widened, so if you want to gather more palettes together, use this one as your home base so the tabs (palette names) will be readable across the top.

To **open** a palette, choose Show [palette name] from the Window menu. The palette will appear in front in its group.

To **display** an open palette at the front of its group, click its tab (palette name).

Resize any palette other than Color, Options, or Info by dragging its size box (lower right corner).

Press Tab to hide or display all open palettes and the Toolbox. Press Shift-Tab to show/hide all open palettes except the Toolbox.

To shrink a palette, double-click its tab or click the palette zoom box (upper right corner, to the left of of the close button). If the palette is not at its default size, click the zoom box once to restore its default size, then click a second time to shrink the palette.

If the Save Palette Locations box is checked in the File menu > Preferences > General dialog box, palettes that are open when you exit Photoshop will appear in their same location when you re-launch Photoshop. To restore the palettes' default groupings when you launch Photoshop, click Reset Palette Locations to Default in the same dialog box.

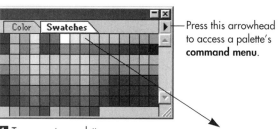

Press this arrowhead to access a palette's **command menu**.

1 To separate a palette from its group, drag the tab (palette name) away from the palette group.

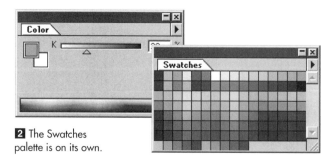

2 The Swatches palette is on its own.

You can resize a palette by clicking once on its Zoom box.

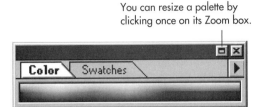

You can further shrink a palette by double-clicking its name or by Alt-clicking its Zoom box.

Color palette

The Color palette is used for mixing and choosing colors to apply with the painting, editing, and fill tools. Choose a color model for the palette from the palette command menu. Click the Foreground or Background color square to access the Color Picker, from which you can also choose a color. You can quick-select a color from the color bar on the bottom of the palette.

Foreground color square.
The currently active square
has a white border.

Background color square.

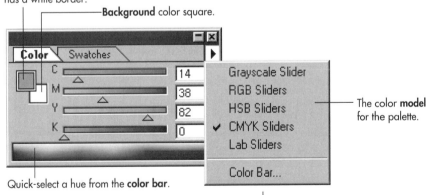

The color **model**
for the palette.

Quick-select a hue from the **color bar**.

Choose Color Bar from the Color palette command menu or Control-click the color bar on the Color palette to open the Color Bar dialog box, then choose a **display style** for the color bar from the Style drop-down menu. Or Shift-click the color bar to cycle through the Styles.

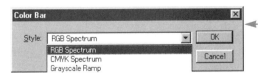

13

Swatches palette

The Swatches palette is used for selecting already mixed colors to be applied with the painting, editing, and fill tools. Individual swatches can be added to and deleted from the palette. Custom swatch palettes can also be loaded, appended, and saved using Swatches palette commands.

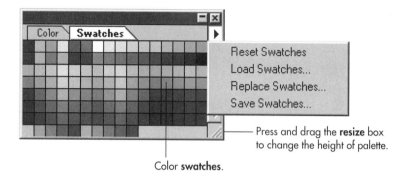

Press and drag the **resize** box to change the height of palette.

Color **swatches**.

Channels palette

The Channels palette is used to display one or more of the channels that make up an image and any specially created alpha channels, which are used for saving selections. The Channels palette can also be used to display layer masks.

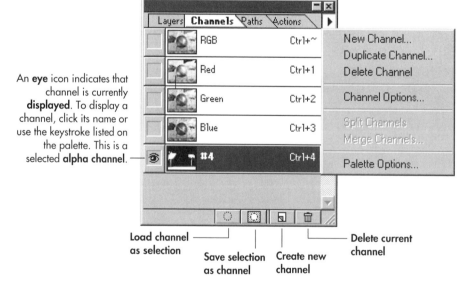

An **eye** icon indicates that channel is currently **displayed**. To display a channel, click its name or use the keystroke listed on the palette. This is a selected **alpha channel**.

Load channel as selection

Save selection as channel

Create new channel

Delete current channel

Brushes palette

The Brushes palette is used for defining a tool's tip size, edge, and angle. You can choose from preset brushes or you can create your own brushes. You can also load, append, and save brushes using the Brushes palette command menu.

Hard-edged tips in this row.

Soft-edged tips in these rows.

Large brush tips. The number is the tip diameter in pixels.

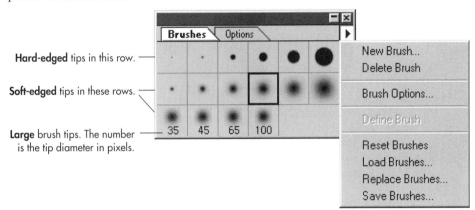

Options palette

The Options palette is used to define attributes for a tool, such as its Opacity, Fade distance, or mode. Options are set for each tool individually. You can reset the currently selected tool or all tools using Options palette commands. If the Brushes palette is in front of the Options palette, click the Options tab, or double-click a tool to bring the Options palette to the front, or press Enter if the tool is already highlighted.

The **Pressure** or **Opacity** slider.

The **mode** drop-down menu.

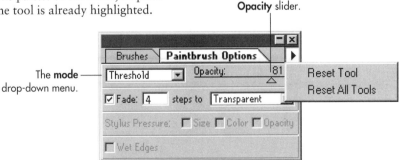

The Options palette when the Paintbrush tool is selected.

Layers palette

Normally, when you create a new image, it will have an opaque Background. Using the Layers palette, you can add, delete, hide/show, duplicate, and rearrange layers on top of the Background. Each layer can be assigned its own mode and opacity and can be edited separately without changing the other layers. You can also attach a mask to a layer. (To specify that the bottommost tier of a new image be a layer with transparency instead of an opaque Background, click Content: Transparent in the New dialog box.)

If you're using Photoshop 4 or later, you can also create **adjustment layers,** which are temporary layers that are used for trying out various color or tonal adjustments using the Adjust commands. An adjustment layer's effects do not become permanent until it's merged with the layer below it.

Only the currently highlighted layer, called the **target layer,** can be edited. Click on a layer name on the Layers palette to highlight it. The name of the target layer will be listed on the image window title bar.

Layers take up storage space, so when you're done with your multi-layer image, you can merge or flatten the layers into one.

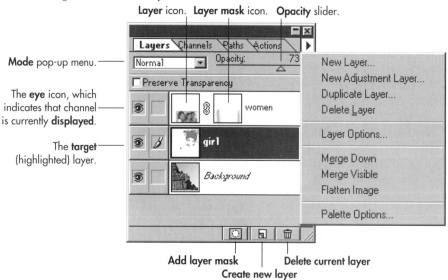

Layer icon. **Layer mask** icon. **Opacity** slider.

Mode pop-up menu.

The **eye** icon, which indicates that channel is currently **displayed**.

The **target** (highlighted) layer.

Add layer mask   Delete current layer
        Create new layer

Paths palette

Paths are composed of curved and straight line segments connected by anchor points. A path can be drawn directly with the Pen tool or a selection can be converted into a path. The Pen tool and its relatives, the Add-anchor-point tool, Delete-anchor-point tool, and Convert-anchor-point-tool, can be used to reshape a path. Paths are saved and accessed via the Paths palette.

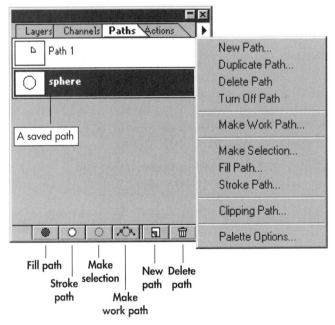

Navigator palette

The Navigator palette is used for moving an image in its window, and for changing an image's display size.

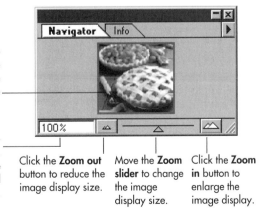

Drag in the preview box to **move** the image in the image window. Control-drag in the preview box to marquee the area you want to magnify.

Enter the desired **zoom percentage** (or ratio, like 1:1 or 4:1), then press **Enter**. To zoom to the percentage and keep the field highlighted, press Shift-Enter.

Click the **Zoom out** button to reduce the image display size.

Move the **Zoom slider** to change the image display size.

Click the **Zoom in** button to enlarge the image display.

Info palette

The Info palette displays a breakdown of the color of the pixel currently under the pointer. The Info palette also shows the x/y position of the pointer on the image. If a color adjustment dialog box is open, the palette will also display before and after color readouts. Other information, such as the distance between points when a selection is moved or a line is drawn, the dimensions of a crop marquee, or the angle of a selection as it's rotated, may display on the palette, depending on which tool is being used.

An exclamation point indicates the color currently under the pointer is **out of gamut** (isn't printable on a four-color press).

RGB and **CMYK readouts** for the pixel currently under the pointer.

Choose a **color model, Total Ink**, or **Opacity** for the readout by pressing this arrowhead.

Press on this arrowhead to choose a different **unit of measure** for the palette.

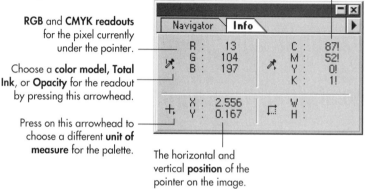

The horizontal and vertical **position** of the pointer on the image.

Actions palette

Alas, the Commands palette is no longer. You can use the Actions palette, however, to create and access command shortcuts. The Actions palette's main purpose is to automate image processing by recording a series of commands and then replaying those commands on one image or on a batch of images.

Turn an action command on or off

A recorded command

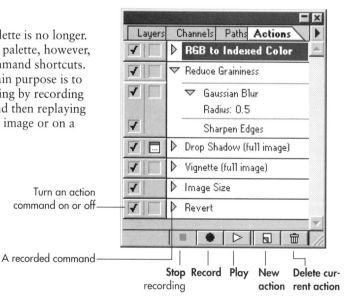

Stop recording　Record　Play　New action　Delete current action

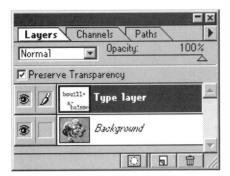

Build your image using layers

You can work on one layer at a time without affecting the non-target layers, and discard any layers you don't need. Merge two or more layers together periodically as you work, though, to conserve memory for large images. And using a **layer mask**, you can temporarily hide pixels on an individual layer so you can experiment with different compositions. When you're finished using a layer mask, you can discard the effects or permanently apply them to the layer.

To speed up screen redraw

Choose small **thumbnails** or no palette thumbnails for Layers, Channels, and Paths. Choose Palette Options from the palette command menu, then click Thumbnails: None or the smallest thumbnail option.

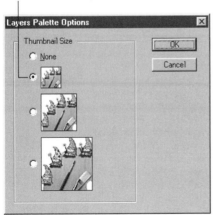

Production techniques

- To undo the last modification, choose the Edit menu > **Undo** (Control-Z) (some commands can't be undone).

- To restore the last saved version of an image, choose File menu > **Revert**, then click Revert.

- Restore part of the last saved version of an image by dragging across it using the **Rubber Stamp** tool with its **From Saved** option, or using the **Eraser** tool with its **Erase to Saved** option, or by applying the **Fill** command with its **Saved** option to a selected area.

- Save flattened versions of an image as you work on it using the **Save a Copy** command. When you're satisfied with one of the versions, discard the copies.

- Use **adjustment layers** to try out tonal and color adjustments, and then merge the adjustment layer downward to apply the effect or discard the adjustment layer. Use the Layers palette Opacity slider to lessen the effect of an adjustment layer. Create a clipping group with the layer directly below the adjustment layer to limit the adjustment effect to that layer.

- Use the Filter > **Fade** command (Control-Shift-F) to lessen a filter effect or Adjust command without having to undo and redo, and also choose a mode or opacity for the filter or color adjustment while you're at it.

- **Interrupt screen redraw** after executing a command or applying a filter by choosing a different tool or command. (To cancel a command while a progress bar is displayed, press Esc.)

- Choose the lowest possible **resolution** and **dimensions** for your image, factoring in your output requirements. You can create a practice image at a low resolution, saving the commands you use in an **action**, and then replay the action on a higher resolution version.

- Make sure your **hardware** requirements are sufficient for your production needs (see pages 1–3).

- Display your image in **two windows** simultaneously, one in a larger display size than the other, so you don't have to change displays sizes constantly.

- Save a complicated selection to a special grayscale channel called an **alpha channel,** which can be loaded and reused on any image whenever you like. Or create a **path,** which occupies significantly less storage space than an alpha channel, and can be converted into a selection.

- Since CMYK Color files process more slowly than RGB Colors files, use the **CMYK Preview** command to preview your image as CMYK Color mode, and convert to the real CMYK Color mode when the image is completed.

- Memorize as many **keyboard shortcuts** as you can. Start by learning the shortcuts for choosing tools (see page 6) or the shortcut for accessing a particular tool while another tool is chosen. Use on-screen tool tips to refresh your memory (rest your pointer on the icon of the tool you're interested in), or refer to Appendix B. Shortcuts are included in many instructions in this book. Use the **Actions** palette to organize and quickly execute frequently used commands.

- If color accuracy isn't critical, you can speed up screen redraw by choosing 256 color/**8-bit display** for your monitor.

- Use **Quick Mask** mode to turn a selection into a mask, which will cover the protected areas of the image with transparent color and leave the unprotected area as a cutout, and then modify mask contours using painting tools. Turn off Quick Mask mode to convert the cutout area back into a selection.

Open and edit part of an image to speed up processing

Using **Quick Edit**, you can open and edit part of an image in the uncompressed TIFF, Scitex CT, or Photoshop 2.0 file format. Choose File menu > Import > Quick Edit, highlight the image you want to open, click Open, marquee the area of the image you want to work on, then click OK. Other techniques you can use to zero in on an area of an image: click Grid in the Quick Edit dialog box, then click on a tile 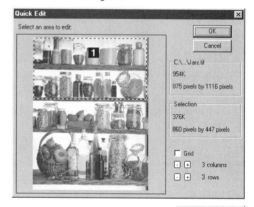, or press F to choose the first tile, or press N to cycle through the tiles. Click a plus or minus button to change the number of tiles. When you're ready to save the edited portion back to its original file, choose File menu > Export > Quick Edit Save. But be careful: changes will save instantly, and without a save dialog box.

Context menus save time

To choose from an on screen context menu, right-click on a Layers, Channels, or Paths palette thumbnail or name or other area of a palette. Or, choose a tool, then right-click the pointer over the image window to access options for that tool .

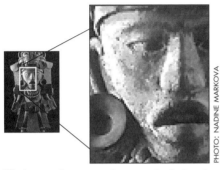

1 Close-up of an image, showing individual pixels.

PHOTO: NADINE MARKOVA

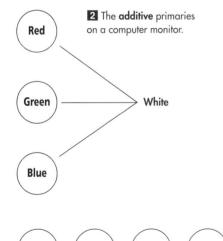

2 The **additive** primaries on a computer monitor.

Red

Green ——→ White

Blue

Cyan Magenta Yellow Black

3 The **subtractive** primaries—printing inks.

THE **FOLLOWING** is a brief explanation of color basics: color models, image modes, and blending modes.

Pixels

The screen image in Photoshop is a bitmap, which is a geometric arrangement (mapping) of a layer of dots of different shades or colors on a rectangular grid. Each dot, called a pixel, represents a color or shade. By magnifying an area of an image, you can edit pixels individually **1**. Every Photoshop image is a bitmap, whether it originates from a scan, from another application, or entirely within the application using painting and editing tools. (Don't confuse Bitmap image mode with the term "bitmapped.") Bitmap programs are ideal for producing painterly, photographic, or photorealistic images that contain gradations of color.

If you drag with a painting tool across an area of a layer, pixels below the pointer are recolored. Once modified, the pixels' original attributes can be restored only by choosing Undo or Revert or by using the Rubber Stamp tool with its From Saved option.

RGB vs. CMYK color

Red, green, and blue (RGB) light are used to display a color image on a monitor. When these additive primaries in their purest form are combined, they produce white light **2**.

The three subtractive primary inks used in four-color process printing are cyan (C), magenta (M), and yellow (Y) **3**. When combined, they produce a dark, muddy color. To produce a rich black, printers usually mix black (K) ink with small quantities of cyan, magenta, and/or yellow ink.

The display of color on a computer monitor is highly variable and subject to the variables of ambient lighting, monitor temperature, and room color. All monitors display color using the RGB model, and simulate the display of CMYK colors. Many colors seen in nature cannot be printed, some colors that can be displayed on screen cannot be printed, and some printable colors can't be displayed on screen. You don't need to worry about RGB-to-CMYK conversion if you're doing multimedia work or are going to output your file to a film recorder.

An exclamation point will appear on the Color palette if you choose a non-printable (out of gamut) color **1**. An exclamation point will also display on the Info palette if the color currently under the pointer is out of gamut **2**. Using Photoshop's Gamut Warning command, you can display nonprintable colors in your image in gray, and then, using the Sponge tool, you can desaturate them to bring them into gamut.

You can use the grayscale, RGB (red-green-blue), HSB (hue-saturation-brightness), CMYK (cyan-magenta-yellow-black), or Lab (lightness-a axis-b axis) color model when you choose colors in Photoshop via the Color Picker or Color palette.

Channels

Every Photoshop image is a composite of one or more semi-transparent, colored-light overlays called channels. For example, an image in RGB Color mode is composed of red, green, and blue channels. To illustrate, open a color image, choose Show Channels from the Window menu, then click Red, Green, or Blue on the Channels palette to display only that channel. Click RGB (Control-~) to restore the full channel display. (For this exercise, choose File menu > Preferences > Display & Cursors, then check the Color Channels in Color box.)

Web graphics

If you're creating an image for a Web site, use the RGB color model. Bear in mind that RGB colors—or colors from any other color model, for that matter—may not match the color palette of your Web browser (see pages 271–272). For the best results, load in the Web palette color table from the Indexed Color mode onto the Swatches palette.

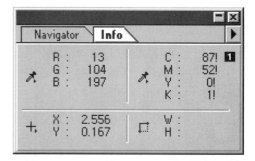

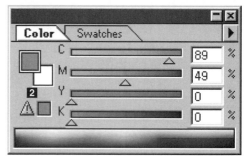

Default number of channels for each image mode

One	Three	Four
Bitmap	RGB	CMYK
Grayscale	Lab	
Duotone		
Indexed Color		

Only currently highlighted channels can be edited.

1 An Alpha channel

Image / Mode submenu:

Image
- Mode ▶
  - Bitmap...
  - ✔ Grayscale
  - Duotone...
  - Indexed Color
  - RGB Color
  - CMYK Color
  - Lab Color
  - Multichannel
  - ✔ 8 Bits/Channel
  - 16 Bits/Channel
  - Color Table...
- Adjust ▶
- Duplicate...
- Apply Image...
- Calculations...
- Image Size...
- Canvas Size...
- Crop
- Rotate Canvas ▶
- Histogram...
- Trap...

2 The **Mode** submenu.

Color adjustments can be made to an individual channel, but normally modifications are made and displayed in the multichannel, composite image (the topmost channel name on the Channels palette), and affect all of an image's channels at once. Special grayscale channels that are used for saving selections as masks, called alpha channels, can be added to an image **1**.

The more channels an image contains, the larger its file storage size. The storage size of an image in RGB Color mode, which is composed of three channels (Red, Green, and Blue), will be three times larger than the same image in Grayscale mode, which is composed of one channel. The same image in CMYK Color mode will be composed of four channels (Cyan, Magenta, Yellow, and Black), and will be even larger.

Image modes

An image can be converted to, displayed in, and edited in eight image modes: Bitmap, Grayscale, Duotone, Indexed Color, RGB Color, CMYK Color, Lab Color, and Multichannel. Simply choose the mode you want from the Image menu > Mode submenu **2**. To access a mode that is unavailable (whose name is dimmed), you must first convert your image to a different mode. For example, to convert an image to Indexed Color mode, it must be in RGB Color or Grayscale mode.

Some mode conversions cause noticeable color shifts; others cause subtle color shifts. Very dramatic changes may occur if an image is converted from RGB Color mode to CMYK Color mode, because printable colors are substituted for rich, glowing RGB colors. Color accuracy may diminish if an image is converted back and forth between RGB and CMYK Color mode too many times.

Medium to low-end scanners usually produce RGB scans. If you're creating an image that's going to be printed, for faster editing and to access all the filters, edit it in RGB

Image Modes

Color mode and convert it to CMYK Color mode when you're ready to imageset it. You can use the CMYK Preview command (Control-Y) to preview an image in CMYK Color mode without actually changing its mode. You can CMYK preview your image in one window and open a second window to display the same image without the CMYK preview. Also bear in mind that some conversions cause layers to be flattened, such as a conversion from Indexed Color mode to Multichannel or Bitmap mode. For other conversions, you'll have the option to click Don't Flatten if you want to preserve layers.

High-end scanners usually produce CMYK scans, and these images should be kept in CMYK Color mode to preserve their color data. If you find working on such large files is cumbersome, you can work out your image-editing scheme on a low resolution version of an image, save the commands using the Actions palette, and then apply the action to the high resolution, CMYK version. You will still, however, have to perform selection, painting, and editing tool operations manually.

Some output devices require that an image be saved in a particular image mode. Commands and tool options in Photoshop also vary depending on the currently selected image mode.

These are the image modes, in brief:

In **Bitmap** mode 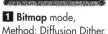, pixels are 100% black or 100% white only, and layers, filters, and Adjust commands are unavailable, except the Invert command. An image must be in Grayscale mode before it can be converted to Bitmap mode.

In **Grayscale** mode **2**, pixels are black, white, or up to 255 shades of gray. If an image is converted from a color mode to Grayscale mode and then saved, its luminosity (light and dark) values remain intact, but its color information is deleted and cannot be restored.

1 **Bitmap** mode, Method: Diffusion Dither.

2 **Grayscale** mode

The **Channels** palette for an image in various modes:

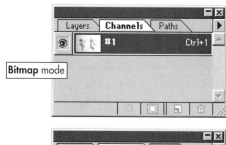

Bitmap mode

Grayscale mode

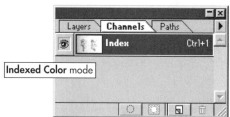

Indexed Color mode

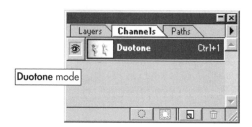

Duotone mode

Image Modes

The **Channels** palette for an image in various modes:

RGB Color mode

CMYK Color mode

Lab Color mode

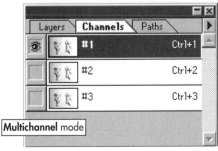

Multichannel mode

An image in **Indexed Color** mode has one channel and a color table containing a maximum of 256 colors or shades. To display a Photoshop image on a Web page or in certain painting or animation programs, it is sometimes better to first convert it to Indexed Color mode. You can also convert an image to Indexed Color mode to create arty color effects.

RGB Color is the most versatile mode because it is the only mode in which all Photoshop's tool options and filters are accessible. Some video and multimedia applications can import an RGB Photoshop image, and the GIF89a Export command, which is one of the best options for Web graphics, is available only for an RGB image.

Photoshop is one of few Macintosh programs in which images can be displayed and edited in **CMYK Color** mode. You can convert an image to CMYK Color mode when you're ready to output it on a color printer or color separate it (unless the output device is a PostScript Level 2 printer, in which case you'd choose Lab Color mode).

Lab Color is a three-channel mode that was developed for the purpose of achieving consistency among various devices, such as printers and monitors. The channels represent lightness, the colors green-to-red, and the colors blue-to-yellow. Photo CD images can be converted to Lab Color mode or RGB Color mode in Photoshop. Save an image in Lab Color mode to print it on a PostScript Level 2 printer or to export it to another operating system.

A **Duotone** is a printing method in which two or more plates are used to add richness and tonal depth to a grayscale image.

A **Multichannel** image is composed of multiple, 256-level grayscale channels. This mode is used for certain grayscale printing situations. You could use multichannel mode to assemble individual channels from several images before converting the new image to a color mode.

Image Modes

The blending modes

You can select from 16 blending modes from the Options palette, the Layers palette, the Fill, Stroke, or Fade dialog box, or the Fill Path dialog box. The mode you choose for a tool or a layer affects how that tool or layer modifies underlying pixels, which in the following text is called the base color. "Blend layer" refers to the layer for which a layer mode is chosen.

NOTE: If the Preserve Transparency box is checked on the Layers palette for the target layer, only non-transparent areas can be recolored or otherwise edited.

Opacities add up

When you choose a mode and an opacity for a tool, be sure to factor in the mode and opacity of the target layer you're working on. If you choose 60% opacity for the Paintbrush tool on a layer that has a 50% opacity, for example, your resulting brush stroke will have a 30% opacity.

NORMAL
All base colors are modified.

DISSOLVE
Creates a chalky, dry brush texture with the paint or blend layer color. The higher the pressure or opacity, the more solid the stroke or color area.

BEHIND
(Paint color only) Only transparent areas are modified, not existing base color pixels. The effect is like painting on the reverse side of clear acetate. Good for creating shadows.

CLEAR
(Paint color only) Makes the base color transparent where strokes are applied. Only available for a multi-layer image when using the Line or Paint Bucket tool, the Fill command, or the Stroke command. Cannot be used on the Background.

MULTIPLY
A dark paint or blend layer color removes the lighter parts of the base color to produce a darker base color. A light paint or blend layer color darkens the base color less. Good for creating semi-transparent shadow effects.

SCREEN

A light paint or blend layer color removes the darker parts of the base color to produce a lighter, bleached base color. A dark paint or blend layer lightens the base color less.

OVERLAY

Multiplies (darkens) dark areas and screens (lightens) light areas of base color. Preserves luminosity (light and dark) values. Black and white are not changed, so detail is maintained.

SOFT LIGHT

Lightens the base color if the paint or blend layer color is light. Darkens the base color if the paint or blend layer color is dark. Preserves luminosity values in the base color. Creates a subtle, soft lighting effect.

HARD LIGHT

Screens (lightens) the base color if the paint or blend layer color is light. Multiplies (darkens) the base color if the paint or blend layer color is dark. Greater contrast is created in the base color and layer color. Good for painting glowing highlights and creating composite effects.

COLOR DODGE

Lightens the base color where the paint or blend layer color is light. A dark paint or blend layer color tints the base color slightly.

COLOR BURN

A dark paint or blend layer color darkens the base color. A light paint or blend layer color tints the base color slightly.

Blending Modes

27

DARKEN

Base colors lighter than the paint or blend layer color are modified; base colors darker than the paint or blend layer color are not. Use with a paint color that is darker than the base colors you want to modify.

LIGHTEN

Base colors darker than the paint or blend layer color are modified; base colors lighter than the paint or blend layer color are not. Use with a paint color that is lighter than the base colors you want to modify.

DIFFERENCE

Creates a color negative effect on the base color. When the paint or blend layer color is light, the negative (or invert) effect is more pronounced. Produces noticeable color shifts.

EXCLUSION

Grays out the base color where the paint or blend layer color is dark. Inverts the base color where the paint or blend layer color is light.

HUE

The paint or blend layer color hue is applied. Saturation and luminosity values are not modified in the base color.

SATURATION

The paint or blend layer color's saturation is applied. Hue and luminosity values are not modified in the base color.

COLOR

The paint or blend layer color's saturation and hue are applied. The base color's light and dark (luminosity) values aren't changed, so detail is maintained.

LUMINOSITY

The base color's luminosity values are replaced by tone (luminosity) values from the paint or blend layer color. Hue and saturation are not affected in the base color.

Blending Modes

STARTUP 3

IN THIS CHAPTER you will learn how to get started in Photoshop: launch the application, scan an image, create a new image, open an existing image, and place an Illustrator image into Photoshop. You'll also learn how to change an image's dimensions, resolution, or file storage size; apply the Unsharp Mask filter to resharpen after resampling; enlarge an image's canvas size; crop, flip, rotate, save, copy, and close an image; and exit the application.

To launch Photoshop:

In Windows 95, click the Start button on the Taskbar **1**, choose Progams, choose Adobe, then click Adobe Photoshop 4.0. If you don't have a shortcut icon for Photoshop on your desktop, open the Photoshop folder, then drag the Photoshop application icon to the desktop.
or
Open the Adobe Photoshop folder in My Computer, then double-click the Photoshop application icon **2**.
or
Double-click a Photoshop file icon **3**.

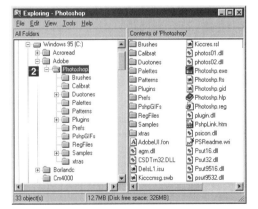

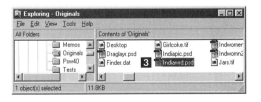

Where images come from

An image can be created, opened, edited, and saved in 18 different file formats in Photoshop **1**. Of these, you may use only a few, such as TIFF, PICT, EPS, and the native Photoshop file format. Because Photoshop accepts so many formats, images can be gathered from a wide variety of sources, such as scans, drawing applications, PhotoCDs, still image and video captures, and other operating systems—and they can be output from Photoshop on many types of printers. And, of course, images can also be created entirely within the application.

Scanning

Using a scanning device and scanning software, a slide, flat artwork, or a photograph can be translated into numbers (digitized) so it can be read, displayed, edited, and printed by a computer. You can scan directly into Photoshop or you can use other scanning software and save the scan in a file format that Photoshop opens.

To produce a high-quality scan, start with as high quality an original as possible. Some scanners will compress an image's dynamic range and increase its contrast, so use a photograph with good tonal balance, and, if you're doing your own scanning, set the scanning parameters carefully, weighing such factors as your final output device and storage capacity.

The quality of a scan will partially depend on the type of scanner you use. If your print shop is going to use the original photograph for printing and the scan will only be used to indicate the image's position or you're going to dramatically transform the image in Photoshop, you can use an inexpensive flat-bed scanner, which will produce an RGB scan. If color accuracy and crisp details are critical, scan a transparency on a slide scanner. An image that is going to be printed electronically should be scanned by a service bureau on a high-resolution CCD scanner, such as a Scitex Smart-Scanner,

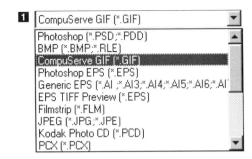

or on a drum scanner. High end scanners usually produce CMYK scans. Unfortunately, high-resolution scans also usually have very large file sizes.

Scanning software basics

Scanning software usually offers most of the following options, although terms may vary. The quality and file storage size of a scan are partially defined by the mode, resolution, and scale you specify, and whether you crop the image.

Preview: Place the art in the scanner, then click Preview or PreScan.

Scan mode: Select Black-and-White Drawing (no grays), Grayscale, or Color (choose millions of colors, if available). An image scanned in Color will be approximately three times larger in file size than the same image scanned in Grayscale.

Resolution: Scan resolution is measured in pixels per inch (ppi). The higher the resolution, the finer the detail in the image, but the larger its file size. Choose the minimum resolution necessary to obtain the best possible printout from your final output device. Don't choose a higher resolution than required, because the image will be larger in storage size than necessary, it will take longer to render on screen, display on the Web, or print, and there will be no improvement in output quality. On the other hand, too low a resolution will cause a printed image to look coarse and jagged, and its details will be lost.

Before selecting a resolution for print output, determine the resolution of the printer or imagesetter and the halftone screen frequency your print shop plans to use. (The scan resolution is different from the resolution of the output device.)

As a general rule, for a grayscale image, you should choose a resolution that is one-and-a-half times the halftone screen frequency (lines per inch) of your final output device, twice the halftone screen frequency

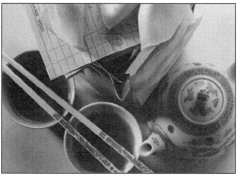

72 ppi

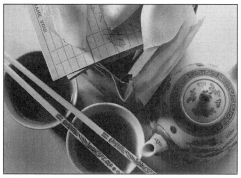

150 ppi

300 ppi

Scanning

for a color image. Use a high scanning resolution (600 ppi or higher) for line art. For example, if your print shop intends to use a 133-line screen frequency for black-and-white printing, you should use 200 ppi as your scan resolution. Ask your prepress shop if they're using an imagesetter that doesn't use the halftoning technology, in which case you should ask them to recommend an appropriate scan resolution. To calculate the appropriate file size for a scan, see the instructions on page 34.

Cropping: If you plan to use only part of an image, reposition the handles of the box in the preview area to reduce the scan area. Cropping can significantly reduce the storage size of a scan.

Scale: To enlarge an image's dimensions, choose a scale percentage above 100%. Enlarging an image or increasing its resolution in Photoshop or any other software program may cause it to blur, because the program uses mathematical "guesswork" (interpolation) to fill in additional information. An image's original information is recorded only at the time of scanning.

Scan: Click Scan and choose a location in which to save the file.

Scanning

NOTES: To scan into Photoshop, the scanner's plug-in module or Twain module must be in the Import folder inside the Photoshop Plugins folder. The first time you choose a scanning module from the File > Import submenu, choose select Twain_32 Source and choose a Twain device (the scanner), then choose Twain_32 Source. Thereafter, to access the scanning software, just choose Twain_32 Source. (See the Photoshop documentation for information about scanning modules.)

If your scanner doesn't have a Photoshop compatible scanner driver, scan your image outside Photoshop, save it as a TIFF, then open it in Photoshop as you would any other image.

To calculate the proper resolution for a scan, follow the instructions on the next page.

To scan into Photoshop:

1. Choose a scanning module or choose File menu > Import > Twain_32 Source.

2. Following the guidelines outlined on the previous two pages, choose a Mode or Type **1**.
and
Choose a Resolution or Path.

3. *Optional:* Choose a different Scale percentage.

4. *Optional:* Crop the image preview.

5. Click Scan or Final. The scanned image will appear in a new, untitled window.

6. Save the image (see pages 49–51). If the image requires color correction, see pages 248–261.

Note how the **file size** changes as you change the mode, resolution, and scale settings.

Scan into Photoshop

The resolution of a Photoshop image, like any bitmapped image, is independent of the monitor's resolution, so it can be customized for a particular output device, with or without modifying its file storage size. An image whose resolution is greater than the monitor's resolution (96 ppi for a typical PC monitor) will appear larger than its print size when it's displayed in Photoshop at 100% view. It's always best, though, to scan your image at the final size and resolution that are required for your final output device.

To calculate the proper resolution for a scan or for an existing image:

1. Create a new RGB document and choose 96 ppi, and enter your final width and height dimensions, if you know what they are.

2. Choose Image menu > Image Size.

3. Click the Auto button on the right side of the dialog box.

4. Enter the screen resolution of your final output device (i.e., the lines per inch (lpi) setting that your print shop will use) **1**.

5. Click Draft (1x screen frequency), Good (1½ x screen frequency), or Best (2 x screen frequency).

6. Click OK.

7. Jot down the Print Size: Resolution value, which is the proper value to enter when you scan your image.
   NOTE: If you're going to scale the final image up or down in Photoshop, you should multiply the resolution by the scale factor to calculate the proper resolution for the scan. You don't need to multiply the resolution if you scale the original image when you scan it.

8. Click OK or press Return.

Is the Web the final destination for your image?

Create the appropriate image size by settting the resolution to 96 ppi in the Image Size dialog box and entering the pixel dimensionss (height and width) for the maximum desired view size of the image. For an online image, determine the most common monitor size and pixel dimensions your viewers will use. Images are usually formatted for a 13-inch monitor—640 by 480 pixels. The total number of pixels in the image determines the file size.

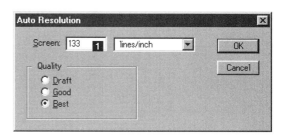

To calculate scanning parameters based on the required file size

Some scanners require that you enter the final file storage size in order to produce the necessary number of pixels for the image. To determine the final file size, choose File menu > New, enter the final width and height, choose RGB Color mode, then click Cancel. Now, keep increasing the resolution until the Image Size figure at the top of the dialog box reaches the size recommended by your print shop or service bureau, and enter that Image Size figure when you scan the image. You can readjust the width and height of the scanned image later in Photoshop, if necessary.

Calculate Resolution For a Scan

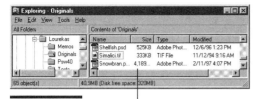

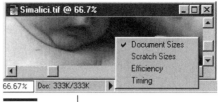

Storage size

If you're courious to know the actual **storage size** of an image, use Windows Explorer to open the folder that contains the file you are interested in, and look in the Size Column. Or, for an even more accurate figure, right-click the file icon and click on Properties.

RAM

To see how much **RAM** an image requires, choose Document Sizes from the bottom of the image window. The figure on the left is the RAM required for the flattened image with no extra channels; the figure on the right is the RAM size for the image with layers and extra channels, if any.

File storage sizes of scanned images

Size (In inches)	PPI (Resolution)	Black/White 1-Bit	Grayscale 8-Bit	CMYK Color 24-Bit
2 x 3	150	17 K	132 K	528 K
	300	67 K	528 K	2.06 MB
4 x 5	150	56 K	440 K	1.72 MB
	300	221 K	1.72 MB	6.87 MB
8 x 10	150	220 K	1.72 MB	6.87 MB
	300	879 K	6.87 MB	27.50 MB

Potential gray levels at various output resolutions and screen frequencies

Output Resolution (DPI)	Screen Frequency (LPI)				
	60	85	100	133	150
300	26	13			
600	101	51	37	21	
1270	256*	224	162	92	72
2540		256*	256*	256*	256*

Laser printers: 300, 600
Image-setters: 1270, 2540

Note: Ask your print shop what screen frequency (lpi) you will need to specify when image-setting your file. Also ask your prepress shop what resolution (dpi) to use for imagesetting. Some imagesetters can achieve resolutions above 2540 dpi.

*At the present time, PostScript Level 1 and Level 2 printers produce a maximum of 256 gray levels.

To create a new image:

1. Choose File menu > New (Control-N) .

2. Enter a name in the Name field **2**.

3. Choose a unit of measure from the drop-down menus next to the Width and Height fields.

4. Enter Width and Height values.

5. Enter the Resolution required for your final output device—whether it's an imagesetter or the Web (resolution issues are discussed on page 34).

6. Choose an image mode from the Mode drop-down menu. You can convert the image to a different mode later (see "Image modes" on pages 23–25).

7. Click Contents: White, Background Color, or Transparent for the Background. To choose a Background color, see pages 112–114. If you choose the Transparent option, you can only save the image in the Photoshop file format, because the background will actually be a layer. Photoshop's layer transparency cannot be read by any other software. (More about layers and transparency in Chapters 7 and 12).

8. Click OK or press Enter. An image window will appear **3**.

TIP If you want the New dialog box settings to match those of another open document, with the New dialog box open, choose the name of the image that has the desired dimensions from the Window menu.

TIP If there is an image on the Clipboard, the New dialog box will automatically display its dimensions. To prevent those dimensions from displaying, hold down Alt when you choose File menu > New.

1 Choose **New** from the File menu.

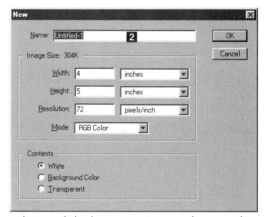

In the New dialog box, enter a **Name** and enter numbers in the **Width, Height,** and **Resolution** fields. Also choose an image **Mode** and click a **Contents** type for the **Background**.

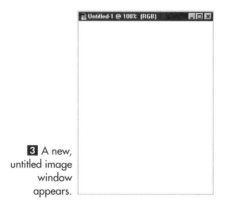

3 A new, untitled image window appears.

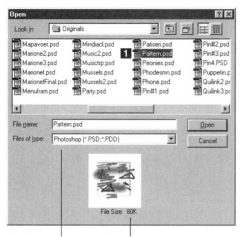

The file's **format**.   The file's **size**.

Double-click a file name in the Open dialog box. If the name of the file you want to open doesn't appear on the scroll list, click the drop-down button in the Files of type box, then choose a format.

Thumbnails

To create image icons for **Windows Explorer** when the View menu is set to Large Icon, click the Save Thumbnail checkbox for individual files as you save them. Thumbnail icons appear only if the file extension is PSD.

To create a thumbnail of any subsequently saved image for display in the Open dialog box, choose File menu > Preferences > Saving Files, then choose Image Previews: Always Save **2**. A thumbnail icon will only appear for an image that has a PSD, JPG, or TIF file extension.

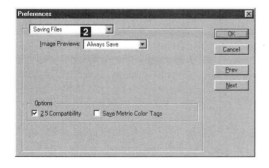

NOTE: To open an Adobe Illustrator file, follow the instructions on page 40 or 41.

To open an image within Photoshop:

1. Choose File menu > Open (Control-O).

2. Locate the file you want to open **1**.

> **NOTE:** If the name of the file you want to open doesn't appear on the scroll list, it means the plug-in module for its file format isn't installed in your system, so you'll have to convert the file to a format that Photoshop supports. To do this, choose the All file format from the Files of type drop-down menu. Once opened, an image can be saved in any format that Photoshop supports. Don't leave the format as Raw.

4. Highlight the file name, then click Open.

or

Double-click the file name.

For some file formats, a further dialog box will open. For example, if you open a file saved in the EPS or Adobe Illustrator format that hasn't yet been rasterized (converted from object-oriented to bitmap), the Rasterize Generic EPS Format dialog box will open. Follow steps 4–9 on page 40.

TIP To open a QuarkXPress page in Photoshop, save it in QuarkXPress using the Save Page as EPS command, then follow the steps on page 40.

TIP To open images in some file formats, like Scitex CT, you must use a special plug-in module, which will be accessed via the File menu > Import submenu.

To open a Photoshop image from Windows Explorer:

Double-click a Photoshop image file icon in Windows Explorer **1**. Photoshop will launch if it hasn't already been launched.

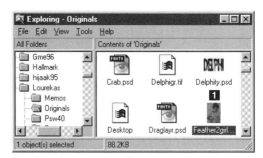

Double-click a Photoshop file icon.

To open Kodak Photo CD images, Photoshop uses the Kodak CMS Photo CD plug-in, which is accessed from the File menu. Kodak's Color Management System is used to enhance the accuracy of image translation from the Kodak file format into Photoshop's RGB Color or Lab Color mode.

To open a Kodak Photo CD file:

1. Choose File menu > Open (Control-O).

2. Locate and double-click the Photo CD file name **2**.

or

Highlight the Photo CD file name and click Open.

3. Choose a Resolution **3**. The base resolution is 512 by 768 pixels, which will produce an image about 7 by 10.5 inches at 72 pixels/inch. A higher resolution will produce a larger image at 72 pixels/inch.

Leave the Landscape box checked to open the image quickly. (Use one of Photoshop's Rotate commands if you need to change the orientation of the image after opening it.)

4. Click Image Info to read about the original film medium. Make a note of the Medium of Original and Product Type of Original info (the type of film used to create the image) **4**. Color Reversal is the term for a color slide; 52/xx is Ektachrome slide; and 116/xx is Kodachrome slide. Click OK.

5. Click Source.

Double-click a Photo CD file name in the Open dialog box. The Format will be listed as Kodak CMS Photo CD.

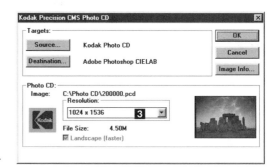

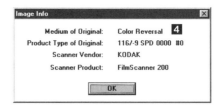

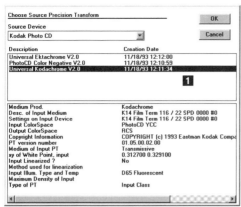

Click on the **Description** that most closely matches the film medium of the original photo that was listed in the Image Info dialog box. The image info dialog box for this image listed Color Reversal as the Medium of Original and the Product Type as 116/-XX, so we chose Universal Kodachrome V2.0 as the profile. Kodak recommends choosing Universal Ektachrome when the Medium of Original is Color Reversal and the Product Type of Original is unknown.

6. Click on the closest available match to the Image Info description **1**, then click OK.

7. Click Destination.

8. From the Device drop-down menu, choose Adobe Photoshop RGB or Adobe Photoshop CIELAB (Lab) as the color mode for the image in Photoshop **2**, then click OK.

9. Click OK in the Photo CD Plug in dialog box. The image will open in Photoshop.

Stop press!

Kodak has upgraded its film scanners to the 4045 and 4050 models and has also upgraded its PhotoCD transform descriptions (version 3.x instead of version 2.x). The product types and film choice for the new upgrades are as follows:

052/72 4050E6
116/72 4050K14
052/xx Universal Ektachrome
116/xx Universal Kodachrome

Open Kodak Photo CD File

When an EPS or Adobe Illustrator file is opened or placed in Photoshop, it is rasterized, which means it's converted from its native object-oriented format into Photoshop's pixel-based format. Follow these instructions to open an EPS file, such as an Adobe Illustrator graphic, as a new document. Follow the instructions on the next page to place an EPS file into an existing Photoshop file.

To open an EPS or Illustrator file as a new image:

1. Choose File menu > Open (Control-O).

2. If the file name isn't listed, click on All Formats in the Files of type box.

3. Locate and highlight an EPS image to be opened, then click Open.
   or
   Double-click a file name.

4. *Optional:* In the Rasterize Generic EPS Format dialog box, check the Constrain Proportions box to preserve the file's height and width ratio **1**.

5. *Optional:* Choose a unit of measure from the drop-down menus next to the Height and Width fields, and enter new dimensions.

6. Enter the final resolution required for your image in the Resolution field. Entering the correct final resolution before rasterizing produces the best rendering of the image.

7. Choose an image mode from the Mode drop-down menu. (See "Image modes," beginning on page 23.)

8. Check the Anti-aliased box for optimal rendering of the image, and soft edge transitions.

9. Click OK or press Enter.

Drag-and-drop from Illustrator 7

You can drag-and-drop an object from an Illustrator 7 image window into a Photoshop 4 image window. The object will automatically become bitmapped in Photoshop, and it will appear on its own layer. If you want to import an Illustrator shape as a path in Photoshop, hold down Control as you drag-and-drop.

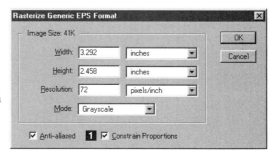

PHOTO: E. WEINMANN

1 The word "Delphi" was created in Adobe Illustrator, and then placed in a Photoshop file.

When you place an object-oriented (vector) image into a Photoshop image, it becomes bitmapped and is rendered in the resolution of the Photoshop image. The higher the resolution of the Photoshop image, the better the rendering (200 ppi minimum).

NOTE: You can also drag a path from an Illustrator 7 image window into a Photoshop image window, where it will appear on a new layer.

To place an Adobe Illustrator image into an existing Photoshop image:

1. Open a Photoshop image.

2. Choose File menu > Place.

3. Locate and highlight the Illustrator file you want to open.

4. Click Place. A box will appear on top of the image. Pause to allow the image to draw inside it **1**.

5. *Perform any of these optional steps (use the Undo command to undo any of them):*

To resize the placed image, drag a handle of the bounding border. Hold down Shift while dragging to preserve the proportions of the placed image.

To move the placed image, drag inside the bounding border.

To rotate the placed image, position the pointer outside the bounding border, then drag.

6. To accept the placed image, press Enter or double-click inside the bounding border. The placed image will appear on a new layer.

TIP By default, the Anti-alias PostScript box is checked in the File menu > Preferences > General dialog box, and this setting produces the most optimal, but slowest, rendering of placed images.

TIP To remove the placed image, press Esc before or while it's rendering. If the image is already rendered, highlight its layer name on the Layers palette, then click the trash icon.

To produce this image, artist Wendy Grossman created the musical notes and other shapes in Illustrator and then imported them into Photoshop.

Place an Adobe Illustrator Image

NOTE: Changing an image's dimensions in Photoshop while preserving its current resolution (leaving the Resample Image box checked) will cause resampling, which degrades image quality. That's why it's always best to scan or create an image at the desired size. If resample you must, apply the Unsharp Mask filter afterward to resharpen (see pages 44–45).

To change an image's dimensions for print output:

1. Choose Image menu > Image Size.

2. To preserve the image's width-to-height ratio, check the Constrain Proportions box **1**. To modify the image's width independently of its height, uncheck the Constrain Proportions box.

3. *Optional:* To preserve the image's resolution, check the Resample Image box **2** and choose Nearest Neighbor, Bilinear, or Bicubic as the interpolation method. Bicubic causes the least degradation in image quality.

4. Choose a unit of measure from the drop-down menu next to the Print Size: Width and Height fields.

5. Enter new numbers in the Width and/or Height fields. The Resolution will change if the Resample Image box is unchecked.

6. Click OK or press Enter.

TIP To restore the original Image Size dialog box settings, hold down Alt and click Reset.

TIP If you modify an image's dimensions and/or resolution with the Resample Image box checked, you will not be able to use the Rubber Stamp tool with its From Saved option to restore a portion of it. Save an image immediately after modifying its dimensions and/or resolution to establish a new From Saved reference.

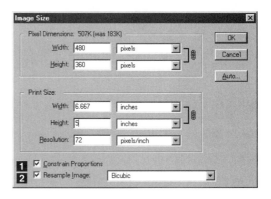

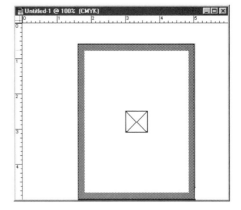

Print preview

To see the image size relative to the paper size, press and hold on the sizes bar at the bottom of the image window. To display the image on screen at the size it will print, choose View menu > Print Size. (By the way, at 100% view, the on-screen display size will match the print size only if the image resolution is the same as the monitor's resolution, which is usually 72 ppi.)

Change Dimensions for Print

Cashing in on too high a resolution

An image contains a given number of pixels after scanning, and its print dimensions and its resolution are interdependent. If an image's resolution or dimensions are changed with the Resample Image box unchecked (Image Size dialog box), the file's total pixel count is preserved. Increasing an image's pixels per inch resolution will shrink its print dimensions; lowering an image's pixels per inch resolution amount will enlarge its print dimensions.

If your file has a higher resolution than needed (more than twice the screen frequency), you can allocate the extra resolution to the print size dimensions by unchecking the Resample Image box (the width, height, and resolution are now interdependent), and then lowering the resolution to twice the screen frequency. The width and height values will automatically increase, and the file size will remain constant—no pixels will be added or deleted from the image.

If you must further enlarge the image's dimensions, click in the Width field, check the Resample Image box, and enter a new Width value. The Height will change proportionately, and the file size will increase, but you'll be resampling, so after clicking OK, apply the Unsharp Mask filter to resharpen (see pages 44–45).

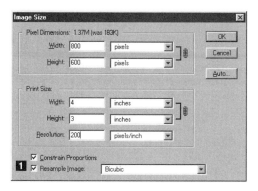

To change an image's pixel dimensions for on-screen output:

1. Choose Image menu > Image Size.

2. Make sure the Resample Image box is checked.

3. To preserve the image's width-to-height ratio, leave the Constrain Proportions box checked.

4. Set the Resolution to 96 ppi, the resolution commonly used for PC on-screen display.

5. Enter new values in the Pixel Dimensions: Width and/or Height fields.

6. Click OK or press Enter.

NOTE: If you increase an image's resolution (resample up) with the Resample Image box checked, pixels will be added and the image's file storage size will increase, but its sharpness will diminish. If you decrease an image's resolution (downsample), information is deleted from the file and it can't be retrieved once the image is saved. Blurriness caused by resampling may only be evident when the image is printed; it may not be discernible on screen. It's best to scan or create an image at the proper resolution. Follow the instructions on the next page to resharpen a resampled image. (And see "Resolution" on page 34.)

To change an image's resolution:

1. Choose Image menu > Image Size.

2. *Optional:* To preserve the image's dimensions (Width and Height), check the Resample Image box **1**. To preserve the total pixel count in the image, uncheck Resample Image. The Width and Height dimensions must change to preserve the current pixel count.

3. Enter a number in the Resolution field.

4. Click OK or press Enter.

On-Screen Dimensions; Change Resolution

If you change an image's dimensions or resolution with the Resample Image box checked, convert it to CMYK Color mode, or transform it, blurring may occur due to the resampling process. Despite its name, the Unsharp Mask filter has a focusing effect. It increases contrast between adjacent pixels that already have some contrast. You can specify the amount of contrast to be created (Amount), the number of surrounding pixels that will be modified around each pixel that requires more contrast (Radius), and determine which pixels the filter effects or ignores by specifying the minimum degree of existing contrast (Threshold).

NOTE: The Unsharp Mask effect is more discernible on screen than on high-resolution print output.

To apply the Unsharp Mask filter:

1. Choose Filter menu > Sharpen > Unsharp Mask.

2. Enter a number in the Amount field (the percentage increase in contrast between pixels) or move the Amount slider ■. Use a low setting (below 45) for figures or natural objects and a higher setting if the image contains sharp-edged objects. Too high a setting will produce obvious halos around high contrast areas. The larger the image, the less sharpening may be required.

3. To choose an appropriate Radius value, which is a little trickier, you need to consider the final size, the resolution, and the subject matter of the image. Enter a number between 0.1 and 100 in the Radius field or move the Radius slider to specify the number of pixels surrounding high contrast edges that will be modified. Try between 1 and 2. Higher values will produce too much contrast in areas that already have high contrast.

The higher the resolution of the image, the more pixels there are on the border

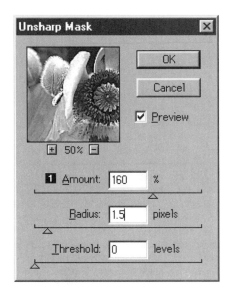

The original image, a bit blurry.

After Unsharp Masking with a high Amount (160%). Radius 1.5, Threshold 0. Notice the halos around the edges and the centers of the flowers.

After Unsharp Masking with a high Radius (6.0). Amount of 130, Threshold of 0. The soft gradations have become choppy and the image has an unnatural contrast and sharpness.

After Unsharp Masking with a high Threshold (15). Amount of 160, Radius of 1.5. Even with the same Amount setting as in the top image, the soft gradations in the petals and the background are preserved.

between high contrast areas, so the higher the Radius setting is required. Try a high Radius setting for a low contrast image, and a lower Radius setting for an intricate, high contrast image.

NOTE: The higher the Radius setting, the lower the Amount setting can be, and vice versa.

4. Enter a number between 0 and 255 in the Threshold field or move the Threshold slider. The Threshold is the minimum amount of contrast an area must have before it will be modified. At a Threshold of 0, the filter will be applied to the entire image. A Threshold value above 0 will cause sharpening along already high contrast edges, less so in low contrast areas. If you increase the Threshold value, you can then increase the Amount and Radius values without adding sharpening noise to areas that require less sharpening. To prevent noise from distorting skin tones, specify a Threshold between 10 and 20.

5. Click OK or press Enter.

TIP To soften a grainy scan, apply the Gaussian Blur filter (Blur submenu) at a low setting (below 1) and then apply the Sharpen Edges filter (Sharpen submenu) once or twice afterward to resharpen.

TIP If you're Unsharp Masking a large image, uncheck the Preview box to avoid waiting for full screen previews. First, get close to the right settings using just the preview window, then check the Preview box to preview the results on the full screen, and finally, readjust the settings, if needed.

TIP Try applying the Unsharp Mask filter to one or two individual color channels (the Red or Green channel, for example, in an RGB image). If you sharpen two separate channels, use the same Radius value in both.

The Canvas Size command changes the live, editable image area.

NOTE: If you want to crop right on the image, use the Crop tool or the Crop command.

To change the canvas size:

1. If the image has a Background, choose a Background color (see pages 112–114).

2. Choose Image menu > Canvas Size.

3. *Optional:* Choose a different unit of measure from the drop-down menus.

4. Enter new numbers in the Width and/or Height fields **1**. Changing the Width won't change the Height, and vice versa.

5. *Optional:* To reposition the image in its new canvas size, click on a gray Anchor square. The white square represents the existing image relative to the new canvas area.

6. Click OK or press Enter. Any added areas will automatically fill with the current Background color (unless the background is a layer with transparency, in which case added canvas areas will also be transparent) **2**–**3**.

Note the new and current file sizes as you change the canvas size.

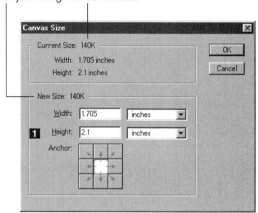

PHOTO: E. WEINMANN

2 The original image.

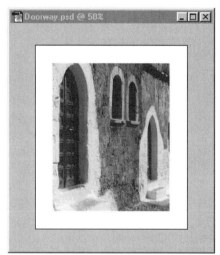

3 The same image with added canvas pixels.

Change the Canvas Size

To specify dimensions and resolution as you crop

Double-click the Crop tool, check the Fixed Target Size box on the Cropping Tool Options palette, enter values in the Width, Height, and Resolution fields, then follow steps 2–4 at right. Click Front Image to insert the current image's Width, Height, and Resolution values into the fields.

Having clicked Front Image, the crop marquee will match the current width-to-height ratio. The cropped image's resolution will increase or decrease to fit the width and height values you enter. If you increase only the resolution, the print size won't change, but the image's pixel count will increase. Entering a higher resolution value will cause pixel resampling, and will probably add distortion to the image.

To crop one image to fit exactly inside another image

Open both images, activate the destination image, choose the Crop tool, check the Fixed Target Size box and click Front Image on the Cropping Tool Options palette, activate the image you want to crop, then draw a marquee. After cropping, drag-and-drop the layer or copy and paste the layer onto the destination image.

To crop an image:

1. Choose the Crop tool (C) ⌗, from the Marquee tool pop-out menu.

2. Drag a marquee over the portion of the image you want to keep **1**.

3. *Do any of these optional steps:*

   To resize the marquee, drag any handle (double-arrow pointer) **2**. Hold down Shift while dragging to preserve the marquee's proportions.

   To reposition the marquee, drag from inside it.

   To rotate the marquee, position the cursor outside the bounding box, then drag in a circular direction.

4. Press Enter **2**.
   or
   Double-click inside the marquee. If you rotated the marquee, the rotated image will be squared off in the image window.

TIP To stop the cropping process before accepting it, press Esc.

TIP To resharpen an image after cropping, apply the Unsharp Mask filter (see pages 44–45).

1 Drag a marquee over the portion of the image you want to keep.

PHOTO: PAUL PETROFF

2 The cropped image.

Crop an Image

NOTE: The Rotate Canvas command flips all the layers in an image. To flip one layer at a time, use the Layer menu > Transform > Flip Horizontal or Flip Vertical command.

To flip an image:

To flip the image left to right, choose Image menu > Rotate Canvas > Flip Horizontal **1**–**2**.

or

To flip the image upside-down to produce a mirror image, choose Image menu > Rotate Canvas > Vertical **3**.

1 The original image.

2 The image flipped horizontally.

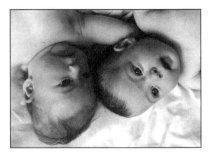

3 The image flipped vertically.

NOTE: The Rotate Canvas commands rotate all the layers in an image. To rotate one layer at a time, use a Layer menu > Transform submenu rotate command.

To rotate an image a preset amount:

Choose Image Menu > Rotate Canvas > Rotate 180°, 90° CW (clockwise), or 90° CCW (counterclockwise).

To rotate an image by specifying a number:

1. Choose Image Menu > Rotate Canvas > Arbitrary.

2. Enter a number between -359.9° and 359.9° in the Angle field **4**.

3. Click °CW (clockwise) or °CCW (counterclockwise)

4. Click OK or press Enter **5**.

5 After rotating an image 180°. Compare with the flipped images, above.

What the Photoshop format does and doesn't do

Photoshop is the only format in which multiple layers are available. You'll also need to use the Photoshop format if you want to work with adjustment layers, grids, guides, or the KP Color Management profiles. Few other applications can read an image in the Photoshop file format, though, so you should keep a copy of your layered RBG image if you think there's any chance you'll want to rework it, and flatten the copy or the second version (see pages 51 and 98). Painter versions 4 and later will import a layered Photoshop image with its layers intact; they'll appear as floaters.

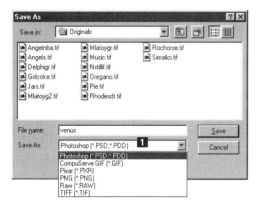

Special instructions for saving in the EPS, PICT, and TIFF file formats are on pages 244–245. Other file formats are covered in the Photoshop User Guide.

To save a new image:

1. Choose File menu > Save (Control-S).
   or
   If the image contains multiple layers, follow the Save a Copy instructions on page 51.

2. Type a name in the "File name" field **1**.

3. Choose a location in which to save the file. If you need to locate a drive, choose My Computer from the Save in drop-down list. Double-click a folder in which to save the file or create a new folder by clicking the Create New folder icon.

4. Choose a file format from the Save As drop-down list. If the document contains more than one layer, only the native Photoshop format will be available.

5. Click Save.

The prior version of a file is overwritten when the Save command is chosen.

To save an existing image:

Choose File menu > Save (Command-S).

To revert to the last saved version:

1. Choose File menu > Revert.

2. Click Revert when the prompt appears **2**.

TIP To revert only a portion of an image, use the Rubber stamp tool with its From Saved option.

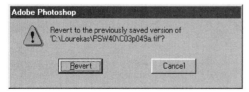

2 Click **Revert** when this warning prompt appears.

Using the Save As command, you can save a copy of an image in a different image mode or use the copy to do a design variation. For example, you can save a version of an image in CMYK Color mode and keep the original version in RGB Color mode.

NOTE: Use the Save a Copy command to copy a file and continue working on the original (instructions on the next page).

To save a new version of an image:

1. Open a file. If the image contains layers and you want to save it in a format other than Photoshop's native file format, flatten the image now.

2. Choose File menu > Save As (Control-Shift-S).

3. Enter a new name or modify the existing name in the File name field **1**.

4. Choose a location in which to save the new version.

5. Choose a different file Format (available for a single-layer document only). Hold down Alt while choosing a format to append the format's three-character extension to the file name.

6. Click Save. For an EPS file, follow the instructions on page 244. For a TIFF or PICT file, follow instructions on page 245. Consult the Photoshop manual for other formats. The new version will remain open; the original file will close automatically.

TIP If you don't change the name of the file and you click Save, a warning prompt will appear. Click Yes to save over the original file or click No to return to the Save As dialog box.

TIP Your image may need to be in a particular mode for some formats to be available.

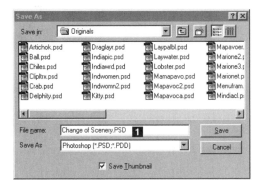

What does the Duplicate command do?

The Image menu > Duplicate command copies an image and all its layers, layer masks, and channels into currently available memory. A permanent copy of the file is not saved to disk unless you then choose File > Save. An advantage of the Duplicate command is that you can use the duplicate to try out variations quickly without altering the original file. HOWEVER, Duplicate should be used with caution, because if an application freeze or a system crash occurs, you'll lose whatever's currently in memory, including your duplicate image. (The original image probably occupied a considerable amount of memory and the duplicate occupied even more memory. If you're curious, both sizes are reflected in the Scratch Sizes on the Info bar.)

Save a New Version of an Image

The Save a Copy command creates and saves a flattened version of a multi-layer image in any file format you choose. The multi-layer version of the image will stay open so you can continue to work on it. The flattened version of an image will be smaller in file size than its multi-layer counterpart.

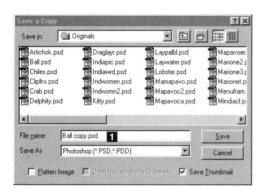

To copy a file and continue to work on the original:

1. With the file open, choose File menu > Save a Copy (Control-Alt-S).

2. *Optional:* Type a new name or change the name in the File name field **1**. The word "copy" will automatically append to the file name.

3. Choose a location in which to save the copy.

4. *Optional:* For an image in the Photoshop file format, check the Flatten Image box to flatten all layers.

5. *Optional:* Choose a different file Format. If you choose any format other than Photoshop, the Flatten Image box will be checked automatically and layers will be flattened.

6. *Optional:* You can delete alpha channels from a Photoshop, PDF, Pixar, PNG, Targa, or TIFF file by checking the Don't Include Alpha Channels box.

7. Click Save. For an EPS file, follow the instructions on page 244. The original file will remain open.

Copy a File, Keep Working on Original

To close an image:

Click the close box in the upper right
corner of the document window **1**.
or
Choose File menu > Close (Control-W).

1 Click the close box.

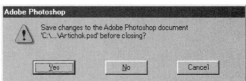

If you attempt to close an image and it was modified
since it was last saved, a warning prompt will appear.
Click **No** to close the file without saving, click **Yes** to save
the file before closing, or click Cancel to cancel the Close
operation.

To exit Photoshop:

Choose File menu > Exit (Control-Q).

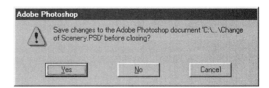

If you exit Photoshop, all open Photoshop files will close.
If changes were made to an open file since it was saved,
a prompt will appear. Click **No** to close the file without
saving, click **Yes** to save the file before exiting, or click
Cancel to cancel the Exit operation.

Close an Image; Exit Photoshop

THIS **CHAPTER** covers how to change the display size of an image, how to move an image in its window, how to display an image in two windows simultaneously, and how to switch screen display modes. The new Navigator palette can be used to move an image in its window or to change the view percentage.

You can display an entire image within its window, or magnify part of an image to work on a small detail. The display size is indicated as a percentage on the image window title bar, in the lower left corner of the image window, and in the lower left corner of the Navigator palette. The display size of an image neither reflects nor affects its printout size.

To change the display size using the Navigator palette:

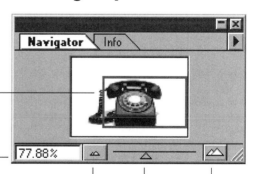

Drag in preview box to **move** the image in the image window. Control-drag in the preview box to marquee the area you want to **magnify**.

Enter the desired **zoom percentage** (or ratio, like 1:1 or 4:1), then press **Enter**. To zoom to the percentage and keep the field highlighted, press Shift-Enter. (You can also change the display size by typing the desired zoom percentage, and then presssing Enter.)

Click the **Zoom out** button to reduce the image display size.

Move the **Zoom slider** to change the image display size.

Click the **Zoom in** button to enlarge the image display.

To change the display size using the Zoom tool:

1. Choose the Zoom tool (Z). ⚲

2. To **magnify** the image, click in the image window . Or, drag a marquee across an area to magnify that area.
or
To **reduce** the display size, Alt-click on the image ❷.
or
To display the entire image in the largest possible size that will fit on your screen, click Fit on Screen on the Zoom Tool Options palette ❸.

TIP Uncheck the Resize Windows To Fit box on the Zoom Tool Options palette if you want to prevent the image window from resizing when you change the image's display size.

TIP To display the image at actual pixel size, click Actual Pixels on the Zoom Tool Options palette or double-click the Zoom tool. An image's display size equals its actual size only when the display ratio is 100% (1:1) and the image resolution and monitor resolution are the same.

TIP Control-Space bar-click to magnify the display size when another tool is selected or a dialog box with a Preview option is open. Control-Alt-Space bar-click to reduce the display size.

TIP You can also change the display size by choosing Zoom In or Zoom Out from the View menu.

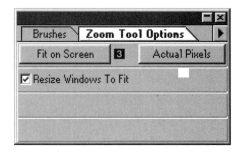

❶ Click on the image with the Zoom tool to enlarge the display size. Note the plus sign in the magnifying glass pointer.

❷ Alt-click on the image with the Zoom tool to reduce the display size. Note the minus sign in the magnifying glass pointer.

Shortcuts for changing the display size

Magnify	Control +
Zoom Out	Control –
Zoom in (window doesn't resize)	Control Alt +
Zoom out (window doesn't resize)	Control Alt –
Actual pixels/100% view	Control Alt 0
Fit on screen	Control 0

1 Click on or drag the preview box on the Navigator palette to move an image in its window.

2 Standard Screen Mode

3 Full Screen Mode with Menu Bar

4 Full Screen Mode

5 Full Screen Mode with Menu Bar

NOTE: If the scroll bars aren't active, the entire image is displayed, and there is no need to move it.

To move a magnified image in its window:

Click or drag the preview box (image thumbnail) on the Navigator palette **1**.
or
Click the up or down scroll arrow. Drag a scroll box to move the image more quickly.
or
Choose the Hand tool (H) ✋, then drag the image.

TIP To fit the entire image in the largest document window your monitor accommodates, double-click the Hand tool or click Fit on Screen on the Zoom Tool Options palette or choose View menu > Fit on Screen.

To change the screen display mode:

Click the Standard Screen Mode button on the bottom of the Toolbox (F) **2** to display the image, menu bar, scroll bars on the document window. This is the Standard mode.
or
Click the Full Screen Mode with Menu Bar button (F) **3**–**4** to display the image and menu bar, but no scroll bars. The area around the image will be gray.
or
Click the Full Screen Mode button (F) **5** to display the image, but no menu bar or scroll bars. The area around the image will be black.

TIP Press Tab to show/hide the Toolbox and any open palettes; press Shift-Tab to show/hide the palettes, but not the Toolbox.

TIP Use the Hand tool (H) to move the image in its window when the scroll bars are hidden and the image is magnified, or use the Navigator palette. Hold down Space bar to use the Hand tool while another tool is selected.

Move Image in its Window; Screen Modes

55

The number of images that can be open at a time depends on available RAM and scratch disk space. You can open the same image in two windows simultaneously: one in a large display size, such as 400%, to edit a detail and the other in a smaller display size, such as 100%, to view the whole image. Or, leave the image in RGB Color mode in one image window and choose View menu > CMYK Preview for the same image in a second window.

To display an image in two windows:

1. Open an image.

2. Choose View menu > New View. The same image will appear in a second window **1**.

3. *Optional:* Move either window by dragging its title bar, and/or resize either window by dragging its resize box.

To recolor the work canvas

Choose a Foreground color (see pages 111–115), choose the Paint Bucket tool, then Shift-click on the work canvas **2**. You can't undo this. To restore the default gray, choose 50% gray for the Foreground color, then Shift-click the work canvas again.

Work canvas

1 An image displayed in two windows simultaneously: one in a large display size for editing, the other in a smaller display size for previewing.

Display an Image in Two Windows

SELECT 5

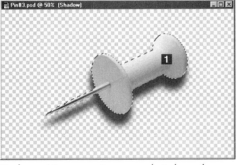

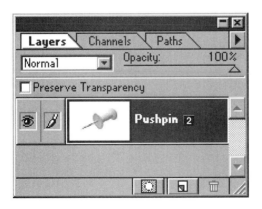

Pixels—**not transparent areas**—selected on a layer.

YOU CAN USE any Photoshop selection tool—Marquee, Lasso, or Magic Wand—to isolate an area of an image. If a command, such as a filter, is applied to a selection, only the selection is affected—the rest of the image is protected. A selection is defined by a moving marquee.

The creation of selections is covered in this chapter, including using the Marquee tool to create rectangular or elliptical selections, the Lasso tool to create irregular or polygonal selections, and the Magic Wand tool and Color Range command to select areas by color or shade. In this chapter you will also learn how to create a frame selection, how to deselect a selection, how to move or hide a selection marquee, how to flip, rotate, resize, add to, subtract from, feather, defringe, and smooth a selection, and how to create a vignette. You can convert a selection into a path for precise reshaping, and then convert it back into a selection (see pages 166 and 172).

The selections covered in this chapter are non-floating—they contain a layer's underlying pixels. If a non-floating selection is moved on the Background ■, the exposed area is covered with the current Background color. If a non-floating selection is moved on a layer, the exposed area will be transparent.

To select an entire layer:

Choose Select menu > All (Control-A). A marquee will surround the entire layer ■.

To select only pixels—not the transparent areas—on a layer, Control-click the layer name on the Layers palette ■.

Select an Entire Layer

To create a rectangular or elliptical selection:

1. Choose a target layer.

2. Choose the Rectangular Marquee or Elliptical Marquee tool **1**. To toggle between those two tools, press M.

3. *Optional:* To specify the exact dimensions of the selection, with the Rectangular or Elliptical Marquee tool highlighted, press Enter to open the Marquee Options palette (or double-click the tool), choose Fixed Size from the Style drop-down menu **2**, then enter Width and Height values. Remember, though, you're counting pixels based on the file's resolution, not the monitor's resolution, so the same Fixed Size marquee will appear larger in a low resolution file than in a high resolution file.

   To specify the width-to-height ratio of the selection (3-to-1, for example), choose Constrained Aspect Ratio from the Style drop-down menu, then enter Width and Height values. Enter the same number in both fields to create a circle or a square.

4. *Optional:* To soften the edges of the selection before it's created, enter a Feather amount on the Options palette. Enter 0 to produce no feathering.

5. If you specified Fixed Size values, click on the image. For any other Style, drag diagonally **3**. A marquee will appear. Hold down Space bar to move the marquee while drawing it. To move the marquee after releasing the mouse, follow the instructions on page 65.

TIP As you drag the mouse, the dimensions of the selection will be indicated in the W and H fields on the Info palette.

TIP To drag from the center of a selection, hold down Alt and drag. Release the mouse, then release Alt.

TIP Hold down Shift while dragging to create a square or a circular selection.

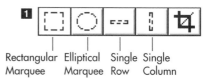

Rectangular Marquee / Elliptical Marquee / Single Row / Single Column

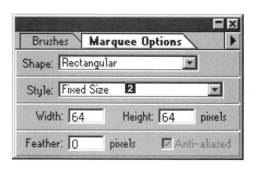

3 Drag diagonally to create a rectangular selection...

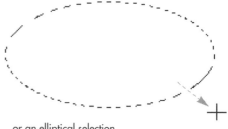

...or an elliptical selection.

Anti-aliasing

Check the **Anti-aliased** box on the Options palette to create a selection with a softened edge that steps to transparency. Uncheck Anti-aliased to create a crisp, hard-edged selection.

 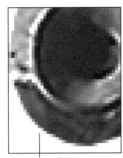

Aliased   Anti-aliased

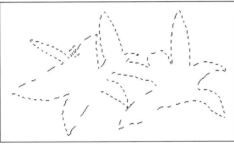

1 A **Lasso** tool selection.

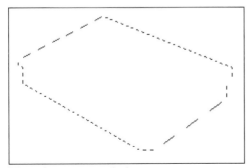

2 A **Polygon Lasso** tool selection.

NOTE: It's a good idea to make all your modifications to a selection before deselecting it, because it is very difficult to precisely reselect an area, unless you save it as a mask in an alpha channel. If the shape you want to select isn't too complex, use the Pen tool to select it instead of the Lasso—you'll get a smoother selection. You can also convert a selection into a path for precise reshaping.

To create a freeform selection:

1. Choose a target layer.

2. Choose the Lasso tool. $\wp$.

3. *Optional:* Enter a value in the Feather field to soften the edges of the selection. This amount will remain in effect until it's changed or the tool is reset.

4. Drag around an area of the layer **1**. When you release the mouse, the open ends of the selection will automatically join.

TIP To feather a selection after it's created, use the Select menu > Feather command (Control-Shift-D).

TIP To create a straight side as you're using the Lasso tool, with the mouse button still down, press Alt, and click to create corners. Release Alt to resume drawing a freehand selection.

To create a polygonal selection:

1. Choose a target layer.

2. Choose the Polygon Lasso tool ⋈ from the Lasso tool pop-out menu.

3. To create straight sides, click to create points **2**. To join the open ends of the selection, click on the starting point (a small circle will appear next to the pointer). Or Control-click or double-click to close the selection automatically.

Alt-drag to create a curved segment as you draw a polygonal selection. Release Alt to resume drawing straight sides.

Freeform or Polygonal Selection

If you click on a layer pixel with the Magic Wand tool, a selection will be created that includes adjacent pixels of a similar shade or color. You can then add similarly colored, non-adjacent pixels to the selection using the Similar command, or non-similar colors by Shift-clicking.

To select by color (Magic Wand):

1. Choose a target layer.

2. Choose the Magic Wand tool (W). ✨

3. Check the Sample Merged box on the Magic Wand Options palette to sample from colors in all the currently displayed layers to create the selection. Only pixels on the current target layer can be edited, but you can apply changes within the same selection marquee through successive target layers.
or
Uncheck the Sample Merged box to sample from colors on the target layer only.

4. Click on a shade or color on the target layer.

5. *Optional:* To enlarge the selection based on the current Tolerance setting on the Magic Wand Options palette, choose Select menu > Grow one or more times.

6. *Optional:* To select other, non-contiguous areas of similar color or shade on the layer, choose Select menu > Similar.

7. *Optional:* To specify a different Tolerance range, enter a number between 0 and 255 in the Tolerance field on the Magic Wand Options palette **1**, then click on the image again (see "Tolerance," at right).

TIP Choose Edit > Undo to undo the last created selection.

TIP To quickly select all the pixels on a target layer (not the Background), Control-click the layer name.

TIP If you have created a floating selection by moving a selection using the Move tool, you can Alt-drag with

To silhouette an object on a flat-color background

Select the background of the image using the Magic Wand tool, choose Select menu > Inverse (Control-Shift-I), choose Edit menu > Copy, then Edit menu > Paste. The object will paste onto its own layer. You can then fill the layer the object originally came from with a flat color.

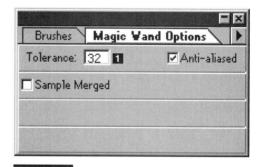

Tolerance

To expand or narrow the range of shades or colors the Magic Wand tool selects, enter a number between 0 and 255 in the **Tolerance** field on the Magic Wand Options palette. With a Tolerance of 32, the Magic Wand will select within a range of 16 shades below and 16 shades above the shade on which it is clicked. Enter 1 to select only one color or shade. To gradually narrow the range of shades or colors the Magic Wand tool selects, modify the Tolerance value between clicks.

another selection tool to remove pixel areas from the selection, if necessary.

TIP To add to a selection with the Magic Wand tool, Shift-click outside the selection. To subtract from a selection, Alt-click inside the selection. You can also use another selection tool, such as the Lasso, to add to or subtract from a selection (see page 67).

TIP To Expand or Contract the selection by a specified number of pixels, choose either command from the Select menu > Modify submenu.

PHOTO: PAUL PETROFF

A Magic Wand selection using a Tolerance of 10.

A Magic Wand selection using a Tolerance of 40.

Select by Color (Magic Wand)

Using the Color Range command, you can select areas based on existing colors in the image or based on a particular luminosity or hue range.

To select by color (Color Range):

1. Choose a target layer. The Color Range command samples colors from all the currently visible layers, but, of course, only the target layer will be available for editing. You can limit the selection range by first creating a selection.

2. Choose Select menu > Color Range.

3. Choose from the Select drop-down menu. You can limit the selection to a color range (Reds, Yellows, etc.), to a luminosity range (Highlights, Midtones, or Shadows), or to Sampled Colors (shades or colors you'll click on with the Color Range eyedropper).

4. Choose a Selection Preview option for the image window.

5. To preview the selection, click the Selection button; to redisplay the whole image, click the Image button. Or, hold down Control with either option selected to toggle between the two. If the image extends beyond the edges of your monitor, use the Image option—

the entire image will be displayed in the preview box to facilitate sampling.

6. If you chose Sampled Colors in step 3, click in the preview box or in the image window with the eyedropper cursor to sample colors in the image.

7. *Optional:* Move the Fuzziness slider to the right to expand the range of colors or shades selected, or move it to the left to narrow the range.

8. *Optional:* If you chose Sampled Colors in step 3, Shift-click with the eyedropper cursor in the image window or in the preview box to add more colors or shades to the selection. Alt-click to remove colors or shades from the selection. Or, click the "+" or "-" eyedropper icon button in the Color Range dialog box, then click on the image or in the preview box without holding down Shift or Alt.

9. Click OK or press Enter.

Choose a color or luminosity range from the **Select** drop-down menu, or choose **Sampled Colors** to sample colors from the image using the Color Range eyedropper.

Move the **Fuzziness** slider to the left or to the right to reduce or expand the range of colors selected.

Choose a **Selection Preview** method for the image in the image window.

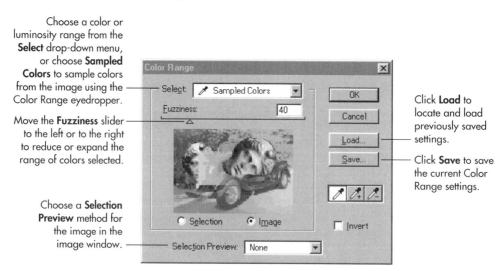

Click **Load** to locate and load previously saved settings.

Click **Save** to save the current Color Range settings.

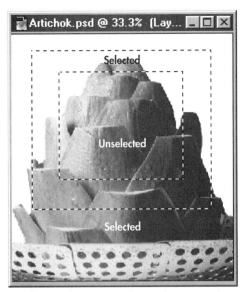

1 A **frame** selection created using the Rectangular Marquee tool.

To create a frame selection:

1. Choose a target layer.

2. Choose the Rectangular or Elliptical Marquee tool (M), then press and drag to create a selection, or choose Select menu > Select All (Control-A).

3. Alt-drag a smaller selection inside the first selection **1**.

To produce this image, a frame selection was created a different way: First the Marquee tool was used to select the center area, then the Inverse command was used to reverse the selected and non-selected areas so the outer area became the selection. The Levels command was used to screen back the selected area.

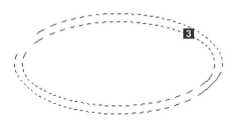

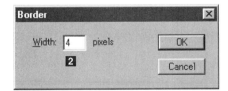

To select a narrow border around a selection:

1. Create a selection.

2. Choose Select menu > Modify > Border.

3. Enter the desired Width of the border in pixels **2**. The allowable range is 1 to 64.

4. Click OK or press Enter. The new selection will evenly straddle the edge of the original selection **3**.

Frame Selection; Border Selection

To deselect a selection:

With any tool selected, choose Select menu > None (Control-D).

or

Click anywhere on the layer using a Marquee tool or the Lasso tool , but not the Polygon Lasso tool.

or

Click **inside** the selection with the Magic Wand tool. (If you click outside the selection with the Magic Wand, you will create a new selection.)

TIP It's difficult to reselect the same area twice, so deselect a selection only when you're sure you've finished using it. If you unintentionally deselect, choose Edit menu > Undo immediately. If you think you might want to reuse a selection, save it as a path or in an alpha channel.

■ Click **outside** a selection to deselect it with a Marquee or Lasso tool. Click **inside** a selection to deselect it with the Magic Wand tool.

PHOTO: NADINE MARKOVA

A selection deleted from a **layer**.

If you delete a non-floating selection from a layer, the original selection area will become transparent. If you delete a non-floating selection from the Background, the selection area will fill with the current Background color.

To delete a selection:

Press Delete.

or

Choose Edit menu > Clear.

or

Choose Edit menu > Cut (Control-X) if you want to place the selection on the Clipboard.

A selection deleted from the **Background**.

1 **Moving** a marquee.

PHOTO: E. WEINMANN

To move a selection marquee:

1. *Optional:* To aid in positioning the marquee, choose View menu > Show Grid or drag a guide or guides from the horizontal or vertical ruler, and also turn on Snap to Guides (View menu > Snap to Guides, or Control-Shift-;).

2. Choose any selection tool.

3. Drag inside the selection **1**. Hold down Shift after you start dragging to constrain the movement to 45° increments.
or
Press any arrow key to move the marquee one pixel at a time.

TIP If you drag a selection on a layer using the Move tool, the selection will be cut from its layer and the empty space will be replaced by layer transparency. If a selection is moved from the Background, the empty space will be filled with the current Background color. In either case, the selection will become a floating selection.

2 The original selection—the **angels** are selected.

3 The selection **inverted**—the **background** is selected.

To switch the selected and unselected areas:

Choose Select menu > Inverse (Control-Shift-I) **2**–**3**.

TIP Choose Inverse again to switch back.

TIP It's easy to select a shape on a flat color background: Choose the Magic Wand tool, enter 5 in the Tolerance field on the Magic Wand Options palette, click on the flat color background to select it entirely, then choose Select menu > Inverse.

Move Selection Marquee; Inverse Selection

To hide a selection marquee:

Choose View menu > Hide Edges (Control-H). The selection will remain active.

TIP To redisplay the selection marquee, choose View menu > Show Edges.

TIP To verify that a selection is still active, press on the Select menu. Most commands will be available if a selection is active.

TIP You can choose the Hide Edges command while some Image menu and Filter menu dialog boxes are open.

To transform a selection:

To apply the transform commands (flip, rotate, or scale) **1**–**2**, follow the instructions for transforming a layer on pages 89–91.

If you transform a selection on a layer, any remaining empty space will be replaced by layer transparency. If the selection was on the Background, the empty space will be filled with the current Background color. In either case, if you transform a selection—unlike if you transform a layer—the selection will automatically turn into a floating selection.

To resize a selection marquee using a command, choose Select menu > Modify > Expand or Contract, enter a number of pixels in the Expand By or Contract By field, then click OK.

1 Scaling a selection.

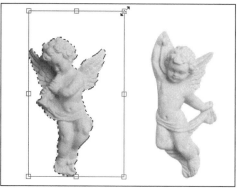

2 The selection enlarged.

Hide Selection Marquee; Transform Selection

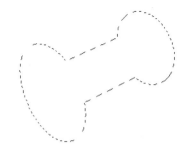

1 The original selection.

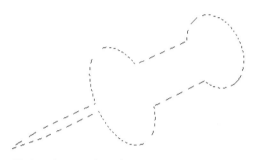

2 The selection enlarged.

To add to a selection:

Choose any selection tool other than the Magic Wand, position the cursor over the selection, then Shift-drag to define an additional selection area **1**–**2**.
or
Click the Magic Wand tool, then Shift-click on any unselected area.

TIP If the additional selection overlaps the original selection, it will become part of the new, larger selection. If the addition does not overlap the original selection, a second, separate selection will be created.

To subtract from a selection:

Choose any selection tool other than the Magic Wand, then Alt-drag around the area to be subtracted.
or
Choose the Magic Wand tool, then Alt-click on the area of shade or color in the selection to be subtracted.

TIP Alt-Shift-drag to select the intersection of an existing selection and the new selection.

Add to or Subtract from a Selection

To vignette an image:

1. For a multi-layer image, choose a target layer, and uncheck the Preserve Transparency box. The vignette you create is going to appear to fade into the layer or layers below it.

For an image with a Background only, choose a Background color (see pages 111–115) for the area around the vignette.

2. Choose the Rectangular Marquee ⬚, Elliptical Marquee ⬭, or Lasso tool ⌒.

3. On the Options palette, enter 15 or 20 in the Feather field. Or to feather the selection after it's created instead, choose Select menu > Feather after step 4.

4. Create a selection **1**.

5. Choose Select menu > Inverse (Control-Shift-I).

6. Press Delete **2**.

7. Deselect (Control-D).

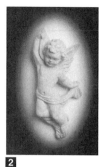

1 **2**

The original image.

The vignette.

Vignette an Image

COMPOSITING 6

1 Moving a selection on a **layer**...

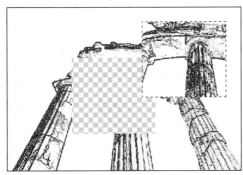

2 ...a **transparent** hole is left behind.

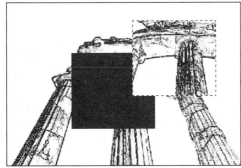

3 Moving a selection on the **Background**: the exposed area fills with the current **Background color**.

THIS **CHAPTER** covers methods for rearranging image elements using the Move tool and using the Clipboard commands: Cut, Copy, Paste, and Paste Into. Compositing is accomplished using layers. In order to place imagery on its own layer, you'll need to learn how to select pixels in a one-layer document so you can move them from one layer to another or copy them between images. (Instructions for moving a selected area of a layer or a whole layer to another document are on pages 94–96.)

To move a selection:

1. *Optional*: To help you position the selection, choose View menu > Show Grid (Control-") or drag a guide or guides from the horizontal or vertical ruler, and also turn on Snap to Guides (View menu > Snap to Guides, or Control-Shift-;).

2. If the selection is on the Background, choose a Background color. The area the moved selection exposes will fill with this color automatically. If the selection is on a layer, the exposed area will fill with transparency.

3. Choose the Move tool (V). Or hold down Control to access the Move tool while any tool other than the Pen or Hand tool is chosen.

4. Position the cursor over the selection, then drag. The selection marquee and its contents will move together **1**–**3**. A floating selection layer will be created. Read about floating selections on the next page.

TIP Press any arrow key to move a selection in 1-pixel increments.

If you follow the instructions on the previous page to move a selection or the instructions below to drag-copy a selection, a new, temporary Floating Selection layer will be created automatically **1**. You can modify floating selection pixels without changing pixels in the layer below it.

What to do with a floating selection:

To merge a floating selection into the layer below it, click on any other layer. Any areas that extend beyond the selection will be preserved and can be dragged into view using the Move tool. The selection marquee will remain active, though now it will surround pixels on the new target layer. Deselect the marquee if you're done with it.

or

To turn the floating selection into its own layer and leave pixels on the underlying layer unchanged, double-click the Floating Selection layer name, enter a name, then click OK.

or

To remove the floating selection altogether, with the "Floating Selection" name active, click the Layers palette Trash icon, or press Delete, or choose Edit menu > Cut or Edit menu > Clear, or choose Delete Selection from the Layers palette command menu.

To drag-copy a selection:

1. Choose the Move tool. (Use the Control key to access the Move tool while another tool is selected.)

2. Hold down Alt before and as you drag the selection you want to copy. Release the mouse before you release Alt. The copied selection will appear on the Layers palette as a floating selection **2**–**3**.

What's the difference between a floating and a non-floating selection?

A **non-floating selection** is created when any selection tool or the Color Range command is used. If you Delete or Cut selected non-floating pixels from the Background, the area left behind will automatically fill with the current Background color. If you remove pixels from a layer, the area left behind will be transparent.

A **floating selection** layer is created automatically if a selection is dragged or Alt-dragged with the Move tool. Pixels in a floating selection are temporarily suspended above the former target layer.

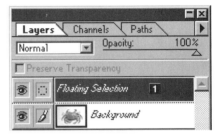

PHOTO: E. WEINMANN

2 Alt-dragging a selection. **3** A copy of the selection is moved.

An object in motion

Hold down **Alt** and press an **arrow** key a bunch of times to generate multiple copies of a selection, one pixel apart: Each time you create a new copy, the prior floating selection layer copy will merge into the underlying layer. Hold down **Alt** and **Shift** and press an **arrow** key to offset each new copy by ten pixels.

Know your image dimensions and reso-lution before copying between images

■ Before using the Clipboard commands, compare the **dimensions** of the image to be Cut or Copied with the dimensions of the layer onto which it will be pasted (the "destination layer"). If the image on the Clipboard is larger than the destination layer, the Clipboard image will extend beyond the image window. You can use the Move tool to reposition the extended areas after pasting.

■ The size of a selection may change when pasted, because it is rendered in the **resolution** of the destination layer. If the resolution of the destination layer is higher than that of the imagery you are pasting, the Clipboard image will become smaller when pasted. Conversely, if the resolution of the destination layer is lower than the resolution of the Clipboard imagery, the Clipboard image will be enlarged when pasted. You can use the Image Size dialog box to choose the same resolution (and dimensions, if desired) for both images. Follow the instructions on page 74 to paste into a smaller image.

Clipboard facts

You can use the Cut or Copy command to save a selection to a temporary storage area called the Clipboard, and then use the Paste or Paste Into command to paste the Clipboard imagery onto another layer in the same image or in another image. The Cut, Copy, and Paste Into commands are available only when an area of a layer is selected.

If you create a selection and choose the Cut command, the selection will be placed on the Clipboard. (The Clear command doesn't use the Clipboard.) If you Cut or Clear a non-floating selection from the Background, the exposed area will be filled with the current Background color. If you remove pixels from a layer, the area left behind will be transparent. For the most seamless transition, check the Anti-aliased box on the Options palette for your selection tool before creating your selection.

The Paste command pastes the Clipboard contents into a new layer and preserves any areas that extend beyond the selection. You can move the entire layer to reveal the extended areas. If you then save your document, the extended areas will save with it. If you crop the layer, however, the extended areas will be discarded.

The Clipboard can contain only one selection at a time, and it is replaced each time Cut or Copy is chosen. The same Clipboard contents can be pasted an unlimited number of times, and will be retained if you exit Photoshop. They will also be retained if you switch to another application if the Export Clipboard box is checked in the General Preferences dialog box.

One more info bite: The dimensions in the New dialog box automatically match the dimensions of imagery on the Clipboard.

TIP If the Clipboard imagery is large, the remaining available memory for processing is reduced. To reclaim memory, empty the Clipboard by choosing Edit > Purge > Clipboard.

To copy and paste a selection in the same image:

1. Select an area on a layer or the Background. To feather the selection, choose Select menu > Feather, and enter a value.

2. Choose Edit menu > Copy **1** (Control-C) (or choose Edit menu > Cut to cut the selection).

3. Choose a target layer.

4. Choose Edit menu > Paste (Control-V) **2**.

5. *Optional:* Restack, move, or defringe the new layer.

If you drag selected pixels from one image to another, presto, those selected pixels will be copied onto a new layer in the destination image. This drag-and-drop method bypasses the Clipboard, so it both saves memory and preserves the Clipboard contents. If your monitor it too small to display two image windows simultaneously, use the copy-and-paste method instead.

To drag-and-drop a selection between images:

1. Open the source and destination images, and make sure the two image windows don't completely overlap.

2. Select an area of a layer.

3. Choose the Move tool.
   or
   Hold down Control.

4. Drag the selection into the destination image window, and release the mouse where you want the pixels to be dropped. You can always move the new layer around later using the Move tool.

TIP Hold down Shift before and as you drag to automatically drop the selection in the exact center of the destination image. You can release the mouse when the pointer is anywhere inside the destination image window.

TIP To drag-and-drop a whole layer to another image, see pages 95–96.

1 An area of the Background is placed on the Clipboard via **the Copy** command.

2 The **pasted** imagery appears on the target layer.

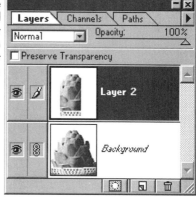

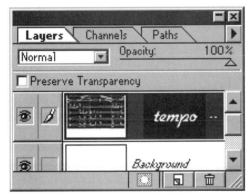

1 The music layer was selected in another image, then pasted into a Type Mask tool selection.

2 The layer contents can be repositioned within the layer mask, since the two aren't linked together. For this image, the music layer icon was activated, and then the layer contents were moved upward using the Move tool.

Layers	Channels	Paths	
Normal		Opacity:	100%

☐ Preserve Transparency

3 The pasted image appeared on a new layer and the layer mask was created automatically when the Paste Into command was chosen. The pasted image (the music) is only visible within the white areas in the layer mask, in this case, the letter shapes.

If you use the Paste Into command to paste the Clipboard contents into the boundary of a selection, a new layer is created automatically and the active marquee becomes a layer mask. The pasted image can be repositioned within the boundary of the visible part of the layer mask, and the mask itself can also be edited.

To paste into a selection:

1. Select an area of a layer. If you want to feather the selection, choose Select menu > Feather and enter a value.

2. Choose Edit menu > Copy to copy pixels only from the target layer, or choose Edit menu > Copy Merged (Control-Shift-C) to copy pixels within the selection area from all the currently visible layers.

3. Leave the same layer active, or activate a different layer, or activate a layer in another image.

4. Select an area (or areas) into which the Clipboard image will be pasted.

5. Choose Edit menu > Paste Into (Control-Shift-V). A new layer and layer mask will be created **1**–**3**.

6. *Optional:* The entire Clipboard contents were pasted onto the layer, but the layer mask may be hiding some of them. Use the Move tool to reposition the imagery within the area the layer mask reveals.

To select the layer mask, click on the layer mask thumbnail. Drag the layer mask to reposition the area the layer mask reveals. Paint on the layer mask with white to reveal parts of the image, or with black to hide parts of the image.

To move the layer and layer mask in unison, first, on the Layers palette, click in the space between the layer and layer mask thumbnails to link the two layer components together. (Click the link icon to unlink the layer and layer mask.)

Paste Into a Selection

Normally, in Photoshop 4.0 or later, if you move a large selection or layer or paste into another image, all the pixels on a layer are preserved, even those that may extend beyond the visible edge of the layer (Adobe calls this "Big Data"), regardless of the dimensions of the image into which the layer is moved. If you want to trim the pasted imagery as it's pasted, follow the instructions below, but please read the sidebar on page 71 before proceeding.

To paste into a smaller image:

1. Click on the destination image, then hold down Alt and press and hold on the Sizes bar in the lower left corner of the image window. Jot down the image's dimensions.

2. Create a selection on another (larger) image.

3. Choose Edit menu > Copy.

4. Choose File menu > New.

5. Type a name in the Name field, then click OK. The Width, Height, Resolution, and Mode will automatically conform to that of the Clipboard imagery.

6. Choose Edit menu > Paste.

7. Choose Image menu > Image Size.

8. Check the Resample Image box to make the resolution the same as that of the destination image **1**. Enter smaller numbers than the dimensions of the destination image (step 1, above) in the Width and Height fields **2**, then click OK or press Return.

9. Choose Select menu > All to reselect the pasted layer.

10. Choose Edit menu > Copy, click in the destination image, then choose Edit menu > Paste.
    or
    Shift-drag the layer name into the destination image window.

Trim or include Big Data

- To **remove** pixels that extend beyond the edge of a layer, make sure the layer is active, choose Edit menu > Select All, then choose Image menu > Crop. Trimming off Big Data will reduce a file's storage size.

- If you apply an image editing command, like a filter, to a whole layer, any big data that is part of the layer will also be modified. To **include** Big Data by making it visible in the image window, use the Canvas Size command.

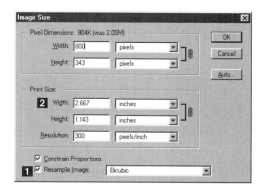

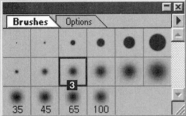

4 The original image.

5 After using the **Sharpen** tool on the strawberry in the center, and the **Blur** tool on the rest of the image.

The Blur tool decreases contrast between pixels. Use it to soften edges between shapes. The Sharpen tool increases contrast between pixels. Use it to delineate edges between shapes. Neither tool can be used on a image in Bitmap or Indexed Color mode.

To sharpen or blur edges:

1. Choose the Blur tool ◊ or the Sharpen tool △ (R to toggle between the two). Each tool has its own Options palette settings.

2. On the Focus Tools Options palette, choose a Pressure percentage **1**. Try a setting of around 30% first.
and
Choose a mode **2**. Choose Normal to sharpen or blur pixels of any shade or color. Choose Darken to sharpen or blur only pixels darker than the Foreground color. Choose Lighten to sharpen or blur only pixels lighter than the Foreground color. (The blending modes are described on pages 26–28.)

3. *Optional:* Click the Sample Merged box on the Options palette to pick up pixels from other visible layers under the pointer to place on the target layer.

4. Click the Brushes tab on the palette, then click a hard-edged or soft-edged tip **3**.

5. Drag across the area of the image that you want to sharpen or blur **4**–**5**. Stroke again if you want to intensify the effect.

TIP To avoid creating an overly grainy texture, use the Sharpen tool with a medium Pressure setting and stroke only once on an area.

Sharpen or Blur

Grids, rulers, and guides can help you position objects precisely.

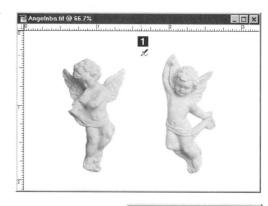

To hide or show rulers:

Choose View menu > Show Rulers (Control-R). Rulers will appear on the top and left sides of the image window, and the current position of the pointer is indicated by a dotted marker on each ruler **1**. To hide the rulers, choose View menu > Hide Rulers.

TIP To quickly access the Units & Rulers Preferences dialog box to change the ruler units, double-click inside the either ruler.

To change the rulers' zero origin:

1. To make the new ruler origin snap to gridlines, choose View menu > Snap to Grid (Control-Shift-"). To make the ruler origin snap to guidelines, choose View menu > Snap to Guides (Control-Shift-;).

2. Drag from the intersection of the rulers in the upper left corner of the image window diagonally into the image **2**–**3**.

TIP To reset the ruler origin, double-click where the rulers intersect in the upper left corner of the image window.

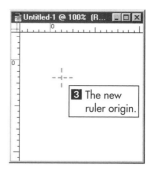

2 Dragging the **ruler origin**.

3 The new ruler origin.

The grid is a non-printing framework that can be used to align image elements. Guides are individual guidelines that you drag into the image window yourself. With View > Snap To Guides turned on, selections and tool pointers will snap to a guide if it's moved near (with 8 screen pixels of) a guide. Ditto for View > Snap to Grid.

To hide or show the grid:

Choose View > Show Grid (Control-") **4**. To hide the grid, choose View > Hide Grid.

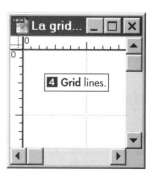

4 Grid lines.

Rulers; Grid

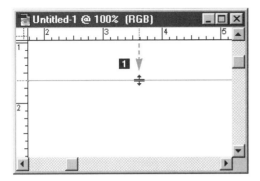

Untitled-1 @ 100% (RGB)

2 The original image.

3 We applied the Glass filter to a layer, chose Undo, selected the area around the tree, and then filled the selection (Use: Snapshot). Try doing the same thing using the Distort > Wave or Ripple filter or an Artistic or Sketch filter.

To create a guide:

Make sure the rulers are displayed, then drag from the horizontal or vertical ruler into the image window **1**. Hold down Shift as you drag to snap the guide to ruler increments as you drag. If the grid is displayed and View > Snap to Grid is turned on, the guide can be snapped to a grid line.

TIP To lock all ruler guides, choose View menu > Lock Guides (Control-Alt-;).

TIP To switch a guide from vertical to horizontal, or vice versa, hold down Alt as you drag.

TIP To move an existing guide, drag it using the Move tool.

TIP File menu > Preferences > Guides & Grid to choose a new guide color or style.

To remove guides:

To remove one guide, drag it out of the image window using the Move tool.
or
To remove all guides, choose View menu > Clear Guides.

Take Snapshot copies the contents of the target layer into the snapshot buffer. The buffer contents can be recouped manually by dragging the Rubber Stamp tool (From Snapshot option) or into a selection using the Fill command (Use: Snapshot option).

To use the Take Snapshot option:

1. Edit or apply a filter to a target layer.

2. Choose Edit menu > Take Snapshot. Choose Take Merged Snapshot to copy the contents from all visible layers.

3. Choose Edit menu > Undo.

4. Use the Rubber Stamp tool, Option: From Snapshot, to restore parts of the prior effect manually.
or
Select part of a layer and use the Edit menu > Fill (Use: Snapshot) command **2**–**3**. Choose Edit menu > Purge > Snapshot when you're finished.

Create, Remove Guides; Take Snapshot

Cloning

The Rubber Stamp tool can be used to clone and rearrange imagery from one layer to another within an image or to clone imagery from one image to another. The same tool can be used with its From Saved option to restore part of the last saved version of an image.

To clone areas within an image:

1. Choose the Rubber Stamp tool (S). 🔨

2. On the Rubber Stamp Options palette, choose a mode.
and
Choose an Opacity percentage.
and
Choose "Clone (aligned)" from the Option drop-down menu ❶. The other options are explained at right.

3. Check the Sample Merged box on the Options palette to have the Rubber Stamp tool sample pixels from all currently visible layers that you Alt-click over. Uncheck Sample Merged to sample pixels from only the current target layer.

4. Click the Brushes tab, then click a small brush tip to clone a small detail or a medium- to large-size tip to duplicate larger areas.

5. Activate the layer you want to clone from.

6. In the image window, Alt-click on the area of the layer you want to clone from to establish a source point. Don't click on a transparent part of a layer—nothing will be cloned.

The other Rubber Stamp options

No source point is needed for these steps.

■ To Rubber Stamp a **pattern**, before step 1, at left, select a rectangular area to become the pattern tile, choose Edit menu > Define Pattern, choose Pattern (aligned) or Pattern (non-aligned) from the Rubber Stamp Options palette drop-down menu, then drag on the layer to stamp the pattern. Choose Pattern (aligned) to stamp pattern tiles in a perfect grid, regardless of how many separate strokes you use. If you don't want the tiles from each stroke to align, choose Pattern (non-aligned).

■ To clone areas from the last saved version of the image, choose **From Saved**.

■ To create Impressionistic strokes, choose **Impressionist**, and use short strokes as you clone.

PHOTO: CARA WOOD

1 Drag the mouse where you want the clone to appear. To produce this illustration, **Clone (aligned)** was chosen for the Rubber Stamp tool.

2 Choose **Clone (non-aligned)** for the Rubber Stamp tool to create multiple clones from the same source point.

3 An opacity of 45% was chosen for the Rubber Stamp tool to create this double exposure effect.

7. On the same layer, drag the mouse back and forth where you want the clone to appear **1**.

or

For the most flexibility in editing the image layer, choose another target layer, then drag the mouse.

NOTE: If the Preserve Transparency box is checked on the Layers palette, cloning will only appear where existing pixels are on that layer.

Two cursors will appear on the screen: a crosshair cursor over the source point and a Rubber Stamp cursor where you drag the mouse. Imagery from the source point will appear where the mouse is dragged, and it will replace the underlying pixels.

TIP Using the Rubber Stamp tool with the Clone (aligned) option, you can clone the entire layer, as long as you don't change the source point. The distance between the source point cursor and the Rubber Stamp cursor will remain constant, so you can release the mouse and drag in another area. To establish a new source point to clone from, Alt-click on a different area of the source image.

TIP Choose Clone (non-aligned) for the Rubber Stamp tool to create multiple clones from the same source point. The crosshair cursor will return to the same source point each time you release the mouse. You can create a pattern with Clone (non-aligned) chosen by cloning an image element over and over **2**.

TIP You can change the Options palette settings for the Rubber Stamp tool between strokes. To create a "double exposure" on one layer, choose a low Opacity percentage so the underlying pixels will partially show through the cloned pixels **3**.

Clone Areas Within an Image

To clone from image to image:

1. Open two images, and position the two windows side by side.

2. If both images are color, choose the same image mode for both. You can also clone between a color image and a Grayscale image. **NOTE:** Choose the Don't Flatten option to preserve layers.

3. Choose the Rubber Stamp tool. 🖫

4. From the Rubber Stamp Options palette, choose Option: Clone (aligned) to reproduce a continuous area from the source point **1**.
   or
   Choose Clone (Non-aligned) to produce multiple clones from the source point.
   and
   Choose an Opacity and a mode.

5. Click the Brushes tab, then click a brush tip.

6. Click on the image where the clone is to appear, and choose a target layer for the clone.

7. Alt-click on the area of the source (non-active) image that you want to clone from **2**.

8. Drag back and forth on the destination (active) image to make the clone appear.

TIP To create a brush stroke version of an image, clone to a new document with a white or solid-colored background **3**.

TIP To test a mode for the Rubber Stamp tool, create a new document with a white background, make part of the background black, choose Clone (non-aligned) and choose a mode from the Rubber Stamp Options palette, then clone to the new document. Choose Darken mode to clone onto a light background, Lighten mode to clone onto a dark background, Luminosity mode to produce a grayscale clone from a color image, or Dissolve mode with an opacity below 100% to produce a grainy, chalky clone.

Destination image.   Source image.

PHOTO: PAUL PETROFF

2 **Alt-click** on the non-active image to establish a source point, then drag back and forth in short strokes on the active (destination) image to make the clone appear.

3 To create this effect, an image was cloned to a new document with a white background.

Physique Medley, David Humphrey. To produce this image, Humphrey composited scanned embroidery and his own charcoal drawings and photographs, among other things. He adjusted luminosity levels of the various components on individual layers using blending modes (Darken, Multiply) and the Eraser and Burn tools.

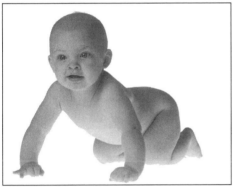

1 A selection copy with a Feather Radius of 0.

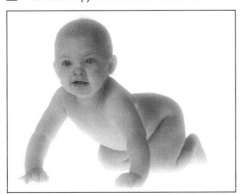

2 A selection copy with a Feather Radius of 30 pixels.

Apply the Feather command to fade the edge of a selection a specified number of pixels inward and outward from the marquee. A feather radius of 5, for example, would create a feather area 10 pixels wide.

NOTE: The feather won't appear until the selection is modified with a painting tool, copied, pasted, moved, or filled, or a filter or an Image menu command is applied to it.

To feather a selection:

1. Choose Select menu > Feather (Control-Shift-D).

2. Enter a number up to 250 in the Feather Radius field. The actual width of the feather is affected by the image resolution. A high resolution image will require a wider feather radius to produce the same degree of feathering than a low resolution image will require.

3. Click OK or press Enter **1**–**2**.

TIP To specify a feather radius for a selection before it's created, choose a Marquee or Lasso tool and enter a number in the Feather field on the Options palette.

If you save an image and then modify one of its layers, you can restore portions of the saved version to contrast with the modifications using the Rubber Stamp tool with its From Saved option. Save your image at the stage at which you would like it restored.

NOTE: The From Saved option cannot be used if you added or deleted a layer or a layer mask from the image, cropped the image, or changed its mode, dimensions, or resolution since it was last saved.

To restore part of the last saved version of an image:

1. Save the image.

2. Modify a layer.

3. Choose the Rubber Stamp tool. ♨

4. Choose From Saved from the Options drop-down menu on the Rubber Stamp Options palette.
and
Choose an opacity. Choose a low opacity to restore a faint impression of the saved image.
and
Choose a mode.

5. Click the Brushes tab, then click a brush tip.

6. Drag across any area of the layer **1**–**2**. Each subsequent stroke over the same area will restore it more. To undo the last stroke, choose Edit menu > Undo (Control-Z) immediately.

1 The original image, to which we applied the Graphic Pen filter.

2 The Rubber Stamp tool was used with 95% opacity to restore part of the image.

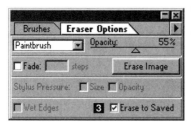

Erase to saved

You can also use the Eraser tool (E) ⌫ with its Erase to Saved option **3** to restore pixels from the last saved version of an image. An advantage of using the Eraser is that in addition to choosing an opacity and mode for the tool, you can also choose a tool type (Paintbrush, Airbrush, Pencil, or Block) and other options from its Options palette.

[sidebar, vertical text] **Restore Part of the Last Saved Version**

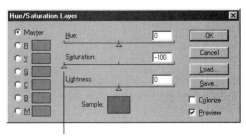

1 In the Hue/Saturation dialog box, move the Saturation slider all the way to the left to remove the color from the layer.

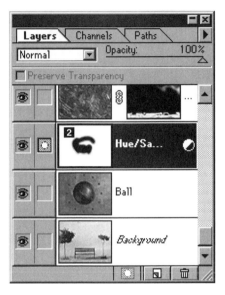

Another nifty technique

Duplicate a color layer, use the Hue/Saturation command to make the layer grayscale, choose Image menu > Add Layer Mask > Hide All to create a layer mask for that layer, and then paint with white to reveal parts of the grayscale layer above the color layer. You can gradually reshape the mask this way, alternately painting with black to add to the mask or white to remove the mask.

To convert a color layer to grayscale and selectively restore its color:

1. Choose a target layer in a color image. Layers below this layer will be affected by the adjustment layer you're about to create.

2. Control-click the Create New Layer button on the Layers palette to create an adjustment layer, choose Type: Hue/Saturation, then click OK.

3. Move the Saturation slider all the way to the left (to -100) **1**.

4. Click OK or press Enter.

5. Set the Foreground color to black.

6. On the adjustment layer, paint across the image where you want to restore the original colors from the underlying layers **2**. (Paint with white to reset areas to grayscale.)

7. *Optional:* You can also move a layer above the adjustment layer to fully restore that layer's color.

TIP Choose any of the following mode and opacity combinations for the adjustment layer:

Dissolve with a 40%–50% Opacity to restore color with a chalky texture.

Multiply with a 100% Opacity to restore subtle color in the darker areas of the image layers.

Color Burn to darken and intensify color in the image layers.

TIP To limit the adjustment layer effect to just the layer directly below it, Alt-click the line between them on the Layers palette to create a clipping group.

Convert to Grayscale, then Restore Color

To eliminate a noticeable "seam" after pasting or moving layer pixels, use the Defringe command. It recolors pixels from the edge of the selection with pixel colors from just inside the edge within a specified radius. (If the edges of the selection or pasted imagery were originally anti-aliased and were originally on a black or white background, use the Select menu > Matting > Remove Black Matte or Remove White Matte command, respectively, to remove unwanted remnants from the original background.)

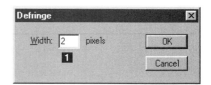

To defringe a layer:

1. With the target layer or floating selection layer chosen, choose Layer menu > Matting > Defringe.

2. Enter a Width for the Defringe area **1**. Try a low number first (1, 2 or 3) so your edges don't lose definition. Some non-edge areas may also be affected.

3. Click OK or press Enter.

3 The original Magic Wand tool selection.

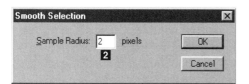

The Smooth command adds unselected pixels to a selection from within a specified radius.

To smooth a selection or a layer:

1. Choose Select menu > Modify > Smooth.

2. Enter a Sample Radius value between 1 and 16 **2**. The larger the Sample Radius, the more unselected pixels will be added to the selection.

3. Click OK or press Enter **3**–**4**.

4 After applying the Smooth command, Sample Radius of 3.

Defringe a Layer; Smooth a Selection

LAYERS 7

Topics that are covered in this chapter
- Create a new layer
- Turn a selection into a layer
- Show or hide a layer
- Duplicate a layer
- Flip or rotate a layer
- Transform a layer
- Convert the Background into a layer
- Restack a layer
- Move a layer within an image
- Drag-and-drop a layer to another image
- Delete a layer
- Merge down a layer
- Flatten layers

Topics that are covered in Chapter 12, More Layers
- Blend pixels between layers
- Create and modify layer masks
- Link layers to move them as a unit
- Create a clipping group of layers

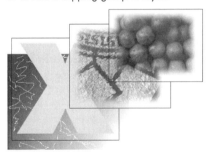

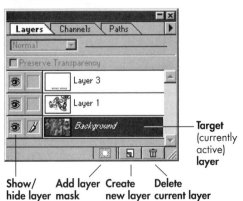

Show/hide layer — Add layer mask — Create new layer — Delete current layer — Target (currently active) layer

LAYERS ARE LIKE clear acetate sheets: opaque where there is imagery and transparent where there is no imagery. You can assign to each layer a different opacity and choose a mode to control how each layer blends with the layers below it. You can change the stacking order of layers, and you can also assign a layer mask to any layer.

If you choose Contents: White or Background Color for a new image, the bottommost area of the image will be the Background, which is not a layer. If you choose Contents: Transparent, the bottommost component of the image will be a layer. Other layers can be added to an image at any time using the Layers palette or the Layer menu. Only one layer can be edited at a time, so you can easily modify one part of an image without disturbing the other layers.

Layers are listed on the Layers palette from topmost to bottommost, with the Background, of course, at the bottom of the list. The target layer, which is the layer currently highlighted on the palette, is the only layer that can be edited. Click on a layer name to make it the target layer. The target layer name is listed on the image window title bar.

If you're using Photoshop version 4.0 or later, you can create an adjustment layer to see how various color adjustments affect the layers below it, and then you can make the effect permanent or discard the adjustment layer altogether if you want to leave the underlying layers unchanged.

VERY IMPORTANT NOTES: Only the Photoshop file format supports multiple layers and the option to create a transparent bottommost layer. If you save your image in any other file format via the Save a Copy command, all the layers will be flattened, and any transparency in the bottommost layer will become opaque white. If you change image modes (i.e. from RGB to CMYK), click Don't Flatten to preserve layers.

An image can contain as many layers as available memory and storage allow, but since the pixel (non-transparent) areas on each layer occupy storage space, when your image is finished, you can merge two or more layers together or flatten all the layers into one to reduce the file's storage size.

To create a new layer:

1. To create a layer with 100% opacity and Normal mode, simply click the Create New Layer button at the bottom of the Layers palette **1**.

To choose options for the new layer when it's created, choose New Layer from the Layers palette command menu or Alt-click the Create New Layer button at the bottom of the palette, and then follow the remaining steps.

2. *Optional:* Enter a new name for the layer in the Name field **2**.

3. *Optional:* Choose a different opacity or mode (they can be changed later).

4. *Optional:* Click the Group With Previous Layer box to make the new layer a part of a clipping group (see pages 154–155).

5. Click OK or press Enter. The new layer will appear directly above the previously active layer.

TIP To change the size of the Layers palette thumbnails or turn off thumbnail display altogether, choose Palette Options from the Layers palette command menu, then click a different Thumbnail Size **3**. Choose None or the smallest size thumbnail to improve Photoshop's performance speed.

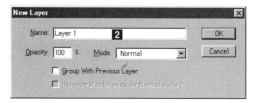

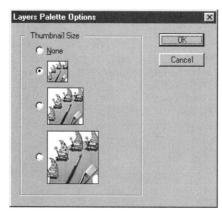

3 You can click a different **Thumbnail Size** or turn off thumbnail display altogether (None) via the Layers Palette Options dialog box.

Before adding a new layer to your image, choose **Document Sizes** from the Sizes bar pop-up menu and note the current **image size**.

The second figure is the amount of **RAM** the layered, unflattened file is using. Note how much the file's storage size increases when you add a new layer. The image in this illustration contains three layers.

Create a New Layer

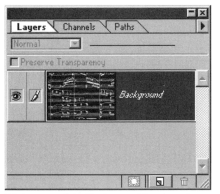

1

2 An area of the Background is selected.

3 After choosing the **Layer Via Cut**, the selection is cut from the Background and placed on **its own layer**.

If you create a floating selection by dragging or Alt-dragging a selection with the Move tool, the selection will automatically be placed on a new, temporary layer above the target layer (the layer currently highlighted on the Layers palette), and will bear the name "Floating Selection." You can edit a floating selection, but it's better to convert it into a layer right away, because simply clicking on another layer name will cause a floating selection to merge with the layer directly below it.

To turn a floating selection into a layer:

1. With the "Floating Selection" name highlighted, Alt-click the Create New Layer button on the Layers palette **1**.
   or
   Double-click the "Floating Selection" layer name on the Layers palette.

2. *Optional:* Rename the layer, choose a different opacity or mode for it, or check the Group With Previous Layer box to make the new layer part of a clipping group (see page 155).

3. Click OK or press Enter.

TIP To delete a floating selection, with the "Floating Selection" name active, click the Layers palette Trash icon, or choose Delete Selection from the Layers palette command menu, or press Delete.

To turn a selection into a layer:

1. Create a selection.

2. To place a copy of the selected pixels on a new layer and leave the original layer untouched, choose Layer menu > New > Layer Via Copy (Control-J).
   or
   To place the selected pixels on a new layer and remove them from the original layer, choose Layer menu > New > Layer Via Cut (Control-Shift-J) **2**–**3**.

Turn a Selection into a Layer

You can hide layers you're not currently working on if you find them distracting. Remember, as you're working, that only currently visible layers can be merged (or printed). And when layers are flattened, hidden layers are discarded.

To hide or show layers:

Click the eye icon on the Layers palette for any individual layer you want to show or hide **1**–**3**. Click again where the eye icon was to redisplay the layer.

or

Drag in the eye column to hide or show multiple layers.

or

Alt-click an eye icon to hide all other layers except the one you click on. Alt-click again to redisplay all the other layers.

To duplicate a layer in the same image:

To create a new layer without naming it, drag the name of the layer you want to duplicate over the Create New Layer button at the bottom of the Layers palette. The duplicate layer will appear above the original target layer, and it will be the active layer.

or

To name the duplicate as you create it, on the Layers palette, activate the Layer you want to duplicate, choose Duplicate Layer from the Layers palette command menu or choose Layer menu > Duplicate Layer, type a name for the duplicate layer, then click OK or press Enter.

To flip a layer:

1. On the Layers palette, activate the layer you want to flip. Any layers that are linked to the active layer will also flip.

2. Choose Layer menu > Transform > Flip Horizontal **4** or Flip Vertical.

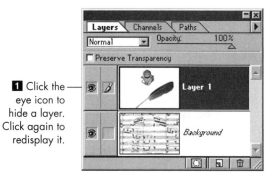

1 Click the eye icon to hide a layer. Click again to redisplay it.

2 Layer 1 hidden.

3 Layer 1 redisplayed.

4 Layer 1 flipped horizontally.

Hide/Show, Duplicate, Flip Layer

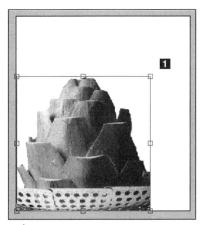

Scale

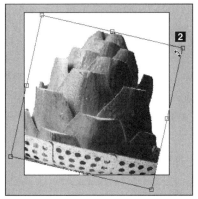

Rotate

Distort

To transform (scale, rotate, skew, distort, or apply perspective to) a layer by dragging:

1. On the Layers palette, activate the layer you want to transform. Any layers that are linked to the active layer will also transform. **NOTE:** You can also transform a selection on a layer; it will turn into a floating selection layer automatically.

2. Choose Layer menu > Transform > Scale, Rotate, Skew, Distort, or Perspective. A bounding border box will appear.

NOTE: If you want to perform multiple transformations, to save time and preserve image quality, after performing step 3 for the first command you choose, you can choose and then perform additional transform commands, and then accept them all at once (step 4).

3. To **scale** the layer horizontally and vertically, drag a corner handle ▣. To scale only the horizontal or vertical dimension, drag a side handle. Hold down Shift while dragging to scale proportionately. Hold down Alt to scale from the center of the layer.

To **rotate** the layer, position the cursor outside the bounding border (the cursor will become a curved arrow pointer), then drag in a circular direction ▣. Hold down Shift while dragging to constrain the rotation to 15-degree increments.

To **skew** the layer, drag a corner handle to reposition just that handle ▣, or drag a side handle to skew along the current horizontal or vertical axis. Hold down Alt while dragging to skew symmetrically from the center of the layer.

To **distort** the layer, drag a corner handle to freely reposition just that handle. Drag a side handle to distort the side of the bounding border along the horizontal and/or vertical axis. Hold down Alt while dragging to distort symmetrically

(Continued on the following page)

Transform a Layer

from the center of the layer. The distort transformation relies less on the horizontal/vertical axes than skew does, so it can produce a greater degree of transformation.

To apply **perspective** to the layer, drag a corner handle along the horizontal or vertical axis to create one-point perspective along that axis –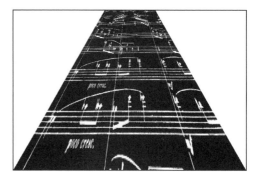. The adjacent corner will move in unison. Or drag a side handle to skew along the current horizontal or vertical axis.

4. To accept the transformation(s), double-click inside the bounding border.
or
Press Enter.

TIP Press Esc to cancel the entire transformation.

TIP Use Edit menu > Undo to undo the last handle modification.

TIP Position the cursor inside the bounding border to move the layer image.

1 The original image.

2 After applying a **Perspective** transformation.

Once you become acquainted with the individual Transform commands, you'll probably want to start using the Free Transform command when you want to perform a series of transform commands. With Free Transform, the various commands are accessed using keyboard shortcuts—you don't have to choose each command from the Layer menu. The image data will be resampled only once—when you accept the changes.

To free transform:

Follow the instructions starting on the previous page, but for step 2, choose Layer menu > Transform > Free Transform (Control-T), and for step 3, the instructions are the same, with these exceptions:

To **Skew**, hold down Control and Shift as you drag.

Transform a Layer; Free Transform

To **Distort,** hold down Control as you drag.

To apply **Perspective,** hold down Control, Alt, and Shift as you drag.

Also hold down Alt to scale, skew, or distort symmetrically from the center of the layer image.

Use the Numeric command if you'd rather transform a layer by entering exact numeric values than by dragging the mouse.

To transform a layer using numeric values:

1. On the Layers palette, activate the layer you want to transform. Any layers that are linked to the active layer will also transform.

NOTE: You can also transform a selection on a layer; it will turn into a floating selection layer automatically.

2. Choose Layer menu > Transform > Numeric (Control-Shift-T).

3. For any of the following transformations that you don't want to perform, just uncheck that transformation's check box.

To **move** the layer, enter *x* and *y* Position values **1**. Choose units for those values from the drop-down menu. Leave the Relative box checked to move the layer relative to its current position. Uncheck the Relative box to position the layer relative to the upper-left corner of the image.

To **scale** the layer, enter Width and/or Height values **2**. Choose units for those values from the drop-down menu. Check the Constrain Proportions box to scale proportionately.

To **skew** the layer, enter degree values (for the amount of slant) in the Horizontal and/or Vertical Skew fields **3**.

To **rotate** the layer, enter a Rotate Angle or move the dial in the circle **4**.

4. Click OK or press Enter.

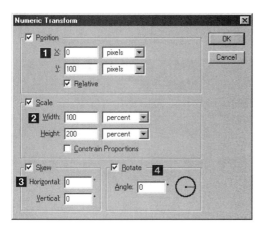

The standard things that you can do to a layer—move it upward or downward in the layer stack, choose a mode or opacity for it, or create a layer mask for it—can't be done to the Background—unless you first convert it into a layer.

To convert the Background into a layer:

1. Double-click Background on the Layers palette **1**.

2. Type a new name **2**, and choose a mode and opacity for the layer.

3. Click OK or press Enter **3**.

TIP If you move the Background using the Move tool, it will turn into a layer.

Let's say you've converted the Background into a layer so you could move it upward in the layer stack or for some other purpose, but now you want a flat, white Background. In other words, your image doesn't have a Background and you'd like to create one.

To create a Background for an image:

1. Choose New Layer from the Layers palette command menu.
or
Alt-click the Create New Layer button at the bottom of the Layers palette **4**.

2. Choose Background from the bottom of the Mode drop-down menu. You can't rename the Background or change its opacity or mode.

3. Click OK or press Enter. The Background will, of course, appear at the bottom of the layer stack.

TIP If you turned the Background into a layer and now you want to turn it back into the Background, do steps immediately above, make sure the former Background is above the new bottommost layer, then choose Merge Down from the Layers palette command menu. It will merge with the new Background.

1 Double-click the Background.

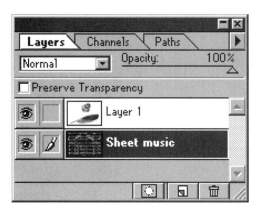

3 The former **Background** is now a **layer**.

4

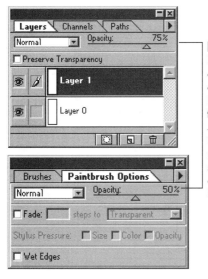

1 Layer 1 has a 75% opacity and the Paintbrush **tool** has a 50% opacity: The resulting stroke opacity will be 37%.

To easily try out different fill colors
2 With **Preserve Transparency** turned on for a type layer, the Fill command recolors only the type shapes, not transparent areas.

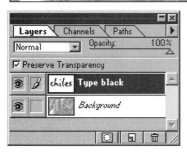

A few more things to know about layers

Tools and the layers

You can use any painting or editing tool to edit pixels on the target layer, but keep in mind that in addition to the Options palette mode and opacity settings for each tool, a tool's effect will also be controlled by the current target layer's opacity and mode **1**. For example, if a layer has a 60% opacity, a painting or editing tool with an opacity of 100% will work at a maximum opacity of 60% on that layer, and less if the tool's opacity is below 100%.

Preserve Transparency

With the Preserve Transparency box on the Layers palette checked, only areas of a layer that contain pixels can be edited **2**; blank areas will remain transparent. You can turn this option on or off for individual layers.

TIP Press / to toggle Preserve Transparency on or off.

If you want to change the size or color of the checkerboard pattern that is used to indicate transparent areas on a layer or turn off the checkerboard pattern altogether, use the File > Preferences > Transparency & Gamut dialog box.

Sample Merged

With the Sample Merged box checked on its Options palette, the Rubber Stamp, Paint Bucket, Blur, Sharpen, Smudge, and Magic Wand sample pixels from all the currently visible layers, though pixels will only be altered on the currently active layer.

Changing image modes

Click Don't Flatten to preserve layers in a multi-layered image if you change its color mode.

To restack a layer:

1. Click on a layer name on the Layers palette.

2. Drag the layer name up or down on the palette, and release the mouse when a dark horizontal line appears where you want the layer to be **1**–**2**.

TIP You can also restack a target layer by choosing Bring to Front, Bring Forward, Send Backward, or Send to Back from the Arrange submenu under the Layer menu.

Dragging the "Puppet" layer downward.

The "Puppet" layer is in a new position in the stack.

To move multiple layers at one time, see page 154.

To move the contents of a layer:

1. On the Layers palette, click the name of the layer that you want to move.

2. Choose the Move tool (V) ▶⊕ or hold down Control.

3. Drag in the image window to move the contents of the target layer. The entire layer will move **3**–**4**.
NOTE: If you move the Background, it will become Layer 0, and the exposed area will become transparent.

TIP Press an arrow key to move a target layer one pixel at a time. Press Shift-arrow to move a layer in 10 screen-pixel increments.

TIP Any part of a layer that is moved beyond the edge of the image will be saved with your image.

TIP With the Move tool selected, Control-Alt-right-click on an object in the image window to quickly activate that object's layer.

3 The original image.

4 After moving the "cow toy" layer with the **Move** tool.

Restack a Layer; Move Layer Contents

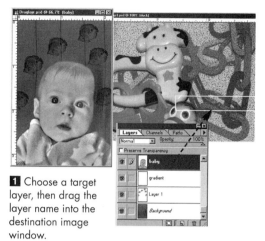

1 Choose a target layer, then drag the layer name into the destination image window.

2 The destination image after dragging the "baby" layer name onto the image.

PHOTOS: E. WEINMANN

3 The new layer name appears on the Layers palette, and is the topmost layer in the destination image.

The method you use to copy a layer (or linked layers) to another image depends on what part of the layer(s) you want to copy. The quickest way to copy a layer to another image is by dragging its name from the Layers palette to the destination image window. With this method, any areas that extend beyond the edge of the image boundary (called the "Big Data") will also move. Use the method on the next page if you want to trim the layer as you copy it. Also, you can't copy linked layers using this method. To copy linked layers, use the method described on page 96.

To drag-and-drop a layer to another image (Layers palette method):

1. Open the image containing the layer you want to move and the image the layer is to be placed into (the "destination image"), and make sure the two windows don't completely overlap.

2. Click in the source image window.

3. Click on the name of the layer you want to move on the Layers palette **1**. Any tool can be selected.

4. Drag the layer name from the Layers palette into the destination image window. Release the mouse when the darkened border is where you want the layer to appear. It will be stacked above the previously active layer in the destination image **2**–**3**.

TIP If the dimensions of the layer being moved are larger than those of the destination image, the moved layer will extend beyond the edges of the destination image window. Use the Move tool to move the layer in the image window. The "hidden" parts will save with the image.

Drag-and-drop a Layer to Another Image

Use this method to copy a single layer or linked layers to another image. In order to drag-copy linked layers, you must use the Move tool and you must drag the source layer from the source image window—not the Layers palette.

To drag-and-drop a layer to another image (Move tool):

1. Open the image containing the layer you want to move (the "source image") and the image to which the layer is to be moved (the "destination image").

2. On the Layers palette, click the name of the layer that you want to copy. (To move multiple layers, link them first. See page 154.)

3. *Optional:* Click in the destination image window, then click on the name of the layer on the Layers palette that you want the added layer to appear on top of.

4. Choose the Move tool (V). ▶⊕

5. Click in the source image window. Drag the target layer from the current image window to the destination image window ◼. The new layer will be positioned where you release the mouse, on top of the target layer in the destination image ◼.

6. *Optional:* Use the Move tool ▶⊕ to move the layer in the destination image window.

7. *Optional:* Restack the new layer or layers (drag them upward or downward).

TIP To copy a layer into the center of another image, start dragging the layer, hold down Shift, then continue to drag. If the two images have the same pixel count, the moved layer will be positioned in the exact *x/y* location as in the source image.

A nifty way to zero in on the layer you want to copy

Position the Move tool over a layer in the image window, right-press to view a menu of layers that are directly below the cursor, then choose a layer from the menu. With any other tool selected, Control-right-press.

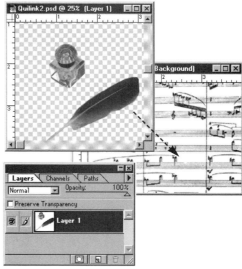

◼ Drag the target layer from the **source image window** into the **destination image window**.

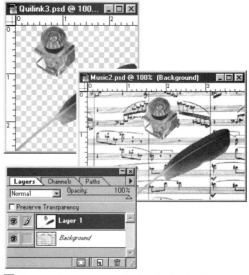

◼ The new layer appears in the destination image.

Not quite as simple as it seems

Bear in mind when you copy and paste that the size of the layer imagery may change when pasted, because it is rendered in the **resolution** of the destination image. If the resolution of the destination image is higher than that of the imagery you're pasting, the Clipboard layer will become smaller when pasted. Conversely, if the resolution of the destination image is lower than the resolution of the Clipboard imagery, the Clipboard layer will be enlarged when pasted. You can use the Image Size dialog box to choose the same resolution (and dimensions, if desired) for both images (see page 42).

Use this copy and paste method if you want to copy only the visible portion of a layer (when displayed at 100% view) and not any Big Data beyond the layer's edge.

To copy and paste only the visible part of a layer to another image:

1. On the Layers palette, activate the layer you want to copy.

2. Choose Select menu > All (Control-A). The areas extending beyond the layer's edge won't be selected.

3. Choose Edit menu > Copy (Control-C).

4. Click in the destination image window.

5. Choose Edit menu > Paste (Control-V). A new layer will be created for the pasted pixels, and it can be restacked, like any other layer, using the Layers palette.

6. Click back in the original image window, then choose Select menu > None (Control-D) to deactivate the selection.

To delete a layer:

1. On the Layers palette, click the name of the layer you want to delete.

2. Click the Trash button, then click Yes.
or
Alt-click the Trash button **1**–**3**.

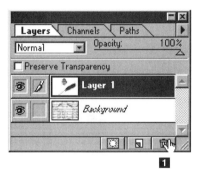

1

2 The original image.

3 After deleting Layer 1.

Merging and flattening

Layers increase an image's file size, so when you've completely finished editing your image, you should merge or flatten it to conserve storage space. Learn the difference between the merge and flatten commands before you choose which one to use.

NOTE: Only the Photoshop file format supports multiple layers. To save your image in any other file format, you must first merge or flatten it down to one layer. To reserve the layered version for future editing, flatten a copy of it using File menu > Save a Copy. The layered version will remain open.

To merge two layers:

1. Activate the topmost layer of the two layers that you want to merge.

2. Choose Merge Down (Control-E) from the Layers palette command menu. The target layer will merge into the layer immediately below it.

The Merge Visible command merges all the currently visible layers into the bottommost displayed layer and **preserves** hidden layers.

To merge multiple layers:

1. Display only the layers you want to merge (all should have eye icons on the Layers palette), and hide the layers you *don't* want to merge. They don't have to be consecutive. Hide the Background if you don't want to merge layers into it.

2. Click on one of the layers to be merged.

3. Choose Merge Visible (Control-Shift-E) from the Layers palette menu.

The Flatten command merges currently displayed layers into the bottommost displayed layer and **discards** hidden layers.

To flatten layers:

1. Make sure all the layers you want to flatten are displayed (have eye icons).

2. Choose Flatten Image from the Layers palette command menu **1**–**2**.

3. Click OK. Any transparent areas in the bottommost layer will turn white.

To merge linked layers or a clipping group

- To merge linked layers, choose **Merge Linked** from the Layers palette command menu or the Layer menu. The Merge Linked command **discards** hidden linked layers.

- To merge layers in a clipping group, activate the underlined layer, then choose **Merge Group** from the Layers palette command menu or the Layer menu. The Merge Group command **discards** hidden grouped layers.

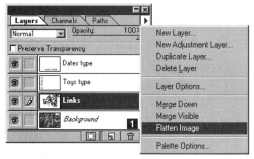

2 The Layers palette for the merged or flattened image.

LIGHTS & DARKS 8

A posterized image.

THIS CHAPTER covers the adjustment of light and dark values. For example, you can invert a layer to make it look like a film negative, posterize it to lower its luminosity levels to a specified number, or change all its pixels to black and white to make it high contrast. You can precisely adjust lightness or contrast in a layer's highlights, midtones, or shadows using features like Levels or Curves. To darken a large or small area of a layer by hand, drag across it with the Burn tool. To lighten an area, drag across it with the Dodge tool. All the commands discussed in this chapter can be applied to a color image, but try applying them to a grayscale image first to learn how they work.

TIP The Fade command (Filter menu > Fade or Control-Shift-F) **1** works for the Adjust commands, not just for filters!

Normally, the Adjust commands affect only the current target layer or a selection on the target layer. If you're using Photoshop version 4.0 or later, however, you can apply most Adjust submenu commands using a different method: via an adjustment layer. Unlike normal layers, the adjustment layer affects all the currently visible layers below it—not just the target layer. The beauty of the adjustment layer is that it won't actually change pixels until it's merged with the layer below it, so you can use it to try out various effects. And if you're not happy with the adjustment layer effect, you can just discard it. Instructions for creating an adjustment layer are on the next page.

TIP If you're really happy with an adjustment layer and you want to use it in another image, just drag-and-drop it from the Layers palette into the destination image window!

1

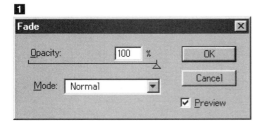

A few things to know before you begin...

■ To apply any of the commands discussed in this chapter to a selected area of a layer rather than to an entire layer, just create a **selection** before you choose the commmand.

■ Dialog boxes opened from the Adjust submenus (Image menu) have a **Preview** box. Changes preview on the entire screen with the Preview box unchecked; changes preview only in the image or in a selection with the Preview box checked. CMYK color displays more acccurately with the Preview option on.

■ To reset the settings in a dialog box, hold down Alt and click the **Reset** button.

■ To open a dialog box with its **last used settings**, hold down **Alt** while choosing the command from the menu bar or include Alt in the keyboard shortcut for that command.

The adjustment layer affects all the currently visible layers below it—not just the target layer, but it doesn't actually change pixels until it's merged with the layer below it. If you're not happy with an adjustment layer effect, just trash it. Read more about adjustment layers on pages 109–110.

To create an adjustment layer:

1. Activate the layer above which you want the adjustment layer to appear.

2. Control-click the Create New Layer button on the Layers palette **1**.
or
Choose New Adjustment Layer from the Layers palette command menu.

3. Choose an adjustment type from the Type drop down menu **2**.

4. *Optional:* Choose other layer options (Opacity, Mode, Group with Previous Layer, or rename the layer). You can change these options later on.

5. Click OK or press Enter.

6. Make the desired image adjustments, then click OK **3**. An adjustment layer can be modified at any time, until it's merged it with the layer directly below it (Control-E).

TIP To limit the adjustment layer effect to just the layer below it, group the two together: Alt-click the line between them on the Layers palette.

The Equalize command redistributes the target layer's light and dark values. It may improve an image that lacks contrast or is too dark.

To equalize a layer:

Choose Image menu > Adjust > Equalize **4**.

TIP To limit the Equalize effect to part of a layer, select the area before choosing the command, then click Select Area Only in the Equalize dialog box. To equalize a whole layer based on the values within the selected area, click Entire Image Based on Area.

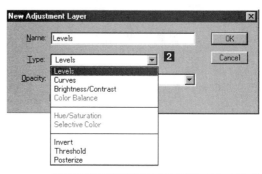

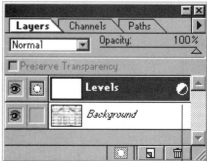

3 The adjustment layer icon.

4 The original image.

After applying the **Equalize** command.

PHOTO: PAUL PETROFF

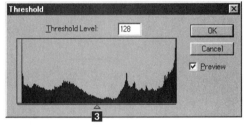 The original image.

 The image **inverted**.

Choose the Invert command to make the target layer look like a film negative, or a negative look like a positive. Each pixel will be replaced with its opposite brightness and/or color value.

To invert a layer's lights and darks:

Choose a target layer, then choose Image menu > Adjust > Invert (Control-I) **1**–**2**.

or

To use an adjustment layer, Control-click the Create New Layer button at the bottom of the Layers palette, choose Type: Invert, then click OK.

PHOTO: NADINE MARKOVA

 **3**

Use the Threshold dialog box to make the target layer high contrast by converting color or gray pixels into black and white pixels.

To make a layer high contrast:

 The original image.

PHOTO: PAUL PETROFF

1. Choose a target layer, then choose Image menu > Adjust > Threshold.

   or

   To use an adjustment layer, Control-click the Create New Layer button at the bottom of the Layers palette, choose Type: Threshold, then click OK.

2. Move the slider to the right to increase the number of black pixels **3**.

   or

   Move the slider to the left to increase the number of white pixels.

   or

   Enter a number between 1 and 255 in the Threshold Level field. Shades above this number will become white, shades below become black.

 After using the **Threshold** command.

3. Click OK or press Enter **4**–**5**.

Invert Layer; High Contrast Layer

Use the Posterize command to reduce the number of color or value levels in the target layer. This effortless command can produce beautiful results.

To posterize a layer:

1. Choose a target layer, then choose Image menu > Adjust > Posterize.
or
To use an adjustment layer, Control-click the Create New Layer button at the bottom of the Layers palette, choose Type: Posterize, then click OK.

2. Make sure the Preview box is checked, then enter a number between 2 and 255 in the Levels field **1**. To produce a dramatic effect, enter a number between 4 and 8.

3. Click OK or press Enter **2**–**4**.

TIP If the number of shades in an image is reduced using the Posterize command, or any other tonal adjustment command is made, and the image is saved, the original shade information will be permanently lost.

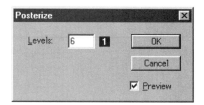

2 The original image.

3 Post **posterization**.

4 posterized image.

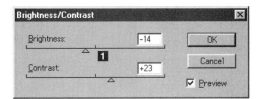

If you use the Levels dialog box to make tonal adjustments, you'll be able to adjust the shadows, midtones, and highlights individually, but the Brightness/Contrast command, discussed below, is simpler to use.

To adjust brightness and contrast (Brightness/Contrast):

1. Choose a target layer, then choose Image menu > Adjust > Brightness/Contrast.

   or

   To use an adjustment layer, Control-click the Create New Layer button at the bottom of the Layers palette, choose Type: Brightness/Contrast, then click OK.

2. To lighten the layer, move the brightness slider to the right **1**.

   or

   To darken the layer, move the Brightness slider to the left.

   or

   Enter a number between -100 and 100 in the Brightness field.

3. To intensify the contrast, move the Contrast slider to the right.

   or

   To lessen the contrast, move the Contrast slider to the left.

   or

   Enter a number between -100 and 100 in the Contrast field.

4. Click OK or press Enter **2**–**4**.

TIP When you move a slider in any of the Adjust submenu dialog boxes, note its position relative to the other sliders and how the layer changes.

PHOTO: PAUL PETROFF

2 The original image.

3 The Brightness slider moved to the right.

4 **Brightness** and **contrast** adjusted.

Adjust Brightness and Contrast

Use the Levels dialog box to make fine adjustments to a target layer's highlights, midtones, or shadows.

To adjust brightness and contrast using Levels:

1. Choose a target layer, then choose Image menu > Adjust > Levels (Control-L).

or

To use an adjustment layer, Control-click the Create New Layer button at the bottom of the Layers palette, choose Type: Levels, then click OK.

2. Do any of the following:

To brighten the highlights and intensify contrast, move the Input highlights slider to the left **1**. The midtones slider will move along with it. Readjust the midtones slider, if necessary.

To darken the shadows, move the Input shadows slider to the right. The midtones slider will move along with it. Readjust the midtones slider, if necessary.

To adjust the midtones independently, move the Input midtones slider.

To decrease contrast and lighten the image, move the Output shadows slider to the right.

To decrease contrast and darken the image, move the Output highlights slider to the left.

3. Click OK or press Enter **2**–**4**.

TIP To make a layer high contrast (black and white), move the Input shadows and highlights sliders very close together. Position them left of center to lighten the image, right of center to darken the image. You can use the Threshold command to produce the same effect.

TIP To adjust levels automatically, choose Image menu > Adjust > Auto Levels (Control-Shift-L) or click Auto in the Levels dialog box.

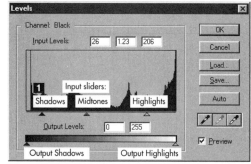

2 The original image.

PHOTO: PAUL PETROFF

3 After **Levels** adjustments.

4 To produce this image, an area of the image was selected before creating an adjustment layer (Type: Levels). The type was added in QuarkXPress.

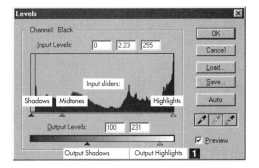

2 The original image.

3 The music layer screened back.

4 The Output slider positions reversed.

To screen back a layer:

1. Choose a target layer, then choose Image menu > Adjust > Levels (Control-L).

or

To use an adjustment layer, Control-click the New Layer button at the bottom of the Layers palette, choose Type: Levels, then click OK.

2. To reduce contrast, move the Output highlights slider slightly to the left **1**.

and

Move the Output shadows slider to the right.

3. To lighten the midtones, move the Input midtones slider to the left.

4. Click OK or press Enter **2**–**3**.

TIP To make a layer look like a film negative, reverse the position of the two Output sliders **4**. The farther apart the sliders are, the more each pixel's brightness and contrast attributes will be reversed. The Invert command produces a similar effect.

The original image.

The **screened back** version.

Screen Back a Layer

Use the Dodge tool to lighten pixels in small areas or use the Burn tool to darken pixels. You can choose different Brushes palette settings for each tool. The Dodge and Burn tools can't be used on a image in Bitmap or Indexed Color mode.

To lighten using the Dodge tool or darken using the Burn tool:

1. Choose a target layer.

2. Choose the Dodge ✹ or Burn ◔ tool. (Press O to toggle between the Dodge, Burn, and Sponge tools.)

3. On the Toning Tools Options palette **1**:

Position the Exposure slider between 1% (low intensity) and 100% (high intensity). Try a low exposure first (20%-30%) so the tool won't bleach or darken areas too quickly.

and

Choose Shadows, Midtones, or Highlights from the pop-up menu to Dodge or Burn only pixels in that value range.

4. Click the Brushes tab on the same palette, then click a hard-edged or soft-edged tip. A large, soft tip will produce the smoothest result.

5. Stroke on any area of the layer. Pause between strokes to allow the screen to redraw **2**–**3**.

TIP If you Dodge or Burn an area too much, choose Edit menu > Undo or choose File menu > Revert. Don't use the opposite tool to fix it—you'll get uneven results.

TIP To create a smooth, even highlight or shadow line, dodge or burn a path using the Dodge or Burn tool and the Stroke Path command (see page 173).

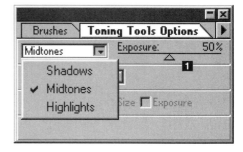

2 The Dodge tool with **Shadows** chosen from the Toning Tools Options palette was used to eliminate dark spots in the background of this image.

3 After dodging.

Dodge or Burn

The original image.

After applying Dodge and Burn strokes to the **neutral gray layer** to create stronger highlights and shadows on the crab.

The neutral gray layer, showing the Dodge and Burn strokes. They appear in shades of black when viewed on their own layer, but they accentuate lights and darks on the underlying layer.

In the following instructions, a new gray layer is created with its own mode, and then the Dodge and/or Burn tools are used to paint shades of gray on that layer, which has the effect of heightening or lessening contrast in the underlying layer. This technique works on a grayscale or color image and allows for unlimited undos.

To create a neutral gray, black, or white transition layer:

1. Choose a target layer in a grayscale or color image above which you want the transition layer to appear.
2. Alt-click the Create New Layer button on the Layers palette.
3. Enter a name for the layer.
4. Choose Overlay mode if you're going to use the Dodge or Burn tool.
5. Check the "Fill with Overlay-neutral color (50% gray)" box.
6. Click OK or press Enter.
7. Follow steps 2–5 on page 106 to create dodge or burn strokes. If you don't like the results, paint over areas with 50% gray (use this like multiple undos) or fill the entire layer again with 50% gray to remove all your changes and start over.

TIP The Sponge tool can't be used on the transition layer, even in a color image.

Neutral Transition Layer

You can adjust lights and darks on a target layer by clicking on thumbnails in the Variations dialog box. (To adjust a color image using the Variations dialog box, see page 125.)

To adjust a grayscale image using thumbnail Variations:

1. Choose a target layer.

2. Choose Image menu > Adjust > Variations.

3. Position the Fine/Coarse slider right of center to make major adjustments or left of center to make minor adjustments **1**. Each notch to the right doubles the adjustment per click. Each notch to the left halves the adjustment per click.

4. Click the Lighter or Darker thumbnail in the Shadows, Midtones, or Highlights column. Compare the Current Pick thumbnail, which represents the modified image, with the Original thumbnail.

5. *Optional:* Check the Show Clipping box if you want to have highlighted the areas of the image that will be converted to white or black from the Variations adjustment.

6. *Optional:* Click the same thumbnail again to intensify the change, or click the opposite thumbnail to undo the modification.

7. Click OK or press Enter **2**–**3**.

TIP Click the Original thumbnail to undo all changes made using the Variations dialog box.

TIP Use the Levels or Brightness/Contrast dialog box to make more precise adjustments, and with the ability to preview adjustments in the image window.

Click the **Original** thumbnail to undo all adjustments.

The **Current Pick** represents the modified image.

The Variations dialog box. The following steps were taken to produce the image at the bottom of this page: The Fine/Coarse slider was moved to the right two notches, the Shadows-Darker box was clicked, the Highlights-Lighter box was clicked, the Fine/Coarse slider was moved to the left four notches, and finally, the Midtones-Darker box was clicked.

2 The original image.

3 After **Variations** adjustments.

PHOTO: PAUL PETROFF

Adjustment layer tips and tricks

■ **Hide** an adjustment layer to temporarily remove its effect.

■ Lower an adjustment layer's **opacity** in increments to progressively reduce its effect.

■ Change an adjustment layer's **blending mode** to produce a variety of visual effects in relationship to its underlying layers. Overlay mode will heighten contrast, Multiply mode will darken the image, and Screen mode will lighten the image.

■ If you don't want an underlying layer to be affected by the adjustment layer, **restack** it above the adjustment layer on the Layers palette.

■ To limit the adjustment layer's effects to a section of its underlying layers, create a **selection** first. Or paint or fill with **black** on the adjustment layer to remove the adjustment effect or **white** to reveal the adjustment effect (instructions on the next page).

To use an adjustment layer to preview different settings for the same command

Create several of the same adjustment layer types, like Color Balance or Levels, hide the adjustment layers, and then show each one at a time to see how they affect the underlying image. You can restack adjustment layers among themselves, and you can place them at different locations within the overall layer stack. If you find using multiple adjustment layers to be confusing, you can adjust and readjust color or tonal values using a single adjustment layer.

More about adjustment layers

An adjustment layer is a special type of layer mask that is used to alter color and tonal characteristics in the layers below it, but those alterations don't permanently affect pixels in underlying layers until the adjustment layer is merged with them. The adjustment layer is really a method for previewing color and tonal adjustments, and it's a great way to experiment with effects before commiting to them.

Normally, an adjustment layer will affect all the currently visible layers below it, but you can use a clipping group to limit an adjustment layer's effect to only the layer or layers it's grouped with.

To edit an adjustment layer:

1. Double-click the adjustment layer name on the Layers palette.
or
Activate the adjustment layer, then choose Layer menu > Adjustment Options.

2. Change the dialog box settings.

3. Click OK.

When you merge down an adjustment layer, the adjustments become permanent for the image layer below it, so you should be certain you want the effect to become permanent before you perform another operation. If you change your mind, un-merge by choosing Edit menu > Undo right away.

To merge an adjustment layer:

1. Activate the adjustment layer.

2. Choose Merge Down from the Layers palette command menu (Control-E).

TIP To merge an adjustment layer with more than one other layer, see the sections on Merge Visible or Flatten Image on page 98. An adjustment layer cannot be merged with other adjustment layers; since they contain no real image pixels, there's nothing to merge.

Edit, Merge Adjustment Layer

Because an adjustment layer is a type of mask, when you activate an adjustment layer, the Color palette automatically resets to Grayscale and the Foreground and Background colors revert to black and white, or vice versa.

To restrict the area a new adjustment layer affects:

1. Create a selection on the layer above which the new adjustment layer will appear **1**.

2. Create an adjustment layer. The adjustment layer thumbnail will be black, with an area of white to indicate where the selection was.

1 In this image, the adjustment layer contains a mask on the left side that is hiding the Threshold effect.

To restrict the area an existing adjustment layer affects:

1. Activate the adjustment layer.

2. Choose black as the Foreground color. (Click the Switch colors icon on the Toolbox to swap the Foreground and Background colors.)

3. To remove the adjustment layer effect:

Create a selection (or selections) and fill them with black.
or
Choose the Paintbrush tool, Normal mode, 100% opacity, then paint with black on the image. Choose a lower opacity to partially remove the adjustment layer effect.

4. *Optional:* To restore the adjustment layer effect, paint or fill with white.

TIP To reveal just a small area of the adjustment effect, fill the entire layer with black and then paint with white over specific areas. Fill the whole adjustment layer with white to display the adjustment effect over the whole image. To diminish the adjustment layer's effect over the whole layer by a percentage, lower its opacity via the Layers palette **2**.

2 In this image, the adjustment layer's opacity was lowered to 60%, which causes the Threshold effect to blend with the overall underlying image.

Layer mask shortcuts

■ **Alt**-click the adjustment layer thumbnail to **view** the mask.

■ **Shift**-click the adjustment layer thumbnail to temporarily **remove** any mask on the adjustment layer.

■ **Control**-click the adjustment layer thumbnail to convert the non-masked area into a **selection**.

Restrict the Adjustment Layer Effect

CHOOSE COLORS 9

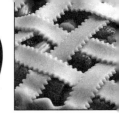

N THIS CHAPTER you will learn how to choose colors using the Color palette, and how to add, delete, save, append, and load colors using the Swatches palette.

What are the Foreground and Background colors?

When you use a painting tool or create type, the current Foreground color is applied.

When you use the Eraser tool, add a border to a picture using the Canvas Size dialog box, or move a selection on the Background using the Move tool, the hole that's left behind is automatically filled with the current Background color. The Gradient tool can produce blends using the Foreground and/or Background colors.

The Foreground and Background colors are displayed in the Foreground and Background color squares on the Toolbox **1** and on the Color palette **2**. (When written with an uppercase "F" or "B," these terms refer to colors, not the overall foreground or background areas of a picture.)

There are several ways to choose a Foreground or Background color, and they are described on the following pages:

- Enter values in fields or click on the big color square in the Color Picker.
- Choose premixed matching system colors using the Custom Colors dialog box.
- Pluck a color from an image using the Eyedropper tool.
- Enter values in fields or move sliders on the Color palette.
- Click a swatch on the Swatches palette.

Foreground and Background Colors

Foreground color square.

Click the **Default Colors** icon (D) to make the Foreground color black and the Background color white.

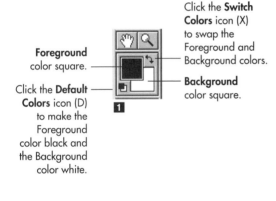

Click the **Switch Colors** icon (X) to swap the Foreground and Background colors.

Background color square.

1

Foreground color square. The currently active square has a double frame.

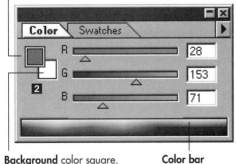

Color	Swatches
R	28
G	153
B	71

2

Background color square.   **Color bar**

To choose a color using the Color Picker:

1. Click the Foreground or Background color square on the Toolbox **1**.

or

Click the Foreground or Background color square on the Color palette if it is already active.

or

Double-click the Foreground or Background color square on the Color palette if it is not active.

NOTE: If the color square you click on is a Custom color, the Custom Colors dialog box will open. Click Picker to open the Color Picker dialog box.

2. To choose from the Photoshop Color Picker:

Click a color on the vertical color bar to choose a hue, then click a variation of that hue in the large square **2**.

or

To choose a specific process color, enter percentages from a matching guide in the C, M, Y, and K fields. For an on-screen image, you can specify specific percentages in the R, G, and B fields. RGB colors range from 0 (black) to 255 (pure R, G, or B). You can also enter numbers in the HSB, or Lab fields.

3. Click OK or press Enter.

TIP To use the Photoshop Color Picker, Photoshop must be chosen from the Color Picker drop-down menu in the General Preferences dialog box (Control-K).

New color. Old color.

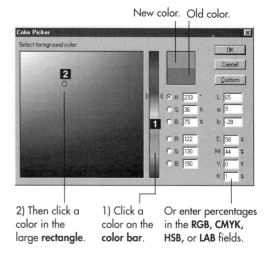

2) Then click a color in the large **rectangle**.   1) Click a color on the **color bar**.   Or enter percentages in the **RGB, CMYK, HSB,** or **LAB** fields.

Out of gamut?

An exclamation point indicates there is no ink equivalent for the color you chose—it is **out of printable gamut**. If you're planning to print your image, choose an in-gamut color or click the exclamation point to have Photoshop substitute the closest printable color (shown in the swatch below the exclamation point). When you convert your image to CMYK Color mode, the entire image will be brought into printable gamut. The out of gamut range is defined by the current settings in the Separation Setup and Printing Inks Setup dialog boxes.

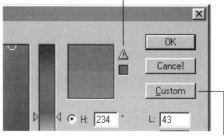

Click **Custom** to choose a predefined color.

All colors are printed as four-color from Photoshop, regardless of whether they are saved as spot or process colors. To save spot colors so they can be color separated from QuarkXPress, Illustrator, or FreeHand, use Pantone colors and also check the Short PANTONE Names box in General Preferences (Control-K).

Don't rely on your monitor to represent matching system colors accurately—you must choose them from a printed Pantone, Trumatch, Toyo, Focoltone, Anpa-Color, or DIC swatch book. And make sure those are the inks that your printer plans to use.

To choose a custom color using the Custom Colors dialog box:

1. Click the Foreground or Background color square on the Toolbox.
or
Click the Foreground or Background color square on the Color palette if it is already active.
or
Double-click the Foreground or Background color square on the Color palette if it is not active.

NOTE: If the color square you click on is not a Custom color, the Color Picker dialog box will open. Click Custom to open the Custom Colors dialog box.

2. Choose a matching guide system from the Book drop-down menu 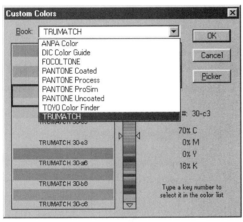.

3. Type a number (it will appear on the "Key #" line).
or
Click a color on the vertical color bar, then click a swatch.

4. *Optional:* Click Picker to return to the Color Picker.

5. Click OK or press Enter.

TIP To load a matching system palette onto the Swatches palete, see page 116.

TIP For the addresses of the various matching system companies (Pantone, Trumatch, etc.), see the Photoshop 4.0 User Guide.

1 In the Custom Colors dialog box, choose a matching system from the **Book** pop-up menu. Then type a number, or click a color on the vertical color bar and click a swatch.

Custom Colors

To choose a color from an image (Eyedropper):

1. On the Color palette, click the Foreground or Background color square if it is not already active.

2. Choose the Eyedropper tool (I). Hold down Alt to use the Eyedropper when the Paintbrush, Pencil, Line, Gradient, Paint Bucket, or Airbrush tool is selected.

3. Click on a color in any open image window ▮.

TIP Alt-click in the image window to choose a Background color when the Foreground color square is active, or to choose a Foreground color when the Background color square is active.

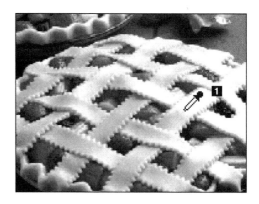

To choose a color using the Color palette:

1. Click the Foreground or Background color square if it isn't already active ▮.

2. Choose a color model for the sliders from the Color palette command menu ▮.

3. Move any of the sliders ▮.
or
Click on or press and drag on the color bar.
or
Enter values in the fields.

TIP In RGB mode, white (the presence of all colors) is produced when all the sliders are in their rightmost positions. Black (the absence of all colors) is produced when all the sliders are in their leftmost positions. Gray is produced when all the sliders are vertically aligned in any other position.

TIP The model you choose for the Color palette does not have to match the current image mode. For example, you can choose the CMYK Color model from the Color palette for a picture in RGB Color mode.

▮ Click the Foreground or Background color square.

▮ Choose a **model** for the sliders.

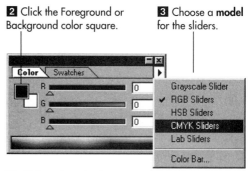

▮ Click on the color bar or move any of the sliders. (Choose Color Bar from the command menu to choose a different **Spectrum style** or Shift-click the color bar to cycle through the styles.)

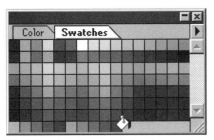

1 Click in the white area below the swatches.

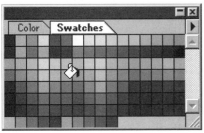

2 Or Alt-Shift-click between two swatches to insert a color between them.

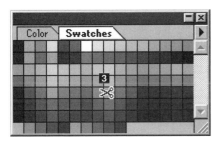

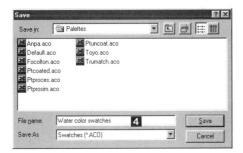

To choose a color from the Swatches palette:

To choose a Foreground color, just click on a color swatch.

To choose a Background color, Alt-click a color swatch.

To add a color to the Swatches palette:

1. Choose a Foreground color.

2. Click the Swatches tab to display the Swatches palette.

3. Position the cursor in the blank area below the swatches on the palette, and click with the paint bucket cursor **1**. The new color will appear next to the last swatch.

TIP To replace an existing swatch with the new color, Shift-click on the color to be replaced.

TIP To insert the new color between two swatches, Alt-Shift-click on either swatch **2**.

To delete a color from the Swatches palette:

Control-click on a swatch (scissors cursor) **3**.

TIP To restore the default Swatches palette, choose Reset Swatches from the Swatches palette command menu, then click OK.

NOTE: If you edit the Swatches palette, and then exit and re-launch Photoshop, your edited palette will reopen.

To save an edited swatches set:

1. Choose Save Swatches from the Swatches palette command menu.

2. Enter a name for the edited palette in the "Save swatches in" field **4**.

3. Choose a location in which to save the palette.

4. Click Save.

Choose, Add, Delete, Save Swatches

Nine preset color swatch palettes are supplied with Photoshop, and they can be loaded onto the Swatches palette. They include ANPA, Focoltone, Pantone (Coated, Process, ProSim, and Uncoated), System, Toyo, and Trumatch.

To replace a swatches set:

1. Choose Replace Swatches from the Swatches palette command menu.

2. Open the Palettes folder in the Photoshop application folder.

3. Double-click a palette **1**. The loaded swatches will appear on the Swatches palette.
or
Highlight a palette, then click Open.

TIP Choose Reset Swatches from the Swatches palette command menu to restore the default palette.

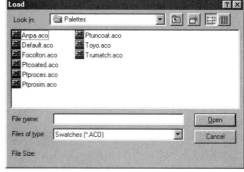

1 Double-click a palette in the Color Palettes folder.

You can append to an existing swatches set any swatches set that you've edited and saved or any of the palettes that are supplied with Photoshop.

To load a swatches set:

1. Choose Load Swatches from the Swatches palette command menu **2**.

2. Open the Palettes or another palettes folder in the Photoshop application folder.

3. Double-click a palette (swatches set) **3**.
or
Highlight a palette and click Open.

4. The appended swatches will appear below the existing swatches.

TIP To enlarge the palette to display the loaded swatches, drag the palette resize box or click the palette zoom box.

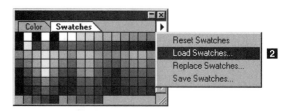

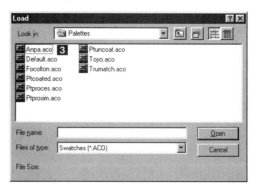

RECOLOR 10

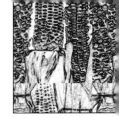

The Preview option...

Image menu > Adjust submenu dialog boxes have a Preview box. If you're working on a normal layer—not an adjustment layer—changes affect the entire screen with the Preview box unchecked. Changes preview in just the image (or selection) with the Preview box checked. CMYK color displays more acccurately with Preview on.

...and a couple of very handy tips

- To display the **unmodified** image in the image window, uncheck the Preview box, and press and hold on the title bar of the dialog box.

- Use the **Save** command in the Levels, Curves, Replace Color, Hue/Saturation, Selective Color, or Variations dialog box to save color adjustment settings, and then apply them to another layer or to another image using the Load command. Or you can drag-copy an adjustment layer between images.

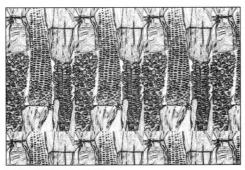

Pattern-making

Each new pattern you create using the **Define Pattern** command replaces the last one. You can, of course, save any image that contains a pattern that you want to reuse, and use the Define Pattern command any time you want to redefine it as a fill pattern.

IN THIS CHAPTER you will learn to fill a selection with color, imagery, or a pattern, color the edge of a selection, tint a Grayscale image, adjust a color image using the Hue/Saturation, Color Balance, Variations, Curves, and Levels commands, replace color using the Replace Color command, saturate or desaturate colors using the Sponge tool, and produce gradients.

All the Adjust submenu commands can be applied to a normal layer via the Image menu > Adjust submenu. Alternatively, many Adjust commands can be applied to an image via an adjustment layer. Unlike submenu commands, which affect only the current target layer, the adjustment layer affects all the currently visible layers below it. The adjustment layer, however, doesn't actually change pixels until it's merged with the layer below it. Adjustment layers are used in this chapter, but they're explained in Chapter 8.

To fill a selection or a layer with a color or a pattern:

1. Choose a target layer.

2. To fill the entire layer, proceed to step 3.

To fill only non-transparent areas on the layer, check the Preserve Transparency box on the Layers palette.

To limit the fill area, create a selection using any method described in Chapter 5.

To create a tiling pattern, select a rectangular or square area using the Rectangular Marquee tool, then choose Edit menu > Define Pattern.

3. To fill with the Foreground or Background color, choose that color now from the Color or Swatches palette.

(Continued on the following page)

(Continued on the following page)

Fill a Selection or a Layer (Color or Pattern)

4. Choose Edit menu > Fill (Shift-Backspace).

5. Choose one of the following: **1**

Use: Foreground Color, Background Color, Black, 50% Gray, or White.

Pattern to fill with the pattern you defined for step 2 on the previous page.

Saved to fill the selection or layer with the last saved version of the image. (Don't add or delete a layer from the image after saving.)

Snapshot to fill with imagery from the Take Snapshot or Take Merged Snapshot command buffer (see page 77).

6. Enter an Opacity percentage.

7. Choose a blending mode from the Mode drop-down menu.

8. *Optional:* If you forgot to check the Preserve Transparency box on the Layers palette, you can check it here.

9. Click OK or press Enter.

TIP If you dislike the new fill color, choose Edit menu > Undo now so it won't blend with your next color or mode choice.

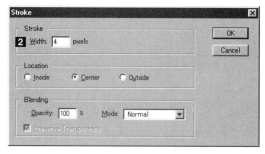

1 In the Fill dialog box, choose a Fill color from the Use drop-down menu, enter an Opacity, and choose a Mode.

Fill shortcuts

Fill selection with Foreground color, 100% opacity	Alt-Backspace
Fill selection with Background color, 100% opacity	Backspace
Fill existing pixels (not transparent areas) with the Foreground color	Alt-Shift-Backspace
Fill existing pixels (not transparent areas) with the Background color	Control-Shift-Backspace

To color the edge of (stroke) a selection or a layer:

1. Choose a target layer, and check the Preserve Transparency box if you want to stroke the edges of existing pixels on the layer, but not transparent areas.

2. *Optional:* Select an area on the layer.

3. Choose a Foreground color.

4. Choose Edit menu > Stroke.

5. Enter a Width between 1 and 16 **2**.

6. Click Location: Inside, Center, or Outside (the position of the stroke on the selection or layer edge).

7. Enter a number in the Opacity field.

8. Choose a blending mode from the Mode drop-down menu.

9. Click OK or press Enter **3**.

TIP To stroke a path, see page 173.

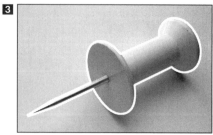

(Stroke a Selection — side tab)

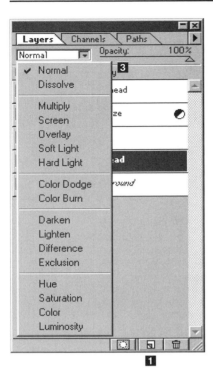

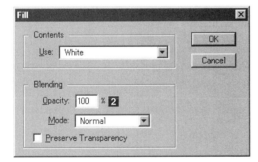

To fill a selection and preview fill modes and opacities:

1. Choose the target layer above which you want the fill layer to appear.

2. Click the Create New Layer button at the bottom of the Layers palette **1**. You will be filling on the new layer.

3. Select an area of the image you want to fill.

4. Uncheck the Preserve Transparency box on the Layers palette.

5. Choose a Foreground color.

6. Choose Edit menu > Fill.

7. Enter 100 in the Opacity field **2**.

8. Choose Normal from the Mode drop-down menu.

9. Click OK or press Enter.

10. To experiment with various color effects, choose an opacity and a mode from the Layers palette **3**.

11. Choose Select menu > None (Control-D).
    or
    Click the selection with the Marquee tool or the Lasso tool.

12. *Optional:* To merge the new layer with the layer below it, choose Merge Down from the Layers palette command menu (Control-E).

TIP To remove the color fill, use the Eraser tool before you merge the layer downward, or delete the layer altogether.

TIP You can continue to modify the new layer using the Layer Options dialog box, opened from the Layers palette, to try different options for blending the new layer with the layer below it (see page 148), or by painting on the new layer with any painting tool.

TIP Restack the layer to see how the color looks above or below different layers.

To colorize a grayscale image using Hue/Saturation:

1. Open a Grayscale image.

2. Choose Image menu > Mode > RGB Color or CMYK Color.

3. Choose a target layer.

4. Choose Image menu > Adjust > Hue/Saturation (Control-U).
   or
   Create an adjustment layer by Control-clicking the Create New Layer button at the bottom of the Layers palette, choose Type: Hue/Saturation, then click OK.

5. Check the Colorize box, and check the Preview box. The image will be tinted red **1**.

6. Move the Hue slider left or right to apply a different tint **2**. Pause to preview.

7. Move the Saturation slider to reduce color intensity.

8. To lighten the image and colorize pure black, move the Lightness slider to the right. To darken the image and colorize pure white, move the Lightness slider to the left.

9. Click OK or press Enter.

TIP To restore the original dialog box settings, hold down Alt and click Reset.

TIP You can also tint a Grayscale image by converting it into a duotone.

TIP See page 146 for tips on painting color on a separate layer over gray layer.

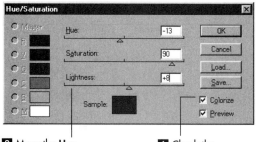

2 Move the **Hue, Saturation**, or **Lightness** slider.

1 Check the **Colorize** box.

Use the Desaturate command to strip color from a layer without actually changing image modes.

To strip color from a layer:

1. Choose a target layer.

2. Choose Image menu > Adjust > Desaturate (Control-Shift-U).

Color adjustments made using the Hue/Saturation command area easiest to discern in an image that has clearly defined color areas.

To adjust a color image using Hue/Saturation:

1. Choose a target layer.

2. Select an area of the layer to recolor only that area.

3. Choose Image menu > Adjust > Hue/Saturation (Control-U).
or
Create an adjustment layer by Control-clicking the Create New Layer button at the bottom of the Layers palette, choose Type: Hue/Saturation, then click OK.

4. Click Master to adjust all colors 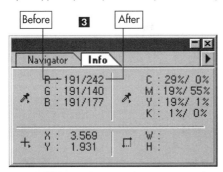.
or
Click a color button to adjust only that color.

5. Move the Hue slider left or right **2**. Pause to preview.

6. Move the Saturation slider to the left to decrease saturation or to the right to increase saturation.

7. To lighten the image and colorize pure black, move the Lightness slider to the right. To darken the image and colorize pure white, move the Lightness slider to the left.

8. Click OK or press Enter.

TIP To restore the original dialog box settings, hold down Alt and click Reset.

■ Click **Master** or click a color button (**R**, **Y**, **G**, **C**, **B**, or **M**).

2 Move the **Hue**, **Saturation**, or **Lightness** slider. In this figure, the B (Blue) button was clicked, and the Hue slider is moved to the left to add more C (Cyan) to the Blue.

Color info

The Info palette displays before-adjustment and after-adjustment color breakdowns of the pixel or area of pixels currently under the cursor while an Adjust submenu dialog box is open **3**. The size of the sample area depends on the current Eyedropper Options palette **Sample Size** setting **4**.

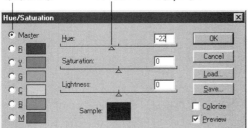

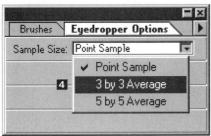

Adjust Color Image (Hue/Saturation)

Use the Replace Color command to change colors in an image without having to first select them.

To replace colors:

1. *Optional:* For an RGB image, choose View menu > CMYK Preview (Control-Y) to see a preview of the actual image and modifications to it in CMYK color. (The Sample swatch in the Replace Color dialog box will continue to display in RGB.)

2. Choose a target layer.

3. *Optional:* Create a selection to restrict color replacement to that area.

4. Choose Image menu > Adjust > Replace Color.

5. Click on the color you want to replace in the preview window in the Replace Color dialog box or in the image window **1**.

6. *Optional:*

Move the Fuzziness slider to the right to add related colors to the selection **2**.
or
Shift-click in the preview window or on the image to add other colors areas to the selection (or just choose the **+** eyedropper icon before you click).
or
Alt-click in the preview window or on the image to subtract color areas from the selection (or just choose the **–** eyedropper icon before you click).

7. Move the Hue, Saturation, or Lightness Transform sliders to change the selected colors. (Only the Lightness slider will be available for a Grayscale image.) The Sample swatch will change as you move the sliders **3**.

The Transform sliders will stay in their current position even if you click on a different area of the image.

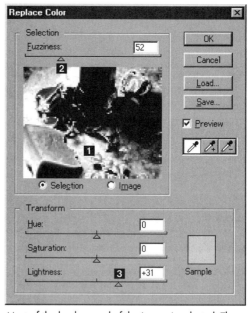

Most of the background of the image is selected. The white areas in the preview window are the **active** areas that will be modified.

8. Click OK or press Enter **1**–**2**.

TIP To restore the original dialog box settings, hold down Alt and click Reset.

TIP Choose Edit menu > Undo (Control-Z) to restore the previous selection in the preview window.

TIP The Sample swatch color from the Replace Color dialog box will display in the currently active square on the Color palette, and the Color palette sliders will reflect its individual components. If the gamut alarm displays, you have produced a non-printable color using the Transform sliders. The Transform sliders won't change the amount of Black (K) in a CMYK color—this component is set by Photoshop's Black Generation function.

TIP Click the Selection button to preview the selection in the preview window or click the Image button to display the entire image. Use the Control key to toggle between the two. If your image extends beyond the edges of your monitor, turn the Image preview option on so you'll be able to sample from the entire image with the eyedropper.

1 The original image.

2 After a **Lightness** adjustment to the background.

Replace Color

Use the Color Balance dialog box to apply a warm or cool cast to a layer's highlights, midtones, or shadows. Color adjustments are easiest to see in an image that has a wide tonal range.

To colorize or color correct using Color Balance:

1. To colorize a Grayscale image, choose an image mode from the Image menu > Mode submenu.

2. Choose a target layer.

3. Choose Image menu > Adjust > Color Balance (Control-B).
or
Create an adjustment layer by Control-clicking the Create New Layer button at the bottom of the Layers palette, choose Type: Color Balance, then click OK.

4. Click Shadows, Midtones, or Highlights **1**.

5. *Optional:* Check the Preserve Luminosity box to preserve brightness values.

6. Move any slider toward a color you want to add more of. Cool and warm colors are paired opposite each other.

Move sliders toward related colors to make an image warmer or cooler. For example, move sliders toward Cyan and Blue to produce a cool cast. Pause to preview.

7. *Optional:* Repeat step 6 with any other button selected for step 4.

8. Click OK or press Enter.

TIP Use a Paintbrush with a light opacity to recolor small areas manually.

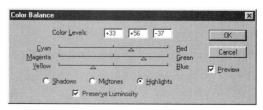

1 Click **Shadows**, **Midtones**, or **Highlights**, then move any of the sliders.

Thumbnail previews in the Variations dialog box represent how an image will look with various color adjustments. To make more precise adjustments and preview changes in the document window, use the Color Balance dialog box.

To adjust color using thumbnail Variations:

1. Choose a target layer.

2. Choose Image menu > Adjust > Variations.

3. Click Shadows, Midtones, or Highlights to modify only those areas ■.
or
Click Saturation to adjust only saturation.

4. Position the Fine/Coarse slider to the right of center to make major adjustments or to the left of center to make minor adjustments ■. Each notch to the right doubles the adjustment per click. Each notch to the left halves the adjustment per click.

5. Click any "More..." thumbnail to add more of that color to the layer ■. Pause to preview. The Current Pick thumbnail represents the modified layer.

6. *Optional:* Click Lighter or Darker to modify the luminosity without modifying the hue ■.

7. *Optional:* Check the Show Clipping box to display neon highlights in areas of nonprintable, out-of-gamut color.

8. *Optional:* Repeat steps 3–6.

9. Click OK or press Enter.

■ First click **Shadows, Midtones, Highlights,** or **Saturation**.

Click the **Original** thumbnail to restore the unmodified layer.

The **Current Pick** thumbnail represents the modified layer.

■ Move the **Fine/Coarse** slider to choose the degree of adjustment.

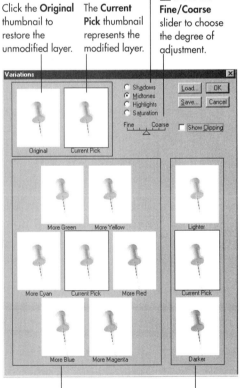

■ Click any "**More**..." thumbnail to add more of that color to the layer. Click the diagonally opposite thumbnail to undo the modification.

■ Click **Lighter** or **Darker** to modify the luminosity without modifying the hue.

Adjust Color using Variations

Curves and Levels

If you use the Curves or Levels command to make color or tonal adjustments, you should adjust the overall image tone first (the composite channel), and then adjust the individual color channels, if necessary (a bit more cyan, a bit less magenta, etc.).

If you adjust an individual color channel, keep in mind that color opposites (cyan and red, magenta and green, yellow and blue) work in tandem. Lowering, cyan, for example, adds more red; lowering red adds more cyan; adding more magenta and yellow decreases the amount of cyan. The moral of the story: you'll probably have to adjust more than one channel to remove an undesirable color cast. If you overzealously adjust only one channel, you'll throw off the color balance of the whole image.

Using the Curves command, you can correct a picture's highlights, quarter tones, midtones, three-quarter tones, or shadows separately. You can use several adjustment layers for color adjustments: use one for the composite channel first and then use one for each individual channel to tweak the color. And you can experiment with the layer opacity or layer mask to remove or lessen the effect in target areas.

To adjust color or values using the Curves command:

1. Choose Image menu > Adjust > Curves (Control-M).
   or
   Create an adjustment layer by Control-clicking the Create New Layer button at the bottom of the Layers palette, choose Type: Curves, then click OK.

2. The Input and Output readouts indicate either brightness values for RGB Color mode or percentage values for CMYK Color mode (light to dark, from left to right). Click on the gradation bar to switch between the two.

3. *Optional:* Choose a channel name to adjust that color separately.

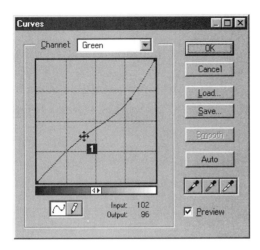

4. Noting where the grid lines meet the gradation bar, drag the part of the curve you want to adjust straight upward to darken or downward to lighten (when in percentage mode) **1**.
and/or

For more precise adjustments, click on the curve to create points to force the curve to remain fixed, then drag between points to produce more subtle adjustments (To remove a point, drag it to the end of the curve or over an adjacent point.)
and/or

Move the extreme end of the curve to reduce absolute black to below 100%, or absolute white to above 0%.

5. Click OK or press Enter **2**–**3**.

TIP We don't recommend using the Curves Pencil tool to draw a curve—it tends to produce a bumpy curve, which in turn produces sharp color transition jumps.

TIP For an image in RGB Color mode, click on the image to see that pixel value placement on the curve. You can then accurately adjust that pixel point. The pixel value will show on individual C, M, Y, and K channels, but not on the composite CMYK channel.

Curves

2 Before Curves adjustment.

3 After Curves adjustment.

To adjust individual color channels using Levels:

1. Make sure the Info palette is open.

2. Choose Image menu > Adjust > Levels (Control-L).

or

Create an adjustment layer by Control-clicking the Create New Layer button at the bottom of the Layers palette, choose Type: Levels, then click OK.

3. Check the Preview box.

4. If there's an obvious predominance of one color in the image (like too much red or green), choose that channel name from the Channel drop-down menu **1**.

Follow any of these steps for a **CMYK** Color image (the sliders have the **opposite** effect in an **RGB** image):

To increase the amount of that particular color, move the black or gray input slider to the right. The black triangle affects the shadows in the image, the gray triangle affects the midtones.

or

To decrease the amount of that color, move the gray or white Input slider to the left. The white slider affects the highlights. The Output sliders are particularly effective for adjusting skin tones in a photograph.

or

To tint the image with the chosen channel color, move the output white slider to the left. To lessen the chosen channel color, move the Black output slider to the right.

Repeat these steps for any other channels that need adjusting, bearing in mind that one channel adjustment may affect another.

5. Click OK or press Enter.

TIP Hold Alt and click Reset to restore the original the dialog box settings.

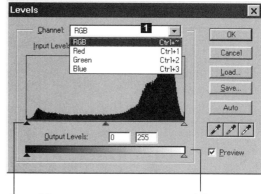

Input sliders   **Output** sliders

In this exercise, you'll be painting shades of gray on a neutral black or white layer with the Color Dodge or Color Burn mode setting to heighten or lessen color in the underlying layer. Though this exercise uses the Color Dodge and Color Burn modes, you can use the neutral color layer option with other layer modes.

To silhouette color areas on black:

1. Activate the layer above which you want the new layer to appear.

2. Choose Layer menu > New > Layer.
   or
   Alt-click the Create New Layer button on the Layers palette.

3. Type a name for the layer.

4. We chose Color Dodge mode for our illustration , but you can choose any mode other than Normal, Dissolve, Hue, Saturation, Color, or Luminosity.

5. Check the "Fill with [mode name]-neutral color" box **2**.

6. Click OK. Our layer was filled with black.

7. Choose the Paintbrush tool. ✐

8. Paint with 60-88% gray. You'll actually be changing the neutral black on the layer. Areas you stroke over will become much lighter.

   If you're displeased with the results, paint over areas or fill the entire layer again with black to remove all the changes, and start over. Repainting or refilling with black will remove any existing editing effects while preserving pixels in the underlying layers.

9. To heighten the color effect, you can choose another mode from the Layers palette. We chose Color Burn mode. Your image strokes will be silhouetted against black **3**-**4**. Paint with a medium gray to restore more original color.

3 The original image.

4 After painting on the Color Dodge mode layer, setting the layer mode to Color Burn, and then painting medium gray strokes on the Color Burn mode layer to heighten contrast between the figures and the black background of the Color Burn mode.

Use the Sponge tool to make color areas on a target layer more or less saturated. (The Sponge tool is also discussed on page 254, where it's used to bring colors into printable gamut.) This tool can't be used on a Bitmap or Indexed Color image.

To saturate or desaturate colors using the Sponge tool:

1. Double-click the Sponge tool.

2. On the Toning Tools Options palette, position the Pressure slider between 1% (low intensity) and 100% (high intensity) **1**. Try a low Pressure first (20%-30%) so the tool won't saturate or desaturate areas too quickly.
   and
   Choose Desaturate or Saturate from the drop-down menu **2**.

3. Click the Brushes tab on the same palette, then click a hard-edged or soft-edged tip. A soft tip will produce the smoothest result.

4. Choose a target layer.

5. Stroke on any area of the layer, pausing to allow the screen to redraw. Stroke again to intensify the effect.

TIP If you Saturate or Desaturate an area too much, choose Edit menu > Undo or File menu > Revert. Don't try to use the tool with its opposite setting to fix it—you'll get uneven results.

TIP You can also adjust saturation in an image using the Image menu > Adjust > Hue/Saturation or Replace Color command.

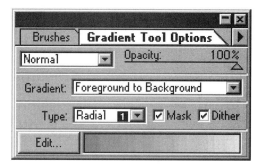

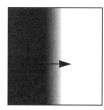

2 The Gradient tool dragged from the middle to the right.

3 The Gradient tool dragged a short distance in the middle using the same colors.

4 The Gradient tool dragged from lower right to upper left.

PHOTO: NADINE MARKOVA

5 The original image.

6 A **radial** gradient in the background. The arrow shows where the mouse was dragged.

Gradients

A gradient is a gradual blend between two or more colors.

The Gradient tool can't be used on an image in Bitmap or Indexed Color mode.

To create a linear or radial gradient:

1. Choose a target layer.

2. *Optional:* Select an area of a layer. Otherwise, the gradient will fill the entire layer.

3. Choose the Gradient tool (G). ▦

4. On the Gradient Tool Options palette, Choose Linear or Radial from the Type drop-down menu **1**.
and
Choose an Opacity.
and
Choose an existing gradient from the Gradient drop-down menu.
and
Choose a mode.

5. *Optional:* Check the Dither box to minimize banding (stripes) in the gradient.

6. *Optional:* Uncheck the Mask box to disable any transparency in the gradient.

7. Choose Foreground and/or Background colors if the gradient Style you chose uses them.

8. For a linear gradient, drag from one side of the image or selection to the other. Drag a long distance to produce a subtle transition area **2**; drag a short distance to produce an abrupt transition **3**. Hold down Shift while dragging to constrain the gradient to the nearest 45° angle. To produce a diagonal gradient, drag from corner to corner **4**.

For a radial gradient, press to establish a center point, then drag outward **5**–**6**.

TIP To delete a gradient fill, choose Edit menu > Undo immediately.

(Continued on the following page)

Linear or Radial Gradient

TIP To reverse the order of colors for a Foreground to Background gradient, drag in the opposite direction. Or, click the Switch colors button on the Toolbox before dragging. ⤺

TIP To produce more of the Foreground color than the Background color in a gradient, click Edit on the Gradient tool Options palette, then move the little Midpoint diamond or click the diamond and enter a percentage above 50 in the Location field **1**.

1 Location

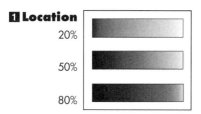

20%

50%

80%

To create your own gradient:

1. Choose the Gradient tool (G). ▓ Open the Swatches palette if you're going to use it to choose colors for the gradient.

2. Click Edit on the Options palette.

3. Click New (Control-N).

4. Type a name for the gradient, then click OK **2**.

5. Click on the leftmost square under the gradient bar to set the starting color **3**.

6. Click a color on the Swatches palette or click in any open image window.
   or
   Click the color swatch in the Gradient Editor **4**, then choose a color from the Color Picker.
   or
   To create a gradient that will use the current Foreground color, click the Foreground selection box **5**.
   or
   To create a gradient that will use the current Background color, click the Background selection box **6**. (Click the plain icon **7** to choose a fixed color.)

Wendy Grossman, in her image, **Guitar with wine**, used gradients, as well as patterns, from Illustrator.

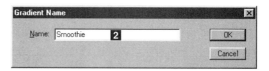

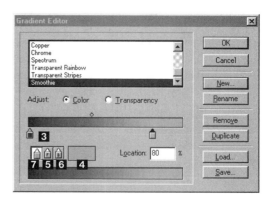

Create a Gradient

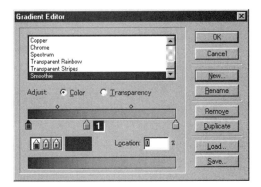

7. Click the rightmost square under the gradient bar to set the ending color, then repeat step 6.

8. *Do any of these optional steps:*

To add intermediate colors to the gradient, click below the gradient bar to create a new square **1**, then choose a color (step 6 on the previous page). Reposition it by dragging.

To reposition a midpoint diamond, which controls where the colors to the left and right of the diamond are 50% each, drag it to a new position or click on it, then enter a percentage in the Location field.

Move the starting or ending square, or enter a new value in the Location field for either square. Moving a square inward will produce more solid color at that edge of the gradient fill. 0% is at the left, 100% is at the right.

To remove an intermediate color, drag its square downward off the bar. You can't remove a starting or ending color.

9. Click OK or press Enter.

TIP Leave the Mask box checked on the Options palette to preserve transparent areas when you fill with a gradient.

More

Click **Save** in the Gradient Editor dialog box to save all the gradients currently on the list to a separate file. This is a good way to organize a bunch of gradients so you can access them easily. Click **Load** to load a previously saved gradient file.

Control-Alt-click Save to save the currently highlighted gradient as a **Curves map**. In the Curves dialog box, load in the gradient file to have the gradient colors replace colors in the image according to their respective luminosity levels.

To edit an existing gradient:

1. Choose the Gradient tool (G). ▣

2. Click Edit on the Options palette.

3. Highlight the name of gradient you want to edit on the scroll list.

4. Follow steps 5–12 in the previous set of instructions.

TIP To remove a gradient, follow steps 1–3, above, click Remove, then click OK.

TIP To duplicate a gradient, follow steps 1–3, above, click Duplicate, enter a name, then click OK. Use this command if you want to edit a gradient and preserve the original.

To change the opacity of gradient colors:

1. Choose the Gradient tool (G).

2. Click Edit on the Options palette.

3. Highlight the name of the gradient you want to edit.

4. Click Adjust: Transparency **1**.

5. Click the leftmost or rightmost square under the transparency bar.

6. Enter an Opacity percentage. Note how transparent that color is in the color bar at the bottom of the dialog box **2**.

7. To add other opacity levels, click just below the transparency bar to produce a new square, then enter an opacity percentage. To delete an intermediate square, drag it downward off the bar. To move a square, drag it or change its Location percentage.

8. To adjust the location of the midpoint opacity, drag the diamond above the transparency bar, or click on it, then enter a Location percentage.

9. Click OK or press Enter.

To create a multicolor wash:

1. Choose a target layer (not the Background).

2. *Optional:* Select an area of a layer.

3. Choose the Gradient tool (G).

4. On the Gradient Tool Options palette, choose an Opacity.
and
Choose Foreground to Transparent from the Gradient drop-down menu, or choose a gradient that you've created that finishes with transparency.

5. Drag from left to right on the image.

6. Choose another target layer or create a new layer, then repeat step 4.

7. Drag from right to left on the image **3**.

8. *Optional:* Using the Layers palette, change the opacity or mode for, or restack, the gradient layers.

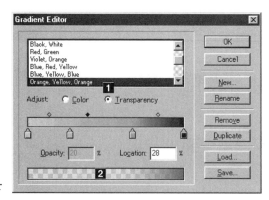

Two gradients, on separate layers, were applied to this image. The middle of the gradients have a 20% opacity, to allow the balloons to peek through. Looks like diddly squat in black and white. Looks nice in color.

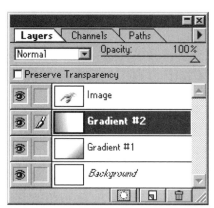

3 Create a subtle painterly effect by placing translucent gradient washes on separate layers.

PAINT 11

I N THIS CHAPTER you will learn to use Photoshop's Line, Airbrush, Pencil and Paintbrush tools. You can paint on a scanned image or you can paint a picture from scratch. You will learn how to create custom brush tips for the painting tools using the Brushes palette, how to save and load brush palettes, and about the Options palette options, like mode and opacity. The Paint Bucket, Smudge, and Eraser tools are also covered in this chapter. Gradients are covered in Chapter 16.

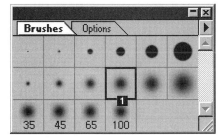

Paintbrush

Airbrush

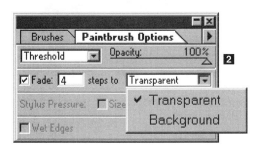

To use the Paintbrush or Airbrush tool:

1. Choose a target layer. Create a selection on the target layer if you want to paint in a restricted area.

2. Click the Paintbrush (B) ✐ or Airbrush (A) tool. ✎

3. Choose a Foreground color (see pages 111–115).

4. Click a hard-edged tip in the first row of the Brushes palette or a soft-edged tip in the second or third row **1**. If a tip is too large to be displayed, its width in pixels will be indicated by a number.

5. Click the Options tab on the palette.

6. On the Options palette, move the Opacity/Pressure slider **2**. At 100%, the stroke will completely cover the underlying pixels.
and
Choose from the mode drop-down menu (see "Blending modes" on pages 26–28).

7. *Optional:* To create a stroke that fades

(Continued on the following page)

as it finishes, check the Fade box and enter a number of steps. The higher the Fade amount, the longer the stroke will be before it fades. Choose Transparent from the "steps to" pull-down menu to fade from the Foreground color to no color, or choose Background to fade from the Foreground color to the Background color.

8. *Optional:* Check the Wet Edges box for the Paintbrush tool to produce a stroke with a higher concentration of color at the edges, like the pooling effect in traditional watercoloring. Use a soft-edged brush tip with this option 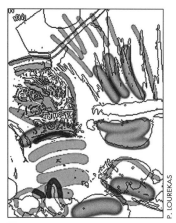–.

9. Drag across any area of the picture. If you press and hold on an area with the Airbrush tool without dragging, the paintdrop will gradually widen and become more saturated.

TIP If you have a stylus hooked up but you're not using it, uncheck all the Stylus Pressure boxes on the Options palette so the Paintbrush tool will work properly with a mouse.

TIP To undo the last stroke, choose Edit menu > Undo immediately. Only the last stroke can be undone.

TIP To draw a straight stroke, click once to begin the stroke, then hold down Shift and click in a different location to complete the stroke.

TIP Alt-click on any open image to sample a color while a painting tool is chosen.

TIP With the Preserve Transparency box checked on the Layers palette, paint strokes will recolor only existing pixels—not transparent areas.

TIP To choose an Opacity level via the keyboard, press any number from 0 through 9 (0 equals 100 percent). You can also enter the actual value numerically (38, 05, etc.), but type it quickly.

1 Strokes created with the Paintbrush tool with the **Wet Edges** box checked on the Paintbrush Options palette.

2 More Wet Edges.

3 The stroke on top was created with the Paintbrush tool, Wet Edges box unchecked. The stroke on the bottom was created with the Wet Edges box checked.

Are you using a stylus?

If you're using a pressure-sensitive tablet and the Control Panel software for the particular tablet you're using is installed, you can choose settings for your stylus for the Airbrush, Paintbrush, Pencil, Blur, Sharpen, Eraser, Rubber Stamp, Smudge, Dodge, Burn, or Sponge tool. Double-click the tool, then click one of the following on the Options palette:

- **Size**: The heavier the pressure, the wider the stroke.

- **Color**: Light pressure applies the Background color, heavy pressure applies the Foreground color, and medium pressure applies a combination of the two.

- **Opacity/Pressure/Exposure**: The heavier the pressure, the more paint is applied.

2 A border created with the Pencil tool (Dissolve mode at 85% opacity), and then the Diffuse filter applied to the border.

To draw straight lines:

1. Choose the Line tool (N). \

2. On the Line Tool Options palette **1**:

Enter a number between 1 and 1000 in the Line Width field.
and
Choose a blending mode from the mode drop-down menu.
and
Choose an Opacity.

3. Choose a Foreground color.

4. Draw a line. The line will fill with the Foreground color when the mouse is released **2**–**3**.

TIP Hold down Shift while dragging to constrain the line to the nearest 45° angle.

TIP To create an arrow, click the Start and/or End box on the Line Tool Options palette. Click Shape, enter numbers in the Width, Length, and Concavity fields in the Arrowhead Shape dialog box **4**, click OK, then draw a line (hold down Shift to constrain the angle).

3 Straight lines added to an image using the Line tool.

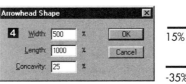

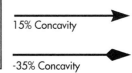

15% Concavity

-35% Concavity

To modify a brush tip:

1. Double-click a brush tip on the Brushes palette **1**.

or

Click a tip, then choose Brush Options from the palette command menu.

2. Move the Diameter slider **2**.

or

Enter a number between 1 and 999 in the Diameter field.

3. Move the Hardness slider.

or

Enter a number between 0 and 100 in the Hardness field (the percentage of the diameter of the stroke that's opaque).

4. Move the Spacing slider.

or

Enter a number between 0 and 999 in the Spacing field. The higher the Spacing, the farther apart each paintdrop will be.

or

Uncheck the Spacing box to have the brush respond to mouse or stylus speed. The faster the mouse or stylus is dragged, the more paintdrops will skip.

5. Enter a number between 0 to 100 in the Roundness field. The higher the number, the rounder the tip.

or

Reshape the tip by dragging either black dot up or down in the left preview box.

6. Enter a number between -180 and 180 in the Angle field.

or

Move the gray arrow in a circular direction in the left preview box.

7. Click OK or press Enter **3**.

TIP Only the Spacing percentage can be changed for the Assorted brushes and most of the Drop Shadow brushes.

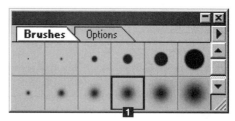

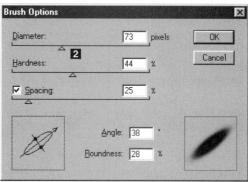

Choose **Diameter**, **Hardness**, **Spacing**, **Angle**, and **Roundness** values in the Brush Options dialog box.

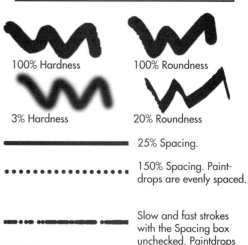

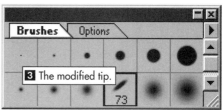

3 The modified tip.

100% Hardness

100% Roundness

3% Hardness

20% Roundness

25% Spacing.

150% Spacing. Paintdrops are evenly spaced.

Slow and fast strokes with the Spacing box unchecked. Paintdrops are unevenly spaced.

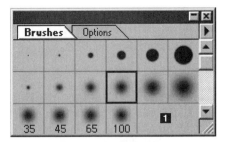

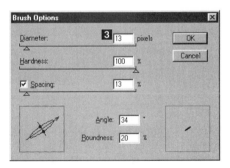

2 The new tip appears after the last tip.

4 A **calligraphic** line added to an image.

To create a new brush tip:

1. Click on the blank area at the bottom of the Brushes palette **1**.
   or
   Choose New Brush from the palette command menu.

2. Follow steps 2–7 on the previous page to customize the tip. The new tip will appear after the last tip on the palette **2**.

To delete a brush tip:

Control-click the brush tip that you want to delete.
or
Click the brush tip on the Brushes palette, then choose Delete Brush from the palette command menu.

You can use the Pencil, Airbrush, or Paintbrush tool to create a linear element, such as a squiggly or a calligraphic line. Use different Angle and Roundness values to create your own line shapes.

To draw a calligraphic line:

1. Click the Pencil, Airbrush, or Paintbrush tool.

2. Choose a Foreground color.

3. On the Brushes palette, double-click a hard-edged brush tip or click on the blank area at the bottom of the palette to create a new tip.

4. The brush will preview in the dialog box as you choose these settings **3**:

   Choose a Diameter between 10 and 15.

   Choose a Spacing value between 1 and 25.

   Position the Hardness slider at 100%.

   Enter 34 in the Angle field.

   Enter 20 in the Roundness field.

5. Click OK or press Enter.

6. *Optional:* Move the Pressure/Opacity slider on the Options palette.

7. Draw shapes or letters **4**.

Monochromatic shades of the Foreground color are applied when you use a brush tip created from an area of a picture.

To create a brush tip from an image:

1. Choose the Rectangular Marquee tool. ⬚

2. Marquee an area of a picture. The selection cannot exceed 1,000 by 1,000 pixels **1**.

3. Choose Define Brush from the Brushes palette command menu. The new tip will appear after the last tip on the palette **2**.

TIP Use the tip with the Paintbrush or Airbrush tool. Click on a white or monochromatic area if you want to see the brush image clearly.

TIP To smooth the edges of the stroke, double-click the custom brush tip, then check the Anti-aliased box. This option is not available for a large brush. You can also specify a Spacing value in the same dialog box. The higher the Spacing percentage, the larger the gap between paintdrops. You can enter a Spacing percentage over 100%.

1 Select an area of an image.

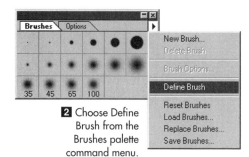

2 Choose Define Brush from the Brushes palette command menu.

A custom brush tip, taken from the necklace of the statue, and used as a brushed-on texture.

A custom brush tip, used like a stamp (various opacities).

Create a Brush Tip from an Image

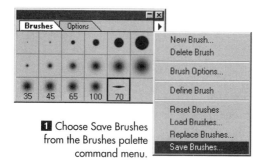

1 Choose Save Brushes
from the Brushes palette
command menu.

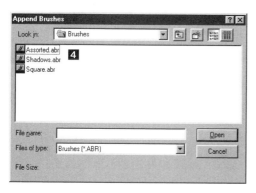

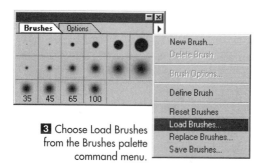

3 Choose Load Brushes
from the Brushes palette
command menu.

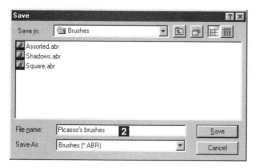

To save a brush set:

1. Choose Save Brushes from the palette command menu **1**.

2. Enter a name in the "File name" field **2**.

3. Choose a location in which to save the palette.

4. Click Save or press Enter.

Three Brushes palettes are supplied with Photoshop in addition to the Default Brushes: Assorted Brushes, which are special shapes and symbols, Drop Shadow Brushes, which are brush tips with soft edges that you can use to make drop shadows, and hard-edged Square Brushes.

To load a brush set:

1. To append a brush set to the existing set, choose Load Brushes from the palette command menu **3**.
or
To have the new brush set replace the currently displayed set, choose Replace Brushes.

2. Open the Brushes & Patterns folder, which is in the Goodies folder in the Photoshop application folder.

3. Double-click a palette name **4**. The brushes will be added to the existing brush set.
or
Click a palette name, then click Open.

TIP The brushes that were on the Brushes palette when you last quit Photoshop will still be there next time you launch Photoshop. To restore the default Brushes palette, choose Reset Brushes from the palette command menu, then click OK.

To create a drop shadow for imagery on a layer:

1. Make sure the object you want to create the shadow for is silhouetted on its own layer 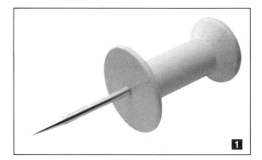, and activate that layer now. (Silhouetting instructions are on page 60).

2. Choose Duplicate Layer from the Layers palette command menu or from the Layer menu, and name it "Image."

3. Double-click the original layer name on the Layers palette, and name it "Shadow" 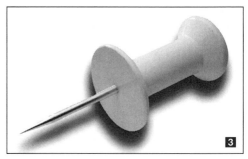.

4. Choose the Move tool.

5. Make sure the Shadow layer is still active, then drag its layer downward and slightly to the right in the image window to reveal some of the shadow.

6. Check the Preserve Transparency box for the Shadow layer.

7. Choose a dark Foreground color.

8. Choose Edit menu > Fill, choose Foreground Color, 80–100% Opacity, Normal mode, then click OK.

9. Uncheck the Preserve Transparency box for the Shadow layer.

10. Choose Filter menu > Blur > Gaussian Blur.

11. Enter a Radius between 4 and 8 pixels.

12. Click OK or press Enter 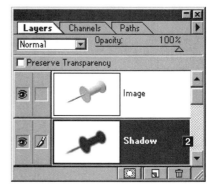.

13. *Optional:* Choose Multiply mode for the Shadow layer to reveal texture, if any, below it.

14. To tweak the shadow layer's position, make sure it's the target layer, then drag it using the Move tool or by pressing an arrow key.

TIP If the entire shadow isn't visible in the image window, use the Image menu > Canvas Size command to expand the canvas to display the shadow fully.

Create a shadow effect via Levels

Create a selection for the shadow shape, and feather its edge. Control-click a silhouetted object's layer if you want to use that shape for the selection. Select the layer to be shadowed, then move the selection marquee. Control-click the Create New Layer button to create an adjustment layer with a mask derived from the selection. Choose Type: Levels, then click OK. Move the black and/or gray Input sliders to the right to darken that part of the layer, choose an individual channel (Channel drop-down menu), move Input sliders to colorize the shadow area, then click OK. Choose Multiply mode for the adjustment layer to reveal more texture or detail from the original layer.

Create a Drop Shadow

The Paint Bucket tool replaces pixels with the Foreground color or a pattern, and fills areas of similar shade or color within a specified Tolerance range. Unlike the Edit menu > Fill command, you can use the Paint Bucket without creating a selection.

NOTE: The Paint Bucket tool won't work on an image in Bitmap color mode.

To fill an area using the Paint Bucket tool:

1. Choose a target layer. If you don't want to fill transparent areas on the layer, check the Preserve Transparency box.

2. Choose the Paint Bucket tool (K). 🖐

3. On the Paint Bucket Options palette **1**:

Enter a number up to 255 in the Tolerance field. The higher the Tolerance value, the wider the range of colors the Paint Bucket will fill. Try a low number first.

and

Choose Foreground or Pattern from the Contents drop-down menu.

and

Choose a blending mode from the mode drop-down menu. Experiment with Soft Light, Multiply, or Color Burn mode.

and

Choose an Opacity.

and

Check the Anti-aliased box to smooth the edges of the filled area.

and

Check the Sample Merged box if you want the Paint Bucket to sample from colors on all the currently visible layers.

4. Choose a Foreground color or define a pattern.

5. Click on the image **2**–**3**.

TIP To undo the fill, choose Edit menu > Undo (Control-Z) immediately.

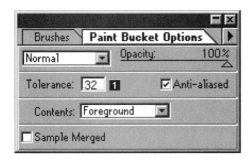

PHOTO: PAUL PETROFF

2 The original image.

3 After clicking with the **Paint Bucket** tool.

NOTE: If you use the Eraser tool on a layer with the Preserve Transparency box checked, or on the Background of an image, the erased area will be replaced with the current Background color. If you use the Eraser on a layer with Preserve Transparency unchecked, the erased area will be transparent.

To erase part of a layer:

1. Choose a target layer.

2. Choose the Eraser tool (E). ✐

3. Choose Paintbrush, Airbrush, Pencil, or Block from the drop-down menu on the Eraser Options palette ∎. Or press "E" to cycle through the tools.

4. Choose an Opacity/Pressure percentage.

5. Click a brush tip on the Brushes palette. (Don't bother to choose a tip for the Block option; its size won't change.)

6. If you're going to erase the Background of the image or if Preserve Transparency is checked on the Layers palette, choose a Background color.

7. Click on or drag across any pixels on the layer ∎–∎.

TIP To restore areas from the last saved version of an image, use the Eraser tool with the Erase to Saved box checked on the Eraser Options palette or use the Rubber Stamp tool with its From Saved option. Neither method will work if you changed the mode, dimensions, or resolution of the image or added or deleted a layer or layer mask from it since it was last saved.

TIP To erase a whole image if it doesn't contain layers, click Erase Image on the Options palette. To erase only the entire target layer, click Erase Layer. Bug fix: If either option is dimmed, force the palette to redraw: Click another tool or hide, then redisplay the palette.

TIP To produce a wet-edged eraser effect, choose Paintbrush from the drop-down menu and check the Wet Edges box.

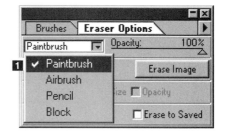

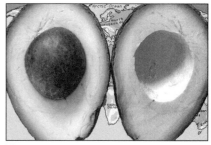

∎ The original image.

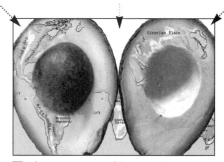

∎ After erasing part of the avocados layer to reveal the map underneath it (Airbrush option, 55% opacity), and erasing part of the map layer to white (Paintbrush option, 100% opacity).

∎ A detail of the partially **erased** map layer.

(side margin) **Erase Part of a Layer**

The Smudge tool can't be used on a image in Bitmap or Indexed Color mode.

To smudge colors:

1. Choose the Smudge tool (U). 🖎

2. On the Smudge Tool Options palette **1**, move the Pressure slider below 100%.
and
Choose a blending mode (see page xx), such as Normal to smudge all shades or colors, or Darken to push dark colors into lighter colors, or Lighten to push light colors into darker colors.

3. *Optional:* To start the Smudge with the Foreground color, check the Finger Painting box on the Smudge Tool Options palette. Otherwise, the smudge will start with the color under the cursor where the stroke begins. The higher the Pressure percentage, the more Foreground color is applied.

Hold down Alt to temporarily turn on the Finger Painting option if the Finger Painting box is unchecked.

4. *Optional:* Check the Sample Merged box on the Options palette to start the smudge with colors from all the currently visible layers in the image (uncheck Finger Painting if you use this option). Uncheck Sample Merged to smudge only with colors from the target layer. In either case, of course, pixels will only smudge on the currently active layer.

5. Click the Brushes tab on the palette, then click a hard-edged or soft-edged tip.

6. Drag across an area of the image **2**–**4**. Pause to allow the screen to redraw.

2 Smudge— **Normal** mode.

3 Smudge— **Darken** mode.

4 Smudge— **Lighten** mode.

Smudge Colors

By drawing colored strokes on a separate layer to apply tints to a grayscale image, you'll have a lot of flexibility: You can change the blending mode or opacity for the Paintbrush or Airbrush tool or the color layer, and erase or dodge tints here or there without affecting the underlying gray image.

To apply tints to a grayscale image:

1. Open a Grayscale mode image, and convert it to RGB Color mode (Image menu > Mode > RGB Color).

2. Alt-click the Create New Layer button on the Layers palette to create a new layer above the grayscale image, and select Color mode for the new layer.

3. Choose the Paintbrush or Airbrush tool.

4. Choose a Foreground color.

5. Choose an Opacity/Pressure percentage below 100% from the Options palette. Choose a low-ish opacity for a subtle tint. You can change opacities between strokes. And remember, you can lower the opacity of the whole layer via the Layers palette.

6. Paint strokes on the new layer.

7. *Optional:* Use the Eraser tool to remove areas of unwanted color (uncheck the Preserve Transparency box for this), then repaint, if desired. Or use the Dodge tool at a low Exposure percentage to gently lighten the tints by hand.

8. *Optional:* Choose a different blending mode for the color layer. Soft Light, Color Burn, and Multiply can produce exquisite effects.

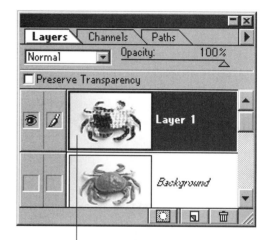

This layer contains the **color tints**.

MORE LAYERS 12

IN **THIS CHAPTER** you will learn
to blend between layers using the
Layers palette opacity and mode controls and the Layer Options dialog box.
You will also learn how to create, modify,
and move layer masks, link layers to move
them as a unit, save a copy of a layer in a
separate document, use layers as a clipping
group, merge layers, and flatten layers.
(Basic layer operations are covered in
Chapter 7, Layers)

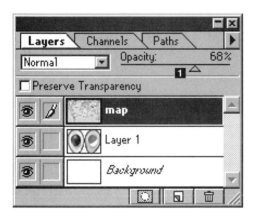

To change the opacity of a layer (or a floating selection):

Move the Opacity slider on the Layers
palette **1**. The lower the opacity, the more
pixels from the layer below will show
through the target layer **2**–**3**.

TIP You can also choose an opacity for a
layer using the Layer Options dialog
box (see the following page).

2 The map layer, 100% Opacity, on top of the
avocados layer.

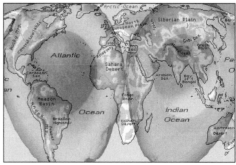

3 The map layer **opacity** reduced to 68%.

You can control which pixels in a pair of layers will be visible using the Underlying sliders in the Layer Options dialog box.

To blend pixels between two layers:

1. Double click a layer name on the Layers palette **1**.

or

Choose a target layer, then choose Layer Options from the Layers palette command menu.

2. Make sure the Preview box is checked **2**, then move the black Blend If: This Layer slider to the right to remove shadow areas from the target layer **3**.

and/or

Move the white This Layer slider to the left to remove highlights from the target layer.

and/or

Move the black Underlying slider to the right to restore shadow areas from the layer below the target layer **4**.

and/or

Move the white Underlying slider to the left to restore highlights from the layer below the target layer.

3. Click OK or press Enter **5**–**6**.

TIP To eliminate white in the topmost of the two layers, move the white This Layer slider to about 245.

TIP To blend or restore colors from one channel at a time, choose from the Blend If drop-down menu before moving the sliders.

TIP To adjust the midtones independently of the shadows, Alt-drag the right part of the black slider (it will divide in two). To adjust the midtones independently of the highlights, Alt-drag the left part of the white slider.

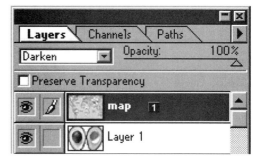

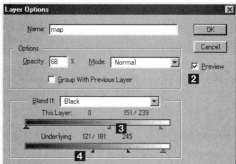

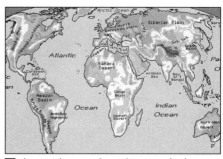

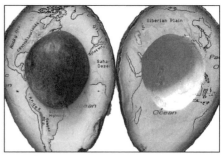

5 The map layer is above the avocados layer.

6 The same image after dividing and moving the white **This Layer** slider and the black **Underlying** slider in the Layer Options dialog box.

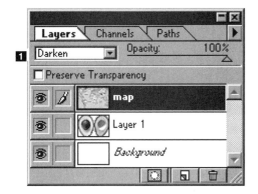

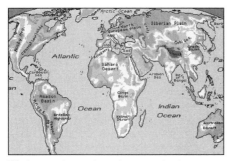

2 The map layer above the avocados layer.

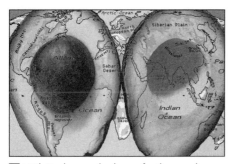

3 With Darken mode chosen for the map layer.

Layer blending modes

The layer blending mode you choose for a target layer affect how that layer's pixels blend with the pixels in the layer directly below it. Some modes produce subtle effects (Soft Light mode, for example); others produce dramatic color shifts (try Difference mode). Normal, of course, is the default mode.

The easiest way to choose a blending mode for a layer is from the mode drop-down menu on the Layers palette **1**–**4**. The modes are discussed in detail on pages 26–28. You can also choose a mode for a layer in the Layer Options dialog box (double-click a layer name to open it).

TIP For the Paintbrush, Airbrush, Paint Bucket, Pencil, and Line tool, you can choose an additional mode, called Behind, that you can't choose for a layer. Behind mode creates the effect of painting on the back of the current layer. For the Line and Paint Bucket tool, you can also choose Clear mode, which works like an eraser. Uncheck Preserve Transparency to access either mode.

4 The layer **blending modes**

Layer masks

A layer mask is simply an 8-bit grayscale channel that has White or Black as its Background color. By default, white areas on a layer mask permit pixels to be seen, black areas hide pixels, and gray areas partially mask pixels. You can use a mask to temporarily hide pixels on a layer so you can view the rest of the composite picture without them. Later, you can modify the mask, remove the mask and make the effect permanent, or discard the mask altogether.

An advantage of using a layer mask is that you can access it from both the Layers palette and the Channels palette. You'll see a thumbnail for the layer mask on the Layers palette and on the Channels palette when a layer that contains a mask is highlighted. Unlike an alpha channel selection, however, which can be loaded onto any layer, a layer mask can only be turned on or off for the layer or clipping group (group of layers) it's associated with.

To create a layer mask:

1. On the Layers palette, click on the name of the layer to which you want to add a mask.

2. If you want to create a mask in the shape of a selection, leave the selection active.

3. To create a white mask in which all the layer pixels are visible, choose Layer menu > Add Layer Mask > Reveal All or click the Add Layer Mask button at the bottom of the Layers palette **1**.
or
To create a black mask in which all the image layer pixels are hidden, choose Layer menu > Add Layer Mask > Hide All or Alt-click the Add Layer Mask button at the bottom of the Layers palette.
or
To reveal only layer pixels within an active selection, choose Layer menu > Add Layer Mask > Reveal Selection or

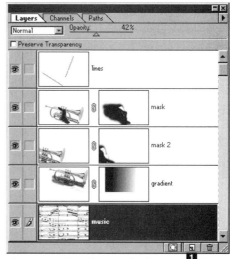

The Layers palette showing the three trumpet layers, each with its own layer mask. Portions of the middle and bottom trumpets are hidden by a black/white layer mask. The topmost trumpet fades out via a gradient in its layer mask.

The trumpets **without layer masks**.

The trumpets **with layer masks**.

click the Add Layer Mask button at the bottom of the Layers palette.

To hide layer pixels within the selection, choose Layer menu > Add Layer Mask > Hide Selection or Alt-click the Add Layer Mask button at the bottom of the Layers palette.

TIP To turn the mask and layer thumbnail display on or off or change the thumbnail size, choose Palette Options from the Layers palette command menu.

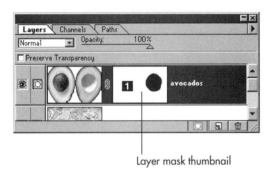

Layer mask thumbnail

To reshape a layer mask:

1. Choose the Paintbrush tool (B). ✐

2. On the Options palette, choose 100% Opacity and Normal mode. (Or choose an opacity below 100% to partially hide layer pixels.)

3. Click a brush tip on the Brushes palette.

4. To reshape the layer mask while viewing the layer pixels, click the layer mask thumbnail on the Layers palette **1** (not on the layer name). The selected thumbnail will have a dark border and a mask icon will appear next to the layer thumbnail.

or

To display the mask channel by itself in the image window, Alt-click the layer mask thumbnail. (Alt-Shift-click the layer mask thumbnail to redisplay the mask over the image layer.)

5. Paint on the picture with black as the Foreground color to enlarge the mask and hide pixels on the layer. (D is the default colors shortcut.)

and/or

Paint with white as the Foreground color to reduce the mask and restore pixels on the layer.

and/or

Paint with gray as the Foreground color to partially hide pixels on the layer.

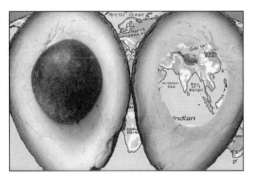

2 The center of the avocado on the right is blocked by a **layer mask**.

6. When you're finished modifying the layer mask, click the layer thumbnail to reselect the pixels on that layer **2**.

Reshape a Layer Mask

By default, a layer and layer mask move together. Follow these steps to move a layer mask independently.

To move a mask without moving its layer:

1. On the Layers palette, click the link icon 🖇 between the layer and the layer mask thumbnails **1**.

2. Click on the layer mask icon.

3. Choose the Move tool (V).⌖

4. Drag the layer mask in the image window.

5. Click again between the layer and layer mask thumbnails to re-link them.

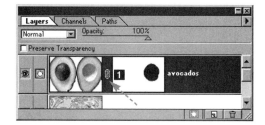

To fill type with imagery using a layer mask:

1. Activate a layer (not the Background).

2. Choose Layer menu > Add Layer Mask > Hide All.

3. Choose the Type Mask tool. T

4. Click on the image, type the letters you want to appear on the image, choose a font and other type specifications, then click OK.

5. Reposition the type selection, if desired, by placing the pointer inside the selection and dragging.

6. Choose Edit menu > Fill.

7. Choose Use: White, 100% Opacity, Normal mode, then click OK.

8. Choose Select menu > None.

9. Reselect the Layer thumbnail **2**–**3**.

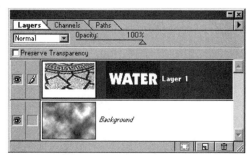

2 The layer mask thumbnail. Layer 1 pixels are revealed through the **white** type in the layer mask.

3 In this image, the water layer is visible only through the letter shapes of the layer mask.

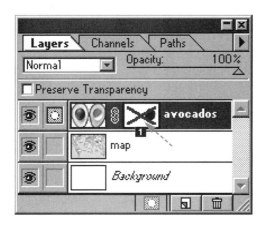

To temporarily remove the effects of a layer mask:

Shift-click the layer mask thumbnail on the Layers palette. A red "X" will appear over the thumbnail and the entire layer will be displayed **1**.

(Shift-click the layer mask thumbnail again to remove the "X" and restore the mask effect.)

TIP For this effect to work, make sure the mask channel is hidden—that no eye icon is showing for the mask on the Channels palette.

TIP To invert the effect of a layer mask, highlight the layer mask icon, then choose Image menu > Adjust > Invert (Control-I). Hidden areas will be revealed, and vice versa.

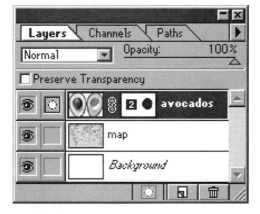

Layer masks that are no longer needed should be discarded, because they occupy storage space.

To apply or discard the effects of a layer mask:

1. On the Layers palette, click on the thumbnail of the mask that you want to remove **2**.

2. Click the Trash icon.
or
Choose Layer menu > Remove Layer Mask.

3. To make the mask effect permanent, click Apply **3**.
or
To remove the mask without applying its effect, click Discard.

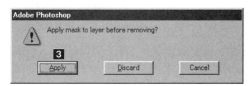

Once layers are linked together, they can be moved as a unit in the image window or drag-copied to another image. Linking is especially useful when the position of the layers in relationship to each other is critical. You can also apply the Transform or Free Transform command to linked layers. In fact, you'll minimize image distortion due to resampling by transforming multiple layers all at once instead of individually.

To link layers and move them as a unit:

1. On the Layers palette, click on one of the layers that you want to move.

2. Click in the second column for any other layer you want to link to the layer you chose in step 1. The layers you link don't have be consecutive. The link icon will appear next to any non-active linked layers **1**.

3. Choose the Move tool (V). ⊹

4. Press and drag the linked layers in the image window.

TIP To unlink a layer, click the link icon.

Click to display the **link** icon in the second column on the Layers palette for any layers you want to link to the active layer. In this illustration, the first three layers are linked.

The bottommost layer of a clipping group of layers (the base layer) clips (limits) the display of pixels and controls the mode and opacity of the layers above it. Only pixels that overlap pixels on the base layer are visible.

To create a clipping group of layers:

1. Click on a layer name.

2. Alt-click on the line between that layer name and the name just above it (the cursor will be two overlapping circles). A dotted line will appear between clipping group layer names, the base layer name will be underlined, and the thumbnail for the topmost layer will be indented **2**. (The layers you choose for a clipping group must be listed consecutively on the Layers palette.)

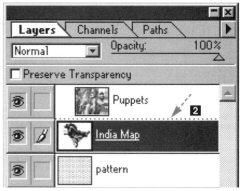

Click between two layers to join them in a **clipping group**. A dotted line will appear, and the **base** layer will be underlined.

1 The map of India is clipping (limiting) the view of the puppets.

3. *Optional:* Repeat step 2 to add more layers to the clipping group **1**.

TIP To remove a layer from a clipping group, Alt-click on the dotted line on the Layers palette. The solid line will reappear.

TIP To create a clipping group using the Layer Options dialog box, double-click the layer name on the Layers palette just above the layer you want to be the base (bottommost) layer, then check the Group With Previous Layer box.

TIP To fill type with imagery using a clipping group, see the instructions on page 183.

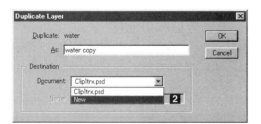

To drag-copy a layer from one image to another

Drag the name of the layer you want to copy from the **Layers palette** into the destination **image window**. It will appear where you release the mouse. Hold down **Shift** while dragging to center the layer in the destination image window.

Use the following technique to save an individual layer in a new document or in an existing, open document. You might want to do this before you perform an operation that requires flattening, such as converting to Indexed Color mode (which does not support multiple layers) or saving your document in a file format other than Photoshop, if you only need to preserve one or two individual layers.

To save a copy of a layer in a separate file:

1. Activate the layer you want to save a copy of.

2. Choose Duplicate Layer from the Layers palette command menu.

3. Choose Destination Document: New **2**.

4. Enter a name for the new document in the As field.

5. Click OK or press Enter.

6. Save the new document.

In these instructions, a filter is applied to a duplicate layer and then the original and duplicate layers are blended using Layers palette opacity and mode controls. Use this technique to soften the effect of an image editing command, like a filter, or to experiment with various blending modes or adjust commands. You can also use a layer mask to limit the area of the effect, a technique that can't be done using the Fade command. If you don't like an effect, you can just delete the new layer and start over.

To blend a modified layer with the original layer:

1. Choose a target layer .

2. Choose Duplicate Layer from the Layers palette command menu.

3. Click OK.

4. Modify the duplicate layer. (Apply a filter or other image editing command.)

5. On the Layers palette, move the Opacity slider to achieve the desired degree of transparency between the original layer and the modified, duplicate layer –.
and/or
Choose a different mode.

6. *Optional:* Create a layer mask to limit the area of effect.

TIP For a beautiful textural effect, duplicate the Background in a color image (preferably, a Background that isn't solid white), highlight the new layer, then choose Image menu > Adjust submenu > Desaturate (Control-Shift-U) to make it grayscale. Next, apply the Add Noise filter or the Pointillize filter . Finally, lower the opacity and choose different modes for the new layer from the Layers palette.

TIP See pages 206–207 of the Filters chapter to learn how to create textures via a layer mask.

1 The original image.

2 To produce the figure below, we applied the Mezzotint filter.

3 After applying the Mezzotint filter to the duplicate layer, then lowering the opacity of the duplicate layer.

4 A blended layer effect using the Pointillize filter.

Blend Layers

MASKS **13**

THIS CHAPTER COVERS two special selection techniques: saving a selection to an alpha channel and working in Quick Mask mode.

If you save a selection to a specially created grayscale channel, called an **alpha channel**, you can load the selection onto the image at any time. If you have, for example, a selection with an irregular shape that would be difficult to reselect, you can save it to an alpha channel. A file can contain up to 24 channels, though from a practical point of view, since each channel increases a picture's storage size, (depending on the size of the selection area), you should be judicious when adding alpha channels. Alpha channels are accessed via the Channels palette **1**, and saved or loaded onto a picture via Select menu commands or the Channels palette. (See our "Tip" on page 166 for converting an alpha channel to a path to conserve file storage space.)

Using Photoshop's **Quick Mask** mode, the selected or unselected areas of an image can be covered with a semi-transparent colored mask, which can then be reshaped using any editing or painting tool. Masked areas are protected from editing. Unlike an alpha channel, a Quick Mask cannot be saved, but the new selection can be saved when you return to Standard (non-Quick Mask) mode.

NOTE: If you're unfamiliar with Photoshop's basic selection tools, read Chapter 5 before reading this chapter.

(Layer masks are covered in Chapter 12.)

Only highlighted channels can be edited.

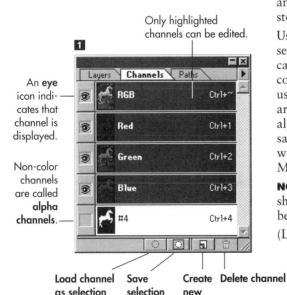

An **eye** icon indicates that channel is displayed.

Non-color channels are called **alpha channels**.

Load channel as selection   Save selection as channel   Create new channel   Delete channel

Masks

157

A selection that is saved in an alpha channel can be loaded onto any image whenever it's needed.

To save a selection to a channel:

1. Select an area of a target layer **1**.

2. Choose Select menu > Save Selection, then click OK.

or

Click the Save Selection as Channel button on the Channels palette **2** (the second icon at the bottom of the palette).

Both alpha channels and Quick Masks are converted to 8-bit grayscale on the Channels palette.

TIP Choose New from the Document dropdown menu in the Save Selection dialog box to save a selection to an alpha channel in a new, separate document **3**.

TIP Choose an Operation option in the Save Selection dialog box to combine a current selection with an existing alpha channel that you choose from the Channel drop-down menu. (Operation options are discussed on page 160.)

TIP You can save an alpha channel with an image only in the Photoshop, TIFF, Pixar, PNG, Targa, or PICT (RGB) file format. To save a copy of a file without alpha channels, check the Don't Include Alpha Channels box, if available.

TIP If you save a floating selection to a channel, the selection will remain floating (it won't replace underlying pixels).

TIP Choose "......Mask" from the Channel drop-down menu in the Save Selection dialog box to turn the selection into a layer mask for the target layer. The layer image will be revealed only where the selection was.

1 Select an area on a layer.

PHOTO: CARA WOOD

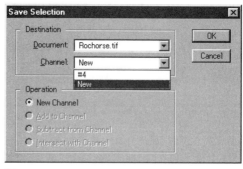

2 Save selection as channel

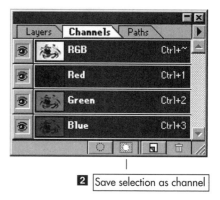

3 Choose Channel: **New** in the Save Selection dialog box. If you are saving to an existing channel, choose an **Operation** option to add to or subtract from white areas on the channel.

Save a Selection to a Channel

1 Click an alpha channel name on the Channels palette.

2 An alpha channel. The **selected** area is **white**, the **protected** area is **black**.

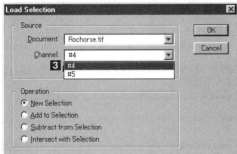

Load selection shortcuts

To load an alpha channel as a selection using the Load Selection dialog box, Alt-click the Load Channel as Selection button on the Channels palette. ⬚ To bypass the Load Selection dialog box, drag the name of the alpha channel you want to load over the Load Channel as Selection button.

An alpha channel can be displayed without loading it onto the image as a selection.

To display a channel selection:

1. Click an alpha channel name on the Channels palette **1**. The selected area will be white, the protected area black **2**.

2. To restore the normal image display, click the top channel name on the palette (Control- ~).

TIP If the selection has a Feather radius, the faded area will be gray and will only be partially affected by editing.

TIP Reshape the mask with any painting tool using black, gray, or white "paint."

To load a channel selection onto an image:

1. If the composite image isn't displayed, click the top channel name on the Channels palette. You can combine the channel selection with an existing selection in the image (see the next page).

2. Choose Select menu > Load Selection.

3. Choose the channel name from the Channel drop-down menu **3**.

4. To load a channel while there's an existing selection in the image, choose an Operation option (see the next page).

5. *Optional:* Check the Invert box to switch what will be the selected and unselected areas in the loaded selection.

6. Click OK or press Enter.

TIP To select only pixels on a layer, and not transparent areas, choose Channel: "[   ] Transparency" or Control-click the layer name.

TIP To load a channel selection onto a different image, make sure the source and destination images have the same dimensions and resolution, activate the destination image, then follow steps 2–6, above, choosing the source image name in the Load Selection dialog box. To load a layer mask selection, activate that layer first in the source image.

Display or Load a Channel Selection

Save Selection Operations

When saving a selection to an existing channel, you can choose from these Operation options in the **Save Selection** dialog box:

Channel and
Selection to be Saved

Resulting Channel

 ADD

New Channel saves the current selection in a new channel.
Shortcut: Click the Save Selection as Channel button on the Channels palette.

Add to Channel adds the new selection to the channel.

Channel and
Selection to be Saved

Resulting Channel

 SUBTRACT

 INTERSECT

Subtract from Channel removes white or gray areas that overlap the new selection.

Intersect with Channel preserves only white or gray areas that overlap the new selection.

Load Selection Operations

If a channel is loaded while an area of a layer is selected, you can choose from these Operation options in the **Load Selection** dialog box:

Selection and
Channel to be Loaded

Resulting Selection

 ADD

New Selection—the channel becomes the current selection.
Shortcut: Control-click the channel name or drag the channel name over the Load Channel as Selection button.

Add to Selection adds the channel selection to the current selection.
Shortcut: Control-Shift-click the channel name.

Selection and
Channel to be Loaded

Resulting Selection

 SUBTRACT

INTERSECT

Subtract from Selection removes areas of the current selection that overlap the channel selection.
Shortcut: Control-Alt-click the channel name.

Intersect with Selection preserves only areas of the current selection that overlap the channel selection.
Shortcut: Control-Alt-Shift click the channel name.

Save and Load Selection Operations

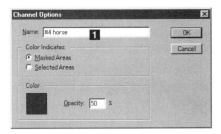

2 The horse is the selected area.

3 The horse is still the selected area, but it is now black instead of white.

To rename a channel:

1. Double-click a channel name on the Channels palette.
or
Click a channel name, then choose Channel Options from the palette command menu.

2. Type a new name in the Name field **1**.

3. Click OK or press Enter.

TIP Normally, the selected areas of an alpha channel are white and the protected areas are black or colored. To reverse these colors without changing which area is selected, double-click an alpha channel name on the Channels palette, then click Color Indicates: Selected Areas **2**–**3**.

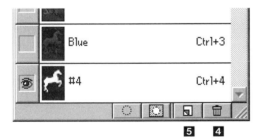

To delete a channel:

1. Click the name of the channel that you want to delete on the Channels palette.

2. Click the Trash icon at the bottom of the palette **4**, then click Yes.
or
Alt-Click the Trash icon.
or
Choose Delete Channel from the Channels palette command menu.

To duplicate a channel:

Drag the name of the channel that you want to duplicate over the Create new channel icon **5**.
or
Highlight the channel name, choose Duplicate Channel from the Channels palette command menu, then click OK.

You can superimpose an alpha channel selection as a colored mask over an image, and then reshape the mask.

To reshape an alpha channel mask:

1. Make sure there is no selection on the image.

2. Click an alpha channel name on the Channels palette. An eye icon will appear next to it **1**.

3. Click in the leftmost column at the top of the palette. An eye icon will appear. There should be only one highlighted channel—the alpha channel name **2**.

4. Choose the Pencil *✏* or Paintbrush tool. *✒*

5. On the Options palette, choose Normal mode.
and
Choose 100% Opacity to create a full mask, or a lower Opacity to create a partial mask.

6. To enlarge the masked (protected) area, stroke on the cutout with black as the Foreground color **3**. (Click the Switch colors icon on the Toolbox to switch the Foreground color between black and white (X) **4**.)
or
To enlarge the unmasked area, stroke on the mask with white as the Foreground color **5**.

7. To hide the mask, click the alpha channel's eye icon.
or
Click the Layers tab, then choose a target layer.

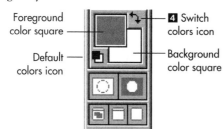

Foreground color square —
Default colors icon —
4 Switch colors icon
Background color square

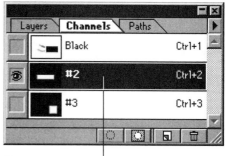

1 Click the alpha channel name on the Channels palette.

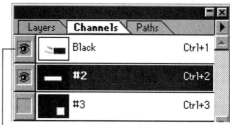

2 Click in the leftmost column at the top of the palette. Make sure the alpha channel name stays highlighted.

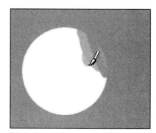

3 Enlarge the **masked** area by stroking on the cutout with **black** as the Foreground color.

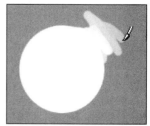

5 Enlarge the **unmasked** area by stroking on the mask with **white** as the Foreground color.

Reshape an Alpha Channel Mask

1 Select an area on a layer.

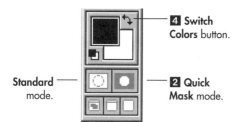

Standard mode.

4 **Switch Colors** button.

2 **Quick Mask** mode.

3 The unselected area is covered with a mask.

If you choose Quick Mask mode when an area of a target layer is selected, a semi-transparent tinted mask will cover the unselected areas, and the selected areas will be revealed in a cutout. You'll still be able to see the image through the mask. The cutout or mask can be reshaped using the Pencil, Airbrush, or Paintbrush tool.

NOTE: You can't save a Quick Mask via Save Selection while your image is in Quick Mask mode, but you can save your selection to a channel when you return to standard screen display mode.

To create a Quick Mask:

1. Select an area of a target layer **1**.

2. Click the Quick Mask mode icon on the Toolbox (Q) **2**. A mask will cover part of the picture **3**.

3. Choose the Pencil *✎* or Paintbrush tool. *✐*

4. On the Options palette, move the Opacity slider to 100%.
and
Choose Normal from the mode drop-down menu.
and
Make sure all check boxes on the palette are unchecked.

5. Click the Brushes tab, then click a tip on the Brushes palette.

6. Stroke on the cutout with black as the Foreground color to enlarge the masked (protected) area. (Press D to reset the default colors to black and white.)
or
Stroke on the mask with white as the Foreground color to enlarge the cutout (unmasked area). (Click the Switch Colors icon on the Toolbox to switch the Foreground and Background colors (X) **4**.)
or
Stroke with gray or a brush with an opacity below 100% (Options palette) to create a partial mask.

(Continued on the following page)

7. Click the Standard mode icon (Q) to turn off Quick Mask. The selection will remain active.

8. Modify the layer. Only the unmasked (selected) area will be affected.

9. *Optional:* Save the selection (the areas that were previously unprotected) to a channel so you can use it later (see page 158).

TIP To create a Quick Mask without first creating a selection, click the Pencil or Paintbrush tool, double-click the Quick Mask icon on the Toolbox, click Selected Areas , click OK, then stroke with black on the layer. The selected areas will be covered with a mask—not the protected areas—so you'll be creating what will be the selected area.

TIP To quickly switch the mask color between the selected and masked areas, Alt-click the Quick Mask icon on the Toolbox.

TIP In the Quick Mask Options dialog box, you can also click the Color box and choose a new mask color, and you can change the opacity of the mask color (both affect display only).

TIP "Quick Mask" will be listed on the Channels palette and on the document window title bar while Quick Mask mode is on .

TIP If you modify a Quick Mask using a tool with a low opacity, that area will be partially affected by modifications.

■ In the Mask Options dialog box, choose whether Color Indicates: **Masked Areas** or **Selected Areas**. Click the **Color** square to choose a different mask color.

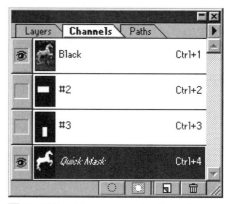

■ "Quick Mask" appears on the Channels palette. To open the Quick Mask Options dialog box, double-click "Quick Mask" or double-click the Quick Mask icon on the Toolbox.

The **Quick Mask** icons on the Toolbox.

Color Indicates:
Masked areas

Color Indicates:
Selected **Areas**

PATHS 14

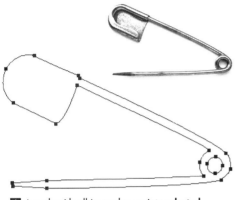

1 A path with all its anchor points **selected**.

LIKE THE PEN tool in Adobe Illustrator, the Pen tool in Photoshop creates outline shapes, called paths, consisting of anchor points connected by curved or straight line segments **1**. A path can be precisely reshaped by adding, deleting, or moving its anchor points. A curved line segment can also be reshaped by adjusting its Bézier direction lines. A path can be used on any layer. If you stroke or fill a path, the color pixels will appear on the currently active layer.

You can convert a selection into a path, reshape it, and then convert it back into a selection. This is a good method for creating a selection with a very exacting fit, which, for certain kinds of shapes, works better than using the Lasso tool or Quick Mask mode. And there's an added bonus: Paths occupy much less storage space than channels.

Paths are displayed, selected, activated, restacked, and deleted using the Paths palette **2**. The Toolbox contains five path-making and reshaping tools **3**.

You can also export a path to Illustrator, where it can also be used as a path, and you can silhouette part of an image using a clipping path in the EPS format to place in an illustration or page layout program.

2 The **Paths** palette.

A **saved** path.

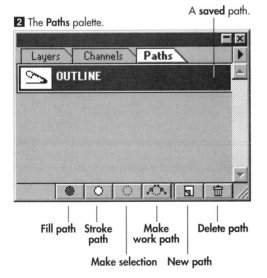

Fill path   Stroke path   Make work path   Delete path

Make selection   New path

3 The Pen tool and its related tools. Press **P** to cycle through them.

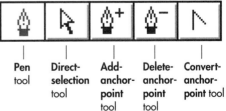

Pen tool   Direct-selection tool   Add-anchor-point tool   Delete-anchor-point tool   Convert-anchor-point tool

If you convert a selection into a path, you can precisely reshape it and then use it as a path or convert it back into a selection.

To convert a selection into a path:

1. Select an area of an image ▮.

2. Alt-click the Make Work Path button at the bottom of the Paths palette ▮.
or
Choose Make Work Path from the Paths palette command menu.

3. Enter 3, 4, or 5 in the Tolerance field ▮. The minimum is 0.5; the maximum is 10. At a low Tolerance value, many anchor points will be created and the path will conform precisely to the selection marquee. At a high Tolerance value, fewer anchor points will be created and the path will be smoother, but it will conform less precisely to the selection.

4. Click OK or press Enter ▮. The new work path name will appear on the Paths palette. Don't leave the path as a work path, though—save it by following the steps on page 168.

TIP To quickly convert a selection into a path using the current Make Work Path Tolerance setting, click the Make Work Path button at the bottom of the Paths palette.

TIP To reclaim storage space occupied by an alpha channel, convert it into a selection and then into a path, save the path, delete the alpha channel, then save the image. Follow the instructions on page 159 to load an alpha channel selection; follow steps 2–4 on this page and then the steps on page 168 to save the path; delete the alpha channel (choose Delete Channel from the Channels palette command menu); then save the image. Later on you can convert the path back into a selection (see page 172) and save the selection to a new alpha channel.

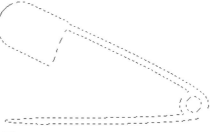

▮ A **selection**.

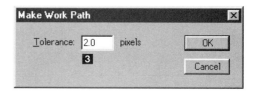

Makes work path from selection

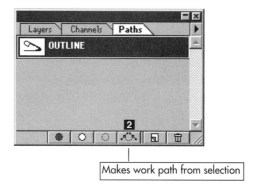

Make Work Path

Tolerance: 2.0 pixels   OK

▮

Cancel

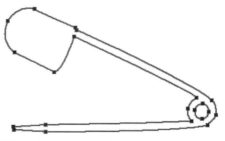

▮ A **selection** converted into a **path**.

Convert a Selection into a Path

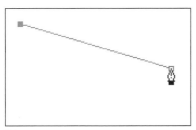

1 Click to create **straight** sides.

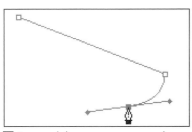

2 Press and drag to create a **curved** segment.

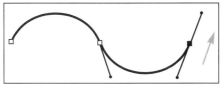

3 Drag in the direction you want the curve to follow. Place anchor points at the ends of the curve, not at the height of the curve. The fewer the anchor points, the more graceful the curves.

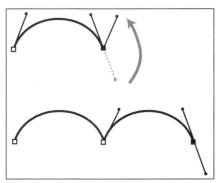

4 To draw **non-continuous** curves, **Alt**-drag from the last anchor point in the direction you want the next curve to follow. Both direction lines will be on the same side of the curve segment.

To create a path (Pen tool):

1. Choose the Pen tool. ♦ **NOTE:** If a path name is currently active, the new path will save under that name.

2. *Optional:* To list the path on the Paths palette before you draw it, click the New Path button at the bottom of the Paths palette. ▣ To name the path before you draw it, Alt-click the New Path button.

3. Check the Rubber Band box on the Pen Tool Options palette to preview the line segments as you draw.

4. Click, move the mouse, then click again to create a straight segment **1**. Hold down Shift while clicking to draw the line to the nearest 45° angle.
or
Press and drag to create a curved segment, then release the mouse. Direction lines will appear **2**–**3**.
or
To create a non-continuous curve, Alt-drag from the last anchor point in the direction you want the next curve to follow, release Alt and the mouse, then drag in the direction of the new curve **4**.

5. Repeat step 3 as many times as necessary to complete the shape.

6. To leave the path open, click the Direct-selection or Pen tool. If you don't deselect the path name or end the path—closed or open—any additional paths you draw will be saved under the same name.
or
To close the path, click on the starting point (a small circle icon will appear next to the pointer).

7. The path will be a Work Path. To save it, follow the instructions on page 168.

TIP Press Backspace to erase the last created anchor point. Press Backspace twice to delete the entire path.

To move a path:

1. On the Paths palette, activate the name of the path you want to move.

2. Choose the Direct-selection tool. ⬉

3. Alt-click the path in the image window to select all its points.

4. Drag the path in the image window.

To copy a path in the same image:

To copy the path and name it, on the Paths palette, Alt-drag the path name over the New Path button at the bottom of the palette **1**, enter a name **2**, then click OK or press Enter. (To copy the path without naming it, drag the path name without holding down Alt.)

To drag-and-drop a path to another image:

1. Open the source and destination images.

2. Choose the Direct-selection tool. ⬉

3. Drag the path name from the Paths palette into the destination image. If there is already an active path in the destination image, the path you drag will be added to its name.

A new path created with the Pen tool will be automatically labeled "Work Path," and it will save with the file, but the next path you create will replace it; the new replaces the old. Follow these instructions to save a path so it won't be deleted by a new path. Once a path is saved, it is resaved automatically each time it's modified.

To save a work path:

1. With the Work Path active, choose Save Path from the Paths palette command menu.
or
Double-click the path name.

2. Enter a name **3**.

3. Click OK or press Enter.

How to scale or rotate a path

You can't scale a path by itself, but here's a work-around: Drag the path you want to scale or rotate to a new document, use the Image menu > Image Size command to resize the document or an Image menu > Rotate Canvas command to rotate it (the path will scale or rotate along with it), and then drag the scaled or rotated path back to the original document.

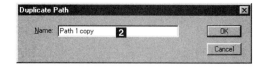

3 Type a Name in the Save Path dialog box.

To quickly save a work path under the default name

Drag the path name over the New Path button 🔲 at the bottom of the Paths palette **1**. To rename it, double-click the path name, then type a new name.

Move a Path; Copy a Path; Save a Path

To display a path, simply click its name on the Paths palette.

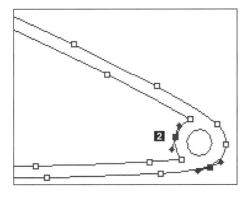

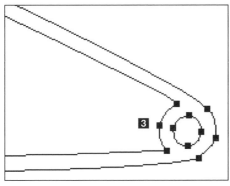

To display a path:

Click the path name on the Paths palette **1**.

To hide a path:

Shift-click the path name on the Paths palette.
or
Click below the path names on the Paths palette.
or
Activate the name of the path you want to hide on the Paths palette, then choose View menu > Hide Path (Control-Shift-H). If you choose this option, you'll have to choose View menu > Show Path to redisplay all the paths.
or
Activate the name of the path you want to hide on the Paths palette, then choose Turn Off Path from the Paths palette command menu.

To select anchor points on a path:

1. Click a path name on the Paths palette.

2. Choose the Direct-selection tool. ⬉

3. Click on the path to select one anchor point.
or
Shift-click to select additional anchor points **2**.
or
Alt-click the path to select all its anchor points **3**. An entire path can be moved when all its points are selected.

TIP To change the stacking position of a path, just drag the path name up or down on the Paths palette.

TIP Hold down Control to use the Direct-selection tool while any Pen tool is selected.

To reshape a path, you can drag, add, or delete an anchor point or move a segment. To modify the shape of a curved line segment, move a direction line toward or away from its anchor point or rotate it around its anchor point.

To reshape a path:

1. On the Paths palette, click on the name of the path you want to reshape.

2. Choose the Direct-selection tool. ↳
To access the Direct-selection tool when any other path tool is active, press Control.

3. Click on the path in the image window.

4. Do any of the following:

Drag an anchor point or a segment **1**.

Drag or rotate a direction line **2**.

To add an anchor point, choose the Add-anchor-point tool ♦⁺ (or hold down Control and Alt if the Direct-selection tool is currently selected), then click on a line segment (the pointer will turn into a plus sign when it's over a segment) **3**–**4**.

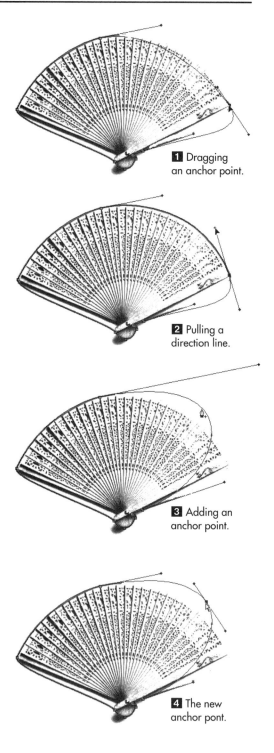

1 Dragging an anchor point.

2 Pulling a direction line.

3 Adding an anchor point.

4 The new anchor pont.

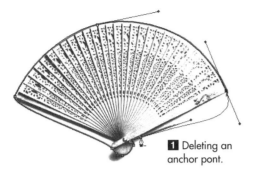

1 Deleting an anchor pont.

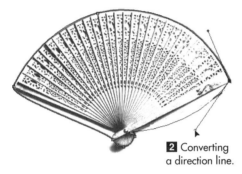

2 Converting a direction line.

To delete an anchor point from a path, choose the Delete-anchor-point tool ⚓ (or hold down Control and Alt if the Direct-selection tool is currently selected), then click on the anchor point (the pointer will turn into a minus sign when it's over a point) **1**.

To convert a curved point into a corner point, choose the Convert-anchor-point tool ⌐, then click the anchor point (deselect the Convert-anchor-point tool by clicking another tool). To convert a corner point into a curved point, click the Convert-anchor-point tool, then drag away from the anchor point.

Use the Convert-anchor-point tool ⌐ to rotate half of a direction line independently **2**. Once the Convert-anchor-point tool has been used on part of a direction line, you can use the Direct-selection tool to move the other part.

To delete a segment, select it using the Direct-selection tool and make sure all the path's anchor points aren't selected, then press Backspace once. Pressing Backspace twice will delete the **entire** path!

5. Click outside the path to deselect it.

To delete a path, click the path name, then click the Trash icon.

NOTE: If the path you want to delete is a Work Path, simply drawing a new work path with the Pen tool will cause the original Work Path to be replaced.

To delete a path:

1. On the Paths palette, activate the name of the path you want to delete.

2. Alt-click the Trash icon on the Paths palette **3**.
or
Click the Trash icon, then click Yes.

To deselect a path:

1. Choose the Direct-selection tool. ⬏

2. Click outside the path. The path's anchor points will be hidden.

To convert a closed path into a selection:

1. *Optional:* You can add, delete, or intersect the new selection with an existing selection.

2. Control-click the name of the path you want to convert into a selection.
or
On the Paths palette, activate the name of the closed path you want to convert into a selection, then click the Make Selection button at the bottom of the palette **1**. Alt-click the Make Selection button if you want to apply a Feather Radius to the selection (enter a low number to soften the edge slightly) **2**, choose whether or not you want edges to be Anti-aliased, or add, subtract, or intersect the path with an existing selection on the image (click an Operation option). Operation shortcuts are listed at right).

3. On the Layers palette, activate the name of the layer you want the selection to be on.

TIP To move the new selection, drag it using any selection tool.

Path-into-selection shortcuts

Make path the current selection	Control-click path name
Add path to current selection	Control-Shift-click path name
Subtract path from current selection	Control-Alt-click path name
Intersect path with current selection	Control-Alt-Shift-click path name

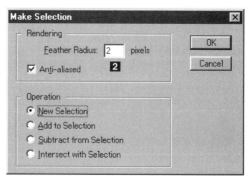

Strokes path with foreground color

When you apply color to (stroke) the edge of a path, the current tool (i.e., Paintbrush, Pencil) and its current Options palette attributes (opacity, mode) are used to produce the stroke.

To stroke a path:

1. On the Paths palette, activate the path to which you want to apply the stroke. The path can be closed or open.

2. Using the Layers palette, activate the layer on which you want the stroke pixels to appear.

3. Choose the Pencil, Paintbrush, Smudge, Airbrush, Rubber Stamp, Blur, Sharpen, Dodge, Burn, or Sponge tool.

4. On the Options palette, choose a mode.
and
Choose an Opacity (or Pressure).

5. Click the Brushes tab on the palette, then click a brush tip. The stroke thickness will match the brush tip diameter.

6. Choose a Foreground color.

7. Click the Stroke Path button at the bottom of the Paths palette **1**. (If you want to switch tools, Alt-click the Stroke Path button, choose from the Tool drop-down menu, then click OK. That tool will be used with its current Options palette settings.)
or
Choose Stroke Path (or Stroke Subpath, for an open Work Path) from the Paths palette command menu, then click OK **2**–**4**.

8. *Optional:* Click the Stroke Path button again to widen the stroke.

2 Soft **Airbrush** stroke.

PHOTO: NADINE MARKOVA

3 The original image.

4 **Smudge** tool stroke.

Stroke a Path

Use the Fill Path command to fill an open or a closed path with a color, a pattern, or imagery.

To fill a path:

1. On the Paths palette, activate the path to which you want to apply the fill.

2. Using the Layers palette, activate the layer on which you want the fill pixels to appear.

3. To fill with a solid color other than white or black, choose a Foreground color.

or

To fill with a pattern, select an area of an image using the Rectangular Marquee tool, then choose Edit menu > Define Pattern.

or

To fill with imagery, activate the layer that you want to use as a fill, then choose Edit menu > Take Snapshot.

4. Alt-click the Fill Path button at the bottom of the Paths palette **1**.

or

Choose Fill Path (or Fill Subpath for an open Work Path) from the palette command menu.

5. Choose from the Contents: Use drop-down menu **2**.

6. Enter an Opacity percentage.

7. Choose a Mode. Choose Clear mode to fill the path with layer transparency.

8. *Optional:* If a layer (not the Background) is active, check the Preserve Transparency box to recolor only existing pixels on the layer, not transparent areas.

9. *Optional:* Choose Rendering options (feathering and anti-aliasing).

10. Click OK or press Enter **3**.

TIP To fill a path using the current Fill Path dialog box settings, with the path name highlighted, click the Fill Path button at the bottom of the Paths palette.

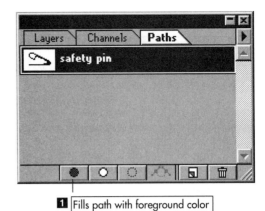

1 Fills path with foreground color

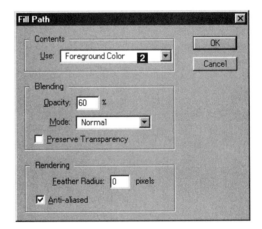

Fill a Path

Partitions, ©1996 Annette Weintraub

Underpinnings, ©1996 Annette Weintraub

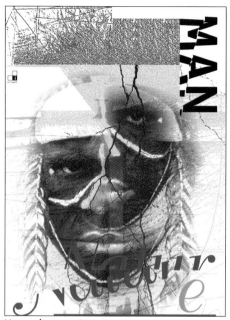

Man and nature, ©Min Wang

Transformation, ©1996 Diane Fenster

Arch, ©Jeff Brice

Sight, ©Alicia Buelow

Koolhaas, ©John Hersey

Webhouserino, ©John Hersey

Video conferencing, ©Wendy Grossman

Seasonal Specialties (tree catalog) ©1996 All Rights Reserved

Seasonal Specialties ©1996 All Rights Reserved

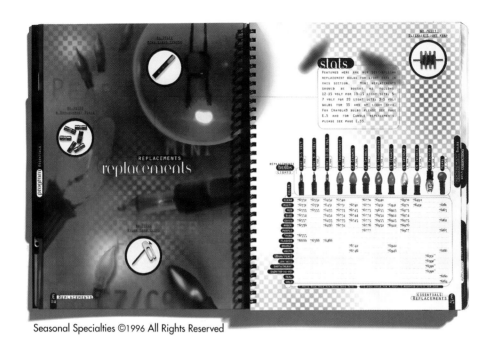

Radiowaver, ©John Hersey

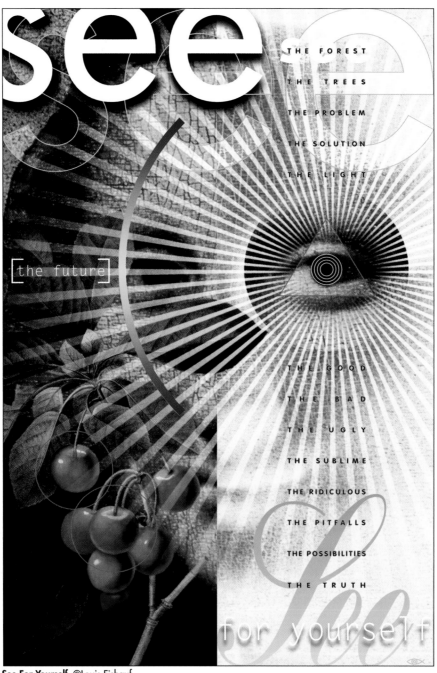

See For Yourself, ©Louis Fishauf

Gate, ©Jeff Brice

Springhead, ©Jeff Brice

Mapping Poem, ©Jeff Brice

Trustfear, ©Alicia Buelow

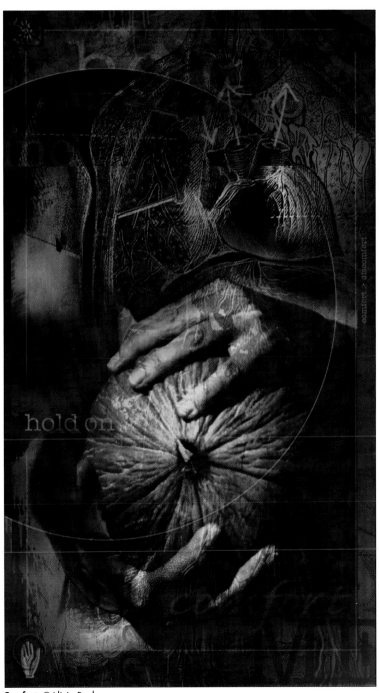

Comfort, ©Alicia Buelow

Taste, ©Alicia Buelow

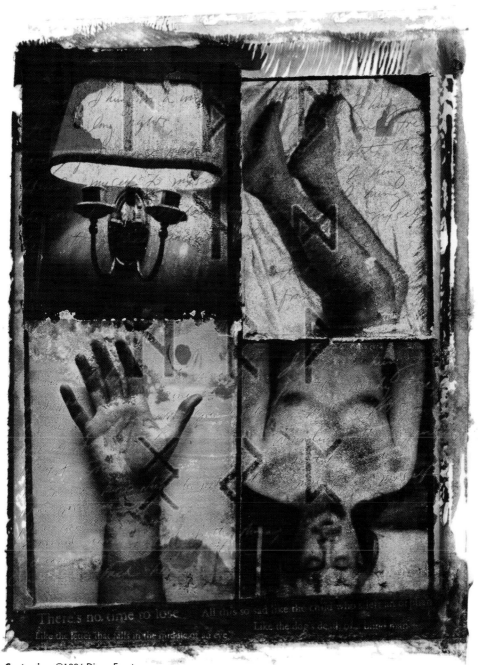

Canto nine, ©1996 Diane Fenster

Labyrinth of Lights, ©1996 Annette Weintraub

Universal Language, ©1996 Annette Weintraub

2 Type wrapping around a Photoshop clipping path using QuarkXPress' Runaround: Auto Image option.

3 A Photoshop clipping path layered over type in QuarkXPress.

4 If the image were imported normally, without a clipping path, it would have an opaque white background.

You can silhouette an image in Photoshop, then open or import it in another application, such as Adobe Illustrator or QuarkXPress. The area outside the image will be transparent, so it can be layered over other page elements, like text.

To clip the background from an image for use in another application:

1. Create a path around the portion of the image you want to keep.

2. Save the path, and keep it active.

3. Choose Clipping Path from the Paths palette command menu.

4. Choose the path name from the Path drop-down menu **1**.

5. Enter a number in the Flatness field. Leave this field blank to use the printer's default setting. Enter 8, 9, or 10 for high-resolution printing; enter 1, 2, or 3 for low resolution printing (300–600 dpi).

6. Click OK or press Enter.

7. Save the document in the Photoshop EPS file format (see page 244). When you open or import it into another application, only the area inside the clipping path will display and print **2**–**4**.

TIP In Adobe Illustrator, you can move, scale, rotate, reflect, or shear the silhouetted image, and the area outside it will remain transparent.

Clipping Path

You can create a path in Photoshop, export it to Adobe Illustrator or Macromedia FreeHand 7, and use it as a path in that program. If you like, you can then place it back into Photoshop (see page 41).

To export a path to Illustrator or FreeHand:

1. Create and save a path.

2. Choose File menu > Export > Paths to Illustrator.

3. *Optional:* Modify the name in the File Name field **1**.

4. From the Paths drop-down menu, choose an individual path name, or choose All Paths to export all the paths in the document.

5. Choose a location in which to save the path file.

6. Click OK. The path can be opened as an Adobe Illustrator document.

TIP To ensure the path fits when you reimport it into Photoshop, don't alter its crop marks in Illustrator.

TIP You may have to choose Artwork view in Illustrator to see the exported path, because it doesn't have a stroke.

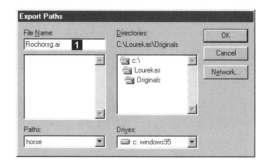

Export Path to Illustrator or FreeHand

TYPE 15

IN **PHOTOSHOP**, type is composed of pixels. Type that is created with the Type tool appears on its own layer automatically (yay!), and can be modified like any other layer. The Type Mask tool creates a type selection, which appears above the current target layer.

This chapter covers how to create type, how to fill type with imagery using a clipping group of layers, and how to screen it back or screen back the background behind it. Special effects techniques include 3D type, fading type, and type with a drop shadow. Type can also be transformed, imported from Adobe Illustrator, filled with a gradient, filled with a pattern, or modified by applying a filter. You'll learn those techniques in other chapters.

Type resolution

Since it's composed of pixels, the resolution of type is the same as the resolution of the image. To create the smoothest possible type for high-resolution output, choose 200 dpi or higher for the image resolution. Unfortunately, increasing a image's resolution causes its file size to increase. If you want to superimpose type over an image for a particular design and you're not creating a special Photoshop type effect, import your Photoshop image into a page layout program or into an illustration program, like Adobe Illustrator, and then layer PostScript type over it.

Check the Anti-aliased box in the Type Tool dialog box for smooth rendering **1**–**2**. Photoshop uses Adobe Type Manager when rendering Adobe PostScript fonts **3**.

1 The side of a character with the **Anti-aliased** box **unchecked** in the Type Tool dialog box.

2 The **Anti-aliased** box **checked** in the Type Tool dialog box.

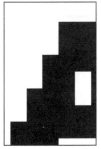

3 Adobe Type Manager turned off or not installed.

Type that is created using the Type tool automatically appears on its own layer, so it can be moved, transformed, recolored, deleted, or otherwise modified without affecting pixels on any other layer.

To create type on its own layer (Type tool):

1. Choose a target layer.

2. Choose a Foreground color. (You can recolor the type later.)

3. Choose the Type tool (T). **T**

4. Click on the image where you want the type to appear. (Don't sweat it—it's a breeze to move it later.)

5. *Optional:* Check the Show: Font and Size boxes to preview the type in the dialog box **1**.

6. Enter characters in the **text** field in the Type Tool dialog box. Press Enter when you want to start a new line, otherwise all the type will appear in one line on the image.
and
Choose a typeface from the **Font** drop-down menu.
and
Choose Points or Pixels from the drop-down menu next to the Size field, then enter a number between 4 and 1000 in the **Size** field.
and
If you entered more than one line of type, enter a number between 0 and 1000 in the **Leading** field (the vertical space between lines of type).
and
Enter a number between -99.9 and 999.9 in the **Spacing** field (the horizontal space between characters).
and
Check any **Style** options. Don't double Style a font, though. For example, if you choose Garamond Italic from the Font menu, don't then apply the Italic style to it.
and

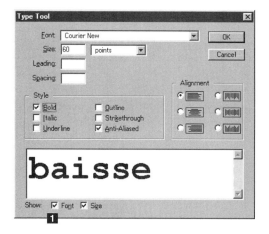

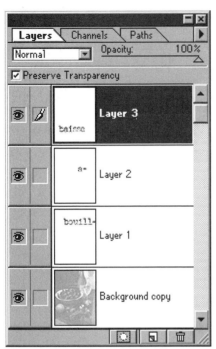

 To produce the image below, type was placed on three separate layers so they could be moved around easily.

Click a horizontal or vertical **Alignment** icon.

and

For most purposes, you'll want to check the **Anti-aliased** box to smooth the type. This option is checked by default. Leave Anti-aliased unchecked if you're planning to output the image to a multimedia program, like Director, where anti-aliased type can appear with an ugly halo around it if it's placed against a non-white or non-uniform background color.

7. Click OK. The type will appear on a new layer and will be colored with the Foreground color **1**.

TIP To change the stacking position of the the type, drag the type layer name up or down on the Layers palette.

TIP Move the Opacity slider on the Layers palette to change the type opacity, or choose a different blending mode for the type layer. To recolor the type, see the instructions on the next page.

TIP With the type layer selected, check the Preserve Transparency box on the Layers palette to restrict painting, filling, editing, or filter effects to the letter shapes. Transparent areas on the layer won't be modified.

TIP To move the type, click the layer name on the Layers palette, choose the Move tool, then drag in the image window, or use the arrow keys to nudge it.

Type on its Own Layer

To recolor type:

1. To fill with a solid color other than white or black, choose a Foreground color.
or
To fill with a pattern, select an area of an image using the Rectangular Marquee tool, then choose Edit menu > Define Pattern.
or
To fill with imagery, activate the layer that you want to use as a fill, then choose Edit menu > Take Snapshot.

2. Click the type layer name on the Layers palette, and check the Preserve Transparency box so only the type pixels on the layer will be recolored.

3. Choose Edit menu > Fill (Shift-Backspace).

4. Choose from the Use: drop-down menu **1**.

5. *Optional:* Enter an opacity value or choose a mode. (You can also choose an opacity and mode for the type layer from the Layers palette.)

6. Click OK or press Enter.

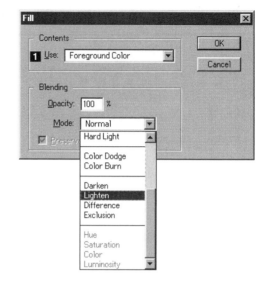

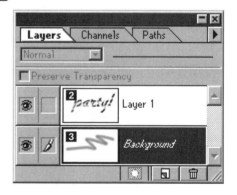

Painterly type

Choose the Paintbrush tool and a Foreground color, make sure the type layer is highlighted and the Preserve Transparency box is checked on the Layers palette, then drag across the type layer in the image window. Only existing pixels will be recolored **2**. To paint behind the type, do it on the layer directly below the type layer **3**.

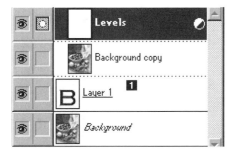

2 Screened back type.

To screen back an image with type, follow the same steps, but use an adjustment layer on the Background to lighten it, and use the topmost Levels adjustment layer to darken the type.

To screen back type:

1. Follow the steps on page 178 to create a type layer.

2. Click the name of the layer that is to be the backdrop image behind the type.

3. Choose Duplicate from the Layers palette drop-down menu, rename the duplicate layer, if you like, then click OK.

4. On the Layers palette, drag the duplicate layer name above the type layer.

5. Alt-click on the line between the two layer names to create a clipping group. A dotted line will appear and the name of the base (bottom) layer of the group will be underlined **1**. The clipping effect won't be visible until you change the duplicate layer.

6. Click on the duplicate layer name.

7. Choose New Adjustment Layer from the palette command menu.

8. Choose Levels from the Type drop-down menu, check the Group with Previous Layer box, then click OK.

9. Move the Input midtones slider to the left to lighten the midtones in the type. Pause to preview.
   and
   Move the Output shadows slider to the right to reduce the contrast in the type. Pause to preview.

10. Click OK or press Enter **2**.

11. *Optional:* Change the blending mode for the adjustment layer or the base layer to restore some background color (try Overlay, Color Dodge, or Hard Light mode). Lower the layer's opacity to soften the Levels effect.

To fill type with imagery from another document:

1. Follow the steps on page 178 to create a type layer.

2. Activate the layer in another document that contains the imagery that you want to fill the type with.

3. Choose All from the Select menu or create a selection.

4. Choose Edit menu > Copy.

5. Activate the image containing the type layer, then Control-click the type layer name.

6. Choose Edit menu > Paste Into (Control-Shift-V) –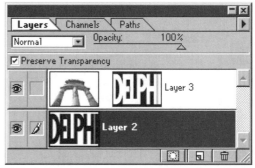. A new layer with a layer mask will be created automatically, and the pasted image will be revealed through the character shapes.

7. *Optional:* With the layer thumbnail selected on the Layers palette, choose the Move tool and drag to move the pasted image within the type shapes. Click in the space between the layer thumbnail and the layer mask thumbnail to link the mask to the layer. The position of the image inside the mask can't be changed as long as they remain linked. (Dragging with the Move tool now would move both the type shape and the image inside it, and expose the type layer underneath.)

1 Type filled with an image using the **Paste Into** command.

2 The bottommost layer is the original type layer; the topmost layer was created after pasting into the type selection.

Other ways to modify a type layer

Since type in Photoshop is composed of pixels, the ways it can be dressed up are almost limitless—just use your imagination! Here are a few suggestions:

TIP Free transform or transform it (see pages 90–91).

TIP Apply a filter to it.

TIP Fill it with a pattern (see pages 117–118) or a gradient (see pages 131–132) (remember to turn on Preserve Transparency for these fill techniques).

Type filled with a pattern, Difference mode.

Type filled with a pattern, Fresco filter applied.

Type filled with a pattern and a gradient.

Type filled with a pattern, the Palette Knife filter applied.

1 The separate layers before being joined a clipping group.

2 The separate layers, pulled apart so you can see their stacking order.

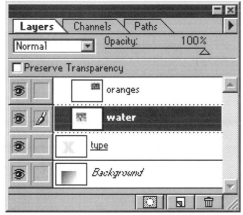

3 The Layers palette after Alt-clicking on the lines above the type layer. The type layer (the underlined name) is the base layer of the clipping group.

To fill type with imagery using a clipping group of layers:

1. Create type using the Type tool.

2. Move the type layer on the Layers palette just below the layer or layers that are to become the type fill **1**–**2**.

3. Alt-click on the line between the type layer name and the layer directly above it to create a clipping group. A dotted line will appear and the base (bottommost) layer of the group will be underlined. Only pixels that overlap the letter shapes will be visible **3**–**4**.

4. *Optional:* Activate the type layer and use the Move tool to reposition the letter shapes in the image window.

5. *Optional:* Alt-click on the lines between other layers directly above the clipping group to add them to the group.

6. *Optional:* Change the mode or opacity for any layer in the clipping group.

TIP To release a layer from a clipping group, Alt-click again on the dotted line.

TIP The opacity and mode for the clipping group are determined by those settings for the base layer (the underlined name on the Layers palette, in our example). Readjust this layer's settings to change the whole group.

4 Type filled with imagery using a **clipping group**.

You can follow these instructions to create a shadow for any object on its own layer.

To create shadow type:

1. Open an image.

2. Create type using the Type tool.

3. With the type layer selected, choose Duplicate Layer from the Layers palette command menu.

4. Click OK or press Enter.

5. Click on the original type layer name (the layer below the duplicate) **1**–**2**.

6. Choose the Move tool ✛, then drag the type slightly away from the duplicate type. You can reposition it later.

7. Choose a Foreground color for the shadow color from the Picker palette. (We chose black for our illustration.)

8. Check the Preserve Transparency box on the Layers palette so only existing layer pixels will be recolored, not the transparent areas on the layer.

9. Choose Edit menu > Fill (Shift-Backspace).

10. Choose Foreground color from the Content/Use pop-up menu, enter 100 in the Opacity field, then click OK or press Enter.

11. *Optional:* Press any of the arrow keys to nudge the type layer.

12. Uncheck the Preserve Transparency box on the Layers palette.

13. Choose Filter menu > Blur > Gaussian Blur.

14. Check the Preview box, then choose the desired degree of blurring by moving the Radius slider **3**. (Drag in the preview window to move the image inside it. Click the **+** button to zoom in or the **–** button to zoom out).

15. Click OK or press Enter (see **1** on the next page). Proceed with the next set of instructions if you want to screen the background behind the type.

1 The original type layer.

2 The Layers palette showing the two type layers that were used to create the shadow type effect.

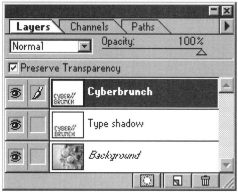

3 Move the **Radius** slider in the Gaussian Blur dialog box to blur the type.

Shadow Type

1 After applying the **Gaussian Blur** filter to the shadow type.

2 After applying the **Levels** command with Input Levels 0, .95, and 255, and Output Levels 92 and 255 to the Background.

3 After filling the adjustment layer with a black-to-white **gradient** (upper right to lower left corner) to mask out the Levels effect in the upper right corner.

Follow these steps to heighten the contrast between the type shadow and the Background.

To screen back the background:

1. Click Background on the Layers palette.

2. Choose Layer menu > New > Adjustment Layer.

3. Choose Levels from the Type drop-down menu, then click OK.

4. Check the Preview box.

5. Move the gray Input slider a little to the left.
and
Move the black Output slider a little to the right.

6. Click OK or press Enter **2**–**3**.

You can further readjust the levels using different blending modes (try Screen mode) and opacities on the Levels adjustment layer.

TIP To create more realistic shadow type on a textured background, choose Multiply mode from the Layers palette for the shadow layer, and move the Layers palette Opacity slider to lighten or darken the shadow.

Shadow Type; Screen the Background

To create fading type:

1. Create type on its own layer, and leave the type layer active.

2. Choose Layer menu > Add Layer Mask > Reveal All. A layer mask thumbnail will appear next to the layer name **1**.

3. Choose the Gradient tool (G).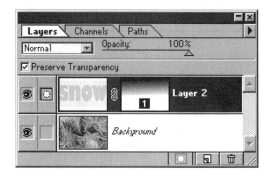

4. Choose 100% Opacity, Normal mode, and Foreground to Background from the Gradient Tool Options palette.

5. Choose black as the Foreground color. (Press D to choose the default colors; press X to switch the Foreground and Background colors.)

6. Drag from the top or bottom of the selection at least halfway across the type. The type layer mask will fill with a black-to-white gradient. Type will be hidden where there is black in the layer mask **2**.

TIP Click on the layer thumbnail on the Layers palette to modify the layer; click on the layer mask thumbnail to modify the layer mask. (Read more about layer masks in Chapter 12.)

2 Fading type.

Fading Type

To keep in mind if you work with a type selection

- To **move** a type selection: Use the Type Mask tool (not the Move tool) to drag it or use the arrow keys to nudge it. Hold down Shift and press an arrow key to move the type selection 10 screen pixels at a time.

- If you drag a type selection using the Move tool, you'll cut away and move pixels from the active layer. You'll be knocking out letter shapes from the image and moving the underlying pixels in the shape of characters. This method creates a floating selection layer. To drop the floating selection onto the active layer and leave the selection marquee active, choose Layer menu > Defloat; to drop and deselect the floating selection, choose Select > None (Control-D).

- You can choose from two methods to **copy** pixels from only within a type selection: Choose Edit menu > Copy to copy pixels only from the active layer or choose Edit menu > Copy Merge to copy pixels from all visible layers below the selection. Position the type selection over the desired pixels before using either copy command.

- To paste imagery into the type selection, activate another layer or another image, copy an area from that image, click back on the image that contains the type selection, then choose Edit menu > Paste Into. The type selection will be deselected.

- If you save the type selection to a new **channel** (click the Save Selection as Channel button ▨ on the Channels palette), it can then be viewed on the Channels palette and loaded onto any layer or layer mask, and at any time.

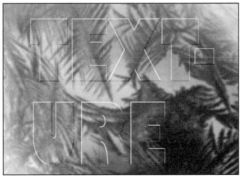

3D type. (For this image, we blurred the Background.)

The Type Mask tool creates a selection in the shape of type characters. You might want to create a type selection for a variety of reasons: to copy layer imagery in the shape of letters; to mask (limit) an adjustment layer effect to a type selection; or to add a layer mask (Reveal All or Hide All).

To create a type selection (Type Mask tool):

1. Activate the layer on which you want the type selection to appear.

2. Choose the Type Mask tool.

3. Click in the image window where you want the selection to appear.

4. Follow steps 4–7 on pages 178–179.

To create 3D type:

1. Create or open an image in RGB mode with a gradient or a texture on the Background.

2. Choose the Type Mask tool and create a type selection.

3. Click the Save Selection as Channel button on the Channels palette. ▨

4. Choose Select menu > None (Control-D).

5. On the Layers palette, activate the texture layer.

6. Choose Filter menu > Render > Lighting Effects.

7. From the Texture Channel drop down menu, choose the number of the channel that contains the type.

8. Choose Spotlight for the Light Type; position the lighting ellipse so it falls nicely across the type; adjust the Height slider for the desired degree of three-dimensionality; and make any other adjustments to the lighting. Uncheck the "White is high" box to make the shadows appear on the lower right.

9. Click OK.

(Continued on the following page)

More stuff to do to the 3D type:

1. After following steps 1–9 on the previous page, activate the channel that contains the type, choose Duplicate Channel from the Channels palette command menu, enter a name ("soft shadow"), then click OK.

2. Activate the duplicate channel.

3. To enlarge the type area, choose Filter menu > Other > Maximum, move the Radius slider to 2, then click OK.

4. To soften the edge of channel, choose Filter menu > Blur > Gaussian Blur. Move the Radius slider to the desired degree of softening.

5. Activate the 3D type effect layer on the Layers palette.

6. Choose Duplicate Layer from the Layers palette command menu.

7. Repeat steps 6–9 on the previous page to create the 3D look, but this time choose the larger type channel as the Texture Channel. For our image, we inverted the layer after applying the Lighting Effects filter. You can also fiddle with the Mountainous slider and other settings in the Lighting Effects dialog box.

8. *Optional:* Lower the duplicate layer's opacity until you reach a pleasing balance between the larger 3D type and the original 3D type.

3D type

To deselect a type mask selection:

Choose Select menu > None (Control-D). (If you press Backspace or choose Edit menu > Clear, you will remove pixels that were within the boundaries of the type selection.)

TIP Double-click the type selection with the Type Mask tool to reopen the Type Tool box (this only works for a Type Mask tool selection).

3D Type; Deselect Type Mask Selection

FILTERS 16

1 Filters are grouped into submenu categories under the Filter menu.

PHOTOSHOP'S FILTERS can be used to produce an myriad of special effects, from slight sharpening to wild distortion. Use filters like Blur or Sharpen for subtle retouching; use filters like Color Halftone, Find Edges, Emboss, or Wind to stylize an image; use the Artistic, Brush Strokes, Sketch, or Texture filters to make a layer look hand-rendered; or create a wide variety of beautiful lighting illusions using the Lighting Effects filter.

This chapter has three components: techniques for applying filters; an illustrated compendium of all the Photoshop filters; and lastly, a handful of step-by-step exercises using filters.

Filter basics

Filters are grouped into thirteen submenu categories under the Filter menu **1**. Any third-party filter added to the program can have its own submenu. (See the Photoshop User Guide for information about installing third-party filters.)

How to apply filters

Filters can be applied to a whole target layer or to a selected area of a target layer. For a soft transition between the filtered and non-filtered areas, feather the selection before you apply a filter.

Some filters are applied in one step by selecting them from a submenu. Other filters are applied via dialog boxes in which one or more variables are specified. Choose Filter menu > Last Filter (Control-F) to reapply the last used filter using the same settings. Choose a filter from its submenu to choose different settings. To open the dialog box for the last used filter with its last used settings, use the Control-Alt-F shortcut.

The **Groucho** filter

Filters cannot be applied to an image in Bitmap or Indexed Color mode, or to a 48-bit RGB or 16-bit grayscale image.

Using a filter dialog box

Some filter dialog boxes have a Preview box, which you should check if you want to display the filter's effects in both the image window and in the preview window in the filter dialog box 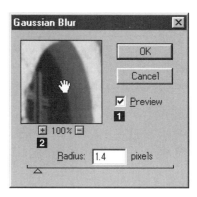. Drag in the preview window to move the image inside it.

With some filter dialog boxes open, the pointer becomes a square when it's passed over the image window, in which case you can click to preview that area of the image.

Click the "+" button to zoom in on the image in the preview box, or click the "–" button to zoom out **2**. Or press the up or down arrow on the keyboard to magnify or reduce a selected field by one unit (or .1 unit, if available).

A flashing line below the preview size value indicates the filter effect is taking its sweet time to render in the preview window. On a slow machine, you might have enough time to go make a sandwich.

A flashing line below the Preview check box means the filter effect is taking its sweet time to preview in the image window.

How to lessen a filter's effect

The Fade command lessens filter effects and Image menu > Adjust effects (not other commands). After applying a filter, choose Filter menu > Fade (Control-Shift-F). Choose an opacity amount, and a mode, if desired **3**, then click OK. If you Undo the Fade command, the complete filter effect will be undone.

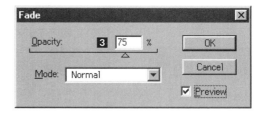

To lessen a filter's effect with an option to test different blending modes, and without limiting yourself to one Undo, do the following:

1. Duplicate the image layer to which the filter will be applied.

To maximize a filter's effect

- To heighten the effect of some filters, like Emboss (illustrated below), make sure the target layer has good brightness/contrast values. To heighten contrast in a layer before applying a filter to it, choose Image menu > Adjust > Levels, move the black Input slider to the right and the white Input slider to the left, then click OK.

- To recolor a layer after applying a filter that strips color (i.e., Charcoal filter), use the Image menu > Adjust > Hue/Saturation dialog box (check the Colorize box).

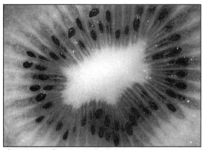

The original image.

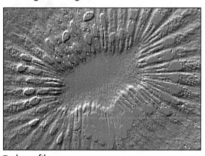

Emboss filter.

2. Apply the filter to the duplicate layer.

3. Use the Layers palette Opacity slider to lessen (fade) the effect of the filter.

4. Choose a different mode from the mode drop-down menu. The instructions on page 156 use this technique.

Because the filter was applied to a copy of the original layer, you can come back later and readjust the mode or opacity of the filter effect layer to blend it differently with the original layer, create a layer mask for the duplicate layer to hide or change the filter effect, or discard the filter layer entirely. When the image is finalized, merge the duplicate layer with the original.

Use a layer mask to control filter effects

A layer mask can be used to limit the effect of a filter. The edge between the white and black areas of the of a layer mask, can be soft, hard, painterly, etc., depending on the type of brush strokes you use to paint the black areas of the mask. By choosing Add Layer Mask > Reveal Selection when a selection is active and then applying a filter (try Brush Strokes > Spatter, Pixilate > Pointillize, Stylize > Wind, Distort > ZigZag or Ripple), the filter effect will be visible on the edge between black and white areas of the layer mask.

Or, create a black-to-white gradient in the layer mask and then apply a filter to the layer image (not the layer mask). The filter effect will apply fully in the image where areas of white are on the mask and fade to nil in areas of the image that correspond to black areas in the mask.

To limit the effect of a filter

Create a selection first on a layer to have a filter affect only pixels within the selection **1**. To achieve a soft-edged transition around the filtered area, feather the selection before applying the filter **2**.

Texture mapping via a filter

For some filters, like Conté Crayon, Displace, Glass, Lighting Effects, Rough Pastels, Texture Fill, and Texturizer, in lieu of using a preset pattern to create a texture effect, you can load in another image to use as the pattern for the texture effect. Lights and darks in the loaded image are used to create the peaks and valleys in the texture. The image you're using for the mapping must be saved in the Photoshop file format.

If the filter dialog box contains a Texture drop-down menu with a load option, select that option, locate a color or grayscale image in the Photoshop format, then click OK.

Apply a filter to an individual channel

To create a subtle effect, modify pixels of a single color component in an image by applying a filter to only one of a target layer's channels (Add Noise is a nice one to experiment with) **1**. Click a channel color name on the Channels palette, apply the filter, then click the top channel on the palette (Control-~) to redisplay the composite image **2**.

To make filter effect look less artificial

If the imagery you're creating lends itself to experimentation, try creating your own formulas by testing different variables in a filter dialog box or by applying more than one filter to the same image. If you come up with a sequence that you'd like to use more than once, save it in an action.

The original image.

1   **2**

The Wind filter applied to type. Check the Preserve Transparency box on the Layers palette for the type layer if you want the filter effect to spread outside the letter shapes. Uncheck Preserve Transparency to limit a filter effect to the letter shapes.

PHOTO: PAUL PETROFF

All the filters illustrated

Artistic filters

Original image

Colored Pencil

Cutout

Dry Brush

Film Grain

Fresco

Neon Glow

Paint Daubs

Palette Knife

Artistic filters

Original image

Plastic Wrap

Poster Edges

Rough Pastels

Smudge Stick

Sponge

Watercolor

Underpainting

Artistic Filters

Blur filters

Original image

Blur More

Gaussian Blur

Motion Blur

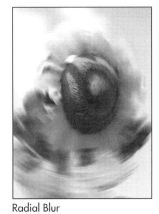

Radial Blur

Smart Blur (Normal)

Smart Blur (Edges Only)

Smart Blur (Overlay Edge)

Brush Strokes filters

Original image

Accented Edges

Angled Strokes

Crosshatch

Dark Strokes

Ink Outlines

Spatter

Sprayed Strokes

Sumi-e

Distort filters

Original image

Diffuse Glow

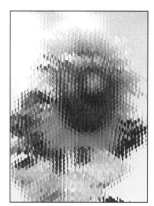

Displace

Glass

Ocean Ripple

Pinch

Polar Coordinates

Ripple

Shear

Distort Filters

197

Distort filters

Spherize

Twirl

Wave (Type: Square)

Wave (Type: Sine)

Zigzag

Noise filters

Original image

Add Noise

Median

Distort Filters; Noise Filters

Pixelate filters

Original image

Color Halftone

Crystallize

Facet

Fragment

Mezzotint (Short Strokes)

Mezzotint (Medium Dots)

Mosaic

Pointillize

Pixelate Filters

Render filters

Original image

Clouds

Difference Clouds

Lens Flare

Sharpen filters

Sharpen Edges

Sharpen More

Unsharp Mask

Sketch filters

Original image

Bas Relief

Chalk & Charcoal

Charcoal

Chrome

Conté Crayon

Graphic Pen

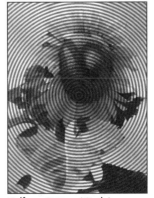

Halftone Pattern (Circle)

Halftone Pattern (Dot)

Sketch filters

Original image

Note Paper

Photocopy

Reticulation

Stamp

Torn Edges

Water Paper

Sketch Filters

Stylize filters

Original image

Diffuse

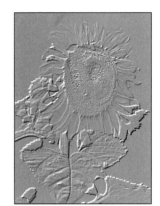

Emboss

Extrude

Find Edges

Glowing Edges

Solarize

Tiles

Tiles, then Fade (Overlay mode)

Stylize filters

Original image

Trace Contour

Wind

Texture filters

Craquelure

Grain Enlarged

Grain Horizontal

Patchwork

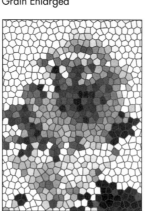

Stained Glass

Texturizer

Image

Selection
marquee

Added
canvas
pixels

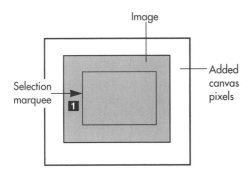

A few filter exercises

Apply the Ripple, Twirl, or Zigzag filter to a target layer with a white border to produce a warped paper texture.

To create a wrinkled edge:

1. Use Image menu > Canvas Size to add a white border around a one-layer image.

2. Choose the Rectangular Marquee tool.

3. Enter 8 in the Feather field on the Marquee Options palette.

4. Drag a selection marquee across about three quarters of the image (not the border) **1**.

5. Choose Select menu > Inverse (Control-Shift-I). The added canvas area will become the active selection.

6. Apply the Filter menu > Distort > Ripple **2**, Twirl **3**, or Zigzag **4**, or a combination thereof. Click the zoom out button (–) in the filter dialog box to preview the whole image.

PHOTO: PAUL PETROFF

2 A wrinkled edge produced using the **Ripple** filter (Amount 100, Medium).

3 A wrinkled edge produced using the **Twirl** filter (Angle -300).

4 A wrinkled edge produced using the **Zigzag** filter (Amount 40, Ridges 8, Around center).

Create a Wrinkled Edge

A variety of textures can be created using the Add Noise filter as the starting point.

To create a texture from nothing:

1. Create a new document, Contents: White.

2. Choose Filter menu > Noise > Add Noise.

3. Move the Amount slider to a number between 400 and 700 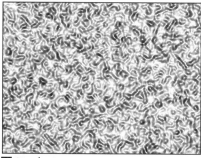, click Gaussian, then click OK or press Enter .

4. Choose Filter menu > Blur > Gaussian Blur.

5. Enter 3 in the Radius field, then click OK or press Enter.

6. Choose Filter menu > Stylize > Find Edges.

7. Choose Image menu > Adjust > Levels.

8. Move the black Input slider a ways to the right and move the white Input slider to left, pause to preview, then click OK or press Enter **3**.

9. Choose Filter menu > Sharpen > Sharpen Edges a few times.

2 A new, blank document, after applying the Add Noise filter.

3 Spaghetti.

By adding an interesting black or gray texture to a layer mask, you can control the blending of what is seen in a layer and the layers below it. Areas of black in a layer mask will hide pixels in the layer and reveal imagery from the layer below.

To use a layer mask to apply a texture:

1. Open an image.

2. Create a new layer, and fill it with a color or shade.

3. Create layer mask for the new layer by clicking the Add Layer Mask button on the Layers palette ▣, and leave the layer mask thumbnail active.

4. Apply a filter or series of filters to the mask **4**–**5**:

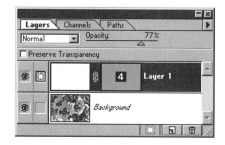

5

Create Texture; Apply Texture

1 The original image.

2 Theirs.

3 Ours.

The Texture filters (Craquelure, Grain, Mosaic Tiles, Patchwork, and Texturizer) will produce a texture effect on a white layer mask. For other filters, first apply the Add Noise filter to the layer mask to create light and dark pixels for the next filter or filters you apply to work with.

Try applying any of the following filters after applying a Texture filter or the Add Noise filter: Artistic > Dry Brush (small stroke size), Palette Knife (small stroke size), Plastic Wrap (use Levels to increase contrast), Sponge, or Watercolor.

5. *Optional:* To intensify a filter's effect, apply the Distort > Twirl or Ripple, or Stylize > Wind filter afterward.

To fade a filter's effect, use the Filter menu > Fade command.

6. *Optional:* Use the Levels command to heighten contrast in the layer mask to achieve a more dramatic light-to-dark contrast.

We've come up with a way to turn a photograph into a watercolor using the Median Noise and Minimum filters. Compare it to Photoshop's Watercolor filter.

Our watercolor filter:

1. Duplicate the layer that you want to turn into a watercolor.

2. With the duplicate layer active, choose Filter menu > Noise > Median.

3. Move the Radius slider to a number between 2 and 8.

4. Click OK or press Enter.

5. Choose Filter menu > Other > Minimum.

6. Move the Radius the slider to 1, 2, or 3.

7. Click OK or press Enter **1**–**3**.

8. *Optional:* Apply the Sharpen More filter.

Our Watercolor

In the following instructions, the Mosaic filter is applied using progressive values to a series of rectangular selections, so the mosaic tiles gradually enlarge as the effect travels across the image. Using a gradient in a layer mask, on the other hand, would gradually fade of the Mosaic effect without changing the size of the mosaic tiles .

To apply the Mosaic filter using graduated values:

1. Choose a target layer.

2. Choose the Rectangular Marquee tool.

3. Marquee about a quarter or fifth of the layer, where you want the mosaic tiles to begin.

4. Choose Filter menu > Pixelate > Mosaic.

5. Enter 6 in the Cell Size field .

6. Click OK or press Enter.

7. With the selection still active and the Rectangular Marquee tool still chosen, drag the marquee to the next adjacent quadrant 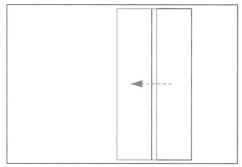. Hold down Shift while dragging to constrain the movement.

8. Repeat steps 4–7 until you've finished the whole image, entering 12, then 24, then 30 in the Cell Size field. To create larger pixel blocks, enter higher numbers—like 8, 16, 28, and 34—in the Cell Size field.

9. Deselect (Control-D) .

1 The Mosaic filter applied using a gradient in the layer mask.

2 Enter a number in the Cell Size field in the Mosaic dialog box. Enter progressively higher numbers each time you repeat step 5.

3 Apply the Mosaic filter to a rectangular selection, move the marquee, then reapply the filter, etc.

4 A graduated mosaic.

Mosaic Filter

1 The original image.

2 The final image.

Turn a photograph into a painting or a drawing:

1. Choose Duplicate Layer from the Layers palette command menu, then click OK.

2. Choose Filter menu > Stylize > Find Edges.

3. With the duplicate layer active, click the Add Layer Mask icon. ▣

4. Paint with black at below 100% opacity on the layer mask to reveal parts of the layer below **1**–**2**.

5. *Optional:* Lower the opacity of the duplicate layer.

6. *Optional:* For a dramatic effect of colors on a dark background, activate the layer icon, then choose Image menu > Adjust > Invert.

TIP To produce magic marker drawing, apply the Trace Contour filter, and apply Filter menu > Other > Minimum (Radius of 1 or 2) in place of step 2, above.

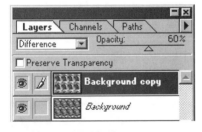

A pattern variation

Fill a layer with a pattern **3**, duplicate the pattern layer, then apply the Find Edges filter to the duplicate layer, fill it with a Foreground color, 60% Opacity, Color Mode. Finally, choose Overlay or Difference mode for the duplicate layer **4**.

3 The original pattern.

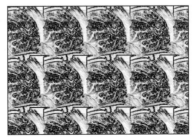

4 A texturized pattern.

Turn a Photograph into a Drawing

To create an illusion of motion, select an object on one layer to be the stationary object, and then apply the Motion Blur filter to the same image on another layer.

To Motion Blur part of an image:

1. Activate the layer that contains the imagery you want to motion blur.

2. Choose Duplicate Layer from the Layers palette command menu, rename the duplicate layer, if you like, then click OK.

3. Activate the Background **1**.

4. Alt-click the Eye icon for that layer to hide all the other layers.

5. Choose Filter menu > Blur > Motion Blur.

6. Enter a number between -360 and 360 in the Angle field or drag the axis line **2**. (We entered -17 for our image.)
and
Enter a number between 1 and 999 in the Distance field (the amount of blur). (We entered 50 for our image.)
and
Click OK or press Enter.

7. Alt-click the Eye icon for the Background on the Layers palette to redisplay all the other layers.

8. Activate the duplicate layer.

9. Select an object on the duplicate layer that you want to remain stationary **3**.

10. Choose Select menu > Feather (Control-Shift-D).

11. Enter 5 in the Feather Radius field, then click OK or press Enter.

12. Choose Select menu > Inverse (Control-Shift-I).

13. Press Delete, then deselect (Control-D) **4**.

14. *Optional:* Move the stationary image on the duplicate layer using the Move tool or change that layer's opacity.

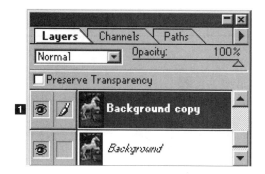

3 Select an object.

PHOTO: CARA WOOD

4 The completed **Motion Blur.**

Motion Blur Part of an Image

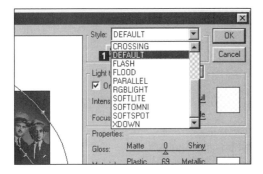

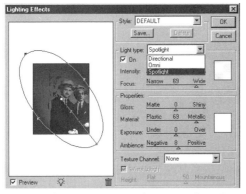

2 Choose from a cornucopia of options in the **Lighting Effects** dialog box to create your own lighting effects.

The Lighting Effects filter produces a tremendous variety of lighting effects. You can choose from up to 17 different light sources and you can assign to each light source a different color, intensity, and angle.

NOTE: For the Lighting Effects filter to work, at least 20 MB of RAM must be allocated to Photoshop.

To cast a light on an image:

1. Make sure your image is in RGB Color mode.

2. Choose a target layer.

3. *Optional:* Select an area on the layer to limit the filter effect to that area.

4. Choose Filter menu > Render > Lighting Effects.

5. Choose Default or choose a preset lighting effect from the Style drop-down menu **1**.

Do any of the following optional steps to adjust the light **2***:*

6. Choose from the Light Type drop-down menu. Choose Spotlight to create a narrow, elliptical light.

7. Move the Intensity slider to adjust the brightness of the light. Full creates the brightest light **3**. Negative creates a black light effect.

8. Move the Focus slider to adjust the size of the beam of light that fills the ellipse shape **4**–**5**. The light source starts from where the radius touches the edge of the ellipse.

3 The default spotlight ellipse with Full Intensity.

4 The default spotlight ellipse with Wide Focus. The light is strongest at the sides of the ellipse.

5 The default spotlight ellipse with Narrow Focus.

(Continued on the following page)

Lighting Effects Filter

211

9. If you want to change the color of the light, click on the color swatch, then choose a color from the Color palette.

10. In the preview window:

Drag the center point of the ellipse to move the whole light.

Drag either endpoint toward the center of the ellipse to increase the intensity of the light **1**.

Drag either side point of the ellipse to change the angle of the light and to widen or narrow it **2**–**3**.

11. Move the Properties sliders to adjust the surrounding light conditions on the target layer.

The **Gloss** property controls the amount of surface reflectance on the lighted surfaces.

The **Material** property controls which parts of the image reflect the light source color—Plastic (the light source color is like a glare) or Metallic (the object surface glows).

The **Exposure** property lightens or darkens the whole ellipse **4**–**5**.

The **Ambience** property controls the balance between the light source and the overall light in the image **6**–**7**. Move this slider in small increments.

Click the **Properties** color swatch to choose a different color from the Color Picker dialog box for the ambient light around the spotlight.

12. Click OK or press Enter.

TIP The Texture Channel option is discussed on page 187.

TIP Shift-drag (the ellipse) to keep the angle constant and change the size of the ellipse. Control-drag to keep the size constant and change the angle or direction of the ellipse.

TIP To create a pin spot, choose Spotlight from the Light Type drop-down menu, move the Intensity slider to about 80,

1 The default spotlight ellipse after dragging the end points inward to narrow the light beam.

2 The spotlight ellipse rotated to the left by dragging a side point.

3 The spotlight ellipse after dragging the radius inward to make the light beam more round.

4 The spotlight ellipse with the Exposure Property set to Over.

5 The spotlight ellipse with the Exposure Property set to Under.

6 The spotlight ellipse with a Positive Ambience Property.

7 The spotlight ellipse with a Negative Ambience Property.

The default Omni light is round. The effect is like shining a flashlight perpendicular to the image.

1 Drag a new light source onto the preview box. A new ellipse will appear where the mouse is released.

move the Focus slider to about 30, and drag the side points of the ellipse inward. Move the whole ellipse by dragging its center point to cast light on a particular area of the image.

TIP If the background of an image was darkened too much from a previous application of the Lighting Effects filter, apply the filter again to add another light to shine into the dark area and recover some detail. Move the Exposure Properties and Ambience Properties sliders a little to the right.

TIP To see the image in the Preview box without the ellipses, drag the light bulb icon just inside the bottom edge of the Preview box **1**. Delete the extra light when you're finished.

TIP To delete a light source ellipse, drag its center point over the Trash icon.

TIP Check the Light Type/On box to preview the lighting effects in the preview box.

TIP To duplicate a light source ellipse, Alt-drag its center point.

TIP The last used settings of the Lighting Effects filter will remain in the dialog box until you change them or exit Photoshop. To restore the default settings, choose a different style from the Style drop-down menu, then choose Default from the same menu.

TIP To add your own Lighting Effects settings to the Style drop-down menu, click Save before clicking OK.

TIP Click Delete to remove the currently selected style from the drop-down menu.

A custom lighting effect

To produce **1**, we chose RGB Color mode, chose a target layer (the figures), and chose Filter menu > Render > Lighting Effects.

In the Lighting Effects dialog box, we:

- Chose Spotlight from the Light Type drop-down menu.

- Set the Intensity halfway toward Full.

- Set the Focus toward Wide.

- Dragged the side points of the ellipse inward to make it narrower.

- Dragged the centerpoint of the ellipse to cast the light over the face on the left in the image.

- Set the Exposure Property slightly toward Over to brighten the light source.

- Moved the Ambience Property slider to 2 to darken the background of the image.

- Dragged the endpoint of the Radius slightly inward to focus the beam of light more intensely on the face.

- When we were satisfied with the light source on one face, we Alt-dragged the centerpoint of the ellipse to duplicate the light, and move the duplicate light over the face on the right **2**.

- To create a subtle backlight, we dragged the light bulb icon into the Preview area to create another light source, rotated the ellipse sideways, and set the Intensity to be less Full than the other lights. We left the Focus setting between Narrow and Wide and left the Properties setting alone **3**.

TIP Apply Lighting Effects to the Background of an image first, then to successive layers above it.

1 The original RGB image.

2 The three ellipses used to produce the image below.

3 The image after applying the Lighting Effects filter with our own settings.

ACTIONS 17

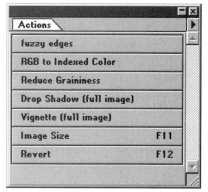

1 Actions palette in **Button** mode. To turn Button mode on or off, choose **Button Mode** from the Actions palette command menu.

An included command has a black check mark; an excluded command has none.

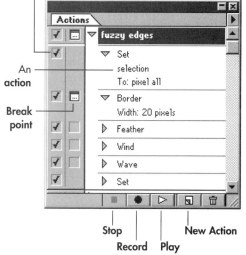

An action

Break point

Stop

Record Play

New Action

2 With the **Actions** palette in **List** mode, you can exclude a command, insert a pause, rearrange the order of commands, record an additional command, rerecord a command, delete a command, or save an action to an action set file.

A **SEQUENCE OF** menu operations can be recorded as an action. The action can then be played back on a single file or on a group of files within the same folder (called a "batch" of files) using the same commands, with the same dialog box settings, and in the same order in which they were recorded. Or, a pause can be inserted in an action, at which point you can choose different dialog box settings during the playback or perform an operation that could not be recorded. You can also add commands to an action after it's recorded.

Actions are particularly useful when you want to produce consistent image editing results on multiple images. You can use an action to apply a series of Adjust commands or a sequence of filter applications. Or, you can save concise steps into an action for preparing a file for print or converting it to a different file format. The Actions palette is used to record, play back, edit, delete, save, and load actions **1**–**2**. Each action can be assigned its own keyboard shortcut for quick access.

By the way, the Commands palette is history. Adobe decided the Actions palette could be used in its place. Some people aren't too happy about that.

Actions

As you create an action, the commands you use are recorded. When you're finished recording, the commands will be appear as a list on the Actions palette.

NOTE: Some operations, like painting brush strokes or using an editing or selection tool, can't be recorded. Sad, but true.

To record an action:

1. Open an image or create a new image.

2. Click the New Action button at the bottom of the Actions palette ■.

3. Enter a name for the action ■.

4. *Optional:* Assign a keyboard shortcut Function key and/or display color to the action.

5. Click Record ■.

6. Execute the commands you want to record as you would normally apply them to any image. When you enter values into a dialog box and then click OK, those settings will record (but not if you click Cancel).

7. Click the Stop button to stop recording ■. The action will now be listed on the Actions palette.

TIP To reorder the sequence of commands in an action, see page 220. To give yourself some leeway for experimentation, record an action on a copy of a file and then replay the action on yet another copy or on the original.

TIP Double-click an action name on the palette to open the Action Options dialog box, where you can rename the action or reset its shortcut or color.

TIP Include the Save command in an action with caution. It's useful if the action will be used for batch processing, but less useful if you're doing creative work. To delete a Save or any other command from an action, see page 220.

Stop Record   New Action

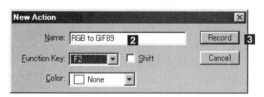

(side margin) **Record an Action**

You can insert a stop into an action that will interrupt the playback, at which point you can manually perform a non-recordable (and *only* a non-recordable) operation, like creating a selection or drawing brush strokes. When the manual operation is finished, you can resume the playback.

To insert a stop in an action:

1. As you're creating an action, pause at the point at which you want the stop to appear.
or
Click the command name in an existing action after which you want the stop to appear.

2. Choose Insert Stop from the Actions palette command menu.

3. Type an instruction for the person replaying the action so they'll know which command to perform 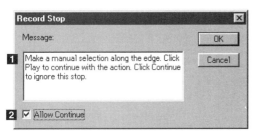. It's a good idea to specify in your stop message that after performing a manual step, the user should click the Play button on the Actions palette to resume the playback.

4. *Optional:* Check the Allow Continue box ▢ to include a Continue button in the stop alert box ▢. **NOTE:** With Allow Continue unchecked, you will still be able to click Stop at that point in the action playback and then click the play icon on the palette to resume the action playback.

5. Click OK or press Enter.

6. The stop will be inserted below the previously highlighted command in the action ▢. To move it to a different position, drag it upward or downward on the Actions palette.

TIP If an action is replayed while the Actions palette is in Button mode, the Play icon won't be accessible for resuming the playback after a stop. Click the action name again to resume play instead. Choose List mode for the palette when you're using stops.

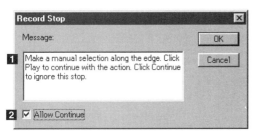

Enter a **message** in the Record Stop dialog box to guide the user during playback. Check the **Allow Continue** box to create a Continue button which the person replaying the action can press to bypass the stop command and resume playback.

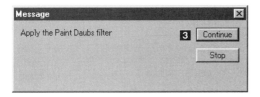

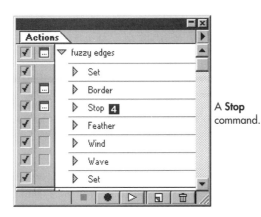

A **Stop** command.

Insert a Stop

To exclude or include a command from playback:

1. Make sure the Actions palette is in List—not Button—mode.

2. On the Actions palette, click the right-pointing triangle next to an action name to expand the list, if necessary.

3. Click in the leftmost column to remove the check mark and exclude that command from playback **1**. (Click in the same spot again to restore the check mark and include the command.)

The "fuzzy edges" action **expanded** on the Actions palette. The Feather step is unchecked to **exclude** it from playback.

A command can be inserted into an existing action. Dialog box settings, however, will not be recorded when you do so. See our the sidebar on this page for a workaround to this limitation.

To insert a menu command into an action:

1. Click the command name in the action after which you want the new menu command to appear.

2. Choose Insert Menu Item from the Actions palette command menu.

3. Choose the desired command from the menu bar.

or

Start typing a command name into the Find field, then click Find **2**.

4. Click OK or press Enter. The menu command will be inserted into the action. When it's played back, the action will automatically pause at this juncture, at which point you can choose dialog box settings, then click OK (or click Cancel). The action playback will resume.

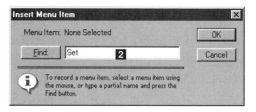

To include dialog box settings in an inserted command

To include dialog box settings with an inserted command, choose Record "[command name]" again, change the dialog box settings, if desired, click OK, then click next to the command name to make the dialog icon ▣ appear. This will insert a pause for the dialog box to open when this step is reached, at which point new settings can be entered.

Or double-click the command name and enter settings in the dialog box. The action will still halt at this point to allow you to accept, change, or cancel the dialog box settings.

More playback options

■ To play an action starting from a specific command on the list, click that command name, then click the Play button or choose Play from "[command name]" from the Actions palette command menu.

■ To play a single command in a multi-command action, click the command name, then Control-click the Play button or choose Play Only "[command name]" from the Actions palette command menu.

2

To replay an action on an image:

1. Open the image on which you want to play back the action.

2. Choose List mode for the Actions palette (uncheck Button mode). (In Button mode, you can only execute the whole action, and any previously excluded commands won't play back.)

3. Click an action name on the palette **1**.

4. Click the Play button on the palette **2**.

NOTE: Batch processing will end at a stop command in an action. Remove inserted stops from the action for batch playback.

To replay an action on a batch of images:

1. Choose List mode for the Actions palette.

2. Make sure all the files for batch processing are contained in one folder.

3. Choose Batch from the Actions palette command menu.

4. Choose Source: Folder **3**.
and
Click Choose.
and
Locate the desired batch folder, then click OK.

5. Choose an action from the Action drop-down menu.

6. Choose Destination: None to leave the files open; or choose Save and Close to save the files over the originals; or choose Folder to save files to a new folder (click Choose to designate the destination folder).

7. *Optional:* If you chose Folder for the previous step and checked the Override Action "Save In" Commands box, the image will save to the folder designated in step 5 during playback when a Save command occurs in the action.

8. Click OK or press Enter. The batch processing will begin.

Using the batch option, you can import non-Photoshop images and process them using an action. This procedure can be used to process images from a digital camera plugged into your computer. The import option is like using File > Import to open an image, except in this case it's automatic.

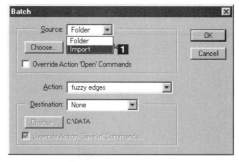

To replay an action on a batch of non-Photoshop images:

1. Choose Batch from the Actions palette command menu.

2. Choose Source: Import **1**.

3. Choose an import option from the From drop-down menu **2**. (These options are the same as in the File > Import dialog box.)

4. Follow steps 5–8 on the previous page.

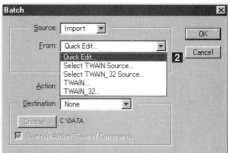

NOTE: To save the current list of actions as a set for later use, follow the instructions on page 224 **before** you clear the palette.

To delete a command from an action:

1. Highlight the command you want to delete.

2. Click the trash icon at the bottom of the Actions palette, then click OK.

NOTE: If commands are reordered, the action may produce a different overall effect on the image on which it is played.

To change the order of commands:

1. On the Actions palette, click the right-pointing triangle next to an action name to expand the list, if it's not already expanded **3**.

2. Drag a command upward or downward on the list **4**–**5**.

The Invert command moved upward on the list.

When a pause (also called a "break point") is inserted into an action, the dialog box for that command will open during playback. When the pause occurs, you can choose different settings or click OK to proceed with the settings used when the action was originally recorded. A pause can only be set for a command that uses a dialog box.

To insert a pause (break point) into an action:

1. Make sure the Actions palette is in List mode (not Button mode).

2. On the Actions palette, click the right-pointing triangle next to the action name to expand the list, if it's not already expanded.

3. Click in the second column from the left (next to the command name) to display the dialog box icon ▇. (Click again in the same spot if you want to remove the icon and remove the pause.)

The action will pause when this command is encountered, at which point you can enter new values, accept the existing values, or cancel out of the dialog box. The playback will resume after you close dialog box.

Actions palette with an action expanded. Click next to the individual command name to insert a pause and show the dialog icon.

Insert a Pause (Break Point)

To add a command (or commands) to an action:

1. On the Actions palette, click the right-pointing triangle next to an action's name to expand the list, if it's not already expanded, then click the command name after which you want the new command to appear.

2. Choose Start Recording from the Actions palette command menu.

3. Perform the steps to record the commands you want to add.

4. Click the Stop button to stop recording 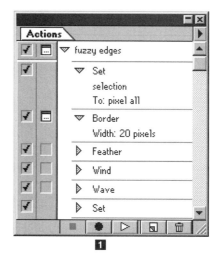. You can drag any command upward or downward to a different position in the action.

TIP To copy a command from one action to another, expand both action lists, then Alt-drag the command you want to copy from one action to the other. If you don't hold down Alt while dragging, you'll cut the command from the original action. Be careful if you copy any Save commands—they may contain particular info for the original action.

To rerecord a whole action using different dialog box settings:

1. Click on the name of the action you want to revise.

2. Choose Record "[action name]" Again from the Actions palette command menu. The action will play back, stopping at commands that use dialog boxes.

3. When each dialog box opens, enter new settings, if desired, then click OK. When the dialog box closes, the Record Again rerecording will continue.

To stop the rerecording, click Cancel in a dialog box or click the Stop button on the Actions palette.

Add Command; Rerecord Action

To rerecord one command in an action:

1. Double-click the command on the action list.

2. Enter new settings.

3. Click OK. Click Cancel to have any revisions be disregarded.

Duplicate an action if you want to experiment with it or add to it and don't want to mess around with the original.

To duplicate an action:

Click on the name of the action you want to duplicate, then choose Duplicate "[action name]" from the Actions palette command menu.

or

Drag the name of the action you want to duplicate over the New Action button at the bottom of the Actions palette **1**.

TIP To duplicate a command in an action, click on the command name, then choose Duplicate "[command name]" from the palette command menu. Or drag the command over the New Action button at the bottom of the Actions palette.

To duplicate an action, drag its name over the New Action button at the bottom of the Actions palette.

To delete an entire action:

1. Highlight the action you want to delete.

2. Click the trash icon at the bottom of the Actions palette, then click OK.
or
Alt-click the trash icon.

Rerecord Command; Duplicate Action

It's a good idea to save actions to a file to guard against loss due to an application or system crash or inadvertent use of the Delete or Clear Actions command.

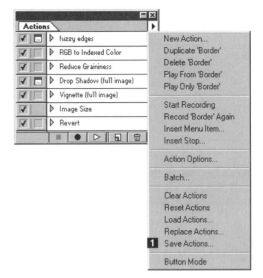

To save all the actions on the Actions palette to a file:

1. Choose Save Actions from the Actions palette command menu **1**.

2. Type a name for the action.

3. Choose a location in which to save the action file.

4. Click Save. The new file will be regarded as one set, regardless of the number of actions it contains. Actions are automatically stored in the Adobe Photoshop 4.0 Preferences file. If this file is deleted to cure a problem in Photoshop, any actions not saved to a separate file will be deleted in the process.

To load an additional actions set onto the Actions palette:

1. Click the action name below which you want the loaded actions to appear.

2. Choose Load Actions from the Actions palette command menu.

3. Locate and highlight the actions set you want to append.

4. Click Open.

To replace the current actions set with a different actions set:

1. Click the action name below which you want the loaded actions to appear.

2. Choose Replace Actions from the Actions palette command menu.

3. Locate and highlight the actions set you want to load.

4. Click Open.

Save, Load, Replace Actions Set

PREFERENCES 18

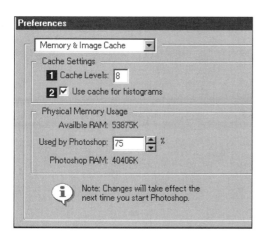

To access the preferences dialog boxes quickly, use the **Control-K** shortcut to open the General Preferences dialog box, then use any of the shortcuts illustrated above to access other dialog boxes, or click **Next** on the right side of the dialog box to cycle through them.

PREFERENCES ARE default settings that apply to the application as a whole, such as which ruler units are used, or if channels display in color. Most preferences changes take effect immediately; a few take effect on re-launching. To access the preferences dialog boxes the fast-and-easy way, see the illustration at left. (Or use the File menu > Preferences submenu.)

NOTE: To reset all the default preferences, open the Prefs subdirectory inside the Photoshop directory, then delete the PHOTOSHO.PSP file.

Image Cache Preferences

1 A Cache Levels value between 1 and 8 helps speed up screen redraw when you're editing or color adjusting high resolution images. A low-resolution version of the image is saved in a cache buffer and is used to update the on-screen image. The higher the Cache Levels number, the more buffers are used, and the speedier the redraw.

2 Check the "Use cache for histograms" box for faster, but slightly less accurate, histogram display in the Levels and Histogram dialog boxes.

General Preferences

1 Choose the Photoshop **Color Picker** to access the application's own Color Picker. If you're trying to mix a color in Photoshop to match a color in Macromedia Director or Netscape Navigator, use the Windows Color Picker.

2 Choose an **Interpolation** option for reinterpretation of an image as a result of resampling or transforming. Bicubic is slowest, but the highest quality. Nearest Neighbor is the fastest, but the poorest quality.

3 Check **Anti-alias PostScript** to optimize the rendering of EPS images in Photoshop.

4 Check **Export Clipboard** to have the current Clipboard contents stay on the Clipboard when you quit Photoshop.

5 Check **Short PANTONE Names** if your image contains Pantone colors and you are exporting it to another application.

A tool tip.

6 Check **Show Tool Tips** to see an onscreen display of the name of the tool or icon currently under the cursor.

7 Check **Beep When Done** for a beep to sound after any command, for which a progress bar displays, is completed.

8 With **Dynamic Color Sliders** checked, the Color palette sliders update as you move them. Turn this option off to speed performance.

9 With **Save Palette Locations** checked, palettes that are open when you exit Photoshop will appear in their same location when you re-launch.

10 To restore the palettes' default groupings when you launch Photoshop, click **Reset Palette Locations to Default**.

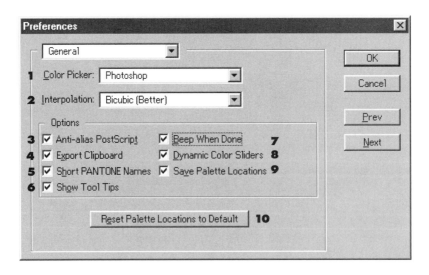

Saving Files Preferences

1 For each **Image Preview** type, choose Never Save to save files without previews, choose Always Save to always save files with the specified previews, or choose Ask When Saving to assign previews for each individual file when you save it for the first time **1**.

2 Check **2.5 Compatibility** to automatically save a flattened, Photoshop version 2.5 copy in every 3.0 document. This option increases the file's storage size. Turn this option off if you don't need it.

3 Check **Save Metric Color Tags** if you are exporting your file to QuarkXPress and are using EFIColor in that program.

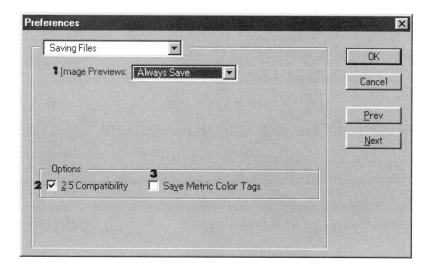

Display & Cursors Preferences

1 Choose whether **CMYK Composites** for the RGB screen version of a CMYK file will be rendered Faster, but simpler, or Smoother and more refined.

2 Check **Color Channels in Color** to display individual RGB or CMYK channels in their particular color. Otherwise, they will display grayscale.

3 Check **Use System Palette** to have the Apple System Palette be used rather than the document's own color palette. Turn this option on to correct the display of erratic colors on an 8–bit monitor.

4 Check **Use Diffusion Dither** to have Photoshop use a grainy dot pattern to simulate transitions between colors that are absent from the limited palette of an 8-bit, 256 color monitor.

5 Uncheck **Video LUT Animation** to disable the interactive screen preview if you are using a video card that is causing conflicts between Photoshop and your monitor. With Video LUT Animation turned on, changes made in a Photoshop dialog box are reflected immediately on the entire screen, not just in the image window or in a selection. With this option unchecked, you must check the Preview box in a dialog box to preview changes in the image window.

6 For the **Painting Cursors** (Gradient, Line, Eraser, Pencil, Airbrush, Paintbrush, Rubber Stamp, Smudge, Blur, Sharpen, Dodge, Burn, and Sponge tools) choose **Standard** to see the icon of the tool being used, or choose **Precise** to see a crosshair icon, or choose **Brush Size** to see a round icon the exact size and shape of the brush tip (up to 300 pixels). For the non-painting tools (Marquee, Lasso, Polygon Lasso, Magic Wand, Crop, Eyedropper, Pen, Gradient, Line, and Paint Bucket), choose **Other Cursors**: Standard or Precise.

| **Standard** cursor | **Precise** cursor | **Brush Size** cursor |

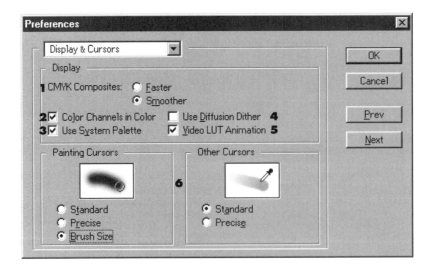

Transparency & Gamut Preferences

1 A checkerboard grid is used to represent transparent areas on a layer (areas that don't contain pixels). You can choose a different **Grid Size**.

2 Change the **Grid Colors** for the transparency checkerboard by choosing Red, Orange, Green, Blue, or Purple from the drop-down menu, or choose Light, Medium, or Dark.

3 To change the color used to indicate out-of-gamut colors on an image if you're using the **Gamut Warning** command, click the Color square, then choose a color from the Color Picker. You can lower the Gamut Warning color Opacity to make it easier to see the actual image color underneath.

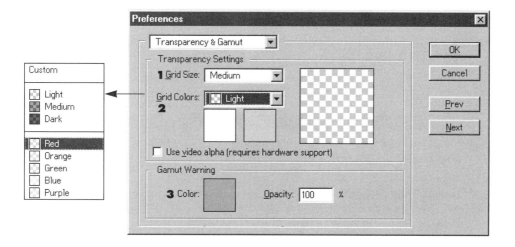

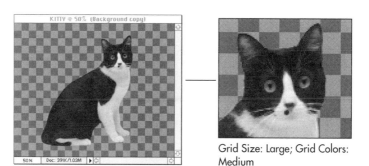

Grid Size: Large; Grid Colors: Medium

Transparency & Gamut Preferences

Units & Rulers Preferences

1 Choose a unit of measure from the Rulers Units: drop-down menu for the horizontal and vertical rulers that display in the image window. (Choose View > Show Rulers to display the rulers.)

2 To create multiple column guides, enter a Column Size: Width and Gutter width.

TIP If you change the measurement units for the Info palette **1**, the ruler units will change in this dialog box also, and vice versa.

TIP You can also open this dialog box by double-clicking either ruler in the image window.

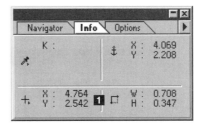

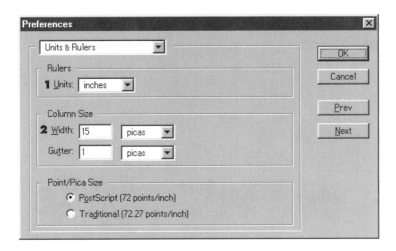

Guides & Grid Preferences

1 Choose a preset color for the removable ruler **Guides** from the **Color** drop-down menu. Click the color square to choose a color from the Color Picker.

2 Choose Lines or Dashed Lines for the **Guides Style**.

3 Choose a preset color for the nonprinting **Grid** from the **Color** drop-down menu. Click the color square to choose a color from the Color Picker.

4 Choose Lines or Dashed Lines for the **Grid Style**.

5 To have grid lines appear at specific unit-of-measure intervals, choose a unit of measurement, then enter a new value in the **Gridline every** field.

6 To add grid lines between the thicker grid line increments chosen in the Gridline every field, enter a number in the **Subdivisions** field.

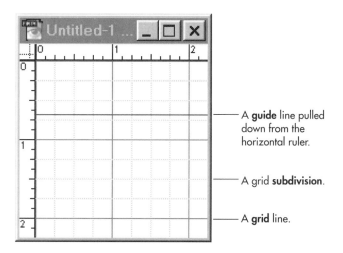

A **guide** line pulled down from the horizontal ruler.

A grid **subdivision**.

A **grid** line.

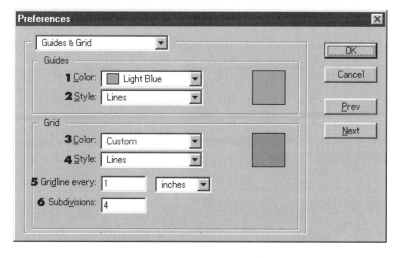

Plug-ins & Scratch Disk Preferences

NOTE: For changes made in this dialog box to take effect, you must exit and re-launch Photoshop.

1 Click **Plug-Ins Folder: Choose** if you need to relocate the plug-ins folder. Photoshop needs to know where to find this folder in order to access the plug-in contents. Photoshop's internal Plug-Ins module shouldn't be moved out of the Photoshop folder unless you have a specific reason for doing so (we're not talking about third-party plug-ins here). Moving it could inhibit access to the Acquire, Export, and File Format commands.

2 The **Primary** (and optional Secondary) **Scratch Disk** is used when available RAM is insufficient for processing or storage. Choose an available hard drive from the Primary drop-down menu. Startup is the default.

3 As an optional step, choose an alternate **Secondary** hard drive to be used as extra work space when necessary. If you have only one hard drive, of course you'll only have one scratch disk.

TIP If your scratch disk is a removable cartridge, removing the cartridge while Photoshop is running may cause the program to crash.

TIP To see how much RAM is currently being used while Photoshop is running, choose Scratch Sizes from the drop-down menu at the bottom of the image window **1**. The number on the left is the amount of memory needed for all currently open images and the Clipboard. The number on the right is the total amount of RAM available to Photoshop.

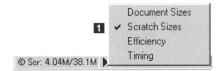

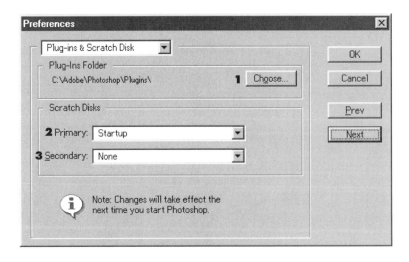

Resolution of output devices

Hewlett Packard LaserJet	300 or 600 dpi
Apple LaserWriter	300 or 600 dpi
IRIS SmartJet	300 dpi (looks like 1600 dpi)
3M Rainbow	300 dpi
QMS Colorscript	300 dpi
Canon Color Laser/Fiery	400 dpi
Linotronic imagesetter	1,200–4,000 dpi

AN IMAGE CAN be printed from Photoshop to a laser printer, to a color printer (thermal wax, dye sublimation, etc.), or to an imagesetter. A Photoshop image can also be imported into and printed from a drawing application, like FreeHand or Illustrator, a layout application, like QuarkXPress or PageMaker, a multimedia application, like Director, or prepared for viewing online.

Printer settings are chosen in the Print dialog box and the Page Setup dialog box (File menu). The following pages contain output tips, information about file compression, instructions for outputting to various types of printers, and instructions for creating duotones or a percentage tint of a Pantone color. Also included is a color separation walk-through, which explains the basic steps for calibrating your system and color correcting an image.

Print

Press and hold on the Sizes bar in the lower left corner of the image window to display a thumbnail preview of the image in relationship to the paper size and other Page Setup specifications.

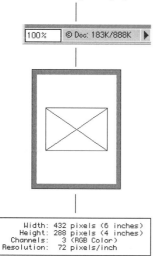

```
Width:   432 pixels (6 inches)
Height:  288 pixels (4 inches)
Channels:    3 (RGB Color)
Resolution:  72 pixels/inch
```

Hold down Alt and press and hold on the Sizes bar to display file information.

NOTE: Only currently visible layers and channels will print.

To print to a black-and-white laser printer:

1. Choose File menu > Print (Control-P).

2. For a picture in Grayscale or RGB Color mode, click Print as: Gray **1**.

For a CMYK Color image, make sure the Print Separations box is unchecked so the composite image will print.

3. Click OK or press Enter.

TIP To print only a portion of an image, select the area with the Rectangular Marquee tool, then click Print Range: Selection in the Print dialog box.

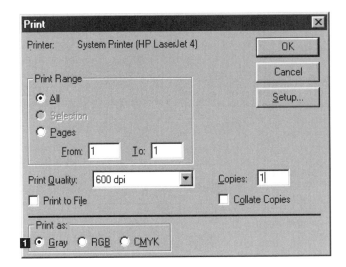

To print to a Hewlett Packard LaserJet with halftone enhancement features:

1. Choose File menu > Page Setup (Control-Shift-P).

2. Click Screens **1**.

3. Check the Use Printer's Default Screens box. (Don't change the default Paper, Layout, Reduce, or Orientation settings. Read about the other Page Setup options on pages 238–239.) Click OK, then click OK again.

4. Choose File menu > Print (Control-P).

5. If the picture is in CMYK Color mode, make sure the Print Separations box is unchecked.

6. Click OK or press Enter.

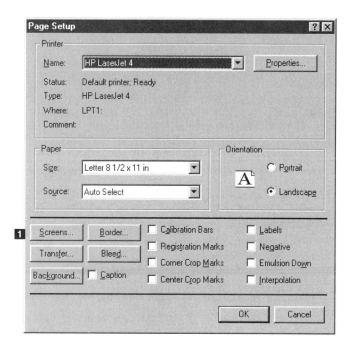

Unless your service bureau tells you otherwise, you should never send an RGB file to a color or high-end printer. To see how an image looks in CMYK mode in Photoshop before you print it, choose Image menu > Mode > CMYK Color before you open the Print dialog box. Clicking Print as: CMYK in the Print dialog box performs the same function without a screen preview.

To print to a PostScript color printer:

1. To print to a PostScript Level 1 printer, choose Image menu > Mode > CMYK Color. CMYK color will be simulated on screen.

or

To print to a PostScript Level 2 printer, choose Image menu > Mode > Lab Color.

2. Choose File menu > Page Setup (Control-Shift-P).

3. Choose the correct color printer driver option from the Name drop-down menu **1**. (A printer driver must be installed in your system to appear on this menu.)

4. Click OK or press Enter.

5. Choose File menu > Print (Control-P).

6. Click Encoding: Binary **2**.

7. Click OK or press Enter.

TIP For a PostScript Level 1 printer, click Screens in the Page Setup dialog box, then check the Use Same Shape for All Inks box. For a PostScript Level 2 printer, check the Use Accurate Screens box, but don't change the ink angles.

TIP If the printout from a CMYK Color file is too dark, lighten the image using the Levels dialog box (Control-L). Move the gray Input slider a little to the left and the black Output slider a little to the right. Save a copy of the file.

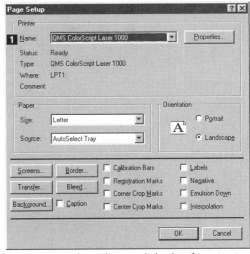

This illustration shows the Print dialog box for a **CMYK** Color image.

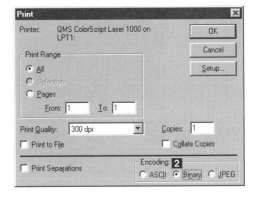

To prepare a file for an IRIS or dye sublimation printer or an imagesetter:

1. To print on a PostScript Level 1 printer, choose Image menu > Mode > CMYK Color.

or

To print on a PostScript Level 2 printer, choose File menu > Page Setup, click Screen, check the Use Accurate Screens box, then click OK twice. Ask your service bureau whether the file should be in CMYK Color or Lab Color mode.

2. Choose File menu > Save a Copy (Control-Alt-S).

3. Choose a location in which to save the file.

4. Choose Photoshop EPS from the Save As drop-down menu, then click Save.

5. Choose Preview: TIFF (8 bits/pixel) **1**.

6. Choose Encoding: Binary. (Leave the DCS option off.)

7. If you've changed the screen settings in the Halftone Screens dialog box, then check the Include Halftone Screen box.

8. Click OK or press Enter.

TIP Ask your service bureau to recommend an image resolution for the color printer or imagesetter you plan to use before saving and printing the file.

TIP If your image is wider than it is tall, ask your service bureau if it will print more quickly if you rotate it first using Photoshop's Rotate Canvas command.

High-End Printer

Photoshop's Trap command slightly overlaps solid color areas in an image to help prevent gaps that may occur due to press misregistration or movement. Trapping is only necessary when two distinct, adjacent color areas share less than two of the four process colors. You don't need to trap continuous-tone or photographic images.

NOTE: Photoshop's Trap command spreads colors, unlike some other applications, which also may use the choke method. Consult with your press shop before using this command, and apply it to a copy of your image; store your original image without traps.

To apply trapping:

1. Open the image to which you want to apply trapping, and make sure the image is in CMYK Color mode.

2. Choose Image menu > Trap.

3. Enter the Width value your press shop recommends **1**.

4. Click OK or press Enter.

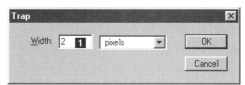

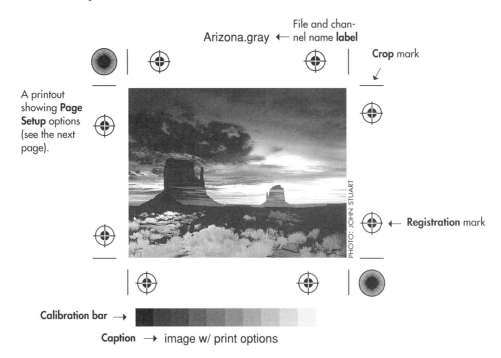

File and channel name **label**

Arizona.gray ←

Crop mark

A printout showing **Page Setup** options (see the next page).

Registration mark

PHOTO: JOHN STUART

Calibration bar →

Caption → image w/ print options

Trapping; Page Setup

The Page Setup dialog box

1 An image will print faster with Portrait Orientation than with Landscape Orientation. If your image is wider than it is tall, choose Image menu > Rotate Canvas > 90°CW. Then you can print it in Portrait Orientation.

2 To print a colored background around the image, click Background, then choose a color.

3 To print a black border around an image, click Border, then specify a measurement unit and a width.

4 Choose Bleed to print crop marks inside the image at a specified distance from the edge of the image.

5 Calibration Bars creates a Grayscale and/or color calibration strip outside the image area.

6 Registration Marks creates marks a print shop uses to align color separations.

7 Crop Marks creates short little lines that a print shop uses to trim the final printed page.

8 Labels prints the document's title and channel names.

9 Ask your print shop whether to choose the Negative or Emulsion Down film option.

10 Interpolation reduces jaggies when outputting to some PostScript Level 2 printers.

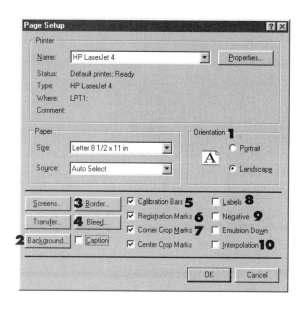

Page Setup Options

Preparing files for other applications

The people at the last stage of your project, ironically, are the people you should chat with first. In order to create printing plates from your file, you'll need to furnish your print shop with paper or film output. Nowadays, many print shops perform this service in house, which makes sense. Before outputting your file, ask your print shop or publisher if they have any specifications for the paper or film output you give them, and make sure the image is saved at the appropriate resolution for the target output device. Also ask what halftone screen frequency (lpi) the print shop will use and output your file at that frequency. You might also ask your prepress shop if you should save your file with special settings for a particular printer, such as in a particular image mode. Let the prepress shop calculate the halftone screen angle settings for you—that's their department.

Photoshop to QuarkXPress

To color separate a Photoshop image from QuarkXPress, first convert it to CMYK Color mode. Different imagesetters require different formats, so ask your prepress house whether to save your image in the TIFF or EPS file format, and whether to turn on the DCS option **1**. The DCS (Desktop Color Separation) option pre-separates the image in Photoshop, and it produces five related files, one for each CMYK channel and one for the combined, composite, CMYK channel. If you need to preview a DCS image in QuarkXPress, choose On (72 pixel/inch grayscale) or On (72 pixel/inch color). A color preview can balloon the storage size of an image.

Leave the Include Halftone Screens and Include Transfer Functions boxes unchecked. Your prepress shop will choose the proper settings for these options.

Photoshop to PageMaker

Save your image in the EPS or TIFF format.

To keep a background transparent

To import a Photoshop image into a drawing or page layout application and maintain its transparent background, save it as a clipping path (see page 175).

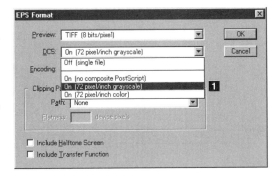

Photoshop and CorelDRAW

To Copy and Paste from Photoshop to CorelDRAW, select an area of a Photoshop layer and copy it, then in a CorelDRAW image window, choose Paste. CorelDRAW will list the pasted object as an image object. You can apply some editing commands to the pasted image object.

To Copy and Paste a CorelDRAW object into Photoshop, select and copy an object in CorelDRAW, then in an Photoshop image window, choose Paste. The object will appear as an area of pixels on a separate layer.

To drag and drop from Photoshop to CorelDRAW, drag a selection from a Photoshop window into a CorelDRAW window. The object will be listed in CorelDRAW as a color bitmap. Most editing commands will be available for the color bitmap object. You cannot drag and drop from CorelDRAW to Photoshop.

Photoshop to a film recorder

Color transparencies, also called chromes, are widely used as a source for high quality images in the publishing industry. A Photoshop file can be output to a film recorder to produce a chrome. Though the output settings for each film recorder may vary, to output to any film recorder, the pixel count for the height and width of the image file must conform to the pixel count the film recorder requires for each line it images. If the image originates as a scan, the pixel count should be taken into consideration when setting the scan's resolution, dimensions, and file storage size.

For example, let's say you need to produce a 4 x 5-inch chrome on a Solitaire film recorder. Your service bureau advises you that to output on the Solitaire, the 5-inch side of your image should measure 2000 pixels and the file storage size should be at least 10 megabytes. (Other film recorders may require higher resolutions.) Choose File menu > New, enter 2000 for the Width (in pixels) and 4 inches for the Height, enter a Resolution value to produce an Image Size of at least 10MB, and choose RGB Color Mode. Click OK to produce the image entirely within Photoshop, or note the resolution and dimensions, and ask your service bureau to match those values when they scan your image.

If the image is smaller than 4 x 5 inches and you would like a colored background around it, click Background in the Page Setup dialog box, then choose the color your service bureau recommends.

Photoshop to Illustrator

To export a **layer**, choose the Move tool, then drag a layer from the Photoshop image window into an Illustrator 7 image window. The layer will arrive as a 72 ppi pixel image in an outlined box.

To export a Photoshop **path**, use the Export > Path to Illustrator command (see page 176). The path does not have to be selected, though it should be a saved path, not a work path. In Illustrator, use File > Open to open the saved Photoshop path file, and use it like any other Illustrator path object. The path will arrive with its own crop marks. If you don't change them, you can save the file in the Illustrator 7 format, then Place the file in Photoshop (but don't rescale or reposition its bounding box, or you'll mess up the registration in Photoshop).

To place a Photoshop image as a **bitmap object** in Illustrator, save it in the Photoshop EPS file format in Photoshop, and use the Open command in Illustrator. Or, use Illustrator's File menu > Place command, and choose the Placed EPS option. Either way, the image will appear in an outlined box, and it can be transformed, but not edited.

You can apply some filters to a Photoshop image if it was opened as an object using the Illustrator's Open command, including the Adjust Color, Invert Color, Object Mosaic, and Photoshop plug-in filters that have been made available as plug-ins to Illustrator.

Photoshop to Painter

When you open a Photoshop image in Painter:

Photoshop **layers** will be converted into floaters in Painter and Photoshop paths will be converted into paths in Painter.

A Photoshop **layer mask** will be converted into a floater with a floater mask in Painter. If you reopen the image in Photoshop, however, the layer mask effect will become permanent and the mask itself will be deleted.

The fourth **channel** in a Photoshop file will become a mask in Painter if there were no paths in the original Photoshop file. To display the mask in Painter and force its name to appear on the Objects: P. List palette, choose the Path Adjuster tool and click in the image window or click the

If your clipping path won't print:

If your high-end printer generates a Limitcheck error when printing a document that contains a clipping path, it may be because the path contains too many points. Follow these steps to reduce the number of points on a path:

1. Activate the clipping path on the Paths palette.

2. Convert the path into a selection.

3. Delete the original clipping path, but leave the selection active.

4. Choose Make Work path from the Paths palette command menu to turn the selection into a path, entering a Tolerance value of 4–6 pixels.

5. Follow steps 2–7 on page 175 to reconvert the path into a clipping path.

third Visibility button on the P. List palette. The channel will be blank if you reopen the file in Photoshop.

If you import a Photoshop file with a transparent **background** into Painter, Painter will create a white background for it. If you reopen the image in Photoshop, it will have a new, white background layer, which will contain any brush strokes that were applied to the background in Painter.

If you apply a **blending mode** to a layer in Photoshop and then open the image in Painter, the mode effect may look different, but the original effect will reappear if you reopen the file in Photoshop.

Painter to Photoshop

You can make a round trip without losing layers or floaters. Choose File menu > Save As, then choose Photoshop 3.0 from the Type drop-down menu. If you save a Painter 4.0 file with floaters in the Photoshop 3.0 file format and then open it in Photoshop, each floater (or floater group) will be assigned its own layer. Painter shapes will also be placed on their own separate layers in Photoshop, and keep its original opacity.

If you save a Painter file with a selection path or mask group in Photoshop 3.0 format (check the Save Mask Layer box in the Save As dialog box) and then open the file in Photoshop, the mask, complete with any feathering, will appear as a mask in channel #4, and any Painter paths will appear on Photoshop's Paths palette. If the Painter image contains more than one selection path, activate the path you're planning to use as a mask in Photoshop before you save it in Painter.

Photoshop produces superior color separations than Painter because Painter doesn't read CMYK files, and because Photoshop offers greater control over print specifications.

The EPS format is a good choice for importing a Photoshop image into an illustration program, like Adobe Illustrator, or a page layout program, like QuarkXPress or PageMaker.

To save an image as an EPS:

1. If the image is going to be color separated from QuarkXPress or Illustrator, choose Image menu > Mode > CMYK.

2. Choose File > Save a Copy (Control-Alt-S). This command saves a flattened version of the image, and discards and any alpha channels in the file.

3. Enter a name in the File name field.

4. Choose a location in which to save the file.

5. Choose Save As: Photoshop EPS.

6. Click Save.

7. Choose Preview: TIFF (1 bit/pixel) for a grayscale preview, or choose TIFF (8 bits/pixel) for a color preview 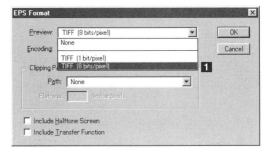.
and
For most purposes, you should choose Encoding: Binary. Binary Encoded files are smaller and process more quickly than ASCII files. However, for some applications, PostScript "clone" printers, or printing utilities that cannot handle Binary files, you'll have to choose ASCII.
and
Click OK or press Enter. The original, non-flattened version of the file will remain open.

TIP If you've changed the frequency, angle, or dot shape settings in the Halftone Screens dialog box, then check the Include Halftone Screen box.

A TIFF file can be imported by QuarkXPress or PageMaker. A CMYK TIFF can be color separated from QuarkXPress.

To save an image as a TIFF:

1. Follow the first four steps on the previous page.

2. Choose Save As: TIFF.

3. *Optional:* Not all programs can import a TIFF with an alpha channel. If your target application does not, check the "Don't Include Alpha Channels" box to discard any alpha channels.

4. Click Save.

5. Click Byte Order: IBM PC **1**.

6. *Optional:* Check the LZW Compression box to reduce the file size. No image data will be lost.

7. Click OK or press Enter.

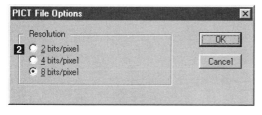

A PICT or BMP file can be opened in most drawing and multimedia applications. Choose whichever format is appropriate for your target application.

To save an image as a PICT or BMP:

1. Follow the first four steps on the previous page.

2. Choose Save As: PICT File.
or
Choose Save As: BMP File.

3. Click Save.

4. Choose a Resolution/Depth option **2**–**3**. (For an image in Grayscale mode, check 2, 4, or 8 bits/pixel.)

5. Click OK or press Enter.

TIP When saving a color image as a PICT for a multimedia application, choose a resolution of 16 bits/pixel or less.

Save as TIFF; Save as PICT

Only about 50 shades of an ink color can be printed from one plate, so print shops are sometimes asked to print a grayscale image using two or more plates instead of one to extend its tonal range. The additional plates can be gray or a color tint, and are usually used to print midtones and highlights. You can convert an image to Duotone mode in Photoshop to create a duotone (two plates), tritone (three plates), or quadtone (four plates).

The Duotones folder in the Photoshop application folder contains duotone, tritone, and quadtone curves that you can use as is or adapt for your own needs (click Load in the Duotone Options box).

NOTE: Duotone printing is very tricky, so you should ask your print shop for advice. **A duotone effect can't be proofed on a PostScript color printer.** In fact, only a press proof will give you accurate feedback.

To produce a duotone:

1. Choose Image menu > Mode > Grayscale. An image with good contrast will work best.

2. Choose Image menu > Mode > Duotone.

3. Choose Type: Duotone **1**.

4. Click the Ink 2 color square **2**. Ink 1 should be the darkest ink, and the lightest ink should be the highest ink number.

5. To choose a matching system color, like a Pantone color, click Custom. Choose from the Book pop-up menu, then type a color number or click a swatch. Subtle colors tend to look better in a duotone than bright colors.
   or
   To choose a process color, click Picker, then enter C, M, Y, and K percentages.

6. Click OK or press Enter.

7. For a process color, enter a name next to the color square.

8. Click the Ink 2 curve **3**.

Threes and fours

Printing a **tritone** (three inks) or a **quadtone** (four inks) requires specifying the order in which the inks will print on press. You can use the **Overprint Colors** dialog box to adjust the on-screen representation of various ink printing orders, but these settings won't affect how the image actually prints. Ask your print shop for advice about printing.

Click a color square to choose a color.

Click a curve to modify it.

Enter a name for a process color.

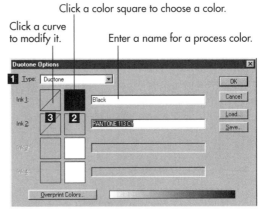

In the Duotone Options dialog box, choose Duotone from the Type drop-down menu, then click the Ink 2 color square.

The image's **highlights**

The image's **midtones**

The image's **shadows**

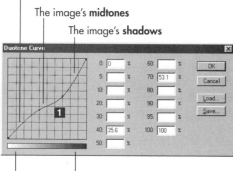

Highlights   Shadows

Reshaping the duotone curve for an ink color affects how that color is distributed among an image's highlights, midtones, and shadows. With the curve shape in screenshot above, Ink 2 will tint the image's midtones. To produce a pleasing duotone, try to distribute Ink 1 and Ink 2 in different tonal ranges (for example, black as Ink 1 in the shadow areas, somewhat in the midtones and a little bit in the highlights; and an Ink 2 color in the remaining tonal ranges—more in the midtones and light areas and less in the darks).

9. Drag the curve upward or downward in the Duotone Curve dialog box **1**. To achieve a duotone effect, the Ink 1 curve must be different from the Ink 2 curve.

10. Click OK or press Enter.

11. Click the Ink 1 curve, then repeat steps 9 and 10.

12. *Optional:* Click Save to save the current settings to use with other images.

TIP To reduce black ink in the highlights, lower the black ink (Ink 1) curve 5 percent setting to zero. To reduce color in the shadows, lower the color ink (Ink 2) curve 100 percent setting to around 85 percent.

TIP If you're using a Pantone color and you're going to output the image from an illustration or page layout program, turn on Short Pantone Names in the File > Preferences > General dialog box.

This is a great low-budget way to expand the tonal range of a grayscale image: it's still printed as a monotone (using one plate).

To print a grayscale image using a Pantone tint:

1. Open a grayscale image.

2. Choose Image menu > Mode > Duotone.

3. Choose Monotone from the Type drop-down menu.

4. Click the Ink 1 color square, then open the Custom Colors dialog box.

5. Choose the desired Pantone color, then click OK.

6. In the Duotone Options dialog box, click on the Ink 1 curve.

7. In the 100% field, enter the desired tint percentage value **2**. Leave the 0% field at 0 and all other fields blank. Click OK.

8. Click OK to close the dialog box.

9. Save the file in EPS format (see page 244).

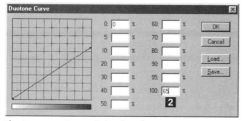

The Duotone Curve dialog box for a monotone print. The 100% field value has been lowered to the desired Pantone tint percentage.

Print Grayscale using Pantone Tints

Color reproduction basics

One of the key—and potentially problematic—issues in output is obtaining good CMYK color reproduction on an offset press. Read this section to familiarize yourself with the various stages in the output process.

The output image will resemble the image you see on screen only if the monitor is carefully calibrated for that output. Each offset press, for example, has its own settings. In order to produce consistent and predictable output, you must enter monitor and press characteristics information into Photoshop.

RGB-to-CMYK conversion

Photoshop determines how to convert an RGB image to CMYK mode and how to display a CMYK mode preview based on the current settings in the File menu > Color Settings dialog boxes, which are discussed on the following pages.

The major steps in color separation are:

■ Calibrate the monitor.

■ Enter Printing Inks and Separation settings.

■ Obtain a color proof using those settings.

■ Match the on-screen preview to the proof.

Monitor settings

Calibrating your monitor involves using either a third-party utility installed in your computer to balance the Red, Green, and Blue components on screen, or using the Gamma control panel to adjust, by eye, the color balance, the white and black areas of color, and neutral gray. See page 253 to learn more about the Gamma control panel.

Once a monitor is calibrated, you need to enter the following info in Photoshop's Monitor Setup dialog box **1**: The Gamma value used to calibrate the monitor, the White Point for that particular monitor,

Questions to ask your print shop about color separations

Color separating is an art. As a starting point, ask your print shop the following questions so you'll be able to choose the correct scan resolution and settings in the Printer Inks Setup and Separation Setup dialog boxes:

What lines per inch setting is going to be used on the press for my job? This will help you choose the appropriate scanning resolution.

What is the dot gain for my paper stock choice on that press? Allowances for dot gain can be made using the Printer Inks Setup dialog box.

Which printing method will be used on press—UCR or GCR? GCR produces better color printing and is the default choice in the Separations Setup box. (GCR stands for Gray Component Replacement, UCR stands for Undercolor Removal.)

What is the total ink limit and the black ink limit for the press? These values can also be adjusted in the Separations Setup box.

Note: Change the dot gain, GCR or UCR method, and ink limits **before** you convert your image from RGB Color mode to CMYK Color mode. If you modify any of these values after conversion, you must convert the image back to RGB Color mode, adjust the values, then reconvert to CMYK Color mode.

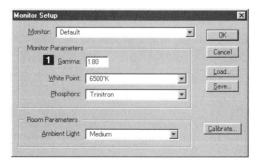

and the room (ambient) lighting around the monitor give Photoshop a clearer idea of the on-screen viewing characteristics. Check with your monitor manufacturer to choose settings for your monitor.

Print and separation settings

Another key factor in color reproduction is the type of output device to be used. In the following section, we discuss offset press output. (Online imaging issues are discussed in Chapter 20.) A monitor is an RGB device that uses light to additively blend colors. An offset press is a CMYK device that uses opaque inks to subtractively blend colors.

In the Printing Inks Setup dialog box, you need to enter the characteristics of the offset press 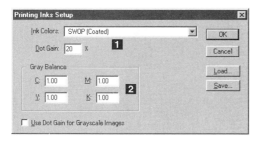, such as the ink type associated with a particular print press and the dot gain for that press. Consult with your print shop for these settings.

You can even match (calibrate) a screen image to a color proof by adjusting the values in the Gray Balance settings in this dialog box **2**. More about this later. Stay tuned.

Other characteristics of the offset press are entered into the Separation Setup dialog box **3**, but since these settings are particular for each press shop, you must consult with your press shop for this information. In short, the Separation Type tells Photoshop about the type of press used: Does the press use the GCR (gray component replacement) or UCR (undercolor removal) method, and how does the print shop handle black ink. The Black Generation amount controls how much black ink is used when translating RGB components of light into CMY inks. Adjustments must be made to prevent inks from becoming muddy when they're mixed together. Black is substituted for areas of CMY ink mixing, and how much black is substituted is determined by the Black Generation amount. Finally, each press shop uses different

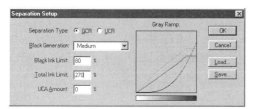

3 In this Separation Setup screen shot, the Black Ink Limit and the Total Ink Limit values have been changed to values suggested by the printshop, and the graph reflects the new values.

Print and Separation Settings

amounts of ink coverage on each separation plate. Some shops use less than 100% maximum ink coverage for each plate. Ask your press shop for these percentage settings.

Separation tables

Once you're satisfied with a set of color proofs from a particular print shop, rather than reenter this information every time you need to do RGB-to-CMYK conversion for that shop, you can use the Separation Tables dialog box to build a table containing the Printing Inks Setup and Separation Setup settings. Click Save **2** in the Separation Tables dialog box to build a table file. Next time you output in that particular press situation, load in the custom Separation Table you created and saved for that press.

But remember, these settings affect RGB-to-CMYK image mode conversions. If you readjust any settings in the Printing Inks or Separations dialog box, you will have to reconvert your image from RGB to CMYK mode again using the new settings. Keep a copy of your image in RGB Color mode so you'll have the option to readjust and reconvert it.

Match the on-screen image to a color proof

After converting your image to CMYK Color mode, ask your output service or press shop to produce a color proof of the image using the Color Settings you just entered.

As we mentioned above, use the Gray Balance settings (Printing Inks Setup dialog box) to match the CMYK preview of an on-screen image to a proof. By matching the two images—on-screen and printed proof—you can then rely more confidently on the accuracy of Photoshop's CMYK Color preview.

Load in any custom Separation Table or reenter all the individual Setup dialog

Total Ink coverage readout

To display total ink coverage percentages on the Info palette for image pixels currently under the pointer, choose **Total Ink** from the pop-up menu next to the leftmost eyedropper on the Info palette **1**. This readout is based on the current Separation Setup settings.

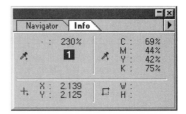

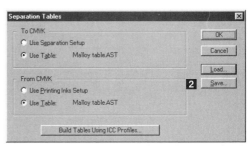

Click **Load** in the Separation Tables dialog box to load in a custom table with specific Printing Inks and Separation Setup settings.

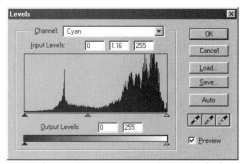

Gray balance adjustments are made to individual channels (Cyan, in this case) using the Levels dialog box. The gray midtones slider is moved to achieve a better color match between the on-screen image and a proof. Jot down the Input Levels value, since you won't be saving these dialog box settings.

File compression

To reduce the storage size of an image, use a compression program like DriveSpace or WinZip. Compression using this kind of software is non-lossy, which means the compression doesn't cause data loss.

If you don't have compression software, choose File menu > Save a Copy, choose TIFF from the Save As drop-down menu, and check the **LZW Compression** box in the TIFF Options dialog box. If you want to save the file without alpha channels, also check the Don't Include Alpha Channels box. LZW compression is non-lossy, which is good, but, and here's the rub, some applications won't import an LZW TIFF, and still other applications will import an LZW TIFF only if it doesn't contain an alpha channel.

If you're saving an image for print output, we don't recommend using the **JPEG** file format or the Compress EPS/JPEG command because JPEG compression is lossy, and additional image data is lost with each compression. The data loss may not be noticeable on screen, but it may be very noticeable on high resolution output. JPEG is more suitable for Web output.

box settings that were used to produce the proof.

Open the CMYK mode image, and adjust the overall light and dark values of the on-screen CMYK mode preview to match the proof by increasing or decreasing the Dot Gain setting in the File menu > Color Settings > Printing Inks Setup dialog box. Increasing the Dot Gain will darken the on-screen preview. Click OK to view the effect.

Next, to match the color of the monitor to the proof, with the CMYK Color mode image open and the proof in hand, open the Image menu > Adjust > Levels dialog box. Choose an individual ink color from the Channel menu and move only the Input Levels gamma slider (the gray triangle) to achieve a better color match between the two images. Repeat, if necessary, for the remaining individual ink colors. Jot down the gamma settings from the top middle field for each ink color on a piece of paper, then click Cancel. **Do not click OK** at this point—you'll **ruin** your CMYK image if you do so.

Open the File menu > Color Settings > Printing Inks Setup dialog box, enter the settings for each ink color that you jotted down from the Levels dialog box in the C, M, Y, and K Gray Balance fields, then click OK. If the original Gray Balance values are not 1.0, then multiply the new values by the old values to arrive at the correct value.

The preview of all CMYK mode images will now reflect the new Printing Inks settings, but the actual image information will only be changed if the image is converted to RGB Color mode and then back to CMYK Color mode.

Follow the instructions on this page and the next page to adjust your monitor for Photoshop. These are the first steps in monitor-to-output calibration. See the Photoshop User Guide for information about calibrating your system. You should do the Monitor Setup and Gamma adjustment before performing the color correction walk-through, which begins on page 255.

NOTE: After choosing monitor specs and making your desktop gray (instructions on the next page), adjust the brightness and contrast knobs on your monitor and do not change them (put tape on them, if necessary). Then follow instructions on the next page to adjust the Gamma.

To choose Monitor Setup options:

1. Choose File menu > Color Settings > Monitor Setup.

2. Choose your monitor name from the Monitor drop-down menu. If it's not listed, consult the documentation that was provided with your monitor to find the closest equivalent **1**.

3. Choose the manufacturer of your CRT from the Phosphors drop-down menu. This information should also be provided with your monitor.

4. Choose Low, Medium, or High from the Ambient Light drop-down menu, whichever is most applicable.

5. Click OK or press Enter.

TIP Leave the Gamma at 1.80 and the White Point at 6500°K, unless you have a specific reason to change it (if you're outputting to videotape, for example, which requires a higher gamma).

TIP The Monitor Setup affects color substitution when an image is converted from RGB Color mode to CMYK Color mode.

TIP Try to keep the light in your computer room consistent while you're working. Not so easy.

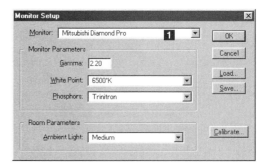

Monitor Setup Options

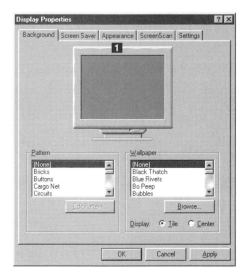

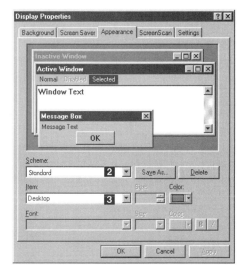

A colored Desktop can influence your perception of colors in a Photoshop image. Make the Desktop gray to alleviate this problem.

To make the Desktop gray:

1. Click the Start button on the Taskbar > Settings > Control Panels.

2. Double-click the Display icon.

3. Choose the Appearance tab **1**.

4. Choose the Windows Standard scheme **2**.

5. Choose Desktop from the Item drop-down list **3**.

6. Choose a gray color from the Color drop-down list.

7. Click OK.

8. Choose File menu > Exit.

Careful adjustment of the Gamma sliders will produce a neutral on-screen gray and will hopefully remove any color cast, if there is one, from your screen.

To adjust the Gamma:

1. Choose File menu > Color Settings > Monitor Setup.

2. Click the Calibrate button.

3. Compare the black, midtone, and white of the Gamma calibration bar grays to a photographic progressive grayscale bar.

4. Click the White Pt button, then move the White Point sliders until the right-most square on the calibration bar matches the photographic bar.

5. Click the Black Pt button, then move the Black Pt sliders until the dark calibration squares look neutral.

6. Click the Balance button, then move the Balance sliders until the gray calibration squares look neutral.

7. Move the Gamma Adjustment slider to blend the light and dark bars.

8. *Optional:* Click Save Settings, then rename and save the Gamma settings.

If you convert an image to CMYK Color mode, its colors are automatically forced into printable gamut. In certain cases, however, you may want to see which areas are out-of-gamut (non-printable) in RGB, and change some of them manually. In the following instructions, you'll choose the Gamut Warning command to display out-of-gamut colors in gray, and use the Sponge tool to desaturate those areas to bring them into printable gamut.

NOTE: The Gamut Warning command uses the current separation table settings, so enter your Setup info first (see page 249).

To correct out-of-gamut colors:

1. Convert your image to RGB Color or Lab Color mode.

2. Choose View menu > Gamut Warning.

3. *Optional:* To select and restrict color changes to the out-of-gamut areas, choose Select menu > Color Range, choose Out of Gamut from the Select drop-down menu **1**, then click OK.

4. Choose the Sponge tool. 🌐

5. Choose Desaturate from the drop-down menu on the Toning Tools Options palette, and choose a Pressure percentage.

6. Click the Brushes tab, then click a tip.

7. Choose a target layer.

8. Drag across the gray, out-of-gamut areas **2**. As they become desaturated, they will redisplay in color. Don't desaturate colors too much, though, or they'll get muddy. (To turn off the Gamut Warning, choose View menu > Gamut Warning again.)

TIP To preview the image in CMYK in a second window, choose View menu > New View. With the new window active, choose View menu > CMYK Preview. Resize and move the new window so both windows are visible.

Desaturate another way

You can use the Image menu > Adjust > Hue/Saturation command instead of the Sponge tool to correct out-of-gamut colors in the selected areas. Move the Saturation slider to the left to desaturate.

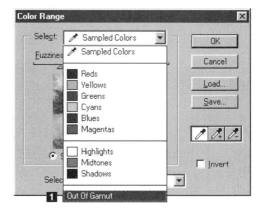

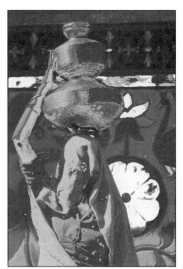

2 For illustration purposes, out-of-gamut colors in this image are shown in white instead of the usual gray.

Correct Out-of-Gamut Colors

A color correction walk-through

The following is a walk-through session to color correct an image using the Levels, Curves, Color Balance, and Unsharp Mask commands. Adjustment layers are used whenever possible so you'll be able to easily readjust the image tone and color later, if your heart desires.

If your image is intended for on-screen output, do all your correction in RGB color mode. If you're working with a CMYK scan, do all your correction in CMYK Color mode. Adobe recommends using RGB color mode for color correction on output intended for separation, converting the image to CMYK Color mode using the proper separation setup settings, and then fine-tuning in CMYK Color mode after you get your color proofs back.

NOTE: Make sure your monitor is calibrated before performing the following steps.

The basic steps

■ Scan or acquire a Photo CD image into Photoshop

■ Set the Black and White points

■ Limit tonal values

■ Adjust the neutral gray

■ Color balance

■ Perform Selective Color adjustments (optional)

■ Unsharp Mask

🖑 The first step

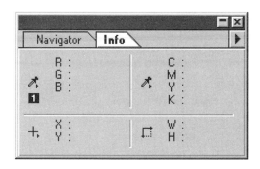

Open a single layer, flattened version of an image in RGB or CMYK Color mode in Photoshop. Use Save a Copy to create a flattened version of the image, if necessary.

On the Info palette, press the leftmost dropper icon and choose RGB Color **1**, and press the rightmost dropper icon and choose CMYK Color. Leave the palette visible and accessible for the following instructions.

The first step in color correction is to set the black and white points (the darkest shadow and lightest highlight values) to preserve image detail in those areas.

🐾 Set the black and white points by eye using Threshold mode (method 1)

1. On the Layers palette, activate the Background of an RGB Color image.

2. Choose Image menu > Adjust > Levels.

3. Uncheck the Preview box, then Alt-drag the black Input slider until small sections of the shadows of the image appear on the white area of the image window ▮.

4. Alt-drag the white Input slider until small sections of the highlights of the image appear on the black area of the image window ▮.

5. Move the gray midtone Input slider (don't hold down Alt) to darken or lighten the midtones.

6. Jot down on paper all the Input readouts that are displayed at the top of the dialog box, check the Preview box, then click Cancel.

7. Activate the Background, Control-click the Create New Layer button, choose Type: Levels, then click OK.

8. Enter all the values noted in step 7, above, into the appropriate Input Levels fields, then click OK.

9. Activate the Background, then set the Info palette readouts to Grayscale. Pass the cursor over the darkest and lightest areas of the image. If the darkest K value falls between 95 and 100%, double-click the adjustment layer to open the Levels dialog box, then move the black Input slider outward. If the lightest K value falls between 5 and 0% white, move the white Input slider outward to lower the contrast. This will lower the percentage values for the Black and White points. Click OK.

1 Alt-dragging the **black** Input Levels slider reveals the **darkest** areas of the image first.

2 Alt-dragging the **white** Input Levels slider reveals the **lightest** areas of the image first.

Double-click the black or white point eyedropper icon to open the Color Picker dialog box, then set target values for the black and white points in the image.

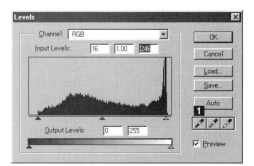

A detail of the **Color Picker** dialog box. The HSB fields have been set to values specified by the press shop for the black point value in an image. Clicking now with the black point eyedropper in the Levels dialog box will lighten the darkest areas of the image to 95% black.

✎ Set the black and white points via the Levels eyedroppers using target values (method 2)

1. Ask your press shop which target values should be entered for the black and white points.

2. To create an adjustment layer above the Background, Control-click the Create New Layer button, choose Type: Levels, then click OK.

3. Double-click the black point eyedropper icon **1**.

4. Click in the area of the image that you want to be the darkest—but not too dark, so some detail is retained. Display the rulers, then drag guides from the vertical and horizontal rulers to that spot so you can quickly relocate it.

5. In the Color Picker, enter the C, M, Y, and K values your press shop recommends or enter 0, 0, and 5, respectively, for HSB values **2**, then click OK.

6. Click the black point eyedropper icon.

7. Click on the same pixel area you clicked on in step 4, above. Use the Info palette and the guides to locate the same pixel values.

8. Double-click the white point (third) eyedropper icon.

9. Click in an area of the image that you want to be the lightest, without sacrificing too much detail. (Set up guides to easily relocate the same spot.) In the CMYK area of the Color Picker, enter C, M, Y, and K values your press shop recommends, or in the HSB area of the picker, enter 0 for H and S and 95 for B, then click OK.

10. Click the White point eyedropper icon. Click on the same pixel area you clicked on in step 9, and find the same

(Continued on the next page)

pixel values using the Info palette and the guides.

11. Move the gray midtone Input slider to darken or lighten the midtones.

12. Click OK.

TIP You can also set target black and white values using the eyedroppers in the Curves dialog box.

TIP Be careful if you're viewing pixel values in the Info palette with the Levels dialog box closed, because the adjustment layer will show the current RGB values on the Info palette, but only the current K value will display in the CMYK part of the Info palette. If the Background is active and the adjustment layer is visible, the Info palette will display all the current pixel readouts.

If you bypassed the steps for setting the Black and White points or were not satisfied with the resulting high and low pixel values, you can further limit the tonal values in the image via the Levels dialog box.

🖎 Limit tonal values

1. Open the Info palette.

2. You can use the existing Levels adjustment layer, or Control-click the New Layer icon to create an adjustment layer above the Background, choose Type: Levels, then click OK. You can perform adjustments on separate adjustment layers, and then show/hide them individually, or show them all together.

3. Move both Output sliders inward slightly to soften the darkest black and lightest white in the image **1**. Or enter 12 and 244, respectively. Use the Info palette to confirm that the adjustments fall within the percentage range your press shop specified (but remember that the Levels dialog box fields don't work in percentage values), then click OK.

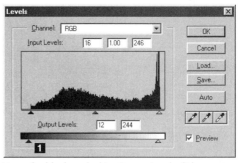

Move the black and white Output Levels sliders inward slightly to tone down the darkest black and lightest white in the image.

Limit tonal values using Curves

To limit tonal values using the Curves dialog box, click on the grayscale bar, if necessary, to make it display percentage values, then drag the low point of the curve upward five percentage points, to 5%, and drag the high point of the curve downward five percentage points, to 95%.

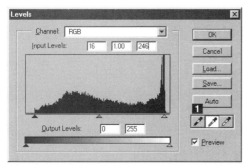

After clicking the gray point eyedropper icon in the Levels dialog box, pass the pointer over the image to find an area with similar RGB readouts.

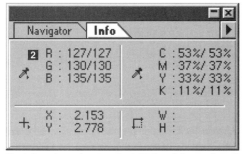

The **Info** palette showing the RGB breakdown of pixels under the pointer. While the Levels dialog box is open, two RGB readouts are displayed: before Levels adjustment and after Levels adjustment. (To reset the Info palette readouts, click on the palette's eyedropper icon and choose RGB color from the drop-down menu.)

✎ Adjust the neutral gray

1. Open the Info palette.

2. Use the existing Levels adjustment layer, or Control-click the Create New Layer button to create an adjustment layer above the Background, choose Type: Levels, then click OK.

3. Click the gray eyedropper **1**.

4. Note the RGB values on the Info palette as you pass the cursor over the image. Reset the palette readouts, if necessary.

5. When you find an area with close to equal R, G, and B readouts **2**, in the range from 100 to 160 (like R=120, G=115, B=110), click on that area with the gray eyedropper.

The overall image color balance will readjust based on the area you clicked on, but the brightness level in that area won't change. Click elsewhere if you want to readjust the neutral gray balance. The Info palette readout should now display similar R, G, and B values.

6. Click OK.

If the image still has an undesirable color cast, you can use the Color Balance or Curves command to correct it. The Color Balance dialog box is easier to use, since it displays the relationship of color opposites, and works on the Shadows, Midtones, and Highlights areas of an image via separate groups of sliders, but you can't use it to adjust individual color channels. Using the Curves command, you can perform adjustments on an individual color channel or on all the channels together, so it provides a greater degree of control over an individual color's adjustment, but the curves are a little tricky to manipulate. Take your pick.

✎ Color balance the image

Control-click the Create New Layer icon to create an adjustment layer above the Background, then follow the steps on page 124 (Color Balance) or page 126 (Curves).

Adjust Neutral Gray; Color Balance

If, after obtaining color proofs, there's still a lingering color imbalance in part of the image, you can correct that color component via the Selective Color command, which adjusts the amount of ink used on press for individual process colors. You can even change the amount of a process color used in specified color combinations (the amount of cyan used in green, for example) without affecting the percentage of that color used in other color combinations.

🔍 Perform selective color adjustments

1. Make sure the image is in CMYK mode.
2. Flatten the image to adjust the whole image, then choose Image menu > Adjust > Selective Color.
   or
   Create an adjustment layer using Type: Selective Color.
3. Choose the color you want to adjust from the Colors drop-down menu 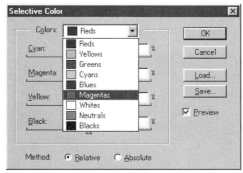.
4. Click Relative to add or subtract a percentage of a process color from the selected color. Using this method, other colors will adjust in tandem with the color you're currently adjusting, but you can't tell which ones.

   Click Absolute to add or subtract an exact process color amount from the selected color. Use this method to adjust individual color components precisely according to your print shop's specifications.
5. Enter the percentages in the Cyan, Magenta, Yellow, and/or Black fields that your print shop specifies, or adjust those sliders.

🔍 Unsharp Mask

Apply the Unsharp Mask filter to the Background (see pages 44–45). Don't merge the adjustment layer into the Background yet.

1 In the Selective Color dialog box, choose an ink color from the **Colors** drop-down menu, then move the sliders to adjust the printing percentage for that color.

WEB & MULTIMEDIA 20

Visit Peachpit Press' web site: http://www.peachpit.com.

THIS CHAPTER covers the preparation of Photoshop images for use in multimedia (on-screen) and on the World Wide Web (online). Conversion to Indexed Color mode is covered first, then, using Photoshop images in Director, and finally, saving images for viewing on the Web.

Some multimedia and video programs and some computer systems will not import a Photoshop image containing more than 256 colors (8-bit color). You can reduce the number of colors in an image's color table by converting it to Indexed Color mode, or to optimize its display on the Web.

NOTE: Converting a multi-layer image to Indexed Color mode will cause its layers to be flattened. Use the Save As command to work on a copy of the image.

To convert an image to Indexed Color mode:

1. Make sure the image is in RGB Color mode.

2. Choose Image menu > Mode > Indexed Color.

3. Choose a Palette **1**:

You can choose Exact if the image contains 256 or fewer colors. No colors will be eliminated.

Choose Adaptive for the best color substitution.

Choose System (Macintosh) if you're going to export the file to an application that only accepts the Macintosh default palette.

Choose System (Windows) if you're planning to export the image to the Windows platform.

(Continued on the followimg page)

Convert to Indexed Color Mode

ARTWORK BY JOHN GRIMES

Choose Web if the image is intended for Web viewing. This option limits the Color Table to only colors available in the most commonly used Web browsers.

To create your own palette, choose Custom, click OK, then edit the Color Table, if you want. (Click Save if you want to save the table for later use. Click Load to load in a previously saved table.) Click OK and skip the remaining steps.

Choose Previous to reuse the custom palette from the last used Custom or Adapative palette option.

4. If you chose the Adaptive palette, you can choose a Color Depth to specify the number of colors in the table **1**. If you choose 4 bits/pixel, the table will contain 16 colors; if you choose 8 bits/pixel, the table will contain 256 colors. The fewer bits/pixel in the image, the more dithered it will be. You can also enter your own value in the Colors field.

5. Choose Dither: None, Diffusion, or Pattern. None will cause areas that contain sharp color transitions to appear posterized, so it's an option that's best suited for flat-color images. Diffusion may produce the closest color substitution, but it can also produce a dotty effect in those areas. The Pattern option, which adds pixels in a more structured arrangement, is available only when the System (Macintosh) palette is used (see step 3).

6. Click OK or press Enter.

TIP If you want to control which colors will be chosen for the palette, create a selection or selections that contain the colors you want to be in the palette before converting your image to Indexed Color mode, then choose the Adaptive palette for step 3 on the previous page.

Painting in Indexed Color mode

In Indexed Color mode, the Pencil, Airbrush, and Paintbrush tools produce only fully opaque strokes. For those tools, leave the Opacity slider on the Options palette at 100%. Dissolve is the only tool mode that will produce a different stroke at a lower opacity.

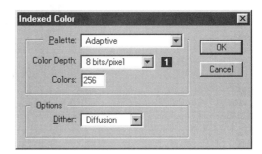

Convert Image to Indexed Color Mode

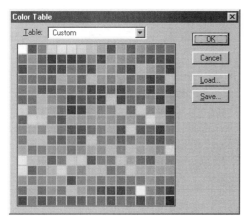

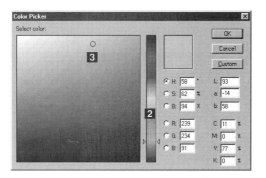

1 Click a color in the Color Table dialog box, or drag across a series of colors.

To edit an Indexed Color table:

1. Choose Image menu > Mode > Color Table. The Color Table will display all the picture's colors.

2. Click on a color to be replaced **1**.
or
Drag Select a bunch of colors by dragging across them.

3. Move the slider up or down on the vertical bar to choose a hue **2**, then click a variation of that hue in the large rectangle **3**.

4. Click OK to exit the Color Picker.

5. Click OK or press Enter.

TIP You can convert a Grayscale picture directly to Indexed Color mode and then modify its color table to add arbitrary color to the image. Try the Black Body or Spectrum table.

For the best results, choose a warm first color and a cool last color, or vice versa, for steps 3 and 5 below.

To reduce an Indexed Color table to two colors and the shades between them:

1. Choose Image menu > Mode > Color Table.

2. Drag across the Color Table from the first swatch in the upper left corner to the last swatch in the lower right corner.

3. Choose a first color from the Color Picker: move the slider up or down on the vertical bar to choose a hue **2**, then click a variation of that hue in the large rectangle **3**.

4. Click OK.

5. Choose a last color from the Color Picker.

6. Click OK to exit the Color Picker.

7. Click OK or press Enter.

You can create a painterly effect by generating an Indexed Color image from an RGB Color image, and then pasting the Index Color image back into the RGB Color picture.

To recolor an RGB image:

1. If the image is not in RGB mode, choose Image menu > Mode > RGB Color.

2. Follow the steps on pages 261–262 to convert the image to Indexed Color mode.

3. Choose Image menu > Mode > Color Table.

4. Choose Table: Spectrum 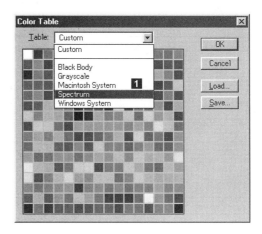.

5. Click OK or press Enter.

6. Choose Select menu > All.

7. Choose Edit menu > Copy.

8. Choose File menu > Revert.

9. Click Revert to restore the image to RGB Color mode.

10. Choose Edit menu > Paste to paste the Indexed Color image onto a new layer.

11. Double-click the new layer name 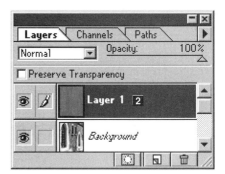.

12. Choose from the Mode drop-down menu **3**. Try Dissolve (at below 80% opacity), Multiply, Soft Light, Difference, or Color.

13. *Optional:* Change the Opacity percentage to reveal more of the original image.

14. *Optional:* Move the black Underlying slider to the right to restore shadows from the underlying layer.
    and/or
    Move the white Underlying slider to the left to restore highlights from the underlying layer.
    and/or
    To restore midtones, Alt-drag to split either slider.

15. Click OK or press Enter.

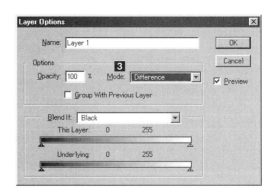

Recolor an RGB Image *(side tab)*

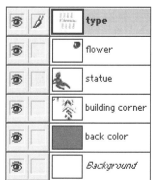

The initial composition of the Director frame in the illustration below was developed using Photoshop's layers (left). Each Photoshop **layer** became a separate **cast member** in Director.

A frame from a Director movie of an interactive map. Each street name is a button link to another point in the movie.

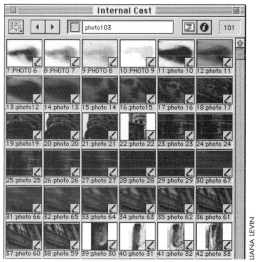

Director's Cast palette. Image and filter sequences were composed using Photoshop layers and then copy-and-pasted onto Director's Cast palette.

From Photoshop to Director

Bitmap imagery, button shapes, bitmap type, and even some transitions can be developed in Photoshop to use in Director, Macromedia's multimedia application. You can use Photoshop's Layers palette like a storyboard to develop an image sequence. Stack, hide, and show picture elements on individual layers, then use each layer as an individual cast member in Director. Assembling an image via layers in Photoshop is like using the Score in Director to assemble cast members on the Stage.

Ways to use the Layers palette as a storyboard

- Show and hide layers in a sequence to preview how you want those objects to appear or disappear in Director.

- Move layers in the image window via the Move tool to test animated motion.

- Lower or increase a layer's opacity to preview a fade-out/fade-in effect.

- To maximize your animation flexibility, select the various elements of a one-layer image, then copy-and-paste them onto individual layers. Each element could become a separate cast member in Director.

- Use a layer's pixels as a separate cast member in Director. Control-click on a layer name (not the Background) to select all the pixels on that layer, and use Edit menu > Copy to copy the pixels to the Clipboard. In Director, choose a cast member window on the Cast palette, then choose Edit menu > Paste Bitmap. The Photoshop pixel imagery will become bitmap imagery in Director, but it may be slightly less smooth in color areas.

  You could also save the Photoshop file in the .PCT (PICT) or .BMP format (choose 16 Bits/pixel) and use Director's Import command to load it onto the Cast palette. A major disadvantage of this method: it flattens all the layers. In Director's Import dialog box, use the appropriate format to import the image.

NOTE: Importing imagery into Director in a non-bitmap format can produce a small file size, but you can't edit the cast member, you can't apply Xtras filters to it, and you may not be able to drop white out using the ink effect of Background Transparent for non-type objects.

RGB vs. Indexed Color images

Either method you use to import imagery from Photoshop into Director—using the copy and paste method or saving a file as a .PCT or .BMP in Photoshop and importing it in Director—will produce an RGB bitmap file with a 16-bit color depth, which is overly large. To find out the file size of a selected cast member, click the info icon on the Cast palette in Director. Use Transform Bitmap to reduce the size of the cast member to 8-bit to speed up the movie's playback.

To reduce the size of the Director bitmap, in Photoshop, you can convert the RGB file to Indexed Color mode using the System palette (Windows) and an 8-bit or lower color depth resolution.

If you use the Adaptive palette, each Photoshop Indexed Color file that you import into Director will arrive with its own color palette. Loading multiple cast members with assorted palettes can slow the movie playback. Use the Copy and Paste option when you have a small number of Indexed Color files to import, and use the File > Import option if you have a large number of Indexed Color files to import that don't have to be edited in Director. Remember to use the appropriate format in the Import dialog box.

While you can use Director to transform a bitmap RGB image from Photoshop and lower its color depth, you'll achieve better

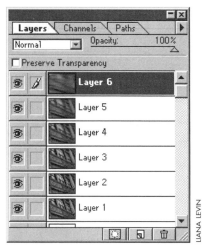

The Layers palette showing a Motion Blur filter sequence. Each layer was copy/pasted into Director as a separate cast member.

This 50K image was saved as an RGB PICT in Photoshop, pasted as Bitmap into Director, and then reduced to 8-bit depth in Director. Note the graininess in the sky.

This 150K image was imported as .PCT and kept at 16-bit depth. It has smooth tone transitions, but it has a larger file size than the image above.

Photoshop to Director

1 This image was converted to Indexed Color mode (8-bit depth) in Photoshop and then pasted into Director as Bitmap, and it's a 50K file. The sky is smooth in this smaller size image, like the 150K image on the previous page.

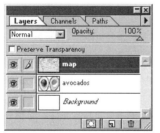

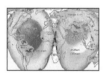

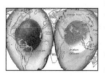

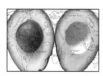

2 This illustration shows a few of the twenty steps that are used to gradually lower the opacity of the map layer. For each opacity level, the Save a Copy command was used to save a flattened copy of the original.

results if you do this in Photoshop via Indexed Color mode **1**.

Creating transitions using transparency

In some multimedia applications, Director 5, for one, you have the option to lower a sprite's opacity. Fade-outs and fade-ins can be created in Photoshop for any object on its own layer above the Background. Follow these steps to create exportable, transparent objects using Photoshop for an application in which you can't change opacities. Create a new document with a white Background, and drag-and-drop or copy-and-paste the chosen object onto its own layer above the Background. With the layer containing the object active, save a flattened version of the image in the .PCT or .BMP format using the File menu > Save a Copy command. You can create a new folder for the series of files you'll be saving **2**.

In the original two-layer document that will remain open, lower the topmost layer's opacity to 95%, and save the image again in the new folder in the .PCT or .BMP format using the Save a Copy command. Repeat these steps to create each separate cast member for the transition, lowering the opacity of the topmost layer each time by 5 or 10 percent. In the multimedia application, use the Import command to load the whole series of files.

How to copy a pixel object with an anti-aliased edge into Director

Director displays an object's anti-aliased edges with a white or colored halo, which will be noticeable if the background behind the object is any color other than white. The halo will also be noticeable if the object moves across a background that isn't uniform or that changes gradually.

This halo problem won't arise if you Import as .PCT to Director for type created in Photoshop. To avoid this problem when using Copy/Paste, select an object in Photoshop without its anti-aliased edge, Control-click on a layer name to select the object, then zoom in to at least 200% view so you can really see the object's edge. Choose Select menu > Modify > Contract and contract the selection by 1 or 2 pixels to remove the anti-aliased edge **1**. Finally, copy the object selection and paste it into Director. A soft-edged shape, like a shadow, will have a dotty dissolve along its edge when it's pasted as Bitmap in Director.

Director and Photoshop filters

Photoshop compatible plug-in filters are now accessable from within Director 5. To use them, make a copy of the Filters folder (Photoshop folder > Plug-ins > Filters), then place it in the Xtras folder within the Director folder. Make sure the Photoshop Filters file was also installed in the Program folder > Macromedia > Dir 5.0 > Dir532 > Xtras folder.

The filters are accessed via the Xtras menu > Filter Bitmap and/or Xtras menu > Auto Filter, and only work on Bitmap cast members.

As of this writing the Gallery Effects filters were working within Director 5, but the new Effects filters were not.

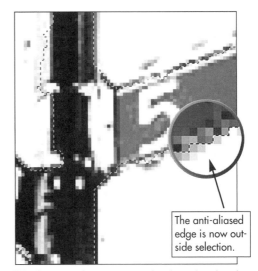

The anti-aliased edge is now outside selection.

1 After using the Magic Wand tool to select the white background around the signpost and then inversing the selection, some of the original anti-aliased edge remained. Select menu > Modify > Contract (by one pixel) was used shrink the selection inward.

Two pasted bitmap cast members in Director 5. The member on the left was copied without contracting the selection in Photoshop. The member on the right was copied after contracting the selection in Photoshop to remove its halo.

Four golden rules for Web image creation

- Let the image **content**—whether it's flat color or continuous-tone—determine which **file format** you use.

- Use as **low** a **pixel size** of the image as is practical, balancing the file size with aesthetics (number of colors). And remember the fail-safe option for flat-color images for viewing on both Mac and Windows browsers: Load the Indexed Color Web palette onto the Swatches palette.

- Try reducing the image's **color depth**.

- View your Web image through a **Web browser** on computers other than your own so you can see how quickly it actually downloads and how good (or bad) it looks.

Photoshop to the World Wide Web

The basic formula for outputting a Photoshop image for on-line viewing may seem straightforward: Design the image in RGB mode, and save it in the file format used by Web browsers (the applications that combine text, images, and HTML code into a viewable page on the World Wide Web). However, when you load and view an image via a Web browser, you may be disappointed to find that not all colors or blends display well on the Web, and your image may take an unacceptably long time to download and render, which is a function of its storage size. If an image looks overly dithered (grainy and dotty), or was subject to unexpected color substitutions, or takes too long to view on a Web page, it means your design is not outputting well.

Four important issues that you'll need to address for on-line output are discussed on the following pages: the pixel size of the image, the color palette, the color depth, and the file format (GIF or JPEG).

Image size

In order to calculate the appropriate image size for your image, you must know beforehand your intended viewers' monitor size and modem speed. In most cases, you should be designing your image for a 13-inch monitor, the most common monitor size, and a 14.4 kbps modem, the most common modem speed. By mid-1997, 28.8 kbps will be the most common modem speed.

The maximum size of an image that can be viewed on a 13-inch monitor is 480 pixels high by 640 pixels wide. The Web browser window will display within these parameters, so your maximum image size will occupy only a portion of the browser window—about 8 inches high (570 pixels) by 7 inches wide (500 pixels).

The image resolution only needs to be 96 ppi, which is the per-square-inch resolution of an IBM PC monitor.

Web Image Size

Assuming dimensions of, say, 500 by 400 pixels (7 by 6 inches), a flattened image in the PICT format will be about 600K, according to its Document Sizes reading on the Info bar in the lower left corner of the image window in Photoshop. This size value, however, reflects how much RAM is occupied when the image is opened in Photoshop. The same file saved in the GIF or JPEG file format will be much smaller due to the compression schemes built into these formats.

To determine a file's actual storage size, highlight the file name in the Explorer, then right-click on the file name and choose Properties. This, by the way, is a more accurate measure of a file's storage size than the View > Details readout in the Explorer.

The degree to which a GIF or JPEG file format compresses depends on how compressable the image is. Both formats cause a small reduction in image quality, but it's worth the size reduction tradeoff, because your image will download faster on the Web. A file size of about 50K traveling on a 14.4 kbps modem with a one second per kilobyte download rate will take about a minute to download, about 30 seconds on a 28.8 kbps modem. (Is this a test question?)

A document with a flat background color and a few flat color shapes will compress a great deal (expect a file size in the range of 20 to 50K). A large document (over 100K) with many color areas, textures, or patterns (an Add Noise texture covering most of the image, for example) won't compress nearly as much. Continuous-tone, photographic images may compress less than flat color images when you use the GIF format. If you posterize a continuous-tone image down to somewhere between four and eight levels, the resulting file size will be similar to that of a flat color image, but you will have lost the continuous color transitions in the bargain. JPEG is the better format choice for a photographic-type image.

Create a browser window layer

Take a screen shot of your browser window, open the file in Photoshop, and paste it into a Web design document as your bottommost layer. Now you can design for that specific browser window's dimensions. (Thanks to Darren Roberts for this hot tip.)

Size comparisons of GIFs

20K GIF, from a 5-level posterized image.

120K GIF, from a continuous-tone image.

To summarize, if an image must be large (500 x 400 pixels or larger), ideally, it should contain large areas of only a few flat colors. If you want the image to be more intricate in color and shape, restrict its size to only a section of the Web browser window.

By the way, patterned imagery that completely fills the background of the browser window is usually created using a tiling method in a Web page creation program or using HTML code.

GIF: the great compromise

GIF is an 8-bit file format, which means a GIF image can contain a maximum of 256 colors. Since a majority of Web users have 8-bit monitors, which can display a maximum of 256 colors, not the thousands or millions of colors that make images look pleasing to the eye, GIF is the standard format to use, and a good choice for images that contain flat color areas and shapes with well-defined edges, like type.

To prepare an image for the GIF format and to see how the image will truly look when viewed via the browser, set your monitor's resolution to 256 colors (not Thousands or Millions), choose File menu > Preferences > Display and Cursors, check the Use Diffusion Dither box, then click OK.

Your color choices for a GIF image should be based on what a Web browser palette can display. Most browser palettes are 8-bit, which means they can display only 256 colors. Colors that aren't on the palette are simulated by dithering, a display technique that intermixes color pixels to simulate other colors. To prevent unexpected color substitutions or dithering, make sure you use the browser palette for your image. Color substitutions are particularly noticeable in flat color areas, and can make you want to disown an image.

Using the GIF89a Export command, you can create an adaptive palette using the

GIF

most common colors in the image—instead of just the colors in the system palette. This concentrates the range of 256 colors to those that are most needed in the image, which helps preserve image quality. Unfortunately, this adaptive palette probably won't match the browser's palette exactly. What to do?! Read on.

Photoshop's Web palette

A more fail-safe approach is to use Photoshop's Web palette, which you can choose if you convert an image to Indexed Color mode. Here's the Web palette's built-in guarantee: colors in the image will display properly on the current browsers on both the Macintosh and Windows platforms. Here's the rub: In order to create a palette that works on both platforms, since the Mac and Windows browser palettes share only 216 out of 256 possible colors, your image will be reduced to 216 colors, even less than in the GIF format. Don't distress. This is a small loss in a continuous-tone image, and it will actually lower its file size. Ready to sign up?

To create a Web palette:

1. Open an image, and if it's not already in RGB Color mode, convert it now.

2. Choose Image menu > Mode > Indexed Color.

3. Choose Palette: Web **1**.

4. Click OK.

5. Choose Image menu > Mode > Color Table.

6. Click Save.

7. Choose a location for and enter a name for the Web color table, click Save, then Click OK.

8. Choose Replace Swatches from the Swatches palette command menu.

9. Locate and highlight the Web table you just saved, then click Open. The swatches will now be the 216 colors common to both Macintosh and

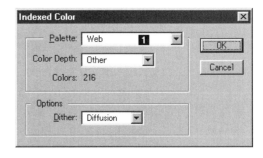

Windows Web browsers. Use only those swatches when you choose flat colors for your Web image.

TIP If you want to apply a gradient fill to a large area of your image and you plan to use the GIF format, create a top-to-bottom gradient. Top-to-bottom gradients produce smaller file sizes than left-to-right or diagonal gradients.

Color depth

If you lower an image's color depth, you will reduce the actual number of colors it contains, which will in turn reduce its file size and speed up its download time on the Web. You can reduce the number of colors in an 8-bit image to fewer than the 256 colors it contained originally in the Indexed Color dialog box or the GIF89a Export dialog box. By choosing the Adaptive palette option, you'll have the ability to reduce the number of colors in the palette and, thus, in the image.

Photoshop provides previews for both Indexed Color and GIF89a exports, so you can test how an image will look with fewer colors. Color reduction may produce dithered edges and duller colors, but you'll get the reduction in file size that you need. Always preview the image at 100% view to evaluate color quality, by the way.

Color depth (and thus, file size) can also be greatly reduced by first using the Hue/Saturation command to colorize the image and make it monotone and then reducing the number of colors substantially (to as low as 4-bit), which won't diminish the quality of the already monotone image.

GIF89a Export

Use the GIF89a format if you require transparency (you want to mask out the image's background or a portion of the image itself) and interlacing (the image displays in progressively greater detail as it downloads onto the Web page). Transparent GIF is a good choice for an image that will display

Color depth

Number of colors	Bit depth
256	8
128	7
64	6
32	5
16	4
8	3
4	2
2	1

Color Depth; GIF89a Export

on a Web page that has a non-uniform background pattern.

To prepare an RGB image for the Web using GIF89a Export:

1. Choose File menu > Export > GIF89a Export.

2. Choose Palette: Adaptive **1**.
   and
   Choose the number of colors (color depth) from the Colors drop-down menu, or enter a specific number.

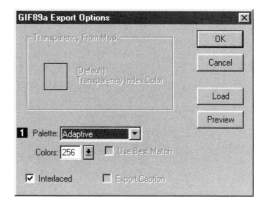

3. Click Preview to preview the image using the present palette and color depth settings. You can drag the image in the preview window, if you like, and you can also zoom in or out using the zoom tool in the dialog box. Click to zoom in, Alt-click to zoom out.

4. Click OK to close the preview window.

5. Try to further lower the color depth level, previewing the results, to see if a lower color depth is tolerable.

6. Leave the Interlaced box checked if you want to display the image in progressively greater detail on the Web page. Uncheck this option if the image contains small type, because interlacing can cause a longer wait for the type to become sharp enough to read.

7. If you're dissatisfied with the image quality, hold down Alt and click Reset to restore the original export settings, then readjust the settings.

8. Click OK when you're satisfied (or as satisfied as you're gonna get) with the GIF export preview.

9. Choose a location in which to save the file, enter a name for the file, then click Save.

The original image.

The cake copied and pasted into its own layer. We hid all the other layers before saving in the GIF format.

To create a transparent GIF:

NOTE: For a one-layer image, do all the following steps. For an image on its own transparent layer, start with step 4.

1. Select the part of the image you want to keep and be non-transparent. If you want to produce a soft-edged transition to transparency, feather the selection using a low value (1 to 3 pixels). Feathering will prevent the fringe of pixels on the edges of areas next to the selection from appearing on the background of your Web page. Don't use feathering if you're selecting a hard-edged, flat color image. A high feathering value will produce noticeable halos along the edge of the image when it's viewed through a browser.

2. Choose Edit menu > Copy.

3. Choose Edit menu > Paste. The imagery will appear on its own layer.

4. Hide any layers that you don't want to be visible in the final GIF image, and also hide the Background, even if it's all white.

5. Choose File menu > Export > GIF89a Export.

6. Choose Palette: Adaptive, and click Preview to preview the GIF file.

7. Try lowering the number of colors via the Colors drop-down menu or by entering a value.

8. Preview again to evaluate the image quality with a lower color depth.

9. The Transparency Index Color—which is the color for transparent areas—is set to the Netscape background color by default. To choose your own color for the transparent areas, click on the Transparency Index Color box, choose a new color, then click OK. This color will only be visible on a large feathered edge when the image is viewed in the browser.

If you want your image to fade or to appear as an irregular shape on a flat color area, create two layers in your Photoshop document, one that contains a flat color chosen with the Web palette loaded into the Swatches palette and one that contains the image with a soft, feathered edge or that has an irregular shape. Hide all the other layers except these two. Use the GIF89a Export command, but don't change the default Transparency color, since transparency isn't created with this type of GIF.

If you're planning to change the background on your Web page using a large flat color background image or via HTML code, though, you must make the Transparency Index Color box match the background the GIF will appear on top of. Otherwise, default gray will display in the soft edge areas of a large feathered edge (yech).

JPEG: the sometimes solution

The JPEG format may be a better choice for preserving color fidelity if your image is continuous tone (contains gradations of color or is photographic) and it's aimed toward viewers who have 24-bit monitors, which have the capacity to display millions of colors.

A JPEG plus: it can compress a 24-bit image to as small a file as the GIF format can compress an 8-bit image.

JPEG's shortcomings: First, a JPEG file has to be decompressed when it's downloaded for viewing on a Web page, which takes time. Secondly, JPEG is not a good choice for flat-color images or type, because its compression methods tend to produce artifacts along the well-defined edges of these kinds of images. And third, not all Web viewers use 24-bit monitors, and a JPEG image will be dithered on an 8-bit monitor, though dithering in a continuous-tone image is less noticeable than in an image that contains flat colors.

You can lower your monitor's setting to 8-bit to preview what the image will look

To match colors between Photoshop and other applications

If you try to mix a color in Photoshop using the same RGB values as a particular color used in Director or Netscape Navigator, you probably won't be able to achieve an exact match, because Director and Navigator use the Windows Color Picker to determine RGB color values (the number attached to each R, G, and B component), whereas Photoshop, by default, uses its own Color Picker.

To be able to mix colors using the RGB sliders on the Color palette in Photoshop to match colors used in Director, you should use the Windows Color Picker rather than Photoshop's own Color Picker: Choose Preferences > General, choose Windows from the Color Picker drop-down menu, then click OK. Remember to reset this preference back to the Photoshop Color Picker when you're finished.

like in an 8-bit setting. If it doesn't contain type or objects with sharp edges, then the JPEG image will probably survive the 8-bit setting conversion.

JPEG format files can now be saved as progressive JPEG, which is supported by the Netscape Navigator browser, and which displays the image in increasing detail as it downloads onto the Web page.

If you choose JPEG as your output format, you can experiment by creating and saving several versions of the image using varying degrees of compression. Open the JPEG versions of the image in Photoshop and view them at 100% or a more magnified view. Decide which degree of compression is acceptable by weighing the file size versus diminished image quality. Be sure to leave the original image intact to allow for potential future revisions.

Each time an image is resaved as a JPEG, some original image data is destroyed, and the more the image is degraded. The greater the degree of compression, the greater the data loss. To prevent this data loss, edit your image in Photoshop format and then save a JPEG copy when the image is finalized.

To save a copy of an image in JPEG format:

1. Choose File menu > Save a Copy (Control-Alt-S).

2. Choose Save As: JPEG.

3. Choose a location and enter a name for the file.

4. Click Save.

5. Enter a number between 0 and 10 for Image Options: Quality or choose from the four drop-down menu options.
   or
   Move the slider left or right to choose from the quality options.

   A Maximum setting will compress the image the least (between 5:1 and 15:1),

(Continued on the following page)

and preserve image quality the most, but the resulting file size from this setting will be larger than with any other setting.

Try all four settings on different versions of the original, and then reopen the JPEGs in Photoshop to weigh the image quality versus file size question.

6. Choose Format Options **1**: Baseline ("Standard") to minimize the amount of data loss during compression.
or
Choose Format Options: Baseline Optimized to optimize image quality during compression.
or
Choose Progressive to produce a progressive JPEG file. This type of file will display in the Web browser in several passes, with more detail revealed with each pass. Choose the desired number of passes (scans) from the Scans drop-down menu.

7. Click OK or press Enter.

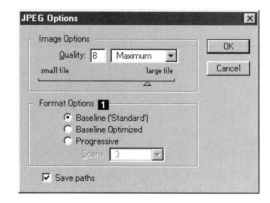

PNG: the future solution?

PNG is a new file format, and it isn't widely supported by Web browsers yet, but it may become more popular in the near future. PNG supports 24-bit color images, it has an interlacing option, and it offers even more impressive compression than the present JPEG format. PNG also supports alpha channels of 256 levels of gray that can be used to define areas of transparency. With 256 levels of masking gray, you can create a very soft fade to transparency, so you'll be able to display soft shadows and glowing shapes on the Web.

To save an image in PNG format:

1. In Photoshop, choose File menu > Save a Copy (Control-Alt-S).

2. Choose a location in which to save the file, enter a name for the file, then choose PNG in the Save As box.

3. Click Save.

4. Choose Interlace: None or Adam7 1.

5. Choose a filter option for the method by which the file will be compressed. (See the Adobe Photoshop User Guide for information on filter options.)

6. Click OK.

Dithering about

Dithering is a technique in which pixels from two palette colors are intermixed to give the impression of a third color, and it's used to make images that contain a limited number of colors (256 or fewer) appear to have a greater range of colors and shades. Dithering is usually applied to continuous-tone images to increase their tonal range, but—argh, life is full of compromises—it can make them look a little dotty.

Dithering usually doesn't produce aesthetically pleasing results in flat color graphics, so these kinds of images usually aren't dithered. The browser palette will dither pixels to create the required color, however, if the palette doesn't contain a color used in the flat graphic. It's best to work with colors from the Web palette loaded into the Swatches palette for those types of images.

Continuous-tone imagery is, in a way, already dithered. Some continuous-tone imagery looks fine on a Web page with no dithering and 256 colors. The fewer the colors the palette of a non-dithered continuous-tone image contains, the more banding will occur in its color transitions; if dithering is turned on, the more dithering you'll see. You can decide which lesser of these two evils your own eye prefers.

One more consideration: Dithering adds noise to the file, so compression with dithering on is not as effective as when dithering is off. So, with dithering on, you may not be able to achieve your desired degree of file compression. As is the case with most Web output, you'll have to strike a balance between aesthetics and file size.

Dithering

In Photoshop, you can access a dithering option when you convert an image to Indexed Color mode. You can't control dithering with the GIF89a Export option; this command dithers an image automatically.

On the fringe: to alias or anti-alias

To make an object anti-aliased, pixels are added along its edge with progressively less opacity to smooth the transition between the object and its background. An object with an aliased edge is sharp, and has no extra pixels along its edge.

When images are composited in Photoshop, anti-aliasing produces smooth transitions between existing shapes and added shapes. Along the edge of a selection created using a tool with an anti-aliased edge, though, there may be a leftover fringe from the color of the former surrounding pixels. If you copy and paste this type of shape onto a flat color background, the fringe may become evident, and it can look mighty peculiar. To eliminate the fringe, before you create your selection, uncheck the Anti-aliased box on the Options palette for the Marquee or Lasso tool. You'll create a hard-edged selection, with no extra pixels along its edge.

To select imagery on its own layer with out selecting semi-transparent pixels on its anti-aliased edge, Control-click the layer name. You'll get a tighter selection this way than you would get using the Magic Wand tool.

When you're initially selecting a shape on a flat color background (all on one layer), use the Magic Wand tool with a low Tolerance setting (1-5). Click on the flat background with Anti-aliased unchecked, zoom in (400-500%) to see the edge of the shape, then choose Select menu > Inverse to select the shape (not its background). At this point, if the edge of the selection created using the Control-click or Magic Wand method still includes too many soft-edged pixels, choose, Select menu > Modify > Contract, and enter a 1 or 2 pixel value for the amount by which the selection edge will shrink inward. Reapply the command until the soft edge is eliminated.

With the GIF89a Export's ability to export a shape on its own layer with a transparent background, the fringe problem is diminished, provided a careful selection was made on the shape initially. If you still detect a fringe edge using the GIF preview, click Cancel, activate the shape's layer, then apply the Layer menu > Matting > Defringe command using a value of 1 or 2 pixels.

In Photoshop, you can produce a tile that can then be used to produce a seamless, repetitive, background pattern on a Web page using HTML code. These instructions get the longest-set-of-instructions-in-the-book award.

To create an almost seamless tile for a repetitive pattern:

1. Create a new 3 x 3 inch document, 72ppi, RGB Color mode, Contents: White.

2. Alt-click the Create New Layer button at the bottom of the Layers palette to create a New layer, and name it "Frame."

3. Choose a Foreground Color.

4. Using the Rectangular Marquee tool, Shift-drag a square selection near the center of the layer.

5. Choose Edit menu > Stroke.

6. Enter Width: 1 pixel, choose Location: Center, then click OK.

7. Choose Select menu > None.

8. Create another new layer, and name it "Design."

9. Draw the pattern. Hard-edge lines will be easiest to work with. Try not to cross more than two edges at a time as you draw.

Anti-Aliasing; Tile Pattern

To *copy the edges of the design:*

1. Make sure the Design layer is active .

2. Choose the Rectangular Marquee tool, Style: Normal.

3. Drag a vertical selection adjacent to and just touching the left edge of the frame, if there are any strokes that extend beyond that edge **2**.

4. Choose Edit menu > Copy.

5. Choose Edit menu > Paste.

6. If necessary, choose the Move tool, then press the up or down arrow to align the new pasted layer strokes with the strokes on the Design layer. Zoom in, if you need to.

7. Repeat steps 1–6 for all edges with strokes that cross them **3**.

To *move the new edge layers over the opposite edge of the design:*

1. Choose the Move tool.

2. Activate an edge layer that resulted from pasting.

3. Shift-drag the layer to position the strokes from one edge across to the opposite edge of the design, stopping so the strokes extend slightly beyond the edge of the frame **4**. Repeat this step for each pasted edge layer.

4. Choose the Magic Wand tool, and choose a Tolerance of 2 on the Magic Wand Options palette.

5. Activate the Frame layer.

6. Click within the Frame shape. The inner part should now be selected.

7. Choose Edit menu > Copy Merged to copy pixels from the visible layers.

8. Choose Edit menu > Paste. The new layer will be positioned above the Frame layer.

9. Activate the Frame layer.

10. Choose the Magic Wand tool.

11. Click again within the Frame shape.

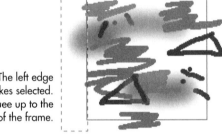

1 The original design pattern with the Frame layer visible.

2 The left edge strokes selected. Marquee up to the edge of the frame.

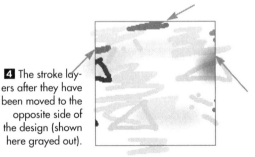

3 The right edge strokes selected. Marquee up to the edge of the frame.

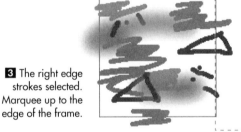

4 The stroke layers after they have been moved to the opposite side of the design (shown here grayed out).

Tile Pattern

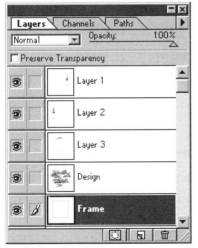 The Frame layer selected with the Copy Merged/Paste layer visible.

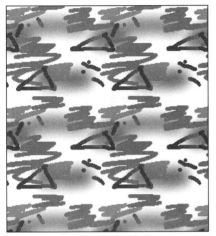

 A new document filled with the pattern.

12. Hide the Design layer and all the edge layers to prevent soft, semi-transparent strokes from combining with their duplicates on the Copy Merged/Paste layer .

13. Choose Edit menu > Define Pattern.

14. Choose Select menu > None.

15. Create a new file whose Width and Height are much larger than the tile document, 72 ppi, RGB mode, Contents: White.

16. Choose Edit menu > Fill.

17. Choose Use: Pattern, 100% opacity, Normal mode.

18. Click OK. The new image will be filled with your pattern tile . If there are any noticeable seams, reopen the tile design file, delete the layer that contains the Copy Merged/Paste view of the design (above the Frame layer), and then reposition the edge layer. Repeat steps 5–18 starting on the previous page.

The Layers palette showing the layers used to produce the pattern fill.

Using layers for Web design

Since you can use Photoshop to create both imagery and special display text effects, it's a good application for designing Web pages. You can use Photoshop's Layers palette to preview and compose the elements of your Web page design. Create separate layers for such items as a particular background color, a tiled pattern, or imagery. And create aliased or anti-aliased headline text in Photoshop, and enhance it in various ways: Add a shadow, distortion, a glow, texture, or fill it with imagery. Photoshop text is rasterized, so, unlike PostScript text, you don't need to worry about whether the desired fonts are installed in the viewer's system. With elements on separate layers, you can restack, reposition, scale down, color adjust (for a screened back effect, for example), or show/hide different elements of the Web page. You can even save different versions of the page and decide later which design to use.

In a layered document, the Copy Merged command will allow you to copy a selection that includes pixels from all visible layers that fall within the selection area. This is a great way to create a "flattened" area of an image. Create a new document, then paste. That flattened area will be on its own new layer. You can duplicate layers to try out different design ideas on the same image, then show/hide individual layers to judge the duplicates.

You can duplicate a layer several times and move the layer imagery to try out an animation sequence (show/hide consecutive layers). Or apply a filter at progressively higher values to preview a filter transition.

When the design is finalized, save the layered version for any future revisions. You can copy-and-paste or drag-and-drop imagery on different layers into a final output document, or duplicate a layer into its own document using the Duplicate Layer command (choose New as the Destination document).

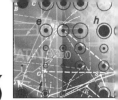

APPENDIX A: KEYBOARD SHORTCUTS

File menu

New...	Control N
Open...	Control O
Close...	Control W
Save	Control S
Save as...	Control Shift S
Save a Copy...	Control Alt S
Page Setup...	Control Shift P
Print...	Control P
Preferences > General...	Control K
Load in last Preferences settings	Alt choose File menu > Preferences > General
Quit	Control Q

Edit menu

Undo	Control Z

The Clipboard

Cut	Control X *or* F2
Copy	Control C *or* F3
Copy Merged	Control Shift C
Paste	Control V *or* F4
Paste Into	Control Shift V
Fill...	Shift-Backspace

Image menu

Adjust commands

Levels...	Control L
Auto Levels	Control Shift L
Curves...	Control M
Color Balance...	Control B
Hue/Saturation...	Control U
Desaturate	Control Shift U
Invert	Control I
Display last dialog box settings	Alt choose command
Make Curves grid larger/smaller	Alt click on grid

Layer menu

New > Layer via Copy	Control J
New > Layer via Cut	Control Shift J
Group with Previous	Control G
Ungroup	Control Shift G
Free Transform	Control T
Transform > Numeric...	Control Shift T
Arrange > Bring to Front	Control Shift]
Bring Forward	Control]
Send Backward	Control [
Send to Back	Control Shift [
Merge Down	Control E
Merge Visible	Control Shift E

Select menu

All	Control A
None	Control D
Inverse	Control Shift I
Feather	Control Shift D

Filter menu

Reapply last filter chosen	Control F
Open last Filter dialog box	Control Alt F
Fade... (last Filter or Image menu > Adjust command)	Control Shift F
Cancel a filter while a Progress dialog box is displayed	Control . (period) *or* Esc

View menu

CMYK Preview	Control Y
Gamut Warning	Control Shift Y
Zoom In	Control +
Zoom Out	Control -
Fit on Screen	Control 0 *or* double-click Hand tool
Actual Pixels	Control Alt 0 *or* double-click Zoom tool
Show/Hide Edges	Control H
Show/Hide Path	Control Shift H
Show/Hide Rulers	Control R
Show/Hide Guides	Control ;

Snap to Guides	Control Shift ;
Lock Guides	Control Alt ;
Show/Hide Grid	Control "
Snap to Grid	Control Shift "

Display sizes

Enlarge display size	Control Space bar click (works with some dialog boxes open)
Reduce display size	Alt Space bar click (works with some dialog boxes open)
Magnify selected area	Drag with Zoom tool
Zoom in (window size unchanged)	Control Alt +
Zoom out (window size unchanged)	Control Alt -

Toolbox

Show/Hide Toolbox and palettes	Tab
Show/Hide palettes but not Toolbox	Shift Tab
Open tool Options palette	Double-click any tool other than Type, Hand, or Zoom

Hand tool

Temporary Hand tool with any other tool selected	Space bar

Eyedropper tool

Select color for the non-highlighted color square (Color palette)	Alt click color
Temporary Eyedropper tool with Paint Bucket, Gradient, Line, Pencil, Airbrush, or Paintbrush tool selected	Alt

Eraser tool

Magic eraser, restores last saved version	Alt drag
Constrain eraser to 90° angle	Shift drag

Gradient Editor

Create New gradient	Control N
Select first or next gradient color marker to the right	Tab
Select last or next gradient color marker to the left	Shift Tab
Save only selected gradient as a file	Control Shift click Save button

Save selected gradient as a Curves map file	Control Alt click Save button

Line tool

Constrain to 45° or 90° angle	Shift drag

Paintbrush, Pencil, Airbrush, Rubber Stamp, Smudge tool

Constrain to 90° angle	Shift drag
Precise crosshair cursor for brushes	Caps Lock

Pen tool

Add anchor point with Direct Selection tool highlighted	Control Alt click line segment
Delete anchor point with Direct Selection tool highlighted	Control Alt click anchor point
Constrain straight line segment or anchor point to 45° angle	Shift drag
Delete last created anchor point	Backspace
Erase path being drawn	Backspace Backspace
Temporary Direct Selection tool with any Pen tool selected	Control
Temporary Convert Anchor Point tool with the Path Select tool	Control
Select whole path (Direct Selection tool)	Alt click path
Switch between Add Anchor Point and Delete Anchor Point tools	Alt (over a point)
Temporary Add or Delete Anchor tool (Pen tool selected) or (Direct Selection tool selected)	Control Alt (over point or segment)
Fill selection with Background color	Control Backspace
Fill selection with Background color and Preserve transparency	Control Alt Backspace

Sharpen/Blur tool

Switch between Sharpen and Blur	Alt drag picture *or* Alt click Sharpen/Blur tool on Toolbox

Smudge tool

Temporary Finger Painting tool	Alt drag

Selection tools

Add to a selection	Shift drag
Subtract from a selection	Alt drag

Intersect a selection	Alt Shift drag
Constrain marquee to square or circle	Drag and press Shift
Draw marquee from center	Drag and press Alt
Move marquee (Marquee tool selected)	Drag marquee
Move marquee in 1-pixel increments	Arrow keys
Move marquee in 10-pixel increments	Shift and Arrow keys
Float selection pixels (Move tool selected)	Control drag selection
Copy (float) selection pixels	Alt drag selection
Drop a floating selection	Control E
Float selection in same position	Control Alt up arrow, then down arrow
Fill selection with Foreground color	Alt Backspace
Fill selection with Foreground color and Preserve transparency	Control Alt Backspace
Switch Masked Areas/Selected Areas (Quick Mask mode)	Alt click Quick Mask icon on Toolbox

Rectangular Marquee and Elliptical Marquee tools

Draw selection from center	Drag and press Alt
Square or circlular selection	Drag and press Shift

Magic Wand tool

Add to a selection	Shift click
Subtract from a selection	Alt click

Lasso tool

Create straight side in a selection	Alt click

Polygon Lasso tool

Create curved side in a straight-sided selection	Alt drag
Constrain to 45°	Shift click

Dialog boxes

Restore original settings	Hold down Alt, click Reset
Delete to the right of the cursor	del
Highlight next field	Tab
Highlight previous field	Shift Tab
Increase/decrease number in highlighted field by 1 unit	Up or down arrow

Increase/decrease number in highlighted field by 10 units	Shift and Up or down arrow
Cancel out of dialog box	Esc

Palettes

Hide/Show Brushes	F5
Show/Hide Picker	F6
Show/Hide Layers	F7
Show/Hide Info	F8
Show/Hide Actions	F9
Shrink palette to a bar	Double-click palette tab *or* Alt click palette zoom box

With any painting or editing tool selected

Move tool	Control
Opacity percentage (Options palette)	Keypad key 0=100%, 1=10%, 2=20%, etc. *or* type two numbers quickly, 41=41%, etc.

Layers, Channels, and Paths

Load a layer, channel, or path as a selection	Control click layer, channel, or path name
Add to current selection	Control Shift click layer channel, or path name
Subtract from current selection	Control Alt click layer, channel, or path name
Intersect current selection	Control Alt Shift click layer, channel, or path name
Delect selected layer, channel, or path	Alt click palette Trash icon
Create new layer, channel, or path and set options	Alt click New [ ] button

Channels palette

RGB Channels

RGB	Control ~
Red	Control 1
Green	Control 2
Blue	Control 3

CMYK Channels

CMYK	Control ~
Cyan	Control 1
Magenta	Control 2

Yellow	Control 3
Black	Control 4

Layers palette

Select/deselect Preserve Transparency option on Layers palette	press /
Select a layer via a pop-up menu in image window (Move tool selected) *or* (any other tool selected)	Control press, choose layer from pop-up menu
Select a layer from the image window (Move tool selected)	Control press object in image
Hide/show all other layers	Alt click layer eye icon
Add new adjustment layer	Control click Create New Layer button
Add new layer mask, but invert mask effect	Alt click Create Layer Mask button
Switch between layer mask view and composite view	Alt click Layer mask thumbnail
Temporarily turn off layer mask effect	Shift click Layer mask thumbnail
Create a clipping group	Alt click line between layers
Merge down a copy of the selected layer	Alt choose Merge Down command
Merge copies of all visible layers into bottommost visible layer	Alt choose Merge Visible command
Merge copies of all linked layers into selected layer	Alt choose Merge Linked command

Channels palette

Open Load Selection dialog box	Alt click Load Channel as Selection button
Open Channel Options dialog box	Alt click Save Selection as Channel button
Switch display between alpha channel and composite (topmost) channel	Shift click alpha channel
Deselect a particular color channel	Shift click a color channel

Swatches palette

Delete a swatch	Control click swatch
Replace swatch with new color swatch	Shift click swatch to be replaced

Insert new swatch between two swatches	Alt Shift click swatch
Select for Background color (Toolbox)	Alt click a swatch

Navigator palette

Zoom in to specific location	Control drag in preview box
Enter a view %, keep text field highlighted	Shift Enter

Actions palette

Turn on current command and turn off all other commands	Alt click check mark
Turn on current command's break point & turn off all other breakpoints	Alt click break point
Start recording an action without opening the New Action dialog box	Alt click Create New Action button
Play an action from a selected command forward to end	Control click Play button
Play an entire action	Control double-click action name

Paths palette

Open Fill Path dialog box	Alt click Fill Path button
Open Stroke Path dialog box	Alt click Stroke Path button
Open Make Selection dialog box	Alt click Load Path as Selection button
Open Make Work Path dialog box	Alt click Make Work Path from Selection button

Brushes palette

Delete selected tip	Control click tip
Select previous tip (Painting tool selected)	press [
Select next tip (Painting tool selected)	press]
Select first tip/last tip (Painting tool selected)	press Shift [or press Shift]

Color palette

Color bar

Choose color for non-highlighted square	Alt click Color bar
Display Color Bar dialog box	Control click Color bar
Cycle through Color bar styles	Shift click Color bar

Free Transform

Move bounding border	Drag inside border
Rotate bounding border	Drag outside border
Scale bounding border	Drag handle
Scale proportionally	Hold Shift and drag handle
Skew bounding border	Control Shift drag handle
Distort bounding border	Control drag handle
Create Perspective effect	Control Alt Shift drag handle
Perform symmetrical transformation	Hold Alt with other shortcuts above
Apply transformation to selected pixels	Press Enter *or* double-click inside border
Cancel transformation in progress	Esc
Undo the last step in transformation	Control Z

Context-sensitive menus

Display context-sensitive menus	Right click on image (any tool selected) *or* Right click on some palette icons for options

Tools

Airbrush	A
Blur/Sharpen	R
Crop	C
Default colors	D
Dodge/Burn/Sponge	O
Elliptical/Rectangular Marquee	M
Eraser	E
Eyedropper	I
Gradient	G
Hand	H
Lasso/Polygon Lasso	L
Line	N
Magic Wand	W
Move	V
Paintbrush	B
Paint Bucket	K
Pen/Direct selection/Add-anchor-point/ Delete-anchor-point/ Convert-anchor-point	P

Pencil	Y
Rubber Stamp	S
Smudge	U
Standard mode/Quick Mask mode	Q
Standard windows/Full screen with menu bar/Full screen with no menu bar	F
Switch foreground/ background colors	X
Type/Type Mask	T
Zoom	Z

Default F key assignments

Cut	F2
Copy	F3
Paste	F4
Hide/show Brushes palette	F5
Hide/show Picker palette	F6
Hide/show Layers palette	F7
Hide/show Info palette	F8
Hide/show Actions palette	F9
Revert	F12
Fill	Shift F5
Feather	Shift F6
Select menu > Inverse	Shift F7

Miscellaneous

| Update font list after opening suitcase | Shift click on image with Type tool |

Print preview box

| Picture information | Alt press on Sizes bar |

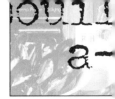

Alpha channel

A special 8-bit grayscale channel that is used for saving a selection.

Anti-alias

The blending of pixel colors on the perimeter of hard-edged shapes, like type, to smoooth undesirable stair-stepping (jaggies).

ASCII

(American Standard Code for Information Interchange) A standard editable format for encoding data.

Background color

The color applied when the Eraser tool is used, the canvas size is enlarged, or a selection is moved on the Background of an image.

Bézier curve

A curved line segment drawn using the Pen tool. It consists of anchor points with direction lines with which the curve can be reshaped.

Binary

In Photoshop, a method for encoding data. Binary encoding is more compact than ASCII encoding.

Bit

(Binary digit) The smallest unit of information on a computer. Eight bits equal one byte. (see Byte)

Bit depth

The number of bits used to store a pixel's color information on a computer monitor.

Bitmap

The display of an image on a computer screen via the geometric mapping of a single layer of pixels on a rectangular grid. In Photoshop, Bitmap is also a one-channel mode consisting of black and white pixels.

Blend (see Gradient)

Brightness (see Lightness)

Burn

To darken an area of an image.

Byte

The basic unit of storage memory. One byte equals eight bits. One kilobyte (K, Kb) equals 1,024 bytes. One megabyte (M, MB) equals 1,024 kilobytes. One gigabyte (G, Gb) equals 1,024 megabytes.

Canvas size

The size of an image, including a border, if any, around it.

Channel

An image component that contains the pixel information for an individual color. A grayscale image contains one channel, an RGB image contains three channels, and a CMYK image contains four channels.

Clipboard

An area of memory used to temporarily store selection pixels. The Clipboard is accessed via the Cut, Copy, and Paste commands.

Clipping

In Photoshop, the automatic adjustment of colors to bring them into printable gamut.

Clone

To copy image areas using the Rubber Stamp tool.

CMYK

(Cyan, Magenta, Yellow, and Black) The four ink colors used in process printing. Cyan, magenta, and yellow are the three subtractive primaries. When combined in their purest form, they theoretically produce black, but in actuality, they produce a dark muddy color. CMYK colors are simulated on a computer monitor using additive, red, green, and blue light. To color separate an image from Photoshop, convert it to CMYK Color mode.

Color correction

The adjustment of color in an image to match original artwork or a photograph. Color correction is usually done in CMYK Color mode in preparation for process printing.

Color separation

The production of a separate sheet of film for each ink color that will be used to print an image. Four plates are used in process color separation, one each for Cyan, Magenta, Yellow, and Black.

Color table

The color palette of up to 256 colors of an image in Indexed Color mode.

Continuous-tone image

An image, like a photograph, in which there are smooth gradations between shades or colors.

Contrast

The degree of difference between lights and darks in an image. A high contrast image is comprised of only very light and very dark pixels.

Crop

To trim away part of an image.

Crop marks

Short, fine lines placed around the edges of a page to designate where the paper is to be trimmed at a print shop.

DCS

(Desktop Color Separation) A file format in which a color image is broken down into five PostScript files: Cyan, Magenta, Yellow and Black for high resolution printing, and an optional low resolution file for previewing and laser printing.

Digitize

To translate flat art or a transparency into computer-readable numbers using a scanning device and scanning software.

Dimensions

The width and height of an image.

Dither

The mixing of adjacent pixels to simulate additional colors when available colors are limited, such as on an 8-bit monitor.

Dodge

To bleach (lighten) an area of an image. Also, a so-so car model.

Dot gain

The undesirable spreading and enlarging of ink dots on paper.

Dpi

(Dots Per Inch) A unit used to measure the resolution of a printer. Dpi is sometimes used to describe the input resolution of a scanner, but "ppi" is the more accurate term.

Duotone

A grayscale image printed using two plates for added tonal depth. A tritone is printed using three plates. A quadtone is printed using four plates.

Dye sublimation

A continuous-tone printing process in which a solid printing medium is converted into a gas before it hits the paper.

8-bit monitor

A monitor in which each pixel stores eight bits of information and represents one of only 256 available colors. Dithering is used to simulate additional colors.

EPS

(Encapsulated PostScript) An image file format containing PostScript code and, in the case of Photoshop, an optional PICT or TIFF image for screen display. EPS is a commonly used format for moving files from one application to another and for imagesetting and color separating.

Equalize

To balance an image's lights and darks.

Feather

To fade the edge of a selection or mask a specified number of pixels (the feather radius).

Fill

To fill a selection with a shade, color, pattern, or blend.

Film negative

A film rendition of an image in which dark and light areas are reversed.

Floating selection

An area of an image that is surrounded by a marquee and can be moved or modified without affecting underlying pixels.

Font

A typeface in a distinctive style, such as Futura Bold Italic.

Foreground color

The color applied when a painting tool is used or type is created.

Gradient fill

In Photoshop, a graduated blend between colors that is produced by the Gradient tool.

Grayscale

An image containing black, white, and up to 256 shades of gray, but no color. In Photoshop, Grayscale is a one-channel image mode.

Halftone screen

A pattern of tiny dots that is used for printing an image to simulate smooth tones.

Highlights

The lightest areas of an image.

Histogram

A graph showing the distribution of an image's color and/or luminosity values.

HSB

See Hue, Saturation, and Brightness.

Hue

The wavelength of light of a pure color that gives a color its name—such as red or blue—independent of its saturation or brightness.

Imagesetter

A high-resolution printer (usually 1,270 or 2,540 dpi) that generates paper or film output from a computer file.

Indexed color

In Photoshop, an image mode in which there is only one channel and a color table containing up to 256 colors. All the colors of an Indexed Color image are displayed on its Colors palette.

Interpolation

The recoloring of pixels as a result of changing an image's dimensions or resolution. Interpolation may cause an image to look blurry when printed. You can choose an interpolation method (Bicubic or Nearest Neighbor) in Photoshop.

Inverse

To switch the selected and non-selected areas of an image.

Invert

To reverse an image's light and dark values and/or colors.

JPEG compression

(Joint Photographic Experts Group) A compression feature in Photoshop that is used to reduce a file's storage size. JPEG can cause some image degradation.

Kern

To adjust the horizontal spacing between a pair of characters.

Lab

A mode in which colors are related to the CIE color reference system. In Photoshop, an image in Lab Color mode is composed of three channels, one for lightness, one for green-to-red colors, and one blue-to-yellow colors.

Leading

The space between lines of type, measured from baseline to baseline. In Photoshop, leading can be measured in points or pixels.

Lightness

(Brightness) The lightness of a color independent of its hue and saturation.

LPI

(Lines Per Inch, halftone frequency, screen frequency) The unit used to measure the frequency of rows of dots on a halftone screen.

Luminosity

The distribution of an image's light and dark values.

Marquee

The moving border that defines a selection.

Mask

An "electronic" paint that protects an area of an image from modification.

Midtones

The shades in an image that are midway between the highlights and shadows.

Mode

A method for specifying how color information is to be interpreted. An image can be converted to a different image mode (RGB to Indexed Color, for example); a blending mode can be chosen for a painting or editing tool.

Moiré

An undesirable pattern that is caused by improper halftone screen angles during printing or when the pattern in an image conflicts with proper halftone patterns.

Object-oriented

(also known as vector) A software method used for describing and processing computer files. Object-oriented graphics and PostScript type are defined by mathematics and geometry. Bitmapped graphics are defined by pixels on a rectangular grid. Photoshop images are bitmapped.

Opacity

The density of a color or shade, ranging from transparent to opaque. In Photoshop, you can choose an opacity for a painting or editing tool or a layer.

Path

A shape that is comprised of straight and/or curved segments joined by anchor points.

PICT

A Macintosh file format that is used to display and save images. Save a Photoshop image as a PICT to open it in a video or animation program. The PICT format is not use for color separations.

Pixels

(Image elements) The individual dots that are used to display an image on a computer monitor.

PPI

(Pixels per inch) The unit used to measure the resolution of a scan or of a Photoshop image.

Plug-in module

Third-party software that is loaded into the Photoshop Plug-ins folder so it can be accessed from a Photoshop menu. Or, a plug-in module that comes with Photoshop that is used to facilitate Import, Export, or file format conversion operations.

Point

A unit of measure used to describe type size (measured from ascender to descender), leading (measured from baseline to baseline), and line width.

Polygon

A closed shape composed of three or more straight sides.

Posterize

Produce a special effect in an image by reducing the number of shades of gray or colors to a specified—usually low—number.

PostScript

The page description language created and licensed by Adobe Systems Incorporated that is used for displaying and printing fonts and images.

Process color

Ink that is printed from four separate plates, one each for Cyan (C), Magenta (M), Yellow (Y), and Black (K), and which in combination produce a wide range of colors.

Quick Mask

In Photoshop, a screen display mode in which a translucent colored mask covers selected or unselected areas of an image. Painting tools can be used to reshape a Quick Mask.

RAM

(Random Access Memory) The system memory of a computer that is used for running an application, processing information, and temporary storage.

Rasterize

The conversion of an object-oriented image into a bitmapped image. When an Adobe Illustrator graphic is placed into Photoshop, for example, it is rasterized. All computer files are rasterized when they're printed.

Registration marks

Crosshair marks placed around the edges of a page that are used to align printing plates.

Resample

Change an image's resolution while keeping its pixels dimensions constant.

Resolution

The fineness of detail of a digital image (measured in pixels per inch), a monitor (measured in pixels per inch—usually 72 ppi), a printer (measured in dots per inch), or a halftone screen (measured in lines per inch).

RGB

Color used to produce transmitted light. When pure Red, Green, and Blue light (the additive primaries) are combined, as on a computer monitor, white is produced. In Photoshop, RGB Color is a three-channel image mode.

Saturation

The purity of a color. The more gray a color contains, the lower its saturation.

Scan

To digitize a slide, photograph or other artwork using a scanner and scanning software so it can be displayed, edited, and possibly output from, a computer.

Scratch disk

(also known as virtual memory) Hard drive storage space that is designated as work space for processing operations and for temporarily storing part of an image and a backup version of the image when there is insufficient RAM for those functions.

Screen angles

Angles used for positioning halftone screens when producing film to minimize undesirable dot patterns (moirés).

Screen frequency

(screen ruling) The resolution (density of dots) on a halftone screen, measured in lines per inch.

Selection

An area of an image that is isolated so it can be modified while the rest of the image is protected. A moving marquee, which denotes the boundary of a selection, can be moved independently of its contents.

Shadows

The darkest areas of an image.

Spot color

A mixed ink color used in printing. A separate plate is used to print each spot color. Pantone is a commonly used spot color matching system. (see Process color) Photoshop doesn't generate spot color plates.

Thermal wax

A color printing process in which a sequence of three to four ink sheets are used to place colored dots on special paper.

TIFF

(Tagged Image File Format) A common file format that is used for saving bitmapped images, such as scans. TIFF images can be color separated.

Tolerance

The range of pixels within which a tool operates, like the range of shades or colors the Magic Wand tool selects or the Paint Bucket tool fills.

Trap

The overlapping of adjacent colors to prevent undesirable gaps from occuring as a result of the misalignment of printing plates or paper.

24-bit monitor

A monitor with a video card in which each pixel can store up to 24 bits of information. The video card contains three color tables for displaying an RGB image, one each for Red, Green, and Blue, and each containing 256 colors. Together they can produce 16.7 million colors. On a 24-bit monitor, smooth blends can be displayed, so dithering isn't necessary.

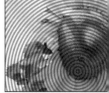

Ten questions and answers about copyright

Written by Tad Crawford

Why is copyright important?

If you are a creator of images (whether Photoshop user, photographer, designer, or fine artist), copyright protects you from having your images stolen by someone else. As the copyright owner, you may either allow or prevent anyone else from making copies of your work, making derivations from your work (such as a poster made from a photograph), or displaying your work publicly. Your copyrights last for your lifetime plus another fifty years, so a successful work may benefit not only you but your heirs as well. If you are a user of images, it is important that you understand the rights and obligations connected with their use so you don't infringe on the copyright of someone else and expose yourself to legal or financial liabilities.

What is an infringement?

Infringement is unauthorized use of someone else's work. The test for infringement is whether an ordinary observer would believe one work was copied from another.

Is it an infringement if I scan an old image into Photoshop and change it?

If the image was created in the United States and is more than 75 years old, it is in the public domain and can be freely copied by you or anyone else. You will have copyright in the new elements of the image that you create.

Is it an infringement if I scan a recent photograph into Photoshop and change it?

The scanning itself is making a copy and so is an infringement. As a practical matter, however, it is unlikely you will be sued for infringement if you change the photograph to the point where an ordinary observer would no longer believe your work was copied from the original photograph.

What does "fair use" mean in terms of copyright?

A fair use is a use of someone else's work that is allowed under the copyright law. For example, newsworthy or educational uses are likely to be fair uses. The factors for whether a use is a fair use or an infringement are: (1) the purpose and character of the use, including whether or not it is for profit (2) the character of the copyrighted work (3) how much of the total work is used and (4) what effect the use will have on the market for or value of the work being copied.

Can I use a recognizable part of a photograph if the entire source photograph is not recognizable?

You would have to apply the fair use factors. Obviously, factor (3) in the previous answer relating to how much of the total work is used would be in your favor, but if the use is to make a profit and will damage the market for the source photograph it might be considered an infringement.

What are the damages for infringement?

The damages are the actual losses of the person infringed plus any profits of the infringer. In some cases (especially if the work was registered before the infringement), the court can simply award between $500 and $20,000 for each work infringed. If the infringement is willful, the court can award as much as $100,000.

Do I have to register my images to obtain my copyright?

No, you have the copyright from the moment you create a work. However, registration with the Copyright Office costs $20 and will help you in the event your work is infringed. To obtain Copyright Application Form VA (for Visual Arts), write to the Copyright Office, Library of Congress, Washington, D.C. 20559 or call (202) 707-9100. Ask for the free Copyright Information Kit for the visual arts and you will receive many helpful circulars developed by the Copyright Office.

Do I need to use copyright notice to obtain or protect my copyright?

It is always wise to place copyright notice on your work, because it is a visible symbol of your rights as copyright owner. Prior to 1989 the absence of copyright notice when the images were published or publicly distributed could, in certain circumstances, cause the loss of the copyright. Since March 1, 1989, the absence of copyright notice cannot cause the loss of the copyright but may give infringers a loophole to try and lessen their damages. Copyright notice has three elements: (1) "Copyright" or "Copr" or "©" (2) your name and (3) the year of first publication.

How do I get permission to reproduce an image?

A simple permission form will suffice. It should set forth what kind of project you are doing, what materials you want to use, what rights you need in the material, what credit line and copyright notice will be given, and what payment, if any, will be made. The person giving permission should sign the permission form. If you are using an image of a person for purposes of advertising or trade, you should have them sign a model release. If the person's image is to be altered or placed in a situation that didn't occur, you would want the release to cover this. Otherwise you may face a libel or invasion of privacy lawsuit.

Digital watermarking

The Embed Digimarc filter embeds nearly invisible copyright information and a contact address into a Photoshop image. The watermark can't easily be removed by reworking the image in Photoshop, it will be present in any copy or any printout of the image, and it will even be retained if the printed piece is redigitized by scanning, so your image will always retain its original copyright.

NOTE: To install the Detect Watermark filter, copy it from the Application CD-ROM (from the Goodies > Optional Plugins > Digimarc/Detect Watermark folder) to the Photoshop Plug-ins folder.

To create a valid copyright, you must register with and pay a fee to Digimarc Corporation. They will enter your personal information into their database and issue you a unique creator ID, so your watermark will contain your personal contact and copyright information.

To embed a watermark:

1. Open a flattened version of the image to be watermarked.

2. Choose Filter > Digimarc > Embed Watermark.

3. If you don't yet have a personal Creator ID, click Personalize **1**, then click Register to connect to the Digimarc Web site or phone Digimarc at the number listed in the dialog box.

4. Enter your Creator ID number **2**, then click OK.

5. Choose Type of Use: Restricted for limited use, or Royalty Free for unlimited use.

6. *Optional:* Check the Adult Content box (this option is not yet available).

7. Enter a Watermark Durability value, or move the slider. Enter 1 or 2 to create a nearly invisible mark that work best

(Continued on the following page)

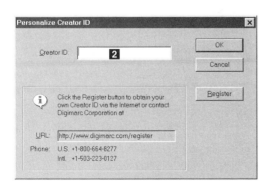

with high-end printing. Enter 3 or 4 for a more visible mark that is more suitable for multimedia or online formats, where you might need to convert the image to various bit depths. Keep in mind that a watermark with a low Durability value might be ruined by image editing.

8. Click OK.

The Digimarc filter must be available to view a watermark symbol already embedded in an image. The title bar of an image that contains a watermark will display a copyright symbol ©.

To read information about a watermark:

1. With the image containing the watermark open, choose Filter > Digimarc > Read Watermark. A dialog box displaying Creator ID and other information will open.

2. *Optional:* If you want to have information faxed back to you, dial the phone number listed in the Watermark Information dialog box.

or

If you're currently hooked up to the Web via a browser, click Web Lookup to open the browser, then navigate to the Digimarc Web site, where you'll see the creator information.

3. Click OK to close the Watermark Information dialog box.

Digital Watermark

APPENDIX D: DIRECTORY OF ARTISTS

Alicia Buelow
336 Arkansas St.
San Francisco, CA 94107
415-642-8083
e-mail: buelow@adobe.com

Jeff Brice
2416 NW 60th Street
Seattle, WA 98107
206-706-0406
e-mail: cyspy@aol.com

Diane Fenster
287 Reichling Ave.
Pacifica, CA 94044
415-355-5007
e-mail: fenster@sfsu.edu
http://www.sirius.com/~fenster

Louis Fishauf
Creative Director
Reactor Art + Design Limited
51 Camden Street
Toronto, Ontario
Canada M5V1V2
416-703-1913 x241
e-mail: fishauf@reactor.ca
http://www.magic.ca/~fishauf/
http://www.reactor.ca

Wendy Grossman
355 West 51st Street
New York, NY 10019
212-262-4497
http://www.renard
represents.com
(pages 41, 132, and color section)

John Hersey
546 Magnolia Avenue
Larkspur, CA 94939
Voice 415-927-2091
Fax 415-927-2092
http://www.hersey.com
e-mail: ultraduc@hersey.com

David Humphrey
439 Lafayette Street
New York, NY 10003
212-780-0512
e-mail: humphrey@is2.nyu.edu
(page 81)

Liana Levin
105-40 63rd Avenue
Forest Hills, NY 11375
718-459-7313
(pages 265, 266)

Min Wang
795 Coastland Drive
Palo Alto, CA 94303
Voice 415-321-4294
Fax 415-321-6246
e-mail: mwang@adobe.com

Annette Weintraub
Professor
Department of Art
City College of New York
138th St. and Convent Avenue
New York, NY 10031
Voice 212-650-7410
Fax 212-650-7438
e-mail: anwcc@cunyvm.cuny.edu
http://www.artnetweb.com/art-
netweb/projects/realms/notes.html

Seasonal Specialties
Jennifer Sheeler, Creative Director
Barbara Roth, Art Director
Lisa Milan, Senior Designer (1997
    catalog)
Seasonal Specialties LLC (@1996
All Rights Reserved)
11455 Valley View Road
Eden Prairie, MN 55344
Voice 612-942-6555
Fax 612-942-1801
jen.sheeler@seasonalspecialties.com
barb.roth@seasonalspecialties.com
lisa.milan@seasonalspecialties.com

Directory of Artists

Lifeline, ©1996 Annette Weintraub

Thank you

Trish Booth, Roslyn Bullas, Corbin Collins, Hannah Onstad, Mimi Heft, Nolan Hester, Keasley Jones, Cary Norsworthy, Gary Paul Prince, and the rest of the gang (hope-we-didn't-leave-anyone-out) at Peachpit Press, for always being helpful and on the ball.

Tad Crawford, attorney, author, and Allworth Press publisher, for contributing the *Ten Questions and Answers About Copyright.*

Adobe Systems, Inc. for technical support.

Gene Chin, instructor at The New School Computer Instruction Center in New York City, for producing the screen captures and revising the text for this edition.

Johanna Gillman, New York City-based artist, wonderful friend, and designer, for her layout services.

Adam Hausman, Macintosh systems specialist, for his layout services.

Darren Roberts and *David McManus,* Parsons School of Design instructors, for their comments on the Web & Multimedia chapter.

Judy Susman and *Dara Glanville* for painstakingly tending to proofreading and copy editing details.

And *Teddy* and *Christ Lourekas,* for all their love and babysitting during this busy, busy, busy year.

Photo credits

Nadine Markova (Mexico City), pages 64, 101

Paul Petroff (Great Neck, New York), pages 47, 61, 63, 80, 100, 102, 205

John Stuart (New York City), page 238

Cara Wood (New York City), page 163

All the other images originated from stock photos (PhotoDisc) or from photographs taken by or owned by the authors.

Excaved, ©1996 Annette Weintraub

Psst! Want to contact the authors?

Call Peachpit Press (1-800-283-9444), and
ask them for our current e-mail address.
By the way, what do you think of this book?
And...what should we write about next?

MOUNTAIN
YEAR

A Southern Appalachian
Nature Notebook

BARBARA G. HALLOWELL

DESIGN BY DEBRA LONG HAMPTON

PRINTED AND BOUND BY R. R. DONNELLEY & SONS

PHOTOGRAPHS BY THE AUTHOR UNLESS OTHERWISE NOTED

*The paper in this book meets the guidelines for permanence
and durability of the Committee on Production Guidelines for
Book Longevity of the Council on Library Resources.*

Library of Congress Cataloging-in-Publication Data

Hallowell, Barbara G., 1924–
    Mountain year : a Southern Appalachian nature
notebook / Barbara G. Hallowell.
        p.   cm.
    Includes bibliographical references and index.
    ISBN 0-89587-222-6 (alk. paper)
    1. Natural history—Appalachian Region, Southern.   I. Title.
QH104.5.A6H35   1998
508.756'8—dc21   98–21685

TO TOM

CONTENTS

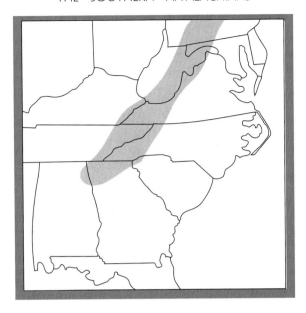

PREFACE

In 1539 Spanish explorer Hernando De Soto landed in Florida and wintered with the Appalache (Apalache) Indians of northwest Florida. They told him of towering mountains to the north. Maybe gold awaited there! Next spring (1540) De Soto headed to the mountains and named them for the Indians who had hosted and guided him, but he found no gold.

The *Appalachian Mountain* chain starts in western Newfoundland, courses across the Gaspe peninsula of Quebec, then extends southwest from Canada and New England to northern Georgia and Alabama.

The *Southern Appalachians* are the portions of the chain from western Maryland southwest to Alabama. In North Carolina and eastern Tennessee they rise as the highest mountains east of the Rockies.

Early explorers saw the mountains as obstacles, massively ugly, describing them as "horrid gloom," "frightful irregularity," "sombrous," with some summits having "naked rocks with the appearance of a scabbed head." What a contrast to the love of these mountains today! Tourists flock to them, hikers and climbers, botanists and zoologists, geologists and naturalists, historians and artists consider them superb areas to explore and enjoy, and people move in, considering them prime living sites.

The Southern Appalachians fire the spirit with their beauty, offer tremendous diversity, and lure with trails and waterfalls and life.

For an introduction to southern mountains, travel the Skyline Drive through Virginia or sections of the nearly 470 miles of Blue Ridge Parkway that connects Shenandoah National Park with Great Smoky Mountains National Park. A land of spectacular vistas awaits. But even better, walk the trails. Then you will truly experience the Southern Appalachians.

ACKNOWLEDGMENTS

My husband, Tom, shared most of these experiences, researched the bird material, took me here and there, up and down, tolerated hours upon hours of my writing labors, advised, encouraged, did errands, read, and edited.

He supported this project faithfully and confidently.

Without him this book would not be.

My sister, Nancy G. Wilson, gave invaluable support which has been meaningful and fruitful.

Information, support, and advice came from some special people: Lincoln Brower, Carlton Burke, Grant W. Goodge, Elton J. Hansens, Charles F. Moore, and Richard M. Smith.

INTRODUCTION

Mountain Year started with questions.

As I taught nature classes, guided walks, held workshops, or walked the outdoors with friends in the Southern Appalachians, the many questions people asked revealed a need. They wanted more than guidebooks on identification and where-to-find-it. They wanted a book *about* the big and little things they saw in nature. For example:

- *How can an earthworm be economically important?*
- *How do a bird's tiny feet keep warm in winter?*
- *Why are so many mountaintop trees dead?*
- *How does rime differ from snow?*
- *Why worry about frogs?*
- *Does a limb move higher on the trunk as a tree grows?*
- *Are there any virgin hardwood forests in the mountains?*
- *Why do I hear northern birds in southern woods in summer?*

My husband, Tom, who taught about birds and led mountain hikes, also received questions. People urged us to write an answer book, one *based especially on our personal observations and experiences.* They could keep it handy at home, and if they forgot an answer heard on the trail, they could look it up.

The writing began.

JANUARY

RHODODENDRON—WINTER'S THERMOMETER

A MOUNTAIN WOMAN once told me, "Each winter morning when I get up, I just look out the winder there at them rhododendrum leaves, and they tell me how to dress."

Anyone unfamiliar with rhododendron might wonder if this is a strange personal quirk. Actually, the remark shows wisdom, resourcefulness, and sensitivity to the natural world around her.

Rhododendron serves as an easily visible, highly dependable indicator of winter temperature. Normally the leathery leaves of this handsome shrub spread wide, but as the temperature drops, they curl under to diminish the exposed lower surface of the leaf. Breezes can no longer cross that surface easily, which apparently controls evaporation. Excess water loss can be fatal for the shrub.

As cold increases, the angle of leaves on the branches changes, too. Rather than flaring widely, leaves droop sharply.

"When them leaves look like cigars ahangin' there, you know it's below freezin'," my rhododendron advisor told me. "That's time to bundle up. When they look like up 'n down danglin' pencils, it's headin' to zero."

She pronounced it "rhododendrum", as it's often heard, though it's "rhodo" from Greek for "rose," plus "dendron" for tree—a rose tree.

"But when sun gets to the curlied

As winter temperatures plunge, rhododendron leaves curl tight.

leaves," the woman continued, "they commence openin' up. A bush'll have closed leaves on its shady side and opened leaves on its sunny side, and that's when you know it'll be sweater weather in a short time. Brrr! Just thinkin' about curlied leaves makes me shiver."

People heap attention on rhododendron in June and July when the showy flower clusters, the "roses" in its name, draw admiring oohs and aahs. At this time the two large-leafed rhododendron species most conspicuous in the mountains contrast sharply with each other.

White rhododendron, *Rhododendron maximum*, also called great laurel and rosebay, displays loosely scattered flower clusters ranging from white to soft pink. Purple rhododendron, *Rhododendron catawbiense*, also called purple laurel, mountain rosebay, and catawba rhododendron, has densely arranged flower clusters, purple-pink.

A mountain abloom with purple rhododendron in the twenties of June, as at Roan Mountain on the North Carolina/Tennessee border, or at high locations along the Blue Ridge Parkway, like Craggy Gardens, represents truly "a mountaintop experience." White rhododendron blooms later, in early July.

But to tell the two species apart when they have no flowers, habitat provides one clue: White rhododendron grows mostly below 3,000 feet elevation and prefers shaded woodlands, especially along streams. Purple rhododendron grows mostly in sunny areas above 3,000 feet.

A leaf of white rhododendron has a pointed base and whitish or rusty underside. A leaf of purple rhododendron has a rounded base and green underside. This identification tip applies only to our native species. It won't do for nursery plants.

The reason goes back to early times. American colonists sent native rhododendron plants back to England. Plant growers there, already breeding varieties of rhododendron imported from the Orient, crossed the American species, especially the purple rhododendron, with them. Nursery stock today offers a wonderful variety of hybrids developed worldwide through many generations of breeding.

Many rhododendron experts revel in retirement in the Southern Appalachians. Conditions of light, soil, temperature, and rainfall enable their private collections of rhododendrons to thrive here.

And come January, experts and amateurs alike use that leafy mountain thermometer. Just look out the window. If rhododendron leaves look like dangling cigars, pile on the down jacket and wool hat.

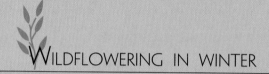

WILDFLOWERING IN WINTER

SOUNDS CRAZY. It's mid-January and I'm going for a wildflower walk. January's a great time for a wildflower walk. Colorful petals won't be showing, and perfumes and butterflies will be missing, but flower parts such as pods, seeds, sepals, and stalks will be everywhere.

I won't let myself be distracted by evergreen mosses, ferns, or lichens. Not even trees, shrubs, or vines will divert me. And certainly not ice toppings on puddles. Today it's strictly wildflowers.

I start by walking into the weedy field. Goldenrod! The field is brown with it, each waist-high stalk topped with fluffy white parachutes, one fluff for each of countless seeds—a feast for winter goldfinches, juncos, sparrows, and siskins.

Between the goldenrod snuggle branched stalks, each tipped with stars. These flower remnants reminded early botanists of stars, too, so they named the plant *aster*, the Greek word for star.

A monster towers above me, a Joe-Pye weed fully twelve feet tall. An early Massachusetts Indian, Joe Pye became well known for his special talents in using this weed to treat many illnesses. His name stuck with the plant.

Queen Anne's lace, so white and delicate

Remnants of many summer and fall flowers create designs and shadows in the snow.

in summer, now bears seed clusters resembling straggly birds' nests. I pull apart the compact mass to examine prickly seeds. Books on wild food suggest steeping them in boiling water to make a good tea. Chewed seeds taste like carrots—not surprising, since Queen Anne's lace is a close relative of the carrot and is often called wild carrot.

Like splotches of bright orange paint on a green field, butterfly weed's flowers bloomed in profusion here last summer. Their nectar attracted hosts of butterflies. I hunt for winter traces of the plant and discover a long, pale pod, empty and tattered, the seeds flown months ago.

I look through a 10X magnifier to examine the flat-topped seed head of yarrow. Surprisingly intricate designs of flower remnants jump out. A dried sprig of yarrow resembles a miniature tree; before the days of plastics, yarrow sprigs were used as trees in model railroad setups and architectural models.

The field is loaded with flowers. Remnants of pigweed and beggar's ticks, agrimony and ragweed, clover and black-eyed Susans mingle like crowds at a bargain sale. And here's a stalk with woody evening primrose pods. Their tips curl backward like four tiny petals. I bend one stalk and shake out the black seeds. One has legs! An insect is wintering in the dark seclusion of a pod.

Like miniature yellow tomatoes, half-inch globes of horse nettle fruits add a sunny touch. Horse nettles belong to the same plant family as tomatoes—the nightshade family.

Here's mullein! In winter, second-year stalks stand prominently, thick, brown, and four or five feet tall; but this mullein plant is in its first year, still a handsome, gray-green rosette with leaves that feel like woolly blankets. Its name derives appropriately from the Latin *mollis*, meaning soft.

Rosettes, flat, circular clusters of leaves, grow all through the field. Many wild plants winter in this form—thistle, yarrow, evening primrose, dock, plantain, even Queen Anne's lace. In spring, stalks will grow from each center, often bearing leaves differently shaped from rosette leaves.

Something jumps. Frost still whitens blades and sprigs in shady spots, but sun warms the unshaded stretches and sure enough. A brown grasshopper. And a wee black beetle.

Though I had intended to explore the woods after the field, time has flown. Maybe I'll visit the woods when an inch or so of snow dusts the ground, setting off winter "flowers" dramatically, full of the wonders of wildflowering in January.

Great-Horned Owl
Master Hunter, Winter Nester

DAYLIGHT LIES an hour away when the mellow, resonant hoo-hoo, hoooooo, hoo-hoo echoes through dark stillness. Silence follows, deep and complete. Though the world of night is active, a vast, dark vacancy hangs across the hollow.

Then the call repeats hoo-hoo, hoooooo, hoo-hoo—notes all the same pitch yet different in length and timing, notes hard to pinpoint for direction. Perhaps they are coming from the dark timbered slopes of the hill beyond the meadow.

Listening for them seems almost an invasion of the owl's privacy, so alone are they in the pre-dawn night. Yet a power-ful message is being broadcast, and all can hear. One wonders if woodland creatures hunch down more compactly or seek closer shelter when they hear it.

An answering call, slightly lower in pitch, suddenly rises from another direction. The message has been received. A pair of great horned owls communicates.

The calls become more frequent and varied in the number of hoos. They come closer together until they overlap in noisy confusion. An argument? More likely an amorous exchange, for the dead of winter is the great horned owl's breeding and nesting season. No other North American owl nests so early.

Early nesting is urgent because incubation

9

While winter still grips the mountains, the great horned owl starts nesting.
Photograph by Mike Hopiak, Cornell Lab of Ornithology

requires nearly a month—twice that of a robin—plus a full three months before the owlets are able to fly. Then, learning to hunt requires still more time, weeks coinciding with summer's most plentiful food supply.

Winter nesting requires true dedication. Those precious eggs—one to three of them—must be kept warm no matter how miserable the weather. The brooding female shields them from chilling rain, pelting sleet, or wind-whipped snow by surrounding them with the feathers and deep warmth of her body. Every so often a vigorous shake flings the drops or flakes from her back.

Even in storm or penetrating cold, the male brings food to her—a squirrel or rat or mouse, maybe nibbled a bit by himself, for he is hungry, too. Both owls are excellent hunters.

By day, the great horned owl, so-named because of its size and "horns," which are merely feathered tufts, sits inconspicuously as if part of a tree or branch. Its browns, blacks, and grays blend perfectly with bark.

But by night, when its great yellow eyes survey the woodland, it becomes the "winged tiger of the woodland."

Larger than a crow and equipped with over a four-foot spread of extra broad wings, this predator swoops to take a wide range of fare—from crawfish, mice, rats, snakes, and birds to groundhogs, rabbits, ducks, and an occasional night-wandering cat. Even skunks are a delight, their scent no problem.

A superb hunter with silent wings in the darkness, this often maligned owl is not the savage, evil creature some people insist. Unlike many of its critics, it does not hunt for fun. It hunts to survive and feed its family. Its prey does not provide sporting supplement to a routine diet; it is the diet.

Observers have watched a great horned owl wade into shallow water to snag a fish or waddle on ground to creep into hiding places inaccessible by air, startling behavior to witness.

The mighty owl occasionally preys on other predators—a roosting red-tail hawk or a hunting screech owl or even the big barred owl. But routinely it preys on what is most available—rats and mice, and consequently is considered highly beneficial to man, who seems prone to shoot it.

When the hoo-hoo, hoooooo, hoo-hoo of the mighty great horned owl carries through icy stillness on a January night, the master of the woodland, provider for a surprisingly early hungry brood, hunts again.

(See also, "Owls: Hunters in Darkness" in February, page 33.)

HAWKS AROUND THE FEEDER

NOT A BIRD MOVES. The cardinal perches like a wooden carving on the platform feeder's ledge. Juncos and towhees crouch on the ground. A song sparrow pauses at the birdbath; a downy woodpecker clings tightly against the suet. Goldfinches freeze on the hanging feeder. Birds become still as statues.

The sky poses no threat, nor do nearby trees and shrubs. But another look catches the erect form of a large bird perched on a low maple limb. Binoculars verify suspicion—a hawk. The birds see it and recognize danger: while they feed on seeds and grains, it might feed on them.

By instantly freezing in position, they hope not to be seen. Most birds of prey attack only moving targets.

For several minutes the small birds stay motionless, watching. One eye blinks, but the strange stillness holds.

Suddenly the hawk flies off through the trees and disappears, diffusing the crisis. As if flipping a power switch, activity resumes. The hawk takes its hunt to another site.

When a hawk threatens feeder birds, one can immediately rule out the red-tail. The largest of the four hawk species that winter in the mountains, red-tails eat rodents (mostly mice), not birds, consuming nearly a quarter pound per day. That's nearly ninety pounds of mice per year. Yet uninformed people insist on shooting them as "enemies."

A red-tail soars against the sky, broad wings sailing on updrafts. Its tail shows rusty-red when the bird banks and flashes its top side or when backlit against the sun. Perched quietly on roadside trees, its splotchy white front tempts trigger-happy people all too frequently.

The kestrel or sparrow hawk, our smallest hawk, might take a look at feeder birds if winter food is unusually scarce. Mostly this dove-sized falcon with long tail and sharply pointed wings favors mice. In summer it dines eagerly on insects, especially grasshoppers. Kestrels hover as they hunt, flapping rapidly above a field or roadside as if suspended in the air. They often perch on telephone poles and wires, making them easy to spot.

The hawk most likely to zoom into our feeder area is the crow-sized Cooper's hawk, though a somewhat smaller sharp-shin hawk might also pay a call. Cooper's and sharp-shinned hawks feed predominantly on small birds and have the short, wide wings and long tail helpful for moving adroitly among tree branches. Lightning fast and powerful, they grab their target, kill it quickly, and fly off to feed in seclusion, leaving behind only a few feather tufts.

We may lament the loss of a feeder friend to a hungry hawk, but hawks are not harmful predators of small birds. They actually help control and improve populations by culling out unhealthy, crippled, or less alert individual birds that would otherwise compete with healthy, strong ones for food.

And hawks control the prolific populations of rodents. Destroy hawks—and their fellow birds of prey, owls—and rodent populations explode. Hawks and owls serve as quiet, behind-the-scenes exterminators.

It's natural to rebel when a hawk grabs a junco, grosbeak, or song sparrow, or more likely, a dove, but the generations of hawks—beneficial, beautiful, and exciting—must eat, too.

A passing hawk sees a feeder bird as an easy meal just as a cardinal sees sunflower seeds as handy fare. When we set out seed for feeder birds, we also set out birds for an occasional hawk.

FINCHES

SEPARATING PURPLE FROM HOUSE

IS IT A PURPLE OR A HOUSE? In the 1960s, the answer would have been easy—a purple. An eastern sparrow-like bird with raspberry-red head, breast, and rump would be a male purple finch, which one bird guide describes as looking "like a sparrow dipped in raspberry juice."

Nowadays the answer is not as easy. Another sparrow-like bird with raspberry red head, breast, and rump, the male house finch, causes many cases of mistaken identity.

This confusion has arisen only recently, and a touch of intrigue lies behind it.

Each fall for eons, purple finches, nesters in northern United States and Canada, have migrated regularly to the South. Since people began feeding birds, purple finches have wintered at feeders, and folks are well acquainted with them.

But house finches come to us by a less than honorable route. Not native to the eastern United States, they belong west of the Rocky Mountains, where they have adapted to human intrusion and thrive in towns and around houses.

In the 1940s bird collectors, eager to make a quick dollar, captured some colorful house finches in California and

Purple finches visit only in winter.
Photograph by Tom Hallowell

shipped them to cage-bird dealers in New York. FOR SALE: HOLLYWOOD FINCHES!

Catching, shipping, and selling songbirds is illegal, a fact the collectors and dealers knew well. Authorities learned of their illicit activity, and the dealers, in great haste to avoid prosecution, destroyed the evidence by releasing the finches on Long Island.

The birds loved their new home. They not only survived, they thrived, multiplied, and extended their range until they now inhabit most of eastern United States. We recall well their exciting first visit to our feeders in New Jersey in the 1950s.

The first North Carolina report came from Wake County in 1963, but they didn't reach our North Carolina mountain home until the mid-1970s. A flock of nearly fifty dined at our feeders for several weeks that winter. Now they are year-round residents, no longer just winter visitors like purple finches. If you see a "purple finch" in summer, it's a house finch.

Both colorful finches are guaranteed to please, but telling one from the other is tough. A bird guide should be helpful, but colors in books can be misleading, and older books on eastern birds often do not include the more recent house finch.

The red of the male purple finch is a strong raspberry; while that of the house finch has a touch more orange. But the difference is subtle, and lighting can play tricks.

Striping helps—in fact, it's the surest, easiest way to tell them apart. On the purple finch, a darker patch with a lighter stripe above and below the eye is particularly noticeable on the brown female, which usually accompanies the male. House finches have plainer faces. The male house finch has heavy lower breast striping, the purple finch less.

Purple finches tend to be chunkier with thicker beaks and higher crowns than house finches, characteristics helpful when the birds are seen in poor light or as silhouettes against the sky.

Unfortunately, a feeder rarely hosts the two species together, so comparison must be by memory rather than direct observation.

House finch population has increased impressively. They are nearly as common in the East as they are in their native West. Like so many introduced species, they compete with native birds for food and nesting sites.

Their songs are undeniably pleasing, but they still strike me as awkwardly "foreign." I wonder if they will become a pest, drive away more desirable native species. The answers lie a few years ahead. Meanwhile, we can only speculate, listen, and try to learn a purple from a house.

BEES AND WASPS
A MATTER OF WAISTLINES

WHEN I STOOP TO INSPECT daffodil shoots along a south wall, something buzzes. A honeybee crawls across a bud, launches, and zooms away. In January? But with temperatures in the fifties and daffodils budding, a honeybee senses spring and flies out to make the most of it.

This tiny event makes me wonder how to tell the difference between a bee and a wasp—and a hornet. I ask an entomologist friend, who chuckles, "It all depends."

"On what?"

"On who you ask. Wasps, hornets— the names are mostly interchangeable. Really, it's a matter of waistlines. Bees barely have 'em, wasps and hornets do— thin ones, very thin."

Appetite whetted, I peruse insect books, seeking information about their differences. As my friend said, the waistline seems significant. The connection between the middle section of the insect's body, its thorax, and its abdomen is thicker in bees; but the distinction between wasp and hornet is flexible: More slender forms tend to be called wasps, the rest hornets—sometimes.

And only the females sting, using an

Mud tubes, meticulously fashioned by a female dauber wasp,
appear pipe-like on an old cabin door.

organ helpful in egg laying. Some sting fiercely, some hardly at all, but when a hornet charges, who pauses to ask, "Are you male or female? Is your sting fierce or mild?"

People often refer to stings as "bites!" A sting is on the rear end of the abdomen. A mouth that bites is on the head end, a whole insect apart.

Honeybees have barbed stings that imbed. As the bee departs, not only the sting but a portion of abdomen stays behind, a fatal event. Wasps and hornets have smooth stings they can use repeatedly, as miserable victims loudly verify.

Stings defend nests where young develop and food is stored, and some wasps and hornets use stings to capture food.

I saw this one day when I pulled several mud tubes of mud dauber wasps off our cabin door to see what hid inside. This exposed a series of four to eight egg chambers or cells in each tube. Within the cells lay tangled, gray-brown debris.

Then it moved. Slowly, carefully, spindly legs disentangled and crawled, a creepy scene in slow motion. Spiders! I counted six in one cell, eight in another. On one spider in each cell clung a gray grub, the wasp's wormlike larva.

A female mud dauber paralyzes spiders with stings, stuffs them into her cells, and lays one egg in each cell. Remarkably, she supplies the precise amount of fresh "meat" to last each grub until pupation.

After changing to an adult, the new wasp chews out of its mud cell, leaving a conspicuous hole.

A whole series of wonders emerged from the books I read. Though we picture busy hives when we think of bees, 99 percent of North America's bees are solitary, living alone, and most rarely sting. Honeybees are not native to North America. Early colonists brought them, using generously the wax and honey from their cells.

Every schoolchild learns the importance of honeybees as pollinators. Before honeybees came to America other bees, especially the bumblebee, flies, moths, and butterflies, even birds and bats took care of pollination.

Carpenter bees look like big bumblebees, but the top of their abdomen is bare, unlike the hairy abdomen of the bumblebee. Carpenter bees buzz around wooden porches, decks, and eaves, seeking sites for boring perfectly round holes. Each hole will lead to a nest channel chewed in the wood.

One day I found several logs on our outside cabin wall with fresh wood exposed. Something had stripped the gray, weathered surface wood. I wondered if mice, squirrels, or insects were the culprits. My entomologist friend stated knowingly, "Wasps or hornets. They strip the wood, chew it with saliva, and use this paste to make papery nests. Have you ever watched hornets building a nest? They pat the paste into place with their front legs."

Bald-faced hornets build the spectacular, gray paper nests we often see. Inside the nest covering hang layers of paper cells for developing larvae. Hornets can be vicious around these nests and inflict a painful sting, all the more challenging for many a mischief-maker who yields to the temptation to pelt a huge nest with rocks or bat it with a long stick—often to his regret.

Paper wasps build similar paper cells but without the gray covering. Their single, flat layer of cells attaches to a beam or branch or overhang by a single stalk. The cells open downward, but the larvae don't fall out. The female glues them in and feeds these upside down young with insects she catches and chews into paste.

Most wasps hold wings at rest, folded lengthwise over their backs. Paper wasps hold them somewhat out to the side.

Many a summer picnic has been ruined when yellow jackets appear to share the feast. "Bees!" someone exclaims—though they're properly wasps or hornets. Many a picnicker's mouth has been stung by a yellow jacket happily sipping soft drink or beer just inside the can's opening.

Yellow jackets plague a picnic fearlessly, persistent to the point of exasperation. Fortunately, they rarely attack unless thoroughly provoked—like a picnicker stepping on their nest! The papery nest usually hides underground, though occasional yellow jackets prefer to build nests above ground.

These bits—and pages more—come to light because a bee buzzed me in January. As I read, I marvel at how little we know and how much we fear. Understanding the characteristics, behavior and waistlines of bees, wasps, and hornets promotes delight, even when we can't tell them apart.

(See also "The Buzzing Board" in November, page 249.)

HOW TINY BIRDS STAY WARM

ORION GLEAMS in winter's night sky. Temperatures plummet. Inside our living room, a crackling fire radiates warmth.

"I'm sure glad I'm not a bird in a bush out there tonight," I comment.

"Oh, they're fine," mutters Tom into his book.

But how do birds keep warm through such bitter cold nights?

Many roost inside tree holes or other cavities where heat from their bodies radiates, warming the confined air space around them. A chickadee we knew roosted in the open horizontal end of a pipe supporting a clothesline.

And one dark night Tom dumped seeds into our hollow coconut bird feeder. A chickadee exploded out of it and nearly startled him off the step ladder. Cozily settled inside for the night, it hadn't expected an avalanche of seed.

The next night it was snuggled and fluffed in the coconut again. A hand held carefully above the sleeping bird could feel the warm air surrounding its body.

Woodpeckers may peck out special

roosting places while chickadees, titmice, nuthatches, wrens, and bluebirds use any pre-existing holes, natural or man-made. Often several birds roost together, hunched tightly, keeping each other warm.

Birds that sleep under the stars often seek the protection of a dense thicket of evergreen. Here, too, birds may roost close together, conserving their vital heat supply. Tom's pre-dawn trips to the newspaper box beneath a white pine often disturb cardinals and doves roosting in its thickly needled branches. Passing a tree trunk laden with dense evergreen ivy at dusk often flushes a flock of juncos that make it a nightly haven.

Birds live inside self-made down "sleeping bags." The colder the temperature, the more a bird fluffs its feathers, creating tiny pockets of air among the down feathers each bird harbors beneath its larger feathers. This layer of pockets, warmed by body heat, makes superb insulation. Frequent preening keeps the larger, covering feathers in good condition to protect the precious down. Loss of the down's insulation qualities can be fatal.

Notice how birds hold feathers close, unfluffed, in hot summer weather, decreasing the insulating air spaces, and how in winter they often look unexpectedly large because of fluffed feathers.

For birds that sleep perched on a limb, a special connection of the leg tendon and toes assures a tight grasp on the limb. The lower the bird squats, the more the tendon tightens its grip. In this position, bare legs and feet are surrounded by body feathers.

Settled for the night, a bird usually sleeps with its beak tucked under a wing or into back feathers, though some, such as doves, hunch heads into shoulders, keeping beaks straight forward.

But in bitter cold weather, how does a bird keep its feet warm as it hops in snow, perches on cold metal, or bathes at the edge of ice? It doesn't. Its feet are cold, but the feet do not freeze.

Birds have an intricate arrangement of arteries and veins called the *rete mirabile*, which means "wonderful network." It controls the flow and temperature of blood to the feet, preventing excessive heat loss. Warm arterial blood flows directly into cool venous blood and warms it. This allows feet to be cold—as low as 37 degrees—but not so cold they will freeze.

Clearly, birds accept cold feet as routine, but just thinking about it makes me grateful for wool socks.

FEBRUARY

Birds That Fly South—To Here

It's easy to name birds that go south *from* here in winter. But name birds that come south *to* here.

Nearly a dozen species migrate here to share our milder winters. Some come from the North, some from north-like areas of our high mountains. Some arrive with precise regularity. Others are highly unpredictable; if they arrive at all, they wander erratically, visit here and there for days, then disappear for weeks.

Recognition for "Most Dependable Winter Visitors" goes to dark-eyed juncos, sometimes called snowbirds, and white-throated sparrows, which tie for this honor. Both arrive without fail, dependable signs of autumn. They visit feeders faithfully, enjoying small seeds and finely cracked corn scattered on the ground.

Recognition for "Most Conspicuous Winter Visitors" goes to evening grosbeaks. Splashed with banana-yellow, black, white, and olive, they deliver strong, insistent calls that proclaim an ecological message: the annual mast crop up north has failed to provide enough food. We've come south for better pickings. Flocks may arrive as early as October and stay till mid-May.

When not even one grosbeak comes our way, the message reverses. The mast, that annual supply of acorns, cones, nuts, and seeds, is providing plentiful food for wildlife. No need to head south.

When a flock of grosbeaks descends on a feeder, the owner initially beams with delight. But when he watches expensive sunflower seeds by the pound disappear into the squabbly gang, he begins to wonder.

The presence or absence of purple finches, easily confused with year-round house finches, also depends on the mast crop. Erratic, too, are flocks of pine siskins, small, pugnacious relatives of the goldfinch. Remarkably tame, these tiny, dark-striped birds sport bits of yellow on the wings.

Two winter residents that appear regularly but are few in number have names that describe unique behavior: creeper and sapsucker.

The brown creeper, a small, inconspicuous bird with dark stripes and down-curved bill, is most often seen creeping up tree trunks as it searches for insects and insect eggs. Up, up, up is its direction. When it gets to the top, it just flies to the bottom of the next tree and heads up.

Yellow-bellied sapsuckers, members of the woodpecker family, drill holes in tree trunks. A prime specialty accounts for their peculiar name. The close rows of tiny holes they drill let sap ooze. As it emerges, the sapsucker "sucks" it. Small bristles on its tongue help lap the sap. The sweet ooze attracts insects, an added feast.

But sap does not flow nor insects swarm in deepest winter. Like other woodpeckers, the sapsucker feeds on berries and bark insects, and also enjoys feeder offerings.

Winter might treat us with glimpses of a red-breasted nuthatch working on suet, or a flock of cedar waxwings dipping into a bird bath. Waxwings thrive on local berries, but rarely dine at feeders.

Juncos, sapsuckers, creepers, red-breasted nuthatches, and waxwings all nest in the highest elevations of our North Carolina mountains. When I watch one at these lower elevations in winter, I wish it could tell me if it came from the North or flew down from a nearby mountain.

Wherever these winter visitors fly from, we welcome them. Their visits in our milder clime vary the local bird population and spark dull days.

P.S. We don't like to wish poor mast crops on the North. But selfishly, they do have their benefits for birdwatchers in southern regions.

(See also "Migration mysteries" in November, page 251.)

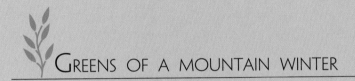

GREENS OF A MOUNTAIN WINTER

HOW GREEN these mountains are in winter! Not as viewed from the heights along the Blue Ridge Parkway, where the forests extend softly gray, almost furry, as far as the eye can see, though spruce and fir poke through the gray at the highest elevations.

And not as one looks down across low valleys. Spires of pine and hemlock stand amid the neutral expanses of bare-twigged forests, but in no way does green predominate. Forest gray rules.

However, a ride beneath trees on any road that snakes along a rocky mountain stream or, better still, a ramble on a streamside trail can trick one into believing the season has suddenly shifted forward. Leaf green rules.

Masses of rhododendron, "laurel" to the mountain people, sprawl up the hillsides, their handsome, polished leaves slapping and clattering noisily as we attempt to push through them. Rhododendron trunks and limbs grow in such profusion that old-timers called thickets of it "hells," and one of a mountaineer's great fears was getting lost in a laurel hell.

Mountain laurel, "ivy" to the mountain people, blankets many hillsides with green, too. Often people confuse laurel with rhododendron, but laurel leaves are much shorter and less leathery—shorter leaves, shorter name.

A few steps into some glossy-leafed shrubs along the stream banks reveal how dog hobble or fetter bush acquired its name. Feet catch in the tangles of its branches, hobbling any dog pursuing a bear, fettering any hunter following his dog, tripping any hiker in pursuit of a short-cut. It frustrates everyone.

Dog hobble goes by a third name, too—Leucothoe—which perplexes plant-lovers, who debate about how to pronounce it. Botany books state *loo-coth' oh-ee*, but remembering that seems to be a problem.

Conspicuous green patches of Christmas fern contrast with forest floor browns. Its fronds appear summertime fresh, though they lie flat in winter rather than stand erect as they do in summer. In earlier times when Christmas decorations were gathered rather than purchased, these rugged fronds provided free, festive touches to dreary rooms.

Tiny whorls of blue-green leaves dot the ground under foot, each flattened leaf patterned with a dainty network of white veins. Indians and early mountain people applied the leaves to rattlesnake bites, convinced they diminished the misery. Logically, the plant was known as rattlesnake plantain, an unpleasant name for

an orchid, especially one that adds such charming leaf designs to a winter woods!

With eyes attuned for green, we spot two more species of orchids. Putty root spreads a single, papery leaf with white parallel veins. Its roots are supposed to taste like putty, so I tried some one time. Awful!

The putty root's faded green differs strikingly from the dark green of its neighbor, the cranefly orchid, which has summer flowers suggestive of—craneflies! This orchid's leaf hides a surprise: the underside wears a splash of rich purple, color startling for so plain a leaf. Once I learned of it, I developed an irresistible urge to flip its leaves just to make sure.

Scalloped galax, oval arbutus, and rounded partridge berry leaves green the drier banks away from the stream; and liverworts and algae, lichens and mosses, other ferns and clubmosses, and, of course, hollies add yet more green.

But perhaps the loveliest greens of all, showing not in dots or clumps but masses, are the needled evergreens—pine and hemlock in the lower elevations, spruce and fir in the upper. They stand as the royalty of winter green, elegantly clad and mighty.

Drab and gray and dreary do not describe a mountain winter. Green sticks out all over.

Leaves of rattlesnake plantain attract attention more than its flowers, even though they are orchids.

STARLINGS, THOSE CONTROVERSIAL IMMIGRANTS

A FLOCK OF BIRDS sweeps into the big dogwood and begins gobbling berries that had escaped earlier consumption. I dash toward the tree, yelling, "Shoo! Go 'way!" as if birds understand English.

My intention isn't to save the red berries because they are beautiful—they have already shriveled and darkened. I balk at these starlings feasting on berries I want for robins, bluebirds, cedar waxwings, and other birds.

I am down on starlings, as are many people.

It's all because of Shakespeare. Poor fellow gets the blame for starlings being in America. However, he's not directly responsible. After all, he lived from 1564 to 1616; colonial America had barely started. But Shakespeare's voluminous writings often mentioned birds, and in one line of one play, there it is—"starling!" That did it.

The reference was caught by a nineteenth-century New Yorker, Eugene Schieffelin, whose burning interests were Shakespeare and birds. He fancied that Americans should know Shakespeare's British birds, so set himself the goal of importing all species mentioned by the bard.

Unfortunately, Schieffelin was unaware of two major principles in nature: 1) birds and animals usually don't survive away from their natural environment, and 2) if they do, they often become serious pests, having no natural enemies to keep them in check. Kudzu, English sparrows, and Japanese honeysuckle are modern examples of imported pests.

Most of Schieffelin's imports died, but eighty starlings, released in 1890 in New York City's Central Park, thrived and multiplied. Enthusiastic, Mr. Schieffelin imported forty more.

As the starling population in New York rose, some moved to less populated areas. By the 1920s starlings had reached Virginia and Ohio; by the 1930s they'd crossed the Mississippi; and by 1950 they lived in all forty-eight states, Canada, and Mexico. North America's millions of starlings today descend from these one hundred and twenty birds.

Historically, Americans have had mixed responses to these short-tailed "blackbirds." At first the newcomers were fun, their antics amusing, their prodigious consumption of insects positive. But when flocks descended on fruit trees or berry patches, it was goodbye fruit crop.

Yet over half the food of adult starlings and all the food of their young is comprised of insects, especially beetles and grubs. When a flock of starlings lands on lawn or field, rejoice! The birds are living insecticides and devour great quantities of weed seeds, too.

To people who feed birds, starlings symbolize greed and aggressive rowdiness. Among birds as among people, we enjoy and respect those who have good manners, which starlings don't. They keep away polite birds and gobble peanut butter concoctions meticulously prepared for bluebirds.

These people often respond to starlings as I do. From indoors they bang windows, flap draperies, yell, and wave arms wildly to chase away the aggressors.

Tough in adaptability as well as personality, starlings tolerate an astonishing variety of living conditions—country-city, hot-cold, wet-dry. They nest in holes or crevices, natural or man-made, a rainspout or skyscraper as acceptable as a tree or cliff.

And cavity nesters beware! Aggressive starlings find flickers particularly easy victims, joining forces against them. While a flicker is briefly absent from its nest cavity, a starling may slip in. Upon its return, the indignant flicker drags the struggling usurper out and chases it away, only to find another starling has sneaked into the hole meanwhile—then another. Overwhelmed by too many battles, the weary flicker departs.

Starlings accept buildings for roosting as well as nesting. At dusk flocks often return to roost in towns or cities after feeding all day in the country, prompting naturalist-writer Rachel Carson to describe them as "commuters in reverse." Roosting starlings become a noisy, dirty nuisance.

Once London's famous clock, Big Ben, perplexed onlookers when it slowed down unexpectedly. Starlings had roosted on its hour hand.

The starling has become a number one success story, but the jury is still out on whether its successful adaptability to America is good or bad.

Owls
Hunters in Darkness

NO MOON LIGHTS OUR WAY. We grope in darkness between car door and house door, stumbling against porch stairs, feeling for doorknob and keyhole.

An owl hoots from the woods. We wonder if it mocks our fumblings in the night. No, the owl has more important business. It's a hunter fully equipped for darkness, fully comfortable in surroundings we find awkward.

From a treetop it can sense a mouse. Through dense woods it can fly without mishap. Its wings can flap silently and carry it unerringly to tiny prey or dark perches.

The owl must be able to catch prey by surprise, hold it tightly, and reduce it to smaller pieces or swallow it whole.

A night hunter must be skillful, must see far more than we see. Owl eyes are big, man-sized, even though a large owl may weigh less than one-fiftieth of an average man's weight. Located on the front of the skull, they provide the binocular vision so important for depth perception.

Because the huge eyes cannot move easily in the tiny skull, the owl must move its entire head to watch a moving object. The head can turn a remarkable 270 degrees of a full 360-degree circle.

Screech owls eat great numbers of mice,
sometimes swallowing them whole—only the tail remains.

But contrary to legend, it can't keep going 'round and 'round. It zips back the opposite way so fast it appears to have turned full circle, a startling effect.

Because the eyes are elongate front to back, they collect extra light and concentrate it on receptor cells in the back of the eye. Our eyes have the same types of receptor cells—cones that act best in bright light and rods that respond best to low light levels. Owls have an unusually high number of rods, boosting night vision.

But they also have many cones. Despite tales to the contrary, owls see as well during daytime as we do. In fact, their daytime vision is better than their nighttime vision.

Tests show they can catch prey even in total darkness, so something in addition to eyesight helps owls find nighttime prey. Perhaps it is ears. The "ears" jutting up on the heads of some owls are not really ears, just tufts of feathers. An owl's true ears are holes on the sides of its head. The right and left ears differ in size and shape, one being higher than the other. This asymmetry helps them locate prey in darkness. A night hunter must hear superbly.

The owl swoops in on its prey silently, taking it completely by surprise. Fine fringe on the margins of its wing feathers and extra soft feathers on the body quiet the rush of air during flight.

With sharp talons on powerful, grasping feet, the owl strikes, holds, and carries the prey, taking it to a perch for eating or to a nest for its young.

To see an owl gulping a full grown rat can impress tremendously, especially at the stage when only the tail sticks out! But the owl may prefer to use its sharply hooked beak to tear prey into small pieces for itself or for its young.

Strong digestive juices break down the soft parts of the food but not the fur or feathers or large bones. These wad into a pellet of indigestible material that the owl burps up and drops beneath its perch.

With these pellets, owls unwittingly contribute to science. Studying them reveals what species the owls ate. When we visited a researcher and inspected tables covered with dissected pellets, remains of mice, rats, and voles, we could see at a glance what superb mouse traps owls are.

Throughout human history, excellent eyesight, exquisite hearing, and silent flight of owls have intrigued and perplexed humans. We yearn to do as well in darkness but must flip light switches and yield to the superiority of these amazing birds of night.

(See also "Great-horned owl: master hunter, winter nester" in January, page 9.)

Rime, snow or hoarfrost?

"I SAW THE STRANGEST THING," announces a visitor new to the mountains. "We drove up to the Blue Ridge Parkway the other day, and the snow on the trees wasn't lined on top the twigs but was stuck on the sides, even on vertical twigs. And it was icy hard."

The first time I encountered this "snow," I was equally perplexed. Then someone explained, "That's not snow; it's rime."

Sometimes super-cool clouds of extremely tiny droplets ride the breezes among the mountaintops. When the droplets bump into a below-freezing object, like a twig, stalk, wire, or pole, they freeze to it. Because they are windborne, the droplets strike the object on its windward side and build up, layer upon layer, toward the wind.

This hard and granular rime ice appears to be pure white because of air pockets between the ice particles. It creates one of the most spectacular shows of the year, competing with other seasonal spectacles across the mountain ranges, such as

Rime ice builds on the windward sides of twigs,
whereas snow settles on top.
Photograph by Tom Hallowell

spring's soft film of green spreading through the forests and autumn's color splash, guaranteed to draw hordes of camera-laden visitors.

But winter's black and white spectacle of rime stands starkly magnificent. Whether the backdrop is cloudy gray or cloudless blue, the patterns and angles of dark twigs outlined in gleaming white present a display beyond easy description.

A climatologist at the National Climatic Data Center in Asheville, North Carolina, remarks that many people call rime "hoarfrost." Even *Webster's Dictionary* lists them as synonyms.

"But they're completely different," the climatologist explains, "like rime and snow are different."

Snow forms in geometric crystals directly from water vapor in clouds. It floats softly to the earth in flakes. If it blows around on the ground, it accumulates in the lee of the wind, contrary to rime, which builds up toward the wind.

Like snow, hoarfrost is crystalline, too. It forms when moisture suspended in still air crystallizes directly onto cold objects, fringing leaves and bordering twigs with feathery or jagged spicules. Unlike rime, hoarfrost involves no cloud or breeze. Hoarfrost often whitens the hollow.

If water droplets in a cloud merge, they become rain. When cold raindrops strike a below-freezing surface, they flow over the surface as they freeze, producing a smooth, clear ice glaze. "An icestorm!" we exclaim. If these droplets freeze on the way down, we have sleet.

Hail completes the list of frozen precipitation, but it comes mostly in spring and summer, usually associated with turbulent thunderstorms. Tiny particles in the towering thunderhead become coated with ice. Within the cloud they are flung up and down, adding more and more layers of ice until they get too heavy and plummet earthward as hailstones, larger than winter's sleet.

To enjoy fully winter's frozen offerings, we must bundle up and experience directly these symbols of winter—the marvel of magnified snow crystals on a coat sleeve, the roughness of rime against fingertips, the magic of frost spicules on a leaf margin, the glitter of icy branches against ominous sky.

But in late February among these frozen wonders sneak warm days when bees buzz among early maple blossoms, daffodil buds pop open, and bluebirds squabble over the bird box. The season is changing.

(See also "A gathering of snow flakes" in December, page 279.)

Vultures
NATURE'S GARBAGE COLLECTORS

MOVIE PRODUCERS, cartoonists, and writers often use them as symbols of ugliness or evil, introduced to evoke feelings of unease, repulsion, fright, threat of death. Vultures! Yet even with their sinister undertones comes beauty.

A vulture beautiful? Just watch it in flight. Giant black wings soaring against sky; wide arcs and sweeping flight circles controlled with infallible precision; hours aloft with scarcely a wingbeat—these impress us as we gaze up at the beauty of a vulture, popularly called a "buzzard."

But there it ends.

The great, dark bird may appear to be relaxed as it soars on a six-foot wingspread, but blustery gusts require continual wing adjustment, and soaring is usually hunting—intense, concentrated, determined. The bird is hungry.

Although considered a bird of prey because it eats flesh and has a sharp, tearing beak, a vulture does not inflict death. Unlike the taloned feet of hawks, owls, and eagles, vulture feet cannot capture active prey any better than a chicken can. It feasts after death or occasionally waits near a dying creature until life fades.

Dinner is carrion—dead rabbit, deer, opossum, bird, snake, dog, cattle, and the like. Isn't it nice that something enjoys a rotting carcass! A hungry vulture and its associates comprise nature's critical cleanup committee, serving man and nature by consuming offensive waste. Animals which could pose a health hazard as they putrefy are removed from the environment—quite eagerly. Associated with death, the vulture enhances life.

When the hide of a dead animal is thick, vultures wait until it decomposes, making it more tender and accessible fare. Rot and stench and bacteria provide choice gourmet touches, boosting appetite and enthusiasm—and occasionally heated battles. Sometimes a vulture's "eyes may be bigger than its stomach." It will eat so gluttonously it can't fly, and sits around stuffed and stuffy.

Feeding is messy, but a vulture's head has no feathers, so keeps properly tidy while poking and pulling within the rib cage of some rotting creature. The head of our common vulture sports red skin like a turkey, earning it the name turkey vulture.

You may wonder if these great birds, so cumbersome and offensive on land, so superb in the air, find their food by sight or by smell. In one ingenious incident, engineers set odorous chemicals of the type found in rotting meat into leaky gas lines. Leaks in a 42-mile line were revealed quickly by vultures circling above. Yet other experiments proved sight to be the important factor. Contradictions tantalize; controversy persists.

Baby vultures could pass as rather cute—well, comparatively. Appearing as tubby blobs of fluffy white down equipped with featherless black faces, they sit awkwardly where they're hatched—on bare ground. Parents can't be bothered with the challenges of nest building. A protected niche by a log, in a hollow stump, against a cliff, or even beside dense brush will do.

The only "nest" I've come across lay between large rocks with a slight overhang. The startled adult leapt up with a great rustle of feathers, while I cringed, fully aware that threatened vultures often regurgitate. This revolting behavior apparently lightens the load for quick escape or discourages with scent. But the bird flew away hastily and politely.

Adults feed the youngsters, usually two, carrion delectables enhanced by partial digestion. The adult regurgitates these into the youngsters' gullets. Compare the picture with a young human father bringing home pizzas and ice cream cones.

Turkey vultures range over most of eastern United States, including these southern mountains, where occasional black vultures fly the skies, too. A short tail, black head, occasional quick wing beats between glides, and large, gray-white patches on each wing identify the black vulture, a more southerly species.

I have overheard visitors on Blue Ridge Parkway scenic overlooks exclaim, "Look, an eagle!" as they point to a soaring vulture. One time a friend eagerly reported that he had seen a whole flock of eagles soaring above the woods. I felt reluctant to say that undoubtedly a dead animal lay in his woods. Would that eagles were as common as vultures!

Ugly yet beautiful, repulsive yet wonderful, the vulture serves us with efficient garbage disposal and inspired flight. It may be just an old buzzard, but we need old buzzards.

Tangling in the Brier Patch

BRE'R RABBIT pops into mind as I struggle to disconnect a sturdy arc of blackberry that has snagged and penetrated the back of my sweater.

When Bre'r Rabbit got thrown into the brier patch, he was delighted; he belonged there. But based on personal experience, I find humans and brier patches thoroughly incompatible. The thorny sprigs and tangles seem determined to make human invasion of their habitat as miserable as possible.

To be grabbed on the sleeve by catbrier, punctured on the hand by blackberry, snared on the leg by multiflora rose, and tripped ignominiously by strands of dewberry produces not only miserable discomfort but fierce thoughts. The human is conquered, the pesky brier stands victorious.

Briers impede our progress and sidetrack projects. Any person captured by them is reduced to the single task of extrication, a tedious procedure during which one's balance can falter and one's instinct is to grab the nearest support. This might easily be a young black locust tree, which tends to hang out with this prickly gang. Black locust sports solid double thorns at the base of each leaf or leaf scar, definitely not something to grab hold of. It adds injury to injury.

All these briery things are pioneer plants, early invaders of untended land. They're mostly sun-lovers, thriving in open fields and along forest edges. Their stems and leaves serve magnificently as protective cover for wildlife. Their flowers and fruits provide a generous food supply. Even so, they persist in dominating land we've

Thorns on stalks can make blackberry patches impenetrable for people.

chosen to keep as open field. They interfere with our comfortable wanderings and encourage reforestation where we don't want it. So we attempt to control the briers, a task best done in winter.

Cutting them off at the base slows them only temporarily. Each lopped plant will send up multiple shoots with astonishing vigor. Digging roots out is a hopeless struggle. Briers run strong, long, and deep—impressively obstinate. Herbicides work, but we don't want to eliminate surrounding plants nor add chemical killers to our environment. Goats help, but zoning rules won't allow them.

So we resort to cutting, knowing we'll have to do it again next year and the next. As we cut, the determined stab-snag-rip-trip team gangs up on us with its "let's let 'em have it" attack. Despite this, we confess to a dash of admiration for these stubborn adversaries and wonder who they are.

Four types of briers are in the lily family, all in the genus *Smilax*, all called catbrier because of their cat-like "claws." *Smilax rotundifolia* (rounded leaves), the most common, grows on trees in a twenty- to thirty-foot vine. Its green stems and heavy thorns earn it the name greenbrier. Also called greenbrier is *Smilax glauca*, which has leaves with whitish undersides. *Smilax bona-nox* has bushy

form with more slender stems. Brown-stemmed *Smilax hispida* displays fine, dense thorns.

Blackberry, dewberry, and multiflora rose are in the rose family. The fierce thorns of common blackberry, *Rubus argutus*, make picking its berries a stimulus for purple vocabulary. But mountain hikers, who often must push through dense stands of blackberry, rejoice to find that the high elevation species, *Rubus canadensis* and *Rubus allegheniensis*, are either thornless or only slightly thorny.

Two dewberries are skilled at tripping, *Rubus flagellaris* and *Rubus hispidus*. Their weak, mildly prickly stems lie on or just above ground, snares for the unwary. *Rosa multiflora* is an import gone wild.

A third plant family, the peas or legumes, has two representatives in our field's prickly population—black locust, a tree, *Robinia pseudo-acacia*, and the deceptively charming sensitive brier, *Schrankia microphylla*. Its blossoms bear a remarkable resemblance to mimosa; but more intriguing, its tiny, fernlike leaves fold tightly when touched—instantly. How nice to know that a plant responds to my touch as I respond to its!

Briers stir mixed emotions. While they stab us and take over our fields, they charm with their beauty, attract wildlife to our premises, and supply us with flowers and berries.

MARCH

Peepers announce spring

"LISTEN TO THE KNEE-DEEPS!"

"You mean peepers?"

"Yeah, little hylas."

Three people on our porch use three different names; yet each knows the bell-like notes of these tiny frogs ring out one of nature's most welcome messages: spring has started.

Country people associate the "yeeps" of spring peepers with pussy willows, crocuses, and warm sun. To be sure, more cold days will come, even snow; but land warms steadily. Peepers respond.

Many people wonder whether birds or bugs make this chorus they hear from dusk into night. They find it incredible that such piercing calls, which carry up to a mile, come from frogs only an inch long.

Years ago a friend gave us several peepers. Delighted, we set them in a terrarium with twigs and soil and puddle. We eagerly anticipated their dusk and nighttime peeps.

That night they serenaded us from several rooms away with doors shut. The music penetrated through closed doors so clearly that sleep was impossible. Next

A spring peeper's throat balloons as he sings ardently to attract a mate.

Photograph by Jim White

morning, we promptly set the terrarium outdoors. The frogs won freedom.

Years ago, too, we were camping with our children in woods by a lake. That warm spring night we stood awhile outside the tent before bedtime, listening to a superb chorus of peepers. "Let's find one!" someone suggested.

Brilliant peeps sounded from shrubs all around us. Within moments, flashlights appeared, and a pajama-clad family crept through the woods, stalking.

Disturbed, the peepers silenced. We waited, scarcely breathing, engrossed in the stalk and the magic of night. Then one peeper dared call, and another, and within moments the din almost hurt our ears.

A peeper's white ballooning throat gleamed in a child's flashlight beam. We watched, entranced, as peep followed peep, every second or two, but when we started to approach, the balloon collapsed into silence.

"Look at his feet!" the children exclaimed. Toe pads that enable the frogs to cling to perpendicular surfaces or sharply angled branches showed clearly.

"Don't get too close and scare them. They can jump twenty times their length."

"Wow! I'd have to jump nearly a hundred feet to match that." That was a night to remember.

Only male peepers sing, their ardor attracting females that lay quantities of single, gelatinous eggs in water. These stick to submerged stalks and pond debris. Wee tadpoles hatch in six to twelve days, feed on pond algae and microscopic creatures for six weeks, then undergo the miracle of metamorphosis, acquiring legs and lungs for life on land as frogs.

The peeper's longtime scientific name, *Hyla crucifer*, means "cross-bearing barker." The "barking" peeper bears a distinctive cross on its back, dark brown in contrast to the frog's pale gray, tan, dull orange, or reddish brown body. Scientists have recently changed its name to *Pseudacris crucifer*.

Home for peepers is woodland, on brushy shrubs or forest floor, occasionally in trees. They dine on insects, tiny snails, or worms, and remain silent through summer. In autumn the male may call a few harsh, half-hearted notes as late as October or early November. Then the tiny frogs burrow under leaf litter or mud to hibernate.

But February brings warmth, and the male peeper judges temperature well. After several consecutive days in the fifties, he crawls from his haven, his mind set on romance, and heads for a watery spot—a pond or marsh or boggy place to join other amorous males. Females appear several days later, and mating occurs as they deposit eggs. If nights get cold, even icy, the frogs just burrow down till warmth returns.

March schedules peepers in prime time, full chorus, full volume. At dusk, beside low meadows or creeks or ponds, a silent, still listener can be overwhelmed by their sound.

And we know it's Spring.

THE TADPOLE SHOW

JUST THE WORD, Spring, brings a smile and a sense of excitement and expectation. Winter sleepers awaken, green creeps into brown, reproduction dominates. Lots is happening out there.

Robins squabble, courting cowbirds usurp the feeder, maple blossoms tint the hollow, and toads trill at dusk. Springtime is frog time.

Around ponds and marshy places the musical chirps of peepers already accompany dusk. Their chorus rises from the pond at the bottom of our mountain. Soon come the clicks, croaks, trills, twangs, and grunts of other frog species, males calling to attract females to water.

Even the most land-adapted frogs must return to water to lay gelatinous egg masses.

Even the youngest school children know that tadpoles hatch from these eggs and turn into frogs. They've probably watched this remarkable change day by day in a classroom or on a video. But as years pass, the wonder of it often fades or stands in danger of becoming ho-hum, another routine event in nature, kids' stuff.

Imagine being given the opportunity to introduce this change to an adult who has never heard of it. One day you two watch tiny tadpoles wriggle free of their gelatinous

*As a tadpole makes the amazing change into a frog, one of the first
obvious events is the appearance of hind legs.*

surroundings. You look through a magnifier at their frail, external gills. Then several days later the gills are gone. How does the tadpole breathe now?

You explain to the tadpole watcher that a fold of skin grew over the gills, leaving a small opening. The gills are on the inside now. Fish-like, the tadpole gets oxygen from water flowing through its mouth and over the gills and out the breathing pore on its left side. "So it's a fish," the tadpole novice declares.

"No wait," you urge.

Every few days you check the tadpoles. They feed and grow. Their horny lips on tiny oval mouths scrape algae from rocks and plants and scavenge dead animals.

"I can see through the skin," says the observer. "What's that coiled thing?"

"That's the intestine, extra long because the animal eats mostly plant food. It coils so it will fit inside. Look at the eyes. They're tiny and flush with the skin surface. And look how the big tail fin helps the tadpole swim quickly."

"And it isn't a fish?"

"Just wait," you once again urge.

Several weeks later two bulges where the tail meets the body signal change. Within days they become legs so tiny they look ridiculous against the plump, oval body.

"What good are silly little legs like that?" the tadpole novice asks.

"Just wait," you persist.

The hind legs grow longer, the intestine grows shorter for digesting insects and tiny animals. It requires less room, so the body slims.

After several days' absence, our observer returns and notices the eyes, now big and bulging. "The mouth's beginning to grin. Everything's changing. What a show! But how can a tadpole eat while its mouth changes?"

People think this is a joke, but it actually eats its tail. Of course, the tadpole doesn't reach around and chomp on it. After all, it can't use its mouth right now. But it receives body nourishment by absorbing the materials of its tail into its blood stream, causing the tail to shrink.

"Why is the tadpole swimming up to the water surface so often?"

"Its lungs are developing off the back of its throat, so it darts up to get much-needed air," you explain.

Then one day, from under the skin, front legs emerge. Unlike the back legs, they push through, fully grown. And day by day the tail, the last tadpole characteristic, shrinks and disappears.

"What a show!" exclaims the observer. "A water thing turns into a land thing; a fish turns into a frog. Why isn't this front-page news?"

"It's too common."

But a sad thing is happening and no one knows why. All over the world, the numbers of frogs and toads and closely related salamanders are plummeting. Various theories implicate pesticides, herbicides, fertilizers, ozone depletion, habitat loss, disease. Some naturalists fear Rachel Carson's "silent spring" may include the chorus of frogs along with the already diminished chorus of birds.

Meanwhile, the tadpole's marvelous show goes on. But for how long?

Spring's Year-Old Buds

March is the time to think buds. Forming nearly a year before going into action, buds grow on trees and shrubs at the base of nearly every leaf, withstand summer's heat and winter's freeze, and symbolize spring.

Tints of yellow-green and fire-chief red on the trees signal action. Blossoms and leaves emerge. A sense of urgency spurs us to take a close last look, for within days many buds will disappear. A magnifier makes their differences jump out.

Whether blunt or pointed, rounded or flat, sticky or hairy, glossy or dull, brown or red, purplish or yellow, tiny or huge, prominent or obscure (what a list of differences), each bud has characteristics special to only its species. For a knowledgeable tree person, a glimpse at a tight bud identifies the tree every bit as exactly as its leaves.

Minute leaves and flowers—precisely rolled, folded, pleated, crumpled, or bent, depending on its species—wait inside each bud, growing now and pressing to burst out. Sturdy bud scales protect these tender, miniature parts from drying and drenching, but offer no protection against birds and squirrels that enjoy gobbling spring buds. If

*Swelling buds of red maple tint woodlands
even while winter persists in the mountains.*

you see a gray squirrel dangling from its hind legs on a maple tree, watch its front legs as they grab buds and pull them toward an eager mouth. Robins, waxwings, towhees, and starlings may join in this feast of fresh veggies.

Because the tree produces far more buds than it needs, losing a few buds does not harm it. Only about half actually open in spring; and if some are eaten or damaged, dormant buds will spring into action as substitutes.

The number and arrangement of bud scales are precise. Oaks and maple buds have many scales, arranged in a tight spiral; tulip tree buds have only two scales, willows only one. That single scale forms the brown base of the "pussy" of those charming, furry, pussy willow blossoms.

As tiny leaves emerge, each adjusts position to assure maximum exposure to the sun, essential for manufacturing food, the leaf's reason to be. Emerging flowers adjust to expose sticky pistil tips. These catch pollen from visiting insects or from the air, assuring fertilization for seed production, the flower's reason to be.

But bud scales shelter something else, something far less obvious—a microscopic group of cells destined for twig growth, particularly active in the larger buds on twig tips. Within that group of cells, growth in length takes place, a strong spurt in early spring, a lesser spurt in summer.

And they shelter yet another group of microscopic cells, the beginnings of next year's bud. But these cells multiply only a little in spring. They wait for summer when the plant shifts its energies from growth and flowering to buds. Their time has come. Each bud develops at the base of a leaf, immediately above the leaf's attachment to the twig, too tiny to see well until midsummer.

Of course, as with almost every rule, there are exceptions. The base of sycamore and sumac leaves actually covers the new buds. Remove the leaf, and there's the bud. Black locust sinks its buds into the bark, making them annoyingly elusive.

When each summer bud has grown to its predetermined size, it stops growing, and for nearly seven months rests on the twig without stirring, a masterful package of potential.

As we look through magnifiers, it's fun to think how these buds we admire formed through spring and summer last year. They waited patiently until now when, a year old, they put all their energies into one spectacular performance— to burst and thereby transform—and vanish.

(See also "Seven Wonders in My Yard" in October, page 230.)

SHADBLOW, JUNEBERRY, SERVICEBERRY, AND SARVIS

OUR FRIEND LOOKS UP at a handsome tree at the edge of the woods. Its mantle of dainty white blossoms sets it apart from the bare trees around it. She remarks on what a handsome serviceberry it is.

"Serviceberry? I've always called that shadbush," comments another friend.

"Or shadblow," I add. "But I grew up calling it Juneberry. It berries in June."

"Sure can tell you folks weren't raised in these mountains," says another. "Here it's sarvis."

According to mountain lore, in the old days, the circuit rider or preacher started spring rounds of mountain slopes and coves about the time these blossoms appeared. He conducted services, baptized and married folks in tiny settlements that had no organized churches. People associated the tree with these services and began calling it serviceberry. Time corrupted it to sarvisberry, then sarvis.

A friend, fascinated by the many common names he'd heard for the tree, collected a list of thirty-one. Scientifically, it's *Amelanchier*, a member of the rose family along with apples, cherries, and strawberries, though its petals are proportionately longer than theirs.

Its plethora of names may be due to its gift of special charm to early spring.

While other woodland trees stand wintry and bare with buds tightly folded, serviceberry presents the first big show of spring. It tints mountainsides and valleys with clusters of white flowers set off by silky reddish bracts. From a distance, the colors merge into soft pink.

Serviceberry starts spring in mid-March in the low elevations, then creeps up mountainsides to reach the high elevations in early to mid-May, blooming only a week or so at each place. Like drifts of pinkish snow, masses of blossoming trees interrupt the bleak gray of winter forests, warming them with a spring message.

Along tidewater rivers of the Atlantic coastal areas, the tree bursts into its annual welcome of spring when the shad fish migrate upstream to lay eggs. Hence, early colonists called it shadbush. I have seen many fisherman on the Delaware River trying their luck as shadbush or shadblows burst buds along the riverside.

Anyone who has shared the seasons with *Amelanchier* appreciates the name Juneberry. In most of its range, the berries ripen from green to magenta to deep purple in June. They provide a gourmet's feast for hordes of birds. Robins, catbirds, mockers, thrushes, jays, thrashers, and their friends and competitors gulp berries greedily, later depositing purple droppings. Mammals, from bears to chipmunks, join the annual feast. If people are lucky enough to claim a share of the berries, they relish jams, cobblers, and pies.

Unfortunately, a tree's usefulness to man often determines its desirability. Serviceberry rates low. Though its wood is harder than oak, tree size is too small, and intense natural competition for its fruits usually leaves man out.

But serviceberry rates high when measured for aesthetic value and for attracting wildlife. Therefore, it makes a good ornamental tree, planted well into a yard, not directly beside a house, where its berries can be messy. In the yard, people can admire its beauty fully, see the wildlife it attracts, and ignore the week or two of untidiness with fallen berries and purple droppings.

When its spring floral display subsides and its early summer berries go, serviceberry retreats into the overshadowing forest community, an inconspicuous, "unimportant" member. It passes quietly through the seasons, growing, storing food, setting buds, waiting, silently preparing every detail.

When its moment comes, its blossom burst restores bleak winter mountains to the glory of spring, useful at last.

(See also "Spring after Spring after Spring" in March, page 63.)

FROM ASPARAGUS TO LILIES

THINK OF A LILY, and what flower do you picture? A white Easter lily, an elegant red garden lily, a roadside day lily?

If you are familiar with mountain woodlands, you may envision a towering Turk's cap lily or a tiny trout lily. If you've had the privilege of exploring special open meadows on high ridges, you may picture the handsome red Gray's lily.

But do you think of asparagus, onions, or catbrier? Do tulips or hyacinths pop into mind? All of these are members of the lily family.

Lily is a familiar flower form. Nearly everyone can picture some member of this plant family. Even city-bred folks who've never set foot in a garden or forest know lilies from street corner vendors and florist shops.

In western North Carolina the lily family presents more than twenty-five groups (genera) of native species, most having the family's bell-like flowers, from huge to tiny. Most have parallel leaf veins, bulbs or rhizomes, and flower parts numbered in threes or sixes. One group (genus) includes the true lilies with large, spectacular blossoms and leaves up the stalk.

Most cultivated lilies originated in the Old World, but North America hosts many native lilies. In the Southern Appalachians Turk's cap, Carolina, Canada, and Gray's lilies represent the family with pride.

Day lilies decorate roadsides with orange. They color gardens with pale yellows to deep reds. But just try to make a

*In southern mountains, the northern bead lily
grows only in the high elevations.*

Photograph by Tom Hallowell

lovely day lily centerpiece for the dining table only to have the flowers close tightly as the guests arrived at dusk. One learns quickly that each flower opens for only a day. Unlike true lilies, the swordlike leaves of day lilies grow in dense clusters from the ground, not up the stalk.

Both of these common lily groups bloom in summer. So why do we discuss the lily family in early spring? Because a big proportion of the family comprises the spring wildflowers for which the Southern Appalachians are famous.

Newspapers enjoy reporting about ramps, one of the first of the lily family to appear in spring. The reporters who cover ramp festivals glory in adjectives describing the strong taste and potent odor of these early, onion-like plants. It makes good reading, and good eating, too. Ramps are a springtime gourmet's delight.

Most spectacular and popular, trilliums carpet early woodlands. The "tri" in their name means three—three leaves, three petals, and three sepals. Mountain species range from pure white through pinks into reds, and some go into ivory, yellow, and green. Unlike the rest of the lily family, trilliums have net-veined leaves.

Along with the trilliums flourish family members with wonderfully descriptive names—trout lilies, Solomon's seal, Solomon's plume, and bellworts of several kinds. Resembling the bellworts are twisted stalk and mandarin. Indian cucumber grows in the same surroundings. Its crisp rhizome is edible and tastes like cucumber.

White clintonia grows in lower elevations and Clinton's lilies in higher. Some folks call both bead lilies because their shiny, deep blue berries in late summer resemble beads.

In higher elevations, too, tiny Canada mayflowers form carpets only several inches high.

Like miniature green lilies, tight clusters of blossoms top the two-to-six foot tall stalks of false hellebore.

With clusters of tiny white flowers atop stalks and later blooming are devil's bit, fly poison, bunch flower, colic root, feather bells, and turkey beard.

Swamp pink, its stalk tipped with a cluster of minute pink flowers, is a rare find. Watch out for wet feet.

So, from asparagus to ramps, from trillium to lilies, from greenbrier to Solomon's plume, the lily family offers tremendous variety. Its many species blossom from early spring through summer, and lower elevation trilliums start in March. "Consider the lilies!"

(See also "Trilliums, a Matter of Threes" in April, page 79.)

Spring After Spring After Spring

I SET THE TRIPOD firmly, frame a pleasing closeup of serviceberry blossoms, and trip the shutter. I have it. The photo has eluded me for years. However, when the pictures arrives back from processing, dismay replaces triumph. I've failed to capture the pristine freshness of these dainty symbols of spring.

Intent on a retake, I hurry back to the serviceberry tree, but instead of blossoming branches, find petals snowing the ground. In flatter places this would mean a delay until next blossom time, a whole year. But in the mountains it means sim-ply, go higher. Spring starts later up there, and farther up, still later, offering spring after spring after spring, all within a few miles!

I haul camera gear to a higher elevation where serviceberry trees blossom in profusion, and there I get the picture. Had I missed the proper photo a second time, a higher elevation would have displayed yet another round of blossoms. Within an hour of my house, serviceberry blooms from mid-March till late May, a two-and-a-half month spread of blossoms—and a month or more for oak

Serviceberry trees patch mountain forests with dainty pink and white.

leaves or trilliums or Dutchman's breeches.

Delightfully, the reverse is true in autumn. In cool, higher elevations, leaf colors show earlier than in lower ones, so one can enjoy autumn on mountain tops, then return to late summer below.

Spring's burst of tree leaf buds shows the effect of elevation most beautifully. A varied pallet of greens sweeps through low valleys and coves and creeps up south-facing slopes; but on north-facing slopes it hesitates for days, even weeks. Eyes scanning up slopes see less and less green until the highest places show only gray, trees tight-budded, all gripped in winter—two seasons at once.

Elevation appears to play tricks with seasons, calling to mind the old statement that in many places every 1,000 feet up a mountain is like traveling a hundred miles north.

The Southern Appalachians' statistics surprise people of the Northeast where New Hampshire's White Mountains dominate mountain lore. North of Virginia and east of Dakota's Black Hills, only one mountain exceeds 6,000 feet, Mount Washington in New Hampshire; and only a dozen reach greater than 5,000 feet.

In the Southern Appalachians 46 peaks rise higher than 6,000 feet, 15 of them higher than Mount Washington, and 288 reach greater than 5,000 feet. It's prime land for chasing spring.

(See also "Shadblow, Juneberry, Serviceberry, and Sarvis" in March, page 58.)

THE WONDER OF EGGS

MENTION EGGS, and most people picture chicken eggs, something to serve with bacon, chop into salad, or break into batter.

But long before Christianity, they symbolized spring and new life. Dyed eggs meant joy. As Christianity spread, people associated the egg—and later, the chick—with resurrection and Easter.

The wonder is that a shelled object with rather gloppy contents transforms into a bird—and quickly. It takes only twenty-one days for a chicken to form (thirteen for a robin, sixteen for a hummingbird, thirty-five for an eagle).

Break a chicken egg into a clear dish and look carefully. Inside the shell lies a membrane, actually two close membranes. Before the break, an air pocket lay between them at the blunt end of the egg. The older the egg, the larger the air pocket. That's why a stale egg tends to float in water.

The yolk is a globe of golden food enclosed in a membrane. Every cook knows how easily that membrane breaks. Between yolk and shell lies the egg white, albumen. On top of the yolk is a white spot containing a single female reproductive cell. If the cell is fertilized by a male cell, this "germ spot" shows prominently—already the bird-to-be has started development.

What a feeling to look at that spot and

realize that within days it can grow into beak and brains, eyes and wings, feathers and feet! But these days a fertilized egg rarely finds its way into a home kitchen, for sad to say, egg-factory hens have no experience with roosters.

How do white and yolk get inside a shell? Deep within the female bird's body, her reproductive cell on its golden yolk pops from the bird's ovary and slips into a tube, the oviduct. If male cells are present from mating, the male cell fertilizes the female cell.

As the egg glides along, the oviduct adds layers of white albumen. Then gland cells secrete layers of mineral substance around the white and yolk, forming the shell. Soft before laying, the shell hardens quickly afterward. When a fertilized egg is laid, development of the chick ceases until heat from hen or incubator penetrates the egg, causing growth to resume.

The bird-to-be needs food, air, and water. After only three days of warmth, a dark red area on the yolk pulsates—the future heart—and blood vessels grow around about one-third of the yolk, absorbing it as food. Eyes and brain show clearly. By Day Five the vessels surround the yolk. Yolk becomes bird.

Both yolk and white supply water, while air and moisture pass through tiny pores in the shell.

By Day Seven an inch-long chick has formed, with heart, brain, beak, legs, and wings.

The hen sits patiently. Occasionally she lifts her body slightly and turns the eggs by poking and pushing them gently with her beak. Some of the albumen inside is twisted into whitish cords, once called "those squiggly things" by our children, but properly termed chalazas. As the parent turns the egg, the chalazas assure that the germ spot, lighter in weight than the rest of the yolk, stays centered.

Turning also keeps the developing bird from sticking to shell membranes. A parent tenderly shifts the eggs every few hours. Commercial incubators turn them automatically.

By Day Thirteen both yolk and white have shrunk, the chick has a coat of down, and the air space between the shell membranes at the large end has enlarged. The chick's head is toward this end.

By Day Twenty much calcium from the shell has transferred into bones. As bones strengthen, shell weakens. The chick's beak penetrates into the air sac; breathing starts—and peeping! The brooding hen hears and becomes excited. She raises her body, pokes gently at the eggs, and "talks" to them. Communication between mother and offspring is established.

On Day Twenty-one the chick labors. Through nearly six hours of alternate struggle and rest, it pecks with its beak, which has a sharp, temporary projection, an "egg tooth," on top. It breaks a band of shell. Strong legs and oversize feet push the shell halves apart, and the chick enters the big, wide world, not the sweet, fluffy chick of commercials and children's stories, but weak, wet, and weary.

It dries and rests, snuggling into its mother's feathers with contented peeps or surrounded by the warm air on the crowded shelf of an incubator. Soon it is up and running, fluffy and charming.

I consider privileged those who have watched a brooding hen fluff protectively over her eggs and heard her concerned clucks. Few people encounter live chickens these days. The free-range chicken has mostly been replaced by the imprisoned factory chicken, which serves as an egg-laying machine. Machines even collect her eggs. Chicks hatch by thousands on tiered shelves, never knowing the contentment of snuggling into warm hen's feathers and hearing her tender clucks.

People wonder how the masses of chicks shipped from hatcheries receive food and water during shipment. A remnant of yolk persists within the chick's body, supplying it with food for its first few days. The figure of speech, "living off the yolk," becomes clear. During this period the chick needs no other food or water, only warmth, so hatcheries ship chicks promptly, packed tightly. Warmth from each others' bodies provides critical heat.

Regardless of species, size, shape, or color, every bird repeats this miracle of new life.

(See also "Precocious Baby Birds" in April, page 90.)

Shortia
LOST AND FOUND

THE ROUNDED LEAVES, dark and evergreen, form a mat close to the ground. They spread widely over the shaded bank by the stream where I planted a small clump in the late 1970s.

A friend gave it to me, explaining that she had salvaged several plants of Shortia when Duke Power Company planned Jocassee Dam in South Carolina in the late sixties. The lake behind the dam was going to flood big areas of Shortia in Pickens and Oconee Counties, so the company let people rescue the plants.

Today in late March, dozens of pink stalks poke above the shiny leaves. Each is topped with an inch-long white or pink flower, so bell-like one almost expects it to ring if nudged. The flower's exquisite proportion and form captivate all who know it. Perhaps even more captivating is the history of Shortia.

Interested in reestablishing French forests that had been decimated by wars, King Louis XVI of France sent André Michaux, a young botanist, to America in 1786. His mission: find and ship appropriate trees and seeds. A dedicated botanist, Michaux spent many years wandering by foot and horseback from Hudson Bay to Florida, but concentrated his collecting in the mountains of western North Carolina. Astonished by the plant diversity there, he shipped not only trees but hundreds of other species.

Around 1788 he shipped a single plant of a species he could not identify. It had two stalks with seed capsules but no flowers. Back in Paris, he set the plant in a herbarium folder marked, "Unknown plant," in French. An attached note read, "High mountains of Carolina. A new genus?" He neglected to record exact date and location of the unusual find, but did describe the nature of the site. Had he stated "in" the high mountains, which could include the valleys, rather than the implied "on," Shortia's history would have been far briefer, even forgotten.

Nearly fifty years later, in 1839, Harvard botanist Asa Gray, studying the herbarium in Paris, came across the unnamed, long-ignored specimen. He described it as "having the habit of pyrola and the foliage of galax." His curiosity fired an intense determination to find this plant in the wild, particularly its flower. In 1840 he started his years of searching. He focused particularly on the high mountain areas, but experienced repeated, discouraging failures.

By 1842 Gray felt certain Michaux's find was a new genus for North America and named it Shortia in honor of his friend, Dr. Charles W. Short, an eminent botanist in Kentucky.

Speculation soared in botanical circles about where Michaux found Shortia. Was it still growing there? The question tantalized. Whenever a botanist visited the Southern Appalachians for any pursuit, Shortia was pursued, too.

The year 1877 stands out in Shortia history. Gray had searched for Shortia off and on for thirty-eight years. That year, seventeen-year-old George M. Hyams, wandering along the Catawba River near Marion in McDowell County, North Carolina, found a strange flower and gave it to his father, an herbalist and collector of medicinal plants. Nearly a year went by before the Hyamses realized the importance of the find. The plant was sent to Dr. Gray at Harvard, whose emotions overflowed with joy.

But a perplexing fact remained. Michaux had noted the location as "high mountains." The Marion area is near but not in the high mountains, so could not have been Michaux's collection site. Some botanists wondered if seeds from a mountain stand upstream had come down to start this Catawba River population. Though aging, Gray renewed search efforts in the mountains upstream, north and east of Asheville, North Carolina, fiercely eager to find the elusive plant.

Then in 1886, Dr. Charles S. Sargent, an authority on trees, was hunting a species of mountain magnolia along the Keowee River headwaters in Oconee

Glossy dark green leaves set off bell-like flowers of shortia.

County, South Carolina. There, he and his local guide, Frank Boynton, happened upon Shortia at a site fitting Michaux's descriptions. Michaux's lost site, Oconee, was rediscovered after nearly one hundred years! For many, Shortia became known as Oconee bells. Within a year they found acres of Shortia, then more sites in the Toxaway and Horsepasture River areas of Transylvania County, North Carolina.

The hunt for Shortia was over, but the threat to Shortia had begun. Wagonloads of it were hauled away in a Shortia craze. Records tell of a train dining car bringing notables to celebrate the opening of the Toxaway Hotel in the early 1900s. Shortia leaves festooned the windows, perched in vases, and decorated tables. Many acres that Sargent and Boynton found in 1889 eventually were destroyed by cultivation, grazing, and road-building.

But natural sites persist. I have wandered in several of these, the forest floor dark and shiny with Shortia leaves. I agree whole-heartedly with botanist Lincoln Foster's statement, "No idea of the beauty of this plant can be formed until it has been seen in its native home. The mass of glossy green and white, once seen, can never be forgotten."

Though Shortia's most favorable habitat was described by Shortia expert P.A. Davies as "a cool, damp, shady stream bank with moist, circulating air," one stand I planted by a stream failed to develop. Another on a dry hillside thrives. It seems backwards. But he was right: my most prosperous plantings lie along another stream bank, darkly shaded by rhododendron. There they blossom in late March and set seeds through late April and May, after which their seed stalks disappear.

Though Gray desperately searched the wild for a blooming Shortia, the plant that obsessed him, he never actually saw one in its natural habitat. However, he did have the joy of seeing a blossoming Shortia plant someone brought him a few years before his death.

APRIL

Violets Are Blue, White, Yellow—And Edible

PRIMROSE-LEAFED, long-spurred, halberd-leafed, round-leafed, birdfoot, sweet white, smooth yellow, marsh blue—to the person who tramps the mountain coves and hills and fields, these adjectives of spring are the descriptive names of violets. I can wander within a few hundred feet of the cabin and find most of them—and even a few others.

Some violets are abundant, some rare, some like tiny pansies—garden pansies are jumbo-sized violets, and some grow with weird, unvioletty-shaped leaves. But all have great appeal for spring wildflower enthusiasts.

Violets love our mountains. A checklist of spring flowers in the Smokies names more than thirty species. All belong to the genus *Viola*, as do pansies.

As if to help a person identify them, violets divide neatly into two groups: "stemless," those with no leaves on the flower stalk; and "stemmed," those with leaves up stem. The former are more

Cheery flowers of round-leaved violets appear, then linger as leaves unfold.

abundant and include our most common blue violet, quite sensibly named the common blue violet.

Adding color—white, yellow, blue, or violet—to the stem type plus using a good flower guide makes identification of many species straightforward. As for the others, I've seen even violet experts argue over several exasperating blue species, many of which interbreed. My approach to these species cannot be called scientific, but simply stated is, relax and enjoy.

Violet flowers have five petals: two upper, two side (usually with patches of hairs or "bearded"), and one lower (usually striped and extending back to form a spur). Mountain youth once made use of the extra-long projection on long-spurred violets. Two boys linked blossoms and pulled. Whoever's spur stayed on got to kiss the girl of his choice.

Violets hide a secret within their foliage. Deep under the leaves at the base of the plant, developing after the familiar showy flowers finish blooming, are strange additional flowers that self-pollinate and never open. A good proportion of the plant's seeds is produced by these.

Botanists describe the two flower types with wonderful-sounding terms: chasmogamous (accent on "mog") flowers are the open, colorful, conspicuous ones we think of as violets; cleistogamous (accent on "tog") flowers are the closed,

secret ones. Of our mountain species, only the birdfoot violet lacks the hidden flowers—"one in every crowd."

How quickly all these facts about identification and reproduction can be tossed aside in that delightful moment when we peer into the cheery faces of spring's round-leafed violets! Their sunny yellow brightens drab winter surroundings.

We need no technical vocabulary to appreciate fully the pristine beauty of the sweet white violet, which often stands "with its feet wet" as it grows in moist places. We need no facts about bearding and petal stripes to admire the pure lavender of birdfoot violet or lush foliage and dark-centered flower of marsh violet. Anyone can revel in a patch of meadow purpled with common violets and accented with yellow mustard and dandelions.

And incidentally, violets taste great. Both flowers and leaves lend colorful excitement to a tossed salad, and a few tender leaves cooked like spinach are loaded with vitamins. A variety of violet recipes can be found in books on edible wild plants. Like violet jello. Its recipe follows.

Whether seriously identifying violets or "just looking," one realizes quickly that the greatest reward is just being out there where violets grow. Each has its favorite habitat—open fields to shady streamsides, deep valleys to high mountain trails, rich woods to scrubby waysides.

VIOLET JELLO

1 envelope unflavored gelatin
½ cup cold water
¼ cup sugar (or a bit less honey)
Dash of salt
½ cup boiling water
¼ cup lemon juice
½ cup purple violet flowers in ½ cup cold water

Sprinkle gelatin onto cold water in bowl. Add sugar, salt, and boiling water; stir till dissolved. Add lemon juice and cool to room temperature. (Heat kills color and flavor of violets.) Blend violets in water and add to mixture. Pour into molds. Chill till set. Scatter extra violet flowers on top before serving. Eat flowers with the jello.

Trilliums, a Matter of Threes

TO IMAGINE a mountain spring without trilliums is unthinkable. Trilliums *are* spring, one of the season's most-loved flowers.

Drawn by the trillium's beauty in red, pink, white, even yellow, people faithfully head for mountain trails each April to indulge in their annual dose. They come to admire not only flowered masses—though even a single plant is perfection—but also the variety of species the mountains offer. Botanists disagree on the exact number, but at least eight grace the southern mountainlands.

Trilliums display their beauty for folks in cars as well as on foot. Along untold miles of winding mountain roads as well as more traveled routes like the Blue Ridge Parkway, trilliums wait, pristine and conspicuous, as if expecting to be enjoyed. White flowers of our largest species, helpfully named large-flowered trillium, *Trillium grandiflorum*, dot forest green in quantities that even disinterested folks cannot fail to notice.

A trillium is made of threes. The single, upright stem supports three leaves and a flower with three petals and three sepals (the small leaves just beneath the petals). The flower has three stigmas for

Single flowers of Vasey's trillium nod beneath the leaves.

receiving pollen and two-times-three stamens for producing its pollen. The word
trillium derives from a Latin word for
three.

Though numbers are usually multiples
of three, fours or fives also can appear. I
once saw and photographed a choice
large-flowered trillium with twenty-seven
petals.

Its leaves make the trillium a noncon-
formist in its plant family, the lily family,
which typically has leaves with parallel
veins. Trillium dares to be different—its
veins grow in a netted pattern.

After blooming, the flower develops
into a handsome green or red fruit. Sticky
seeds cling together and tumble
groundward in clusters. Each seed has
material attached that attracts ants. They
carry seeds to their nests, eat off the attractant, and unwittingly disperse them.
Midsummer most trilliums die back,
gone until spring.

From seed to blossoming plant takes six
or seven years. Not until its third year
does the tiny new plant produce even a
single true leaf. For perhaps two more
years it continues this lone annual leaf,
followed by one or two years with a
whorl of three. At last the plant matures
and produces its wonderful flower.

People who buy trilliums for gardens
need to consider this long growth period.
Whether nurseries that claim to be selling nursery-produced stock cope with

tending young trilliums six or seven years
or dig up mature plants from nature is a
problem that looms heavily in the world
of wild flower merchandising.

People often despair at the trillium's
varied names. Imagine a handsome red
species burdened with such names as
wake robin, stinking Benjamin, and
birthroot.

Early settlers, lacking knowledge of
migration, tied this species to the spring
arrival of robins. Therefore, they became
known as wake-robins, as if the robins
had been asleep all winter and suddenly
woke up. Actually, robins begin arriving
in February, well before trilliums bloom.
Although it's a pleasing, poetic name,
some people confuse things by calling all
trilliums wake-robins.

The unfortunate name stinking Benjamin came about because the flower's
unpleasant smell is detectable only when
putting nose to flower—but it's not clear
who Ben was.

Birthroot derives from a tea the colonists brewed from the flower's underground stem or rhizome and roots. The
tea was offered to new mothers to
staunch bleeding during childbirth.

Botanists avoid confusion by calling it
Trillium erectum because its flower stands
so erect above the trio of leaves.

Nature loves to throw in tricky twists
that confuse the beginner. Wake-robin
comes not only in deep red but also in

white and cream. All can grow together. And large-flowered trillium blossoms initially are pure white; then as they age over a week or two, they turn pink. Catesby's trillium, *T. catesbeii*, can start out white or pale pink, then become deeper pink.

For those who are eager to identify trilliums, colorful drawings or photographs in flower books help. One can't miss, for instance, a painted trillium, with a red "V" painted on each white petal. Its petals have wavy margins—they undulate, so its scientific name is *T. undulatum*.

But if pictures do not lead to a name, check where the flower joins the leaves. In some trillium species, the flower has a stalk, in others no stalk. Noting this can help with identification. The deep red trillium, *T. cuneatum*, called toadshade or little sweet Betsy, has no flower stalk. Also, its flowers appear as if stuck in bud stage, the petals not opening outward like most trilliums do. Mottled light and dark green decorate its leaves.

Its yellow look-alike, *T. luteum*, also has no flower stalk. Most mountain trilliums have a stalk.

Then note whether the flower stalk holds the flower above the leaves, as in *T. erectum* and *T. grandiflorum*, or arches over, dropping the flower under the leaves. Three mountain species "nod"—nodding trillium, *T. cernuum* ("turned towards the earth"), Vasey's trillium, *T. vaseyi*, and sometimes, Catesby's trillium. George Vasey and Mark Catesby were early American botanists.

Trillium lovers have favorites. Some choose large-flowered trillium's ruffly white flowers that turn pink. Some favor painted trillium with its dabs of red. Seldom-seen Catesby's trillium lures with its rarity and delicately proportioned leaves. I choose Vasey's and cannot resist tipping leaves up to see that handsome, deep-red flower nodding beneath, solitary, magnificent, often three inches across.

In Donald and Lillian Stokes's wonderful book, *A Guide to Enjoying Wildflowers*, I found a statement that says it all, "Wherever trilliums are found, they are a treat to encounter."

(See also "From Asparagus to Lilies" in March, page 60.)

THE LOVE OF BLUEBIRDS

WHEN IS A BLUE BIRD not a blue-bird? When it's sparrow-sized and blue all over; that's an indigo bunting. When it's robin-sized and sporting a crest and white stripes, that's a blue jay.

But moments ago, a blue bird perched on a sumac berry cluster beside the porch and proved he was indeed a bluebird. He showed his breast of rusty orange.

A close relative of the robin, the blue-bird is said to carry on its back and head "the hue of heaven," though actually its blue is deeper than the sky. On its breast, it displays "the rich rusty-brown of freshly turned earth," though that depends on where you turn the earth. Rusty orange seems a better definition.

Such vivid description applies only to the male, a spectacular fellow indeed when morning sunlight glows on his blue and orange. I know; I just saw him. The female, on the other hand, appears to have been laundered too often. As with over-washed blue jeans, her colors look severely faded, mere tints of his.

So how can we have the heart to con-fuse the gentle, well-behaved bluebird with rowdy jays that pick noisy squabbles and advertise their presence brazenly?

The bluebird's soft warbles sound

*The usually gentle, friendly bluebird can
turn aggressive against birds that venture too close to its nest.*
Photograph by J. R. Woodward

dignified and confidential, touched with tenderness. A background of them as we work about the yard gives friendly, relaxing accompaniment.

Let's face it—people love a bluebird. Even early English in the Plymouth colony succumbed to its charm. They called it the "blue robin" because its size and rusty breast resembled their beloved English robin. Bluebirds are close relatives of our robin, which likewise received its name because of its rusty breast. Both are thrushes.

Literature, music, and custom chose bluebirds as the symbol of happiness. Maurice Maeterlinck, the Belgian poet-dramatist, solidified this symbolism in his famous play, *The Bluebird*. Northern folks consider the return of the bluebird a happy sign of spring. Older people remember the American World War II song, "There'll be bluebirds over, The white cliffs of Dover, Tomorrow when the world is free." Poignant, well-meant words, but inaccurate. Bluebirds don't live in England. Fortunately, happiness can be anywhere.

Bringing to our yards their shy friendliness and impeccable behavior, as well as their flash of blue, bluebirds seem to like people. That's what we'd like to think, anyway. Actually, yards attract bluebirds, who like to feed in open areas. Perching on a post, sprig, or wire, the birds will spot an insect or worm on the ground and drop down to catch it, a reversal of flycatcher behavior. A flycatcher sits on a similarly exposed perch but flies up to catch its insect in the air.

Bluebirds and old-time orchards belonged together. Orchards provided open ground and nesting cavities. Bluebirds returned the favor by eating great quantities of insects. Modern orchards, pruned and sprayed, enhance apples but obliterate bluebird food. In the early days of spraying, an old orchardist commented to me that he just couldn't understand why he didn't have bluebirds anymore.

For many decades, the number of nest cavities diminished precipitously. The culprits included sterile orchards, fewer wood fence posts with holes, and competition for remaining holes by burgeoning populations of aggressive house sparrows and starlings, both brought from England. The bluebird population plummeted.

People missed them. Their love affair with bluebirds lived on, and campaigns to provide nest boxes bore fruit—or rather, young birds. Through much of the bluebird's range, dedicated workers set boxes six to twelve feet above ground in open areas. Homeowners helped by putting boxes in their yards. Bluebirds accepted the hospitality.

The concept of "bluebird trails" was initiated in Illinois, with a large-scale nest-box program. This involved placing boxes one hundred yards apart in open areas. The program led to the establishment of numerous trails, the longest running six hundred miles in Canada. The boxes stand enough in the open to discourage house sparrows and have small enough entrance holes to keep out starlings. Bluebirds investigate them by late February and settle down to business by late March.

Though not back to their former abundance, a bluebird perched on a topmost twig, roadside wire, or garden chair is once again common. They seem solidly established. We see them at winter feeders, watch them feed young in spring, enjoy family groups in summer, and admire their colors against reds and golds in fall.

Once again the bluebird brings happiness, unwittingly fulfilling its symbolic mission.

Dogwood, a Special Mountain Beauty

IF WE COULD FLY over the mountains in the next two or three weeks, we might be startled to see patches of snow amid the vast spread of mountain woodland below.

Snow in April? This "snow" is dogwood blossoms.

Once again dogwoods' white and pink show plays in yards, city, and forests. Like last year, folks will exclaim that the dogwoods are extra lovely this year. Each year their beauty seems special.

Dogwood offers beauty in all seasons. One tree expert called it "America's most decorative tree." As spring blossoms fade, lustrous green summer leaves unfold and cover the tree's shapely limbs. In autumn the leaves turn deep red, then drop, leaving twigs fruited with fire-engine red berries. Wintry snow trim sets off the pleasing layers of its twigs. And dogwood is tidily small; a forty-foot tree is a giant.

Even in winter, long before blossoms appear, we can glance at a dogwood and predict whether the tree will (or won't) be loaded with flowers this spring. It's easy because dogwood grows two types of buds. Pointed leaf buds are inconspicuous, but flower buds stand out prominently, gray, somewhat fuzzy, and shaped like wee onions. Many buds mean many blossoms.

Choose a flower bud to examine every

As dogwood blossoms open, green tints the white.

few days for the next two weeks. You'll note that each unopened bud is protected by two outer scales, then two inner scales right angled to them. Already this spring, those four scales, called bracts, have pulled apart slightly.

As days pass, the four bracts grow larger, tinted at first with green, then yellow, then cream, finally white. (Pink dogwood's bracts are dark pink at first, becoming lighter as they grow.)

Now for some fun. When the blossom is fully open, we can ask someone the color of a dogwood flower. It seems a silly question, but watch out.

If the four white or pink "petals" are actually bracts, where are the real flower petals?

Look closely in the blossom's center at that cluster of tiny green buds. Each of these opens and spreads four curved, yellow-green petals, and in the center stands a green pistil surrounded by four yellow-green, pollen-bearing stamens. A dogwood flower is yellow-green—and tiny.

Have you ever wondered why each white or pink bract has a dark notch at its tip? If you watch the early bud daily as the bracts enlarge, you'll discover that the remains of the scaly part of the bract which once covered the winter bud become that dark notch.

Dogwood's conspicuous bracts signal insects: "Land here. There's nectar in these little flowers. Come have a sip." Each flower fertilized by insect-carried pollen starts to swell at its base, gradually enlarging into a green oval fruit enclosing a single hard seed. By autumn the fruits, now red, trim the tree.

Then call in the birds. Robins swoop in to feed, as do mockingbirds, waxwings, and cardinals. Starlings can strip a tree in minutes. I watched one fruit-laden dogwood host a dozen or more bluebirds with its bright red banquet.

The beauty of dogwood's spring blossoms nearly led to its extermination early in this century. Markets in towns and cities sold huge sprays for pennies, and people swarmed over the countryside, breaking branches to decorate their home or sell. Fortunately, enlightened people passed laws to protect the tree. North Carolina even chose dogwood as its state flower.

It seems curious that such a charming tree bears the uncharming name of dogwood. Someone will inevitably quip, "Because of its bark!"—an old, old joke. In early Germany the tough hard wood of the European dogwood was used for making skewers and animal prods called "dags" (the "a" sounding as in father). The original name was "dagwood," and the name came to America with the settlers, eventually changing to dogwood.

But another tale persists: A brew of dogwood's bark discouraged fleas and mange on dogs. It's unclear if either story is correct, but I prefer the first. Somehow, skewers and prods appeal more than flea and mange remedies.

Our native white dogwood has the scientific name *Cornus florida*. (Pink dogwood has been developed from it.) *Cornus* is Latin for "horn," referring to dogwood's hard wood, popular for tool parts and, before plastics, for weaving shuttles. *Florida* means "flowering."

A tree so prominent in mountain springs should surely last forever. In recent years, however, a disease has been destroying dogwoods in the Northeast and threatens Southern Appalachian dogwoods, too. It's hard to imagine a spring without dogwood, yet the threat is real. Someday dogwoods, so wonderfully common now, could be scarce, even rare. Someday they may be even more valuable for us.

Meanwhile, when the spring sky spreads extra blue, I plan to sit beneath a dogwood tree and look to the blue through a mass of backlit blossoms. I'll feel again that, even if common, dogwood is special.

PRECOCIOUS BABY BIRDS

AT MY FEET lies a tiny robin, newly hatched, deplorably helpless. Its nest hides in the overhead maple; we watched it being built several weeks ago. The hatchling barely moves. Then it dies. A newly hatched baby chicken would have fared far better.

Words that describe a day-old chick might include cute, fluffy, cuddly, charming. A day-old robin would probably inspire words like ugly, naked, bloated, wobbly. Its charm lies only in its helplessness and size.

A new chick's eyes sparkle as it scurries about, alert and eager. A robin's eyes stay closed and bulging as it sprawls in the nest, weak and dependent. Most baby birds fit neatly into one of two major categories. At hatching, precocial young are, well, precocious. Like the chick, their eyes are open, their down thick, their legs ready to run. If aquatic, like ducks, they swim. They preen, bask in the sun, scratch, pick up food, and leave the nest soon after hatching. *Precocial* derives from Latin meaning "mature before"—before hatching.

Most land precocial young scurry after their mother, who leads them to food. In many species the mother taps the ground with her beak near a likely morsel, and the young rush to it. Within an

A killdeer chick hatches from a large egg open-eyed and nearly ready to run.
Photograph by Warren Greene/VIREO

hour after hatching, a chick from our home incubator ran to my finger as I tapped the ground. Then it scratched the ground several times with each leg, all chicken!

Precocial young of many water and sea birds, such as gulls and puffins, cannot follow a parent that flies to sea to get food. Therefore, adults bring food to them. Some parents poke the food into the young. Others merely set the food down for their precocious young to pick up.

Altricial birds, the second major category of young, include our songbirds. At hatching, they need tender care. Appropriately, *altricial* derives from the Latin for "nurse." Though some young may have slight patches of down, they are mostly naked with eyes tightly closed. Their body heat control doesn't work well yet, so they require heat from the parent's body—brooding.

A parent arriving at the nest is stimulated by great, gaping mouths with brightly colored linings and yellow borders. The babies' feeble cheeping and head wobbling add to the excitement. The parent responds by poking food in and dashing off to get more.

Two local birds, the killdeer (precocial) and the meadowlark (altricial) are approximately the same body size, but the killdeer's egg is nearly three times larger in volume. Precocial birds lay eggs much larger in proportion to the adult's size than those of altricial birds. They incubate much longer—the killdeer for twenty-four days; the meadowlark for fourteen.

Precocial young stay inside their large egg longer because they develop more fully before hatching. Altricial young, less developed at hatching, catch up after hatching. If we add nest-care time to incubation time for the early-hatched meadowlark, it nearly equals the incubation time for the killdeer.

A few familiar birds fit neither precocial nor altricial categories. They lie between. At hatching, young hawks and owls are fully downy and comparatively well-developed, yet they stay in the nest, dependent on close parental care for many weeks.

In our mountains, only a few wild species are truly precocial: ruffed grouse, wild turkey, various ducks, geese, bobwhite, and killdeer. Nighthawks and whippoorwills are precocial, too, but the young stay close to the nest. Precocial, altricial—not words on the tip of the tongue in everyday living, but they describe something special about baby birds. And almost everyone enjoys baby birds.

(See also "The Wonder of Eggs" in March, page 66, and "The Early Days of a Baby Robin" in May, page 104.)

Return of the Hummers

THEY'RE BACK! Tiny bundles of speed and energy, the hummingbirds have returned from the danger and stress of migration. They have journeyed all the way from Central America.

We humans play with the thought that surely they have returned solely to entertain us, because they're highly skilled at that. The swooping dives of courting males, the swirling squabbles, the lightning acrobatics astonish even veteran hummingbird watchers. When they pause a moment, perched on a twig, primping, they startle us with being so birdlike.

Somehow their humming wings and zooming flight make them seem more like insects.

Most of their interests exclude us. Their sights are set on natural food and reproduction. But what an exciting moment when a hummer zooms close and hovers only a few feet away, peering directly at you with naive curiosity, twittering with apparent friendliness. Seeming extra brave, the bird is confident of a fast getaway on wings that blur with motion, beating fifty to sixty times per second, but the encounter is fleeting. Almost as

A whirr of wings and high delicate twitters led to
the discovery of a hummingbird nest with two nearly-grown young.
Photograph by Tom Hallowell

soon as you become aware of it, the hummer has disappeared.

Nectar, the sweet liquid in flowers that attracts insects for pollination, is prime hummingbird food, so a nectar substitute, sugar water, used in special feeders, lures them closer. The recipe is simple: four parts water, one part sugar, boiled five minutes to retard fermentation and mold. (Extra boiled mixture can be stored a few days in the refrigerator.) Though a bit more nourishing, honey water, even if boiled, is subject to quick fermentation. It also encourages a fungus disease. Stick with sugar. Frequent cleaning and fresh refills of feeders are important for keeping hummers healthy.

Many people insist on adding red food dye to the sugar syrup, aware that red attracts hummers. (An ornithologist reported watching a hummer investigating a red traffic light, ignoring yellow and green.) In times when just simple glass bottles and tubes were used, red dye was important. Most modern feeders, however, have a red plastic attractant—part of the container itself or red "flowers" surrounding tube openings. Red syrup is not recommended. After all, that's pouring artificial dyes into the natural perfection of a hummingbird.

The best way to lure hummingbirds is with flowers, particularly reds and oranges. Popular flowers include scarlet sage, trumpet creeper, red-flowered honeysuckle, nasturtium, columbine, impatiens, bee balm, touch-me-not (jewelweed), cardinal flower, gladiolus, and coral bells. Then watch the incredible aerial maneuvers as the bird positions its needle-like bill so that its slender, extendible tongue can reach into the deepest of flowers. That tongue, incidentally, can be seen easily as it pokes into a clear feeder tube.

Watch a hummingbird "work over" the nooks and crannies around a window frame. We might like to flatter ourselves that the birds are being friendly and interested in our activities indoors. Mostly they are lapping up minute insects and spiders with their long tongues. These important bits of live food supplement the nectar.

Even though scientists list over three hundred hummingbird species, we have only one species, the rubythroat, in the eastern United States. (Wandering species from other parts are extremely rare.) Only male rubythroats display the iridescent ruby throat patch, a spectacular contrast to the shimmering green body and white breast. Even the throat can fool us: in certain lighting, it appears jet black.

Meanwhile, our boiled, undyed sugar syrup waits on the porch in clean, freshly filled feeders. It's time for the hummers to dine with us.

THE CHALLENGE OF WARBLERS

FOR BIRDWATCHERS, warblers cause delight or despair—or both. Non-birdwatchers wonder what a warbler is anyway.

According to the dictionary, to warble is to sing melodiously in a trilling manner. A warbler also is a person or bird that sings so. A further definition describes a warbler as any of a large family of small, insect-eating, New World birds, many of which are brightly colored. They're not just any bird that sings.

Thus it may seem surprising that something as delightful as a colorful, singing bird can cause despair. Try finding the one you just heard, and you'll understand quickly. As these notoriously active, elusive little fellows busily search for insects, they stay within the maze of tree tops or dense shrubs, inevitably behind a twig or leaf. You see them dart, but by the time your binoculars focus, they're gone. Exasperating! Moreover, the nondescript glimpse one gets from forty feet below bears dubious resemblance to the static side view in a bird guide.

To complicate things, most warblers are transients, just passing through for a few days during spring migration. They're following the increase of insects as the days become warmer. Their short stay allows no time for the comfortable familiarity we have with common yard birds.

Birdwatchers talk about "warbler waves" when, in late April and early May, mixed warbler flocks flow through the treetops. Sadly, in recent years waves have diminished to trickles, mainly due to habitat loss both in nesting territory in North America and wintering grounds in South America. Forest destruction and housing and commercial development have obliterated warblers' habitats. Adding to their struggle to survive are pesticides, cowbird predation, and deer over-browsing of shrubby places home to insects warblers eat.

One doesn't watch warblers from the house like a flock of robins on the lawn. One must go outdoors and listen. From treetops come high-pitched squeaks, chits, buzzes—and warbles. Only an experienced ear fully appreciates the variety. I've known experts who could identify an impressive list of warbler species without seeing one bird.

One may wonder why people bother with warblers at all. Simply stated, because they're beautiful. Flipping through the warbler pages in any bird book verifies this. Rewards for the struggle to get a good look include the yellowthroat's buttercup throat against its jet black mask; the black-throated blue warbler's clean-cut pattern of blue-black-white; the magnolia warbler's startling black stripes on yellow; the blackburnian warbler's flaming orange throat.

And warblers challenge. In any field of pursuit, the unique challenge lures us on. The white plunging river, the steep rugged mountain, the demanding sonata. . .and the elusive warbler. All dare us to conquer, rewarding success with thrills.

Not all of the approximately thirty-six spring warbler species we might see in our mountains continue north. By mid-May, about twenty settle down to nest here, the nest location influenced by altitude. For example, blackburnian and Canada warblers prefer the high elevations, redstarts the low.

Stop, look, and listen for yellow warblers among willows and alders along water courses, and for yellowthroats in low, bushy fields and wet thickets. Striped black and white warblers "creep" on trunks of deciduous trees, hunting food much as nuthatches and brown creepers do. Black-throated blue warblers choose deciduous woodlands while black-throated greens prefer hemlock or spruce-fir groves.

The ultimate challenge for warbler identification comes in autumn. The birds have lost their colorful plumage through molting and have acquired drab plumage for fall and winter. Species that differ radically in summer look discouragingly similar—olive gray or dull yellowish with few distinguishing features. Roger Tory Peterson in his famous *Field Guide to the Birds* includes several pages appropriately entitled, "Confusing Fall Warblers." The enthusiast who conquered spring warblers suddenly confronts a whole new set.

That dilemma is months away now when the outdoors is atwitter with warbler conversation and these butterflies of the bird world dart amid new leaves and blossoms.

Get out the binoculars. Sharp eyes, discerning ears, a good field guide, and patience will combine to fill you in on that special annual delight—the return of the warblers.

(See also "Migration Mysteries" in November, page 251.)

MAY

Earthworms, Lowly Plowmen

WITH THE BACK of my spade, I knock apart a fresh clump of garden soil. Several long earthworms retract hastily into shortened burrows. Two more lie loosely on crumbled earth, momentarily shocked by unexpected devastation in the quiet world where they serve mankind unwittingly.

Then suddenly they push down into broken soil, spurning sunlight in favor of darkness and moisture. After all, they get their oxygen through moist skins; drying is fatal.

Another worm, bisected by the slicing spade, thrashes wildly. Its contortions attract my attention, and I stoop for a closer look. Within moments, the head end disappears into soil. It will regenerate a new tail end and proceed with life as usual, but the old tail end slows.

I happen to admire earthworms, not because of their appearance, which is deplorably unappealing, but because of the unobtrusive way in which they collectively accomplish marvels. Their work is one of nature's grandest achievements.

The world over, earthworms labor unseen in the topsoil of our earth. The

*An earthworm glides across open moss only briefly, far
preferring the darkness and moisture of its burrow in the soil.*

worth of soil can often be measured in terms of total worms therein. Some people believe that even the economies of nations can be measured in terms of worms—all because worms eat dirt.

Unless the soil is extremely loose, these wiggly tubes of flesh, which lack eyes, legs, ears, faces, or voices, burrow by eating their way through dirt. The soil passes through their digestive canals, where food fragments are broken down chemically and absorbed. Acids and salts even break down particles of rock, and this releases minerals vital to plant growth.

Some earthworm species deposit this dirt mixed with valuable waste materials, known as castings, within the burrows; others expel castings outside the entrance. Either is a boon to farmers. Worm "waste" contains forty-five percent more nitrogen and phosphorus and fifty percent more potassium than most surface soil.

But golfers waste no enthusiasm on castings. A casting on a putting green can send a perfect putt askew.

The average one-acre garden has approximately fifty thousand dirt-eating worms, often dubbed "humus factories." These lowly plowmen pass collectively nearly thirteen tons of soil per year.

Archaeologists long wondered why objects left on the earth's surface sank gradually. They learned to bless the earthworm, master of soil-moving. Walls and even buildings have been undermined, covered, and saved from destruction—by worms.

As we look across the landscape, we can reflect that much of the soil on this earth has been swallowed and passed through earthworms at least once, some possibly hundreds of times.

The quiet worm serves the soil—and therefore nations—in other ways. Its burrows allow air and water to penetrate hardened soil, loosening it, and the worm pulls astonishing quantities of green plant material into its burrow. Some serves as food, but much decays, adding organic fiber and nutrient to soil, as a farmer does when he plows under a cover crop.

Uncountable birds and animals relish the earthworm as food, and no one will argue its value when impaled on a fish hook.

As I ponder earthworms in a spadeful of garden soil, I consider how the accomplishment of each individual seems minuscule, yet how their collective achievement yields results of worldwide economic importance. Hardly the lowly plowman.

(See also "Seven Wonders in My Yard" in October, page 230.)

THE EARLY DAYS OF A BABY ROBIN

DAY 1. With a final, mighty kick, he is free. He shakes loose a last piece of egg shell and sprawls exhausted on the floor of his home, a robin's nest. Hatching out of an egg is a tough job. He's worked all day to break the weakened shell, using his "egg tooth," a sharp, rough projection on the tip of his upper beak.

The pulsing bodies of two nest-mates snuggle close against him in a dark world of warm feathers. His big eyes have not yet opened. Maybe it's just as well, for newly hatched songbirds are not much to see. Nearly naked, with bulging abdomens, they lift wobbly heads on scrawny necks. Baggy skin compounds their appearance problems. Their soon-to-be-marvelous wings hang limp and ineffective.

Suddenly the feathery warmth lifts. The female parent picks up the shell fragment and flies away, then returns to carry off the shell of the fourth egg to hatch. She drops the pieces far from the nest to deceive enemies.

When the nest jiggles again, the baby raises its head with a mighty effort and opens its huge mouth—wide. Dad stuffs a delicious piece of caterpillar down his throat. The mouth has a bright yellow

Helpless robin babies require intense parental care but fly full-grown from the nest in about two weeks.
Photograph by J. R. Woodward

border to excite and guide the parent.

Hunger governs activity as the parents work diligently all day to bring food. They instinctively bring soft food for the babies, items often quite different from their own menu. As long as mouths open, parents poke—worms, flies, caterpillars, grubs, spiders.

One parent offers too big a meal and watches perplexed when the baby doesn't swallow. As she tries to pull the half-swallowed food out, she lifts the baby off the nest floor with it. With a flip, she loosens the caterpillar and pecks to soften it, and pokes it in again. The baby swallows successfully.

Food going in means waste coming out. Just after swallowing, the baby robin passes limey material neatly contained in a soft membrane. Instantly the parent grabs this fecal sac and flies off to drop it at a distance from the nest. The nest stays clean.

The new baby requires frequent brooding, snuggling amid feathers against a parent's warm body. Its body thermostat does not yet function, so it cools or heats according to its surroundings, as with cold-blooded animals.

Day 6. Growth! The baby robin is nearly six times hatching size. His body temperature is constant now; frequent brooding is no longer urgent. The egg tooth fell off several days ago. And he can see. Now if the nest jiggles, he begs only if the parent shows. For anything else, he "freezes."

Feathers are developing in sheaths, "pin feathers." As with most birds, they grow only on eight special skin areas called tracts, which show prominently on the baby. From these, nearly three thousand feathers will develop when the robin reaches maturity. (I wonder who had the patience to count feathers to find that average number.)

Day 9. Feathers make the nestling "cute" by human standards. His fluttering wings while begging for food attract parental attention. Brooding is necessary only during rain, a major enemy.

While struggling to be fed, one overly eager nest-mate tumbles from the nest. He lies on the ground, quite still, but the nest is roomier and competition less acute.

Day 12. Feet and toes have strength-ened enough for perching, and feathering is complete, though tail feathers remain short, requiring less nest room. The young robin is nearly full size, ten times hatching size, and no wonder. Observers estimate that at this stage a young robin can consume fourteen feet of earthworms per day.

A nest-mate climbs onto a tree branch. She likes it and stays. Another follows but tumbles. His calls from the ground distress the parents. He hides in a low bush and yells for food. A parent flies down to feed him.

Day 13. The last baby robin perches on the nest edge. Parents call, urging him out, so he jumps to a limb and squawks. A parent brings a choice grub. He gulps it, then leaps for his first flight, and crash lands on some grass.

A giant creature called a boy runs toward him and grabs. The robin hops into a dense shrub and hides, camouflaged by his speckled tan breast. If only the boy knew that parent birds take better care of their young than even the most well-meaning human!

The nest is empty.

(See also "Precocious Baby Birds" in April, page 90.)

NATURE'S DELICATE BALANCE

EVERYTHING had been so perfect—the cardinals had nested in a shrub directly outside our window, allowing a prime view of their nesting activities. We counted eggs until there were four and watched the patient parents incubate them for twelve days.

We rejoiced in the hatching of three into naked, miserably homely creatures that seemed all mouth, and checked daily as they grew in size, feathering, and charm. By then three pairs of dark beady eyes watched us with interest, too.

Then one little cardinal disappeared, though still far too young to leave the nest naturally. The following day the other two were gone. Disaster had overtaken the cardinal family. Some other creature had needed a meal.

The parents, perplexed, tended the nest a few hours until instincts guided them elsewhere to start another.

Most cardinals have two broods, averaging four eggs. If all eight young survived, that would total four more pairs to breed next spring. If each of them produced eight eggs, and their parents did the same, a total of forty young, twenty-five pairs of cardinals would breed the next season. A yard that supports one pair could not support such mushrooming numbers.

Similarly, if all the thousands of tadpoles that hatch from a single frog's egg

*The number of seeds in a dandelion patch
far exceeds the number that the land can suppport.*

mass survived, the pond would be clogged with tadpoles quickly.

A pine tree produces dozens of seeds on each cone and hundreds of cones. If every seed grew into a new pine tree that matured to produce more cones, if all the hundreds of mosquitoes that hatched from one female's egg laying survived and reproduced, if all squirrel babies lived to produce more babies, the outdoor world would be crammed with life beyond imagination.

In a spare moment, pluck a dandelion seed head, one of those fluffy balls we like to blow. Control the impulse to blow and note the delicate symmetry of the seed arrangement and filmy beauty of the parachutes. Then pluck seeds one by one, counting. Healthy globes might have three hundred seeds, plants frequently lopped by mowers perhaps one hundred and fifty.

A square foot of undisturbed soil can support about three healthy dandelion plants, averaging about twenty flowers per plant—18,000 seeds! What if all 18,000 sprouted and grew?

Nature has a superb check on this phenomenon of overproduction—mortality. It manages a marvelous balance of production versus consumption—rabbit eats clover, crow gulps baby cardinal, and jay consumes song sparrow eggs. Squirrels feast on pine seeds, mice and finches on dandelion seeds, swallows on mosquitoes, caterpillars on leaves, microbes on dead fruit.

Mortality of plants and animals is influenced, too, by where they live, their habitat. A given habitat supports only a given number of any species; any excess is eliminated. It must starve, die of disease, be shaded out, or move away, but often finds no new place to go. The average back yard may support just one pair of cardinals. If six cardinal pairs try to breed there, fights ensue over food supply and territory; five must go. A corner of yard supports one large maple. If all the seedlings that sprout beneath it grow, the struggle for light, space, and food will eliminate most.

This natural adjustment of population is called, quite logically, the balance of nature. It carries on without remorse night and day, year in, year out, eon through eon, never static, fluctuating constantly from natural causes—flood, drought, fire, storm, disease, temperature—and from man-made causes.

If we contemplate a natural environment, we see a harshly beautiful, complex web of life. Each plant, each creature plays its individual role while exquisitely interdependent on others to a degree far beyond our comprehension. Science constantly reveals new aspects of this interdependence and awes us with its complexity—and our dependence on it.

We become upset over the loss of a nest of cardinals, a minuscule, even necessary event among the myriad in nature's everyday balancing routine. It perplexes that evidence of the natural balance unsettles us. Yet we tend to minimize the effects of our own disruption—wasting, over-consuming, obliterating, polluting. As Priscilla urged in Longfellow's "Courtship of Miles Standish," "Look to thyself, John."

Forests with Giants

IN OUR ABANDONED FIELD a seedling forest starts. Up the hill a young forest thrives, above it a mature forest. If only we could walk beyond that into virgin forest, forest undisturbed by man.

Virgin forest—the name seems magic, conjuring visions of forests where every tree towers as a giant, every trunk rises massively. But virgin forests are gone—or so I thought. Indians affected some; white settlers ravaged the rest for land clearing and lumber.

Then I moved to the southern mountains and was thrilled to discover that isolated stretches of virgin forest still exist.

In the Great Smokies and Nantahala Mountains, for example, a few foresighted people, along with the forests' inaccessibility, helped save patches of them. We can walk through virgin forests today. Though exploration and trails have left them no longer undisturbed, they remain uncut.

When we enter a virgin forest, we unconsciously lower our voices, soften our steps in awe and respect. Unlike in my mind's picture, true tree giants are few. Infant, adolescent, and middle-aged trees share the home of patriarchs, renewing the forest.

Giant tulip trees dwarf all else in the cove hardwood forest.

Within moments, the spell of height, serenity, and diversity engulf. Forest grandeur promotes humility. One cannot avoid a sense of reverence in such lush and magnificent surroundings.

In bowl-shaped mountain valleys called coves, the rich, damp soil supports a special forest, the Southern Appalachian cove hardwood forest—tulip tree, buckeye, sugar maple, red oak, ash, walnut, sourwood, silverbell, beech, yellowwood, dozens of others. Here thrives greater temperate zone diversity than almost anywhere in the world. Here grow our nation's last stands of this virgin forest.

Silence pervades—our silence, that is, which magnifies the sounds of nature. A winter wren's brilliant notes tumble above the swirls of a stream's pool; a rosebreasted grosbeak calls; leaves whisper; a chipmunk chirps; a bee zooms.

Spring in the forest offers a visual feast of massed trillium, phacelia, phlox, and violets and a long list of flowering neighbors. Fern carpets set off the flowers. Moss wraps fallen trunks and rocks in plush green.

One massive tulip tree requires six adults with arms outstretched to reach around it. When we stand at the base of a five-person Goliath and look up to confirm its identity, we laugh. We need binoculars to study its lowest leaves.

From time to time, giants fall and decompose for generations, their massive trunks changing to soil. Nurseries of flower, shrub, and tree seedlings and saplings grow on them, so ecologists call them "nurse logs."

As we wander this magnificent tree cathedral, we compare it with a nearby forest we had visited. Labeled "managed demonstration forest," it had signs along its trails explaining forest uses. The demonstration forest cultivated "useful" species and explained how big trees and "junk" trees had been harvested, crooked trees removed, remaining trees thinned so all would be appropriate for cutting at optimum size and time for use. The demonstration was well done, and we fully agreed some forests must be managed as crops to satisfy our need for wood products.

However, one sign proudly exhorted us to look around and learn about this "proper forest." "Proper?" Has nature through the eons failed to manage a proper forest? Does man think he can manage forests more properly?

To understand the inappropriate use of the term "proper forest," simply walk a while and pause a while in the virgin forest. Put your hands on a forest giant, look up into it, sense the diversity, grandeur, and rich life an old forest sustains.

We have stood, sat, walked, and photographed in virgin forest many times since we discovered the trails in Joyce Kilmer Memorial Forest in the

Nantahalas, and of Ramsey Cascade Trail, Greenbrier Cove, and Albright Grove in the Great Smokies. Every time the experience refreshes, offers something new, and every time we wish that people unfamiliar with woods could experience this forest environment so bursting with growth and green.

Peter Farb's excellent book, *The Face of North America*, states, "If a traveler were permitted to see only one forest in eastern United States, that one should be a cove hardwood."

I'll add another word—a virgin cove hardwood.

TREE GROWTH 101

IF YOU EVER RETURN to a tree you knew as a child, chances are you'll be surprised to find that special branch you once loved to hang on lower than you recalled. After all, you've grown taller. Or, you may insist that your favorite limb has moved higher up the tree through the years. There it is—way up there.

Try to convince those caught up in nostalgic remembrance that their claim is impossible, that trees just don't grow that way. A limb at a certain height stays at that height, a limb "way up there" grew way up there originally. The limb swung on in youth has probably died and bro-

ken off or been cut off. Healing bark has obliterated the place where it grew.

Growth centers on trees are isolated and easy to remember. Growth takes place only, 1) at the tips, and 2) around the girth.

First, tips: Growth (adding new cells) occurs at all tips—tree top, twig tips, and root tips.

Pretend you're a tree. Stand and hold arms straight out to the side to represent limbs. Your body is the trunk, your head the top of the tree, your toes the roots.

As a tree, you could add height or

length only at the tips—only on top of your head, at your finger tips, and at the tips of your toes. However, adding at these locations wouldn't affect the level of your arms. They would stay in their original spot.

Second, girth: The tree grows in thickness or girth around its trunk and branches, adding a layer of wood each growing season.

The growing layer that lies beneath the bark around the trunk and branches is only a few cells thick, an incredibly thin growing layer for all that tree. It is called the *cambium* from a Latin word meaning "change." The cells in the cambium divide and change.

To its outer side, the cambium changes into long cells which form tubes. These carry food made in leaves to the rest of the tree.

To its inner side, the cambium changes into long cells which form wood. The most recently grown wood carries water from roots up through the tree to its leaves. Older wood cells die and become hard and strong. Most of a tree's bulk is dead.

In early spring new wood cells grow large; in late spring or early summer, they grow small. The next spring the new cells are large again, followed by small. These alternating large and small cell areas show as rings when a tree is cut across, appropriately called growth rings or annual

rings. We count them to learn a tree's age.

Rings not only tell age, they reveal a history of the tree's growth. A wide ring means the tree grew well, perhaps due to plentiful rainfall or good light. A narrow ring means it grew poorly, perhaps due to drought or poor light. Rings tell of fire, damage, or pressure, as when one tree leans against another.

A fascinating science has developed around the study of tree rings—dendrochronology. It investigates what tree rings tell about history.

Dendrochronologists (nineteen letters in that fine word) have devised calendars of tree rings. Provide them a tree section, and they match it to their calendar of rings to reveal when it grew and what climatic conditions were during its life. Worldwide tree calendars date back even hundreds of years before Christ.

Archaeologists use rings for dating. For example, rings on a log from an ancient pueblo matched to the calendar of rings for that area reveal when the pueblo was built.

The study of forest decline, a current worldwide environmental concern, uses tree growth calendars. Tree rings in recent years show an alarming slowdown in growth.

Strange what tangents hanging on tree limbs can lead to.

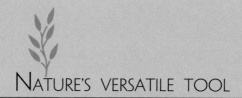

Nature's Versatile Tool

IT CAN REVEAL where a bird lives, how it lives, and who it is. It can serve as a knife, fork, spoon, chisel, trowel, tongs, probe, hammer, needle, forceps, and straw. And there is more: nut cracker, spear, shuttle, hod, comb, pliers, grocery bag, or wood basket. What a magnificent variety of functions this gadget can perform, this simple structure known as a beak or bill. It does many jobs we humans delegate to hands or tools.

We note these beak functions casually because they are what we expect of birds. But ponder the skill of an oriole that weaves a hanging nest at the end of a swaying limb, poking and threading strands of grasses with remarkable know-how. Yet the bird may be building its first nest and has never seen a nest built before.

And consider the skill of a house wren maneuvering a stick several times its own length through a hole in a wren box, all with its tiny beak. Then it wrestles the sprig into proper position within the box. The house wren is one of many species that carry and arrange long strands of grass and sticks for nest construction.

Robins and barn swallows carry mud in their beaks, great wads of it as nesting material. Woodpeckers use beaks as chisels, and blue jays and titmice use them as hammers to pound off seed coats.

Cardinal beaks serve as nut crackers and woodcock beaks as probes, poking deep into the ground to find earthworms. Long heron beaks act as tongs to nab fish and frogs.

Birds carry a delightful assortment of foodstuffs in these grocery bags—cherries, fish, shrimp, nuts, beetles, caterpillars, spiders, moths, worms, for example. (Some birds, like hawks and owls, use feet instead of beaks as carriers.)

And beaks do all the preening, that tremendously important grooming of feathers which keeps them in top condition for flight and weather protection.

The amazing diversity of beak shapes developed to satisfy birds' varying requirements for finding and eating food. Swallows, chimney swifts, and nighthawks, which chase and capture insects in flight, have very short beaks and wide mouths, almost like scoops.

Hummingbirds, seeking nectar deep within flowers, need long, narrow beaks. Warblers and vireos, which glean tiny insects from leaves and twigs, have petite, slender beaks. Their food is soft, so they don't need heavy beaks like the seed eaters—sparrows, finches, cardinals, and grosbeaks.

Hawks and owls have sharply curved beaks for tearing flesh before eating it or before feeding their young.

Because crows and jays eat a wide variety of diets, their beaks are sturdy and fairly long. Crows are famous for their love of corn, yet they'll feed on road kills, grasshoppers, mice, or small birds' eggs with equal enthusiasm.

The fine, pointed beaks of chickadees, titmice, nuthatches, and creepers are excellent for removing insects from tiny crevices.

In bird identification, maybe color and size will catch the eye first. But don't miss the beak. It's revealing.

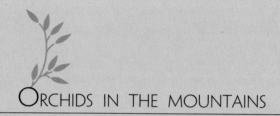

ORCHIDS IN THE MOUNTAINS

A NEWCOMER to the mountains peers in amazement at a tiny orchid plant on the forest floor. "I thought orchids grew only in the tropics—on trees," she says.

She's mostly right. Orchids frequent tropical jungles. The showy forms we see in florist shops and exotic gardens derive from these. And in the tropics they usually do grow on trees. Because those orchids compete with dense vegetation, they are spectacularly colored and fantastic in shape and size to attract proper pollinators.

But we in the Southern Appalachians have orchids, too, ground-growing species. Because they face less competition, they are smaller and less conspicuous.

Our new friend's surprise at finding orchids in the mountains sparks my curiosity. I wonder just how many orchid species do grow here. Perusal of flower books reveals a surprising twenty-eight species in western North Carolina, a wonderful challenge for orchid enthusiasts.

Yet even the most common of them—like rattlesnake plantain, ladies' tresses, and lady slippers—are few in number compared, for example, with dandelions, Queen Anne's lace, and goldenrod. Finding a patch of pink lady slippers certainly

Queen of the woodland, a yellow lady slipper
seems almost unreal in its orchid perfection.

causes more flurry than finding a patch of dandelions. Spotting a rarer yellow lady slipper creates even more excitement. It takes trained eyes and a share of luck to find a three-bird orchid, three minute pinkish flowers that resemble flying birds. Its stalk, only three to eight inches high, grows obscured by leafy litter on the forest floor.

Some species, such as the small green wood orchid, have flowers the same color as their surroundings. The twayblades' brown flowers hide among old, fallen tree leaves. Yet yellow fringed orchids and purple fringed orchids announce themselves brightly.

Consider for a moment the animal world where a frog is more complex than an earthworm, and a raccoon more than a frog, and a human more than a raccoon. In the plant world, a similar progression of advancement places mosses over algae, ferns over mosses, and flowering plants over ferns. Among the flowering plants, buttercups, anemones, and magnolias are among the most primitive. Orchids and the aster family, including daisies and dandelions, are the most advanced.

The highly specialized orchid flower has only three petals, two of which usually flare winglike. The third petal is extremely variable, possibly fringed or spurred or pouched, giving the flower a distinctive, often spectacular appearance.

In a structure unique to orchids, the pistil, which receives pollen from other orchid plants, and the stamens, which produce pollen to be carried away, are fused into a single reproductive organ, the column.

Pink lady slippers are one of our best-known and conspicuous mountain orchids. When looking at its lower petal, folded into a puffy, pink pouch, one wonders how pollination of such an apparently closed flower can possibly occur.

The bumblebee knows. Attracted by color and guided by the pouch's prominent veins, which converge on a vertical slit, the bee shoves, butts, and claws vigorously at this slit. Suddenly, she (the worker bee is a nonbreeding female) disappears into the pouch. Intent on a feast of nectar droplets, she feeds happily, unaware that the entrance door has slammed shut.

Ready to depart, the bee finds the slit not only closed but contoured in such a way that opening it from within is impossible. Frantic buzzing fills the pink prison. Then she spots a dot of light showing through a tiny hole at the far upper end of the pouch. As she approaches this tight exit, pollen deposited on her back by a previous flower scrapes onto the pistil's tip, pollinating the plant. As she squeezes through the exit, pollen from this flower rubs onto her back to be carried to the next.

Like other orchids, pink lady slippers

require certain fungi or molds on their roots. If the soil lacks these, the plant cannot survive. Transplanted lady slippers may last a year or two in a garden, but tragically, many succumb due to lack of this vital fungal association.

The beauty of an orchid lies in more than its exotic appearance or advanced biological status. It lies, too, in the fun of hunting and finding some of the many orchid species in our mountains and, more simply, in just knowing they are here.

GOLDEN DUST RIDES THE AIR

DURING OUR FIRST SPRING in the mountains, we learned about it the hard way. After pine pollen had coated porch chairs with yellow dust late one April, we hosed and scrubbed the porch and its furniture. Proud of our accomplishment, we flopped into chairs, admired the view, and basked in being so ready for summer.

Then in late May, yellow dust coated chairs and porch again. Grimly, we recleaned and resolved to find out more about pollen season. Enthusiasm for more than one major cleaning per spring ran low, very low.

We learned that flowering Virginia pines cause the dusting in April, white pines the one in May—two deluges of pine pollen. The living dust lies as a golden film on puddles and ponds, swirling into strange curves and designs as breezes play with the water surface. It fogs windshields, sifts into living rooms, and causes sneezes. One breezy day we watch pollen blow across the valley in such profusion that at first we mistake the clouds for a summer shower—but no drops fall and the clouds are gold tinted.

This extravagant splurge of pollen starts at the base of pine "candles," the light-colored spikes of spring needles, where special cones grow. Tiny and soft, these male "flowers" cluster in tremendous

Male cones of a white pine produce great quantities of wind-dispersed pollen.

numbers all over the tree. As pollen within their pollen sacs ripens, it yellows. The sacs burst and fling their golden burden to the wind. Shaking a branch stirs a swirling cloud of pollen, each grain a living cell. The air is filled with life.

With pollen gone, the useless cones drop off, often carpeting the ground beneath the tree, clogging gutters, littering pavements. People sweep them up, mostly unaware that they are cones or that they produced all that pollen.

Pines have a second type of cone, rarely seen in its early stages. These female cones grow mostly on uppermost branches of mature trees. On the cone, spirally arranged scales grow on a central stalk, and each scale bears a pair of tiny egg cells.

Only a fraction of the untold billions of airborne pollen cells ever reaches an egg cell to fertilize it. It seems as if most of the leftovers land on my porch.

After fertilization, the white pine's reddish female cones grow to nearly three-quarters of an inch. They stand upright on the twig, hidden way up there, cling-ing through fall and winter and spring.

Not until their second summer do female cones, now green, become pendant (hang down) and grow from six to eight inches long. Now we can see them from below, especially as their scales thicken and turn brown and woody. By late summer, the scales flare, each scale letting two winged seeds slip out. Seeds softly pinwheel earthward and sometimes catch breezes and whisk high in the air. Off they go.

Then the white pine's woody cones fall.

We're into white pine's pollen time now. But have patience, you sneezy people, anti-dust housekeepers, and pollen-count monitors. Pollen time lasts only briefly, and except for sneezes, it's mostly harmless.

Have amazement, too, for the profusion, the purpose, the marvel of those clouds of pollen. Then choose a fine May day to clean it up. And take heart: it won't happen again till next year.

(See also "Conifers for Christmas" in December, page 271.)

JUNE

HONEYSUCKLE, A LOVE-HATE AFFAIR

"IF EVER THERE WERE a plant to be 'on the fence' about," exclaimed one botanist, "it's honeysuckle!"

He referred to the common or Japanese honeysuckle, not to its less frequent, less well-known native cousins, which are modest and better behaved.

The superb fragrance of Japanese honeysuckle's blossoms, easily considered among the most pleasant in nature, can be forgotten quickly as one struggles to yank out its lengthy streamers. They creep over shrubs and gardens in one season. The joy of its flowers festooning late May countryside and the delight of cedar waxwings gobbling its berries collapse as the vine twists around young trees. Its fruits, leaves, and vines reap praise as food and cover for wildlife, and it rates A+ in preventing soil erosion. However, it merits stern condemnation for its stifling effect on native plants, especially those of wildlife value, such as dogwood and blackberry.

While romantically inclined folks surround honeysuckle with rosy adjectives, horticulturists describe it as a major nuisance, elaborating with words like pernicious, aggressive, stifling, "a reject."

So, feelings about honeysuckle are contradictory, strictly "on the fence." It's a love-hate affair, but it started with love.

Nectar in honeysuckle's flowers produces the fragrance
that attracts insects and hummingbirds—and people.

Dr. George Hall was behind it. A doctor in China, he jumped at the opportunity to go to Japan after its ports were opened to western trade in the mid-1800s. Thrilled with the plants he found in Japan, he became a trader, shipping exotic species to the United States after Civil War hostilities had ceased.

Japanese honeysuckle was one of these exotics. It first crossed American shores in New England, where it charmed the populace and still behaves as a respectable vine. But it spread to other states, helped by birds and animals, which dined on its blue-black berries and dispersed its seeds. People also helped it spread by purchasing it for their gardens—unthinkable now.

Growing conditions were particularly favorable in the Southeast. The attractive vines went rampant.

When honeysuckle begins to overwhelm its surroundings, there is really only one effective, admittedly formidable way to deal with it. Unless willing to use herbicides, which can kill or damage other plants in the vicinity, you dig it out by the roots.

Apart from the fact that it's back-breaking work, there's a hitch to this. The slightest remnant of root left behind puts out vigorous new shoots.

Step #2, therefore, is to dig new shoots out as they reveal themselves.

Even this requires follow-up. A conscientious battle through several years will provide victory, though some might question who the real victor is.

Because we've battled honeysuckle everywhere we have lived, we consider ourselves yankers with authority. We're even experts on the feel of the vine and the effects of the extended streamer. As you pull, twigs or dried leaves or grasses ten, fifteen, even twenty feet away quiver and move. You pull steadily, intrigued and impressed by the extent of the effect. Think of the satisfaction of pulling up twenty feet of vine with one mighty yank.

By this time you're glowing with pride in your honeysuckle-pulling skills, as eager to talk about the approaches to them as others are to discuss their operations, beach trips, or techniques for keeping worms off broccoli.

Another solution is goats, if you want goats. They eat honeysuckle with enthusiasm.

Yet quietly, while you might think mean thoughts about the well-intended Dr. Hall, it's impossible not to admire the vigor of the plant, its glorious fragrance in late May and early June, and its graceful flowers and handsome foliage—so sweet, so lovely.

I expect to be riding that fence for a long, long time.

Lightning in Bugs

INSECT BOOKS consistently call them "fireflies." I like "lightning bug."

Possessing a poetic, romantic flair, "fireflies" suggests fairies and flickering nighttime mysteries. But "lightning bug" comes across as substantial and realistic. After all, the lights of these remarkable creatures of dusk flash more like lightning than fire.

Either is acceptable, of course. Yet oddly, the insect is neither fly nor bug. It's a beetle.

Everyone remembers the summer magic of scooping flying lightning bugs from the air into cupped hands. We imprisoned them in mayonnaise jars with ice pick holes in the lid. At bedtime, we slipped the treasured jar beneath the covers. The prisoners illuminated the white interior of our temporary "tents" with an eerie, intermittent glow. We could even read by their light.

Few lightning bug captors have resisted the temptation to hold one between thumb and forefinger, fascinated by the softly glowing abdominal tip. At any moment it might flash as if switched on like a lamp. Occasional captors dared to remove that tip to see if its glow persisted. It did!

Late each spring, we say the lightning bugs are "back" —back from the soil. As larvae they passed the winter in snug underground cells, then gradually changed form through several spring weeks. In late May, they emerged as adult beetles.

Shortly after sundown, over moist

lawns, meadows, and marshlands, countless miniature lightnings of these adults flash. The display continues just into darkness, though a few stragglers may flash well into the night.

There must be some really good reason for this energetic show, and there is—sex. He seeks her for mating. The male flies over places where the usually flightless female perches on tips of leaves and blades. He flashes. If she responds with her flash, which is weaker than his, he heads her way, each signaling as they approach.

After mating, the female stops flashing—though there is one malevolent species in which the female flashes somewhat differently after mating, attracting a male of another species, whom she promptly devours. Mostly, adults do not feed at all.

The female lays eggs in or on the ground around moisture-loving plants. These hatch into odd little larvae which glow but do not flash. Dubbed "glowworms," they are fond of snails, especially slugs. They inject a paralyzing fluid, secrete enzymes that digest prey tissue, and lap the meal. If you are a gardener with slugs competing for your lettuce and chard, admire those blinking lights over your garden. The more, the better.

Ever since humans first encountered fireflies, we've been mystified by their strange, cold light and how certain cells produce it. Perplexing, too, is that no heat is associated with it. Only in recent years has there been an explanation, but one so complex chemically that the non-chemist remains in the dark.

The last few abdominal segments of the male, and usually only one or two segments of the female, contain luciferin, a chemical that glows when it comes in contact with the oxygen in the air. These segments are super-supplied with air tubes.

Nerves control the amount of air in the tubes, and therefore the amount of oxygen reaching the light-producing cells. The more air, the brighter the flash. Behind light-producing segments is a reflective surface that enhances the flash.

Scientists understand many aspects of this remarkably efficient cold light. Duplicating it, particularly in ways that might be economically useful, remains an unattained and tantalizing goal.

About half a dozen kinds of common lightning bugs frequent the eastern United States, each having its individual pattern or rhythm of flashing. The length, intensity, and number of flashes, the interval between, the flight level, the flight direction (some flash only as they rise), all are characteristic for each species.

Tiny sparkles against the shadows of dusk continue to enchant people of all ages. Catch a firefly. Let it crawl to the edge of your hand, spread its wings and take off, flashing. You'll understand.

A ROSE BY ANOTHER NAME

SURELY THE ROSE must be among the most beloved of flowers, yet its kinship goes far beyond the handsome blossom we envision when we hear the word, "Rose."

We squash a strawberry between tongue and palate, photograph mountain ash berries, make blackberry jam, or pull agrimony seeds from pant legs. We uproot multiflora from a pasture, enjoy a cherry pie, or admire a mountainside of serviceberry. We trip over dewberry tangles, gather spires of steeplebush, or bite into a dripping pear. In each case we are dealing with roses—roses by another name, but all belong to the rose family.

Associating apple sauce with a yellow tea rose may seem preposterous, but it is botanically correct. Apples, peaches, pears, cherries, and plums bear close kinship with roses. Each flower on a bough of apple blossoms resembles remarkably a tiny wild rose. It even smells lovely.

The apple blossom develops a fruit similar to a rose hip, though far larger and more palatable. Of course, you can't make great bowls of sauce or racks of pies out of rose hips, but they pack in the vitamin C and have a tang of apple flavor. Books on edible wild plants give pages of recipes for rose hips, especially in jams, jellies, and fruit butters.

Like apples, the flowers of most native rose family trees have that same wild rose form—five roundish petals, five sepals, and many stamens around the center. Crab apple and hawthorn, black cherry and pin cherry, serviceberry and even the tiny blossoms of mountain ash follow this rosy pattern, as do wild strawberry and yellow cinquefoil.

The rose family can impress with statistics. Hawthorns alone in the United States number nearly one hundred and three species, about five of which grow in the southern mountains. Seeking exact statistics causes controversies among botanists, who cannot agree on classification. They tend to frame quoted statistics with such words as "maybe," "about," "around," and "perhaps."

The blackberry crowd numbers over two hundred species in our country. Only a few grow in the mountains. If you have ever tried to eradicate them, you will agree they proliferate appallingly.

Of approximately twenty-five species of serviceberry, the mountains claim two, though one dominates. At warmer, low elevations flower buds burst in March, but not until spring has pushed into May does the serviceberry spectacular start in cooler, high elevations. Just before new leaves appear, amid the soft gray mantle of winter twigs on ridges, slopes, and valleys, patches of pale pink tint the forests as delicately as wisps of fog. Serviceberry's annual glory creeps in, its color the visual merging of white flowers and red bud scales. Blossom masses seem to float on the forests. Each day more appear, adding fragile white and pink here, there, all around—hundreds and more hundreds of them. Each lasts only a few days.

Bees buzz among blossoms of roses and all their relatives, and nectar perfumes the air. The rose family bursts with such life and beauty, it can't help but include favorites.

THE ULTIMATE CREEPY CRAWLY

THOUSAND LEGGER—even the name gives me the creeps. When I was a child, an occasional thousand legger appeared on the wall beside my bed at night. After Dad swatted it with a roll of newspaper, it would drop to the floor, its legs wiggling and jerking. I shivered in revulsion and grew up considering these leggy centipedes the ultimate "creepy crawly"—until I met millipedes.

The first millipede I encountered stretched nearly four inches, slender and wormlike, dark gray with pinkish underparts. It glided slowly and smoothly along the forest floor, unlike a speedy centipede.

I set a stick in front of it. Obligingly, my new acquaintance crawled aboard. I was astonished when I lifted the stick for a closer look. Not only did the incredible flow of leg motion not repel me, its absolute precision and timing were downright exciting, even beautiful. Graceful waves of dozens of legs moved the millipede along the twig perfectly. How could so many legs not get tangled up! Millipedes replaced centipedes as my ultimate creepy crawly—but I liked them.

Leggy centipedes have but one pair of legs on each body segment; millipedes have two, bringing the total number to between thirty and a hundred pairs,

A millipede curls tightly when disturbed,
protecting its softer under parts and making it hard to pick up.

depending on the species. In fact, their greatest claim to fame is legs.

The next time I found a millipede, I tried to pick it up. By that time I'd learned how completely harmless it was, not like the centipede, which is a predator that poisons its insect and worm prey. Though our local centipede's bites are not poisonous to people, they can redden the skin and be painful. But millipedes need no poisonous bite. A diet of decaying plant material requires no attack.

When I touched this millipede, it instantly rolled into a ball. Speed protects the centipede; it zooms and zips around the forest floor—or the walls of a house—with remarkable speed. But a millipede putts along like a slow-plodding turtle, and when threatened, simply curls into a ball to protect its soft underparts. The ball's hard outer surface makes it slippery, which quickly discourages enemies, though a few shrews find millipedes gourmet eating. My slippery ball just didn't want to be picked up, but I was determined and succeeded.

With ball in hand, I noticed a sudden, peculiar scent. Millipedes have another trick for protection. They can manufacture perfume from rotten leaves that in some species smells like almonds, apples, or peaches, in others a veritable stench. Even if something eager to eat a millipede finds the perfume enticing, the taste is dreadful. I get that information secondhand.

Most people are not even aware millipedes exist. Yet within a 200-mile radius of Asheville, North Carolina, live between 200 and 300 species. The Southern Appalachians, especially North Carolina, have been one of the world's prime centers of millipede evolution, so we have a great diversity. Some species are drab, some have touches of bright reds, yellows, and oranges, but all have some brown.

They live unobtrusively all around us, a few even in our homes. I base that latter claim on the evidence of finding their dried bodies in spider webs in my basement and garage.

Because millipedes have problems with water balance inside their bodies, most live in damp places, under forest litter, logs, and rocks. In dry weather, they are inactive; heavy rain drives them into the open. In damp places they thrive on decaying vegetation, or as one writer terms it, on "delicious rotting remnants."

They're finicky, though. A leaf must be in just the right stage of decay and not too dry. They might eat old hornet's nests. Their service as decomposers, nature's inconspicuous clean-up committees, goes unheralded, but when one considers how many millipedes there are, the effect must be tremendous.

Despite millipedes being common, science has spent little time on them. Why so neglected? It's the old story—they're of little apparent economic importance. And they don't bite, sting, or bother humans, homes, or crops—and certainly they aren't cute or endearing. So we—and science in general—ignore them. But who says we can't enjoy them.

Name That Fern

LOOK AT ANY illustration depicting nature. Birds perch on trees, butterflies settle on flowers, a frog with a dragon fly flitting by sits by the stream, and inevitably, ferns carpet the banks.

Though a staple of any woodland scene, ferns are dismissed by most people. "They all look alike," someone complains. "Just green, green, green."

Yet even fern names are intriguing. Climbing fern climbs like a vine. Walking fern propagates new plants at its leaf tips, making the plant "walk." Resurrection fern dries up, turns gray, and "dies" in dry weather. Then in wet weather it "resurrects" to green.

Maidenhair fern leaflets droop in strands resembling flowing (green) hair. Spore cases of cinnamon fern turn cinnamon colored. Appropriately, a fern with spore masses interrupting the green leaflets on its stalk is named interrupted fern. Ferns certainly aren't all alike.

Location inspires the names of some ferns: rock cap, marsh, glade, and wood. Other names reveal a special characteristic, like sensitive, hay-scented, or fragile. Christmas fern is evergreen, used as

Christmas decoration in earlier times.

The Southern Appalachians, a region lush with fern green, host around fifty species of ferns. To identify them, look for these characteristics:

1. Shape. Note where the leaf (frond) is widest and narrowest. New York fern, which carpets many of our mountain forests, has leaflets progressively smaller toward the base until the last pair almost disappears. Broad beech fern's lowest leaflets are its widest, making the frond a broad triangle. Spreading woodfern is handsomely wide, ebony spleenwort fern surprisingly narrow.

2. Size. Cinnamon fern soars to five feet tall, while mountain spleenwort, which thrives in rock crevices, grows only several inches.

3. Division. The leaf of a fern is usually divided into pairs of leaflets. On some ferns, these leaflets are mostly undivided, their margins having few or no indentations or lobes. On many ferns the leaflets are divided, giving them their delicate "ferny" look. Leaves on Christmas fern, for example, are divided into leaflets, but those leaflets are usually undivided. Those on lady fern or hay-scented fern are finely divided.

4. Margins. Leaflet margins may be smooth, toothed, or lobed.

5. Stalk features. Consider whether the stalk is scaly, woolly, smooth, or hairy, and note its color.

6. Range. Range maps can make or break an identification. For example, if you decide on a fern's name and find that its species grows only on the western slopes of the Rockies or near cactus plants in the desert, it's time to reconsider.

7. Color. Consider the shade of green: dark green, yellow green, gray green, blue green.

8. Pattern of spore case clusters. Watch people who know ferns. Invariably they'll check the back of the frond. They're looking at clusters of spore cases. These vary in size, shape, arrangement, and location, but each fern species has its own special pattern.

This list of identification features may seem formidable, but an overall glance at a fern covers most of them in moments. Tied in with a fern guidebook, these "what-to-look-fors" make fern identification a pleasing challenge, tossing out forever that "they-all-look-alike" syndrome.

See also the following essay, "Fern Puzzles, Easy Answers," page 140.)

The wide base of the leafy part of beech ferns contrasts with the narrower bases of some other species, a help in identification.

Fern puzzles, easy answers

WHILE RUMMAGING through an old junk pile in the woods, I found an unusual jar. Its neck was narrow, yet inside thrived a garden of young ferns, some so large they curled over in their limited quarters. Like with ships in bottles, I wondered how the ferns got in there.

An odd association came to mind: the ferns in the jar and several recent phone calls I'd received.

One caller sounded so distressed. "I have the most beautiful maidenhair fern, but something is dreadfully wrong with it. Its leaves are turning brown at the edges." Another upset caller lamented, "The tips of some ferns in my yard are turning brown. Are they dying?"

A third caller asked, "Shall I put insecticide on ferns? They have little brown spots on the backs of the fronds. Are they scale insects?"

I gave good news to all three callers. The ferns were merely trying to multiply. The brown spots were masses of tiny brown cases filled with ripening reproductive cells—spores.

Until scientists solved the mystery of fern reproduction in the mid-1800s, superstition surrounded ferns. No one had ever seen fern flowers or seeds, so people concluded they were invisible. If you found some, you'd become invisible, too. If you scattered fern seeds on the ground, the earth would show buried treasure. If

*Leaflet margins of northern maidenhair fern fold back over
developing spores, protecting them, then unfold
to release them when they are ripe.*

bracken fern were burned, rain would fall and goblins stay away.

People saw that ferns could reproduce from buds on their underground stems (rhizomes). Gardeners could even divide rhizomes with a spade to make more plants. People noted that some ferns could grow from leaf tips that propagate new plants, as in walking fern. Some grow from little buds or "bulbs" that fall off and start new plants, as in bulblet fern.

But no one could find fern seeds—ferns don't have any. And what about all that spore dust ferns produce?

Botanists discovered that after a spore falls to the earth, it divides to add cells and become a new plant. The new plant doesn't look like a fern at all. It's only about the size of a woman's little fingernail, heart-shaped, and extremely delicate. Few people seeing it would call it a fern.

On its under side grows a female cell and many male cells. Male cells swim to the female in a film of moisture. One fertilizes it, and from the union a tiny new leaf grows, then several more, tiny fern fronds.

The development is slow, dependent on moisture, and vulnerable. Reproduction by rhizomes, tips, and bulblets has far greater chance for success.

In most fern species, the spore clusters develop on the back of the frond. With some, they may be on a special separate frond. Clusters may be round or long, in rows broken or connected, along the margin or near the mid-vein of the leaflet. No matter what the arrangement, it is consistent for a species.

So the apparent fern maladies and the ferns in a jar tied together because of fern reproduction. Silt sifted into the jar as it lay on the forest floor. Spore cases on nearby ferns burst spores into the air—and the jar. Moisture stayed intense within the jar due to its narrow neck. A top horticulturist could not have produced more perfect conditions for ferns to grow, and grow they did.

I examined this contained and portable garden, thinking about its hows and whys, then snuggled the jar back into old leaves, as I had found it. It belonged there.

(See also the preceding essay, "Name that Fern," on page 137.)

Eft and Company

I EXPLAIN TO A FRIEND that I found an eft. "A what?" she asks.

"An eft," I repeat. "E-F-T. A red-spotted eft."

I tell her how I hunted efts in the Pennsylvania mountains as a child, but only on rainy days. That's usually when these gentle salamanders creep on forest floors.

Back then I called them "lizards." Finding one was magic, and I found many, compounding the magic. I'd push through dripping ferns, step over bead lilies and wintergreen, and squoosh on soggy leaves. "There's one!" Its bright orange stood out conspicuously against forest floor browns and greens.

I'd take one in my hand and look into its trusting face, so benign, even cute, and watch the creature crawl a few steps on my hand and feel it tickling my skin. Then I'd set it carefully on the ground and wander on to count how many more I could find.

I've never grown up when it comes to efts. Each time I find one in the mountains today, the magic lives on—the appealing face, the splayed toes, three on front feet, four on hind feet, the two rows of red spots ink-lined in black that run down its orange back. They charm me as much today as in childhood.

Maybe even more, because when I

The orange of efts shows up against dark leaves on the woodland floor,
especially when rains make the surroundings wet.

began to learn more about efts, they turned out to be *two* of my childhood favorites, newts and "lizards." Moreover, they weren't lizards at all. Lizards are reptiles with scaly skins and claws on their toes. Efts are amphibians with smooth skins and no claws.

I learned, too, efts are the most common American salamander, though not commonly seen. Most of us don't wander in the woods when it's raining.

Efts aren't efts at all when they are young. They have three lives. Life #1 starts in gelatinous eggs, laid in water on plant stems and leaves. A quarter-inch larva hatches, brown and almost tadpole-like but with miniature legs. It breathes with external gills as it grows in the pond. After three or four months of water life, it develops lungs and creeps onto land.

Life #2 starts as the changing creature turns orange and transforms into a proper red-spotted eft with a long, rounded tail. For two or three years the eft leads a forest life, threatened occasionally by a hungry predator. Its skin has an irritant harmless to humans but distasteful to the creature that chooses an eft for dinner. Predators rarely repeat an eft.

Maturity sends the eft into life #3. Needing to breed, it gradually turns brown again with a yellow underside and returns to the pond. Now called the red-spotted newt, it develops a flattened tail

for swimming, continues to breathe with lungs, and mates. This is the creature I delighted in catching in lakeshore shallows when a child.

Discovering that newts and efts are the same animal tore my allegiance, even as it fascinated me. I loved the drama and challenge of catching newts as they swam and scurried into mud and old leaves. But the eft also lured me into dripping woods for the excitement of solitude and the quest. Suddenly two became one. I had to be loyal to both.

When I moved to the Southern Appalachians more than forty years later, red-spotted efts wandered the forest here as well as in Pennsylvania. Moreover, I read that there are more different species of salamanders in North Carolina than anywhere else in the world. Another writer supported this, proclaiming the area "the salamander capital of the world."

Scientists disagree on exactly how many species there are in the mountains, not sure which are true species and which are races of those species. It's well over thirty, and new ones are being found. The Great Smoky Mountains have the greatest number of species anywhere, in icy streams, rocky gorges, and highest mountains as well as warmer, softer, lower places.

Scientists give complex reasons for the North Carolina mountain's wonderful supply of salamanders. Basically, the great glaciers of the last Ice Age did not reach the southern mountains, allowing salamander life to persist and to continue changing. Coupled with the wide diversity of habitats and often complete isolation, and high rainfall, this allowed tremendous variation. Many mountains have their own species of salamanders; some are found nowhere else.

You may wonder why we don't we see salamanders more often. Unlike the eft or newt, most species have no lungs. They get oxygen through their skins. For this exchange, skins must be moist, so salamanders live in moist places—under rocks and logs, in soggy decaying leaves, along stream edges and beds. Moreover, most come out only at night.

Scientific studies of the clear-cutting method of timber harvest have shown that it drastically reduces salamander populations. It eliminates shade, reduces leaf litter and moisture, and increases soil temperature, all fatal to salamanders.

Many uncertainties exist about salamanders. However, one fact is certain: anyone wanting to learn about salamanders should head for salamander paradise in the Southern Appalachians.

JULY

Mr. Ugly, Mr. Good

TRY TO NAME a four-legged creature that sings more beautifully than some birds, has golden eyes described by Shakespeare as "jewels," feeds with a tongue attached to the front of its lower jaw, and can breathe through its skin.

It closes eyelids up, digs into soil with hind legs, ignores its young, and swallows its skin. It catches food that's more than half the length of its body away without shifting its feet, depresses protruding eyes to help swallow, and breathes through gills as a baby, lungs as an adult.

Such a creature pulls off even more wonders. It puffs up grandly if threatened, hears through flat discs on the side of its head, and can live more than thirty years, though in nature it usually dies in its first or second year. It uses its front feet as "hands" to push slippery or leggy food into its mouth, lays up to eight thousand eggs at a time, and has dry skin with glands that secrete a bitter liquid.

Surely this remarkable animal must live in some exotic foreign land, in the tropics perhaps. Actually, it thrives in our Southern Appalachians, common here as well as over most of eastern United States.

You've probably guessed it by now, but two more clues will give it away. It hops and has "warty" skin.

Though a toad's face makes no claim for beauty, its eye is among nature's loveliest.

Yes, it's the common or American toad, *Bufo americanus*, often called affectionately a hoptoad, a friend to anyone who likes to eat, for its menu features mostly insects and other small creatures that compete with us for our food.

But the mere mention of a toad often causes negative responses. "Ugh! Mr. Ugly!" But wait. Bufo has a truly charming, benign, even comical face. And those eyes! In an era when superstition and mysterious tales about toads ran rampant, Shakespeare saw the truth, bless him, and immortalized the beauty of a toad's eyes.

How can a creature so gentle and harmless be considered obnoxious and hateful, even feared? Sadly, as with snakes, ignorance and misinformation encourage these common attitudes.

That "warty" skin especially turns people off, but those lumps are glands that ooze a bitter liquid, the toad's main protection. Most creatures that grab a toad for a meal hate the taste, particularly dogs. They spit the toad out vigorously. More bitterness lies in the squirt of fluid a toad might release when mishandled.

And how can a toad possibly be fearsome when it has no teeth or no "stinger." And it loves to be tickled—gently. Soft stroking between the eyes causes its head to bow low. Strokes on the side cause it to lean eagerly to that side, as if in blissful enjoyment. Having a wild creature respond so positively to one's touch appeals tremendously. Hardly fearsome.

Sometimes when held, a toad will emit rich chirping sounds, but true toad "singing" is the musical trill of the male, a sound of spring. His throat balloons as he sings to lure a female to the pond where he waits. Though his prospective mate and he are land animals, they return to ponds to mate and lay eggs.

The eggs, laid in gelatinous strands, hatch into tadpoles with gills. As these change later into appealing miniatures of adults, they acquire lungs for breathing. They also absorb oxygen through a film of moisture on their skin. (And toads also drink through their skin. Add this to their list of wonders.)

Toadlets often leave a pond in huge numbers to start life on land, choosing a rain storm, which led to the myth that skies can rain toads. Few survive even the first few hazardous days. They become food for many creatures, their unpleasant taste not yet developed.

As a tiny toad grows, its thin outer skin tightens and must be shed frequently. Even the adult sheds several times a year, always furtively, indulging in an intensely private event. It contorts, pulls, and stretches the skin, which splits down its back and works off over the entire animal in one piece. The new skin displays rich shades of earth tones. In a grand final gesture, the toad stuffs the wad of skin into its mouth, then gulps mightily.

Years ago our pet toad—named Bufo, of course—tolerated my presence during this seldom-seen procedure, a rare and relished privilege.

The usefulness of toads to people cannot be exaggerated. Many dozens of times throughout dusk and night that long, sticky tongue flings out and zap! Another insect vanishes. One study of toad appetite reported a toad eating nearly ten thousand insects in three months, nearly one hundred and fifty a day. An observer watched a toad consume fifty-five army worms in one sitting. Just think of a toad in your garden, so kind to people. If only people were kind to it.

For fun, I offered our pet toad a nightcrawler. She studied the giant worm with great interest, cocked her head for a better look, then faster than my eye, the worm was in her mouth.

But the worm rebelled. Frantically its head end shot out of the mouth. The toad's "hands" shoved it back in. The worm backed out, the toad shoved again. For over a minute, worm and toad struggled. Who would win?

Then Bufo gave a massive gulp followed by an all-encompassing eye blink. The worm did not reappear.

In autumn, when a praying mantis was reaching the end of its life span, I offered one to Bufo. They contemplated each other for a few moments, each a formidable predator. Then the mantis made a mistake. It moved. Toads strike only at moving prey, and instantly the mantis was doubled over inside the toad's mouth, its legs flailing. The mantis, famous for capturing its prey dramatically, became the victim.

Rejected, misunderstood, thankless, often abused, "Mr. Good" hops silently around our yards and gardens, walkways and woods.But nowadays I must qualify that by saying, "Used to hop." Worldwide populations of toads and other amphibians are plummeting. Some scientists suspect increased ultraviolet radiation due to ozone depletion, which can affect development of amphibian eggs. In our quest for perfect lawns, gardens, and crops, we use chemical pesticides and fertilizers freely, and acid rain falls.

How ironic that our need for order and perfection in nature threatens a natural, cost-free pesticide with impeccable qualifications.

Cowbirds—Lazy and/or Clever?

IT'S HARD TO DECIDE whether cowbirds are lazy or just plain clever or both. They don't bother to build nests or raise young. They let someone else do that work. Seems they have a good thing going—though their victims might not agree.

The drab, gray female, larger than a bluebird, smaller than a robin, lays her eggs in other birds' nests, then goes happily on her way. With her brown-headed mate, whose only contribution is mating, she leads a carefree existence. Opportunists they are, not only farming out their responsibilities, but getting away with it. Their "brood parasitism" seems like a mean trick on the birds that built the

nest. But for cowbirds it works fine. Their numbers prosper.

When the female feels the urge to lay, generally while nest owners are off feeding at dawn, she sneaks in furtively. She may have visited the nest the evening before and dumped an egg from it. She doesn't even pick on someone her own size. Her victims are usually smaller species, such as vireos, warblers, wrens, flycatchers, finches, and sparrows, though occasionally she might choose a cardinal or towhee. If host birds spot a cowbird laying, they might scold a bit, but mostly they ignore the uninvited guest, accepting her stoically.

The host bird's response to the strange

egg varies. Some incubate it, some shove it out, some abandon the nest, some build a new nest on top. This last response, most likely that of vireos and warblers, can turn dramatic. Where cowbirds are numerous, yellow warblers have been known to build up to five nests atop each other.

One spring at dusk, Tom and I watched a cowbird hop along a limb toward the nest of a solitary vireo, checking it out. Next morning, slightly past dawn, he held a mirror above the nest to peer into it. Three eggs lay there, one distinctly larger. What a great opportunity to watch the drama unfold! But it ended quickly. Several days later the vireos abandoned the nest due to a heavy infestation of lice, a common problem for birds.

Because the cowbird's egg is larger and hatches a day or two sooner than the host's eggs, the cowbird youngster dominates from the start. An aggressive character, it hogs food, grows fastest, and often shoves its nest-mates overboard. Even if one or two of the host's babies survive till time to leave the nest, the noisy cowbird demands so much attention that other fledglings usually die from neglect.

As I watch a Carolina wren labor to supply the overwhelming needs of an insistent young cowbird twice its size, my emotions confuse. Should I have compassion for the struggling parent, anger at

the lazy (clever) cowbird, or chuckles for the comedy of tiny parent stoking a monster? As I ponder these emotions, the busy wren searches nearby crevices of logs and porch.

From a human viewpoint, the cowbird is one of our most unloved, unpopular birds. It boasts no special beauty, no lovely song, no cute antics, no human friends—except a few researchers who admire the ingenuity of its behavior.

Researchers have struggled to learn how many eggs a cowbird will lay, no small task, for one pair's eggs can be scattered among many nests. Pooled information suggests about five. However, a captive female with ten nests available laid thirteen eggs in fourteen days!

Cowbirds become more and more prominent as research scientists study the alarming decline of many once-common songbirds, especially migrants to the tropics. Though one major reason for decline is loss of habitat, both in United States and the tropics, scientific fingers point at a second major cause—forest fragmentation.

Migrant birds in alarming decline tend to be those that favor large stretches of unbroken forest for feeding and nesting, sites well away from the forest edge and field haunts of cowbirds.

As massive development, wider highways, and logging fragment forests into smaller and smaller plots, forest edge

A cowbird egg is larger than those in the nest of a solitary vireo.
Photograph by Tom Hallowell

increases dramatically. Cowbirds can sneak to far more nests than they once did, decreasing numbers of songbird young while multiplying their own numbers. Too, forest fragmentation allows easy predation by blue jays, grackles, and crows, which often feed on smaller bird eggs and young.

Cowbirds came by their name because they enjoy hanging around cows. As bulky bovines move through pasture grass, insects fly out. Cowbirds gobble these in tremendous numbers, along with their major food, weed and grass seeds.

Love 'em or hate 'em, cowbirds proliferate, and by midsummer both adults and young have joined gangs of starlings, grackles, and redwings, the "blackbird" flocks that swell as summer progresses into fall. Then most head south for winter. No one here will miss them.

ONE OF THE WORLD'S BEST TOYS
A PIECE OF GLASS

WHAT A MARVELOUS discovery! Even though only a blob of curved glass, it lets people see tiny things they've never seen before. It magnifies! Scientists originally named it "lens" because its shape resembles a lentil, a bean. With unabashed fascination, generations of scientists, nature lovers and children from one to one hundred have used it to enter a new and fascinating world. Lines on one's hand look like ditches, skin becomes mountains and valleys, a hangnail looks absolutely dreadful, and a splinter appears as a spike.

Most magnifiers for reading enlarge two to three times (2-3x). They turn colorful Sunday comics into masses of color dots and Cheerios into doughnuts. Hand lenses, often called pocket magnifiers, usually enlarge eight to ten times (8-10x), providing even grander looks.

On a midsummer day, a friend and I each dangled hand lenses from strings around our necks as we wandered fields and forest edges. A light tickle on my hand drew attention to a tiny creature that hopped there. I peered through the lens and laughed out loud, "What a face! Look."

My friend, who knew insects well, exclaimed, "A miniature monster! It's one of the leaf hoppers."

The hopper's eyes bulged, with horns

jutting out behind. Its body shape seemed ridiculously humpbacked. Then it hopped—and vanished.

Within moments another tiny insect jumped aboard my sleeve and underwent hand-lens scrutiny. Long and sleek, it looked as if someone had decorated it for Christmas—red bands alternating with green. "A red-banded leaf hopper," my friend said. "Beautiful!"

That's how leaf hoppers and tree hoppers are—beautiful, comical, quaint, bizarre. "Nature must have been in a joking mood when leafhoppers were developed," commented one insect man.

Usually less than half an inch long, they live by sucking plant juices and hop mightily. Though common, they mimic surroundings so perfectly that seeing them isn't easy. Some look exactly like thorns, others like buds or tiny leaves or sticks.

I caught a grasshopper. As a child, I had captured many to watch them spit "tobacco juice." Now I wondered how it would look beneath the 10x lens. Impressive! The drop of dark brown liquid, spit out because the grasshopper felt threatened, indeed looked like tobacco juice. Apparently its taste discourages many grasshopper enemies. I watched the mouth parts working in the juice, moving sideways, not up and down like ours, then let the captive go.

My friend set a single flower from a milkweed cluster in my hand. A naked eye sees how the five petals curve sharply backward to expose five nectar cups. Insects alight on the cups to sip sweet nectar but have trouble getting a foothold. Between the cups are slits where the insect can set legs well. But watch out! It's a trap. A hand lens reveals why.

At the top of each slit is a tiny black clamp. When the insect's leg touches this, the clamp grabs hold, the insect struggles, pulling the clamp from the flower, and flies away. Occasionally the insect is too small or weak to pull away and dies entrapped.

There's good reason for such an odd arrangement—pollination. Attached to the clamp are two bags with sticky pollen. When the insect flies to the next milkweed plant, it carries these pollen sacs to the next flower, cross-pollinating it. Ingenious!

At the woods I plucked a woodfern leaflet, turned it over, and examined a sorus. Sori are clusters of spore cases that appear as brown dots or lines on the backs of many ferns. Through the lens, the sorus loomed huge, no longer a mere dot but a mass of globular spore cases, each loaded with spores. We looked at several fern species, each with sori different from the rest.

We stopped at a dogwood tree to see if next year's buds were showing yet, searching in the angle where the leaf meets the twig. Yes, they were well started—in July! Though barely visible with the naked eye, the 10x lens showed the new buds clearly.

"How about this!" exclaimed my friend, standing in leafy shade. "Look at this water drop, here, on this leaf. Nature's hand lens. It magnifies the leaf vein beautifully—as we magnify it!"

So simple, a little 10x magnifier, but what discoveries it makes possible. It's one of the world's best toys.

MYSTERY OF THE MONARCHS

ARTICLES ON MONARCH butterflies inevitably show up in mid-September and October, the time of their amazing, much-publicized migration to Mexico. But what are monarchs doing now—in late July? Multiplying.

To lay their eggs, mated female monarchs flutter over milkweeds—only milkweeds. Nothing else will do because their hatchlings eat only milkweed. They lay the cream-colored eggs singly, one here, one there, on the hairy undersides of the leaves. The eggs are tiny. Five fit nicely on the head of a straight pin. I know—I've placed five there to photograph them.

A female might lay up to four hundred eggs in two weeks. Then she dies, but she has started the lives of a new generation of monarchs.

The beady-headed bit of caterpillar (or larva) that emerges from the egg several days later gives no clue to the colorful creature it will become. Almost white, it has only one objective—eat! So it promptly eats the first thing it finds, its egg shell. Then it chomps on what is all around it—milkweed leaves, devouring them at a tremendous rate, growing phenomenally fast. At the same growth rate, a two-week-old human baby would weigh several tons.

A monarch butterfly expands its wings after emerging from the cramped quarters of its chrysalis case.

Growth makes the outer skin too tight, so a larva literally splits out, shedding its skin four times through two weeks of growth. It becomes a handsome, two-inch creature featuring yellow, black, and white stripes.

But change looms. The caterpillar is finished. It stops eating, suspends itself upside down from a milkweed leaf or sprig, and dangles like a wrinkly J. For the last time its skin sheds, and as if by magic, the caterpillar is gone. Instead, an astonishing new form dangles, a lumpy, yellow-green pupa or chrysalis. Within a half hour its surface becomes glistening smooth and the color shifts to jade, studded with shiny gold dots.

Day after day this chrysalis gem hangs immobile, apparently resting, but within the jeweled case one of nature's most sensational transformations takes place. What was once a plump, clumsy, leaf-chewing caterpillar emerges a scant two weeks later as a slender, graceful, nectar-sipping butterfly. You can't help but pause in awe of this change. The butterfly hangs onto the empty chrysalis case until its soft, crumpled wings expand fully and dry. Then off it flies to sip nectar from many kinds of flowers and to seek a mate.

Meanwhile, both parents responsible for this caterpillar-turned-butterfly die, which poses a question. How do the offspring of the dead adult monarchs know to migrate to Mexico in the fall?

The migration story starts on a certain few days in Mexico in March. The monarchs that flew to Mexico and wintered in its high mountains respond to an urge to fly north again. They follow the spring development of milkweeds, first in northern Mexico, then in the southern United States. They mate and lay eggs and most die, though a tattered few might push farther north.

The eggs hatch, transform into butterflies that fly farther north. These mate and lay eggs. Through several generations the monarchs progress northward, breeding and dying.

Then something special happens. The final, late-August generation, those mostly in the northern United States and southern Canada but also in the southern mountains, is stronger, more active, with more stored fat. It feels no urge to reproduce, yielding instead to an inner compulsion to head south.

Flying singly or in loose flocks, the monarchs join millions of their kind—frail, fluttering, vulnerable bits of orange and black, funneling from all over eastern United States into a few special acres of Mexico. There they winter, covering the fir forest acres like a living blanket.

Masses of butterflies turn green branches, even whole trees, to golden gray, the color of the underside of their wings when folded at rest. Their numbers weigh limbs down, even break some.

To walk within this cathedral of life-laden trees, engulfed in the incredible silence and stillness, is awesome. Conversation drops to whispers. The word "wonder" truly comes into its own.

Then the sun breaks from behind a cloud, bathing the forest with patches of warmth. Within moments, warmth raises the body temperature of the monarchs to above fifty degrees. They spread wings, transforming trees to orange. The clouds of fluttering orange lift from the branches, the sky comes alive; and a watcher tingles with thoughts: I am here amid the butterflies, actually seeing this much-storied spectacle. This is real, it is. None of these monarchs has ever been here before. How do they know?

This mystery of the monarchs tantalizes. What leads these inexperienced insects to a few isolated forest acres at nine- to ten-thousand-foot elevation in Mexico? What guides them along the way to roost overnight on the exact trees and shrubs their forebears used? This incredible, annual migration inspires a host of questions as yet unanswerable.

But today in late July, we can examine milkweeds and possibly find eggs, striped larvae, or camouflaged pupae, green against green. We can watch adults flutter among flowers of roadsides, gardens, and meadows, and know that none of these will be migrants. Only their gifted progeny, that final generation of summer, will lift into the air and follow that wonderfully mysterious urge to head for Mexico.

In autumn, when I look up to watch one fly over, I will ask it, "How do you know?"

(See also "Seven Wonders in My Yard" in October on page 230.)

THE PERFECT LEAF

TODAY I SET OUT to find a perfect leaf, no blemishes allowed. I need it for a photography project and tell Tom I'll be back soon.

But I don't come back soon. Later he finds me. "What's up? I got worried."

"I'm having the best time, even though I can't find a perfect leaf. Look. They have either holes or spots, or lumps, rips, squiggles, rolls, folds, or something—imperfections all over the place.

"Hordes of creatures are using these leaves. I call 'em 'the six-legged gang' because most are insects. Each leaves a clue or message that it's been here—or is here. A leaf's like a town with all these characters living on it."

"And in it," adds Tom. "Who's in your gang?"

"Miners, blotch makers, skeletonizers, rollers, tyers, folders—and hole makers and gall makers."

"They sound downright sinister!"

Actually, they're delightfully harmless to people. Most don't even bother the tree. They're just miniature larvae of tiny moths or wasps, plus a few beetle and fly larvae and aphids. All leave some distinct trace on the leaf by going about their everyday business of eating, home building, or changing form.

Skeletonizers eat green tissue in spreading patches, leaving only veins, the intricately beautiful skeleton of the leaf.

Rollers, folders, and tyers perform astonishing feats. Imagine a caterpillar only an eighth- or quarter-inch long rolling a huge leaf around itself. Or another folding over the tip of a leaf and plastering it flat to the leaf surface.

These larvae spin and stretch silk threads between two leaf edges or surfaces. Each uses a thread arrangement special to its species. The elastic threads tighten, then shrink more in moisture, pulling the leaf together. Repetition of this process pulls the leaf into a perfect fold, roll, or mat in which the larva lives. Only insects that spin can do this, mostly tiny moths and a few sawflies.

"Let's see if this roller's at home," I suggest and slowly, gently, unwind a tight roll. We hear the tough threads rip and snap, but when the final roll opens, find nothing but tiny piles of caterpillar droppings. "He's already left. I'll try another."

Inside the second roll hides a barely visible caterpillar. It wiggles, resisting exposure. I re-roll the leaf, though without its threads, the caterpillar's home is looser. The larva will pupate in there, then emerge and fly off.

Leaf miners and blotch makers live between the upper and lower surfaces of a leaf, where they eat or "mine" the leaf's thin layer of green tissue and leave a greenless trail or distinctive blotch.

Hole makers are easy to find, though many will drop or fly if disturbed. For them, the leaf is not home but food. Larvae of beetles, moths, and butterflies make a remarkable assortment of holes.

On some leaves lumps, balls, bristles, or "witch's hats" jut from the surface. Certain aphids, wasps, beetles, and flies, at some stage in their lives, irritate the plant they live on. It responds by producing an abnormal growth called a gall, and the larva lives within it.

This challenge of finding a midsummer leaf without a blemish eats time. But suddenly I spot new sprouts from a felled maple. New leaves! There, perched on its twig, as if waiting for me to find it, hangs that rarity in July, the perfect leaf.

(See also "Mini-miners Work Between Layers," in July on page 166.)

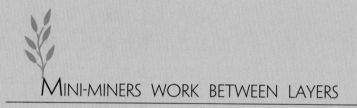

Mini-Miners Work Between Layers

THE INSECT WORLD is a miniature world—no giants like mammoth whales, ponderous elephants, monster sharks, or towering ostriches. The largest insects, such as the Atlas moth of India, measure only about a foot across the wings.

Even Atlas moths loom as giants compared to the insects that live between the layers of a leaf, a leaf nearly as thin as this page. These tiny creatures feed on the moist green cells that lie between a leaf's transparent upper and lower layers. As they munch cells, they work like miniature miners, removing the resources in their paths. Logically, they're called leaf miners.

Where miners eat the green away, they leave behind easily detectable clear, white, or tan trails. Those squiggly white lines on leaves of columbine, nasturtium, beets, and spinach are miner trails, as are many of the spots and blotches on oak leaves, greenbriar, and pileweed. If you look, you'll be surprised by the great variety of plants that play host to miners.

Leaf miners are the larvae of tiny moths, beetles, flies, or sawflies. The majority are moth larvae, merely minute caterpillars. Each has adapted marvelously to existence in a flat, moist environment. With wedge-shaped heads and

*One can trace the trail of a miner from hatching
through growth until it rests and changes into an adult.*

flattened bodies, they push through leaf layers easily, gobbling green. Because they have no need for eyes, legs, and antennae, these features are often reduced.

As miners eat, each traces its signature in the leaf, its mine distinctive to its species. Its mark may be a line, squiggly or straight, or a round or trumpet-shaped or fingerlike blotch. Insect experts can glance at the mark and tell what species made it. They can hold a mine to the light, watch the larva feeding—so can you—and tell from the position and movement whether it is a beetle, moth, fly, or sawfly larva.

Confined between the leaf layers, the larva has a special problem—where to put its waste material, called frass. Some species simply eject it into the tunnel behind, leaving dark streaks in the translucent mines. Some make an opening in the leaf and eject it. Some choose a special location within the mine and always deposit in that one spot. Again, experts can identify a species by its method of frass deposition.

When a larva "grows up," it must pass through a resting or pupa stage, during which it makes an incredible change into the adult form—the moth, beetle, or fly. This often occurs inside the leaf, but some larvae emerge from the leaf first, then pupate on its surface or tumble to the ground first.

If you're looking for a new way to entertain the children or grandchildren or something to fill a few relaxing moments of your own with something different, let leaf miners help.

Find some leaves with winding miner trails and note where each trail is hairbreadth thin. That's where the miner hatched and started to eat. You can follow its trail as it ate and grew. The line gets wider and wider, zigging around, then suddenly stops. Here the miner either pupated and left the leaf or dropped from the leaf to pupate elsewhere.

What a delight to get caught up in tracking miners!

(See also "The Perfect Leaf" in July on page 164.)

Understanding Snakes

WHILE ON HANDS AND KNEES pulling honeysuckle, I hear a gentle rustle in weeds beside me. A small head pokes out, black with white throat. It senses the air and scene, and eyes me. I freeze, eager to see what it will do.

Finding my presence no threat, it emerges from the grass, trailing behind a body that comes on and on, the sleek form of a large black snake. Knowing it is less harmful than a playful kitten, I stay motionless, pleased with the rare chance to observe a snake going about its routine business.

It pokes deftly through grass and weed stalks, its tongue flicking, and changes direction several times. It approaches my hand, curious about this unfamiliar thing, noses it briefly, then glides away silently into the weeds.

Later I describe the incident to a friend who exclaims, "Weren't you brave!"

Brave? The thought had never occurred to me. Watching a harmless creature was not bravery. It was opportunity, unexpected and precious.

Had I leapt to my feet, shrieked, "Snake!" and fled in panic, I would have missed that opportunity. Had I killed the snake, the act would have shown ignorance, revealing that I didn't know the snake was harmless and beneficial, a diner of rodents and insects.

Ignorance breeds fear of snakes, for humans often fear what they do not understand. Lack of information leads to false folklore. Much of what people sincerely believe they "know" about snakes is uninformed or misinformed. Those who understand snakes do not fear them, but they do respect them.

Sadly, people who fear often turn deaf ears to truth, as if they are proud of or secretly enjoy their fearing. They refuse to listen to the exciting information about snakes learned by those who have studied them—not in the classroom, laboratory, or library, but outdoors, out with the snakes.

I know people who never experience the joy of a field or forest walk because they fear snakes. Yet those of us who have walked hundreds of mountain miles have rarely seen a snake, even more rarely a dangerous one.

With the false conviction that "the only good snake's a dead one," people attack a snake. If it can't escape, it defends. It strikes its persecutor—and then is called "mean" or "vicious."

A snake is amazing. Without arms or legs, it glides forward gracefully. Overlapping scales on its underside catch onto any rough surface, and perfectly timed waves of muscle action move scales—and

snake. Some even climb vertically on trees and walls.

Watch as it moves, firm in the knowledge that a snake's forward motion is much slower than a human's. Even a child can easily outrun a snake. Yet an ignorant parent might caution, "Watch out! He'll chase you!"

A snake tests surroundings not with eyes and ears, as we do, nor with nose to the ground like a dog, but with its tongue. And that flicking tongue can't sting. It's an organ of smell. It flicks to "sniff" or sense the surroundings.

Snakes glare, but not because of meanness. A snake certainly cannot look kind and adorable when it has no eyelids to flutter. And people who claim snakes are slimy have never touched one. Snake skin is dry like soft leather, sleek, but in no way slimy.

Anatomically, snakes are strung out, having paired organs, such as kidneys, lying one behind the other. Most have only one lung.

Spectacular! That's the word for their ability to swallow food often thicker than their own diameter. Tiny teeth, pointed inward, keep prey from escaping. Upper and lower jaws, not hinged together like ours, spread far apart; left and right jaws move independent of each other. By working jaws forward, the snake essentially crawls around its food. The body stretches, the swallowed prey often bulging in it.

*Without eyelids or lashes and with a set, smileless mouth,
a gentle, harmless corn snake looks fierce.*
Photograph by Tom Hallowell

Many years ago, when one of our small sons acquired a baby Boa constrictor, some people criticized us for allowing our children to have a poisonous snake. Snakes catch prey in three different ways: 1) by simply grabbing and swallowing, 2) by coiling around prey and constricting it with lightning speed, and 3) by striking with poison fangs and paralyzing the prey. A constrictor has no poison, and a poisonous snake does not constrict. Our baby boa was absolutely harmless.

But people have trouble overcoming prejudice against snakes. Psychologists treat those who yearn to overcome this fear and hatred by teaching true facts about snakes, helping people to learn and understand rather than malign. It's far more fun to watch snakes than fear or kill them. Snakes are a natural part of the outdoors. It's good to know they are there.

(See also "Snakebite" in July on page 172.)

SNAKEBITE

SNAKEBITE! The very word brings chills. The uncertainty of where a snake might be and the chance of a lightning-fast strike unsettle almost anyone. Coming across a snake unexpectedly startles even those who know and understand snakes.

But many people are convinced a snake is out to get them, to chase and bite. The fastest North American snake, the western whip snake, moves barely three miles per hour. A human outruns it easily. If a snake suddenly heads your way, it is frantically seeking to escape the situation and in its terror, heads wildly in any direction.

A snake bites for only two reasons: to catch food or to defend. It certainly isn't interested in us for food, so defense is its only reason to bite.

Solution: Don't threaten it. A snake won't bite unless provoked. Handled quietly, gently, it has no interest in biting. Squeezed, poked, stepped on, or surrounded by fast motion, it panics. Then it defends itself quite properly and understandably—it bites.

The danger of snakebite is astonishingly exaggerated. In 1990, the last year of comprehensive statistics, the entire United States had only four snakebite deaths. By comparison, over forty thousand people died that year in automobile accidents.

This raises the question, Which is more dangerous, a rattlesnake or a car? The answer seems obvious. Yet some people deny themselves outdoor pleasures and suffer miserably because they fear snakebite, though they ride around in cars fearlessly.

Only two species of poisonous snakes live in the southern mountains: copperhead and timber rattler. Some folks insist that the poisonous water moccasin haunts the mountains, too. But names can confuse. Two snakes, the harmless water snake and the poisonous cottonmouth, are both called "water moccasin." The cottonmouth lives only in the coastal plain and lower Piedmont. The common water snake ranges through the entire state. Because of this name confusion and similar size, shape, and habitat, the water snake is one of the most mistreated of all nonpoisonous snakes. It is needlessly feared and regularly killed by those who, in ignorance, insist it is poisonous. Dead specimens are delivered to hospitals, nature centers, and museums as "poisonous moccasins."

The cottonmouth opens its white-lined mouth widely when threatened and quivers its tail. The water snake does neither. A harmless hognose snake also opens its pale mouth widely when threatened, but it does not live around water.

The copperhead has, logically, a copper-colored head. Brown or red-brown bands cross its body, wider on the sides than on top, the "hourglass" design. Ordinarily this quiet, lazy fellow wants only to be left alone. But if it senses threat, watch out!

A friend was lying prone to photograph a tiny flower close up. He suddenly realized that in the background of the blossom, only fifteen inches from his nose, was a head, a copperhead! He inched his way backward slowly until he could get to his feet. The snake, unthreatened, never moved.

But the photographer, much to his regret, never took the picture. It would have been a winner.

Both copperhead and timber rattler have broad heads and vertically elliptical eye pupils. If you're close enough to see these, move! Slowly!

Incidentally, rattles on a rattlesnake's tail warn enemies but do not indicate age. A rattle is added each time the skin sheds, which is several times a year. And rattles can break off.

In the Appalachians, most poisonous bites are by copperheads. The bite is painful but rarely fatal. Rattler bites are more dangerous but often provoked, especially likely when people attempt to kill the snake.

The directions about snakebite read, "If bitten, keep calm." Pain is severe, life can be at stake, so keep calm! What they mean is: don't run around, which only spreads the poison. Ride to a hospital for proper treatment as soon as possible.

Be sensibly wary—avoid threatening a snake and don't poke your hand into crevices. Step carefully over logs and rocks.

Respect for snakes and interest in the true facts about them are far more pleasant than wallowing in unnecessary fear and stress based on misunderstanding and folklore.

Even poisonous snakes just aren't all that bad.

(See also "Understanding Snakes" in July on page 169.)

AUGUST

BLUE RIDGE HAZE—OLD AND NEW

CAMERA SHUTTERS snap and click as summer tourists capture pieces of the vast mountain scene that stretches before us. They pose happily in front of it, and later they'll say, "That's me on the Blue Ridge Parkway."

I feel sad as I watch them. The mountains they want to record will show only faintly in their pictures. Many of the magnificent ranges fade into murk, an artificial murk that lessens the very thing these tourists came to see—scenery.

To those of us acquainted with this view before the mid-1970s, the summer scene often seems woefully limited, sadly partial and inadequate. Gray-white haze diminishes the close mountains, makes the next ones even less visible, and loses the distant expanse of mountains beyond completely.

The tourists smile with pleasure, unaware of the fantastic view they cannot see. I yearn to push a button to have the haze suddenly lift, exposing the real view. They'd gasp in wonder and surprise and whisk out cameras for a new flurry of pictures.

When we moved to the western North

Carolina mountains in 1971, the nearby Blue Ridge Parkway lured us to its heights regularly. Range upon range extended out there, in every direction, the close ones dark, each layer behind a lighter and lighter blue until, perhaps fifty miles away, the last layer merged into sky.

In summer, a gentle blue haze softened the ridges. After all, that's how the Blue Ridge Mountains and Smokies got their names. Haze started mid-May and persisted until mid-September, a natural phenomenon that develops as leaves emerge in spring, produced by a combination of leaf emissions, heat, high rainfall, and still air.

I learned to understand and accept the natural haze as part of the Blue Ridge summer, even learned to love it as in certain lighting it enhanced the wonderful effects of layered mountains. I once wrote, "When sun is high, the mountain layers seem almost one, superimposed and almost monochromatic. But a natural summer haze often separates them, providing wonderful curving patterns of lights and darks in blues and grays. Lowering sun of late afternoon backrims the layers and casts mountain foregrounds into deep shadow."

In those early 1970s, we knew the haze would disappear as leaves fell in autumn. The sublime weather of October overwhelmed it—and me. October became my favorite mountain month—

splendid colors, mild days, clear air, and crisp nights. From mid-September to mid-May, the haze was mostly forgotten.

One January day we drove the Blue Ridge Parkway west, exited at its terminus outside Cherokee, North Carolina, the eastern gateway to the Smokies, and drove up Clingman's Dome, one of the highest mountains in eastern United States.

From its lookout tower, a 360-degree view of superb clarity extended to the horizon fifty, sixty, seventy miles away— mountains, mountains, mountains forever, evergreens and winter grays turning into blues as distance increased, then lavenders and grays. Winter was prime time to see the mountains.

But haze increases. Old timers mutter, "Sure don't look like it used to. Can't see them yonder mountains much at all any more." We agree. Surreptitiously, the haze has crept into all seasons, no longer a summer phenomenon. The finger of blame no longer points to leaves. It points to us.

It points to industry to the west of us and to auto emissions by all of us. The tremendous increase of such pollution in recent years, coupled with the quiet air of mountain valleys, creates a white haze different from the natural blue. We are not alone; the Grand Canyon and many other places have the same problems.

One wonders whether our mountain

air will deteriorate even more or whether fewer people will visit the Blue Ridge Parkway and hosts of other Southern Appalachian sites because the scenery is lost in haze.

Not yet, but science and government and tourist promoters scratch their heads, wondering what to do as more cars hit the road and steer toward the mountains.

(See also "Ghost Forest" in August on page 187.)

NATURE'S REAL-LIFE BLOB

NAME A PLANT. Name an animal. Easy. But a foursome of intelligent, educated, TV game show contestants could not agree on whether a lobster was an animal.

And what about worms and ticks, corals and sand dollars, oysters, owls, sharks, and jellyfish? Because many people assume that animals should have four legs and fur, they have trouble categorizing these creatures. All are animals.

But deciding whether some primitive living things are plant or animal baffles even scientists. For example, consider a common one-celled creature that propels itself by waving a whiplike strand (a flagellum) and takes in microscopic food particles through a gullet. It even has a light sensitive "eye," a prominent red spot. Surely it's an animal.

But close inspection shows it to be full of tiny bodies containing green chlorophyll. Like leaves of green plants, it manufactures food by photosynthesis. Does that make it a plant?

Euglena, as it is called, has perplexed scientists for generations. You may have watched this plant/animal through a microscope in a biology class.

But meet something even more incredible, nature's real life blob—the slime mold. Its name is enough to turn anyone off. But read on. This common thing seems straight out of science fiction. It

Beautiful colors and forms of slime molds overcome the stigma of their unpleasant name.

even frequents secretive places—damp, low-light woods, especially on rotting logs, though in damp seasons it might invade lawns and porches, alarming to the unfamiliar.

In one stage, slime mold is a shapeless, disorganized blob of living material—no cells, no tissue, no structure—a slimy, primitive mass one, two, or three inches across. Though it might come in subdued tones of brown, tan, or white, it can startle with bright yellow, violet, or red, depending on species.

The mass flows, engulfing food par-ticles in its path—spores, bacteria, yeasts, molds. A pin poked into the ground or log at the blob's leading edge will be passed in an hour or so. The thing can ooze through soil like a spoonful of milk, breaking up, reuniting, breaking again. No nerve cells or brain control the flow, yet locomotion is precise as the material willfully migrates, animal-like. Scientists scratch their heads to explain it.

Comes time for reproduction, though, the blob flows to the ground surface. Small bumps appear, a sign that its feeding days are finished. A new, highly organized stage begins.

Within hours, delicate stalks push up from the bumps, wonderfully diverse in shapes and colors, usually about a quarter-inch high, though tall ones might stretch to a half inch. Stalks are tipped with perfect clusters of spore case—definitely plant-like.

Well-known scientist-author Peter Farb describes these fruiting slime molds as "one of the most beautiful objects of the soil, like bouquets of fantastic flowers on wispy stalks."

Clumps of fruiting stalks can be collected, dried, and set into pill or match boxes. They keep almost indefinitely, though one needs a magnifier to fully enjoy their beauty.

The spore cases dry and release reproductive spores to the breezes. Those that alight on moist, decaying wood in dim light release tiny blobs of living material which creep about like amoebas. Those that alight in water develop a flagellum that propels them to a proper location to settle down. Astonishingly, if conditions reverse, each form can change into the other—and later, back again! Eventually, they grow into the wonderfully disorganized blob, all very animal-like again.

For many years, scientists, unable to comfortably place slime molds into either the plant or animal kingdom, classified them as fungi. Indeed, most studies of slime molds have been done by fungus experts. But now scientists have set slime molds into a kingdom called Protoctista, which includes one-celled animals, some algae, and some ex-fungi. It's a rather uncomfortable designation, but the one currently used.

A question arises inevitably: Are slime molds important to us? They have no direct economic importance, but their role as decomposers, as recyclers of nature's materials and therefore as soil conditioners, is by no means a light one.

Best of all is their uniqueness, their baffling, two-stage life, their unobtrusive existence and delicate beauty in spite of the miserable name man has bestowed upon them. A few people find slime molds so intriguing they keep them as pets. Oat flakes provide food, jars or dishes serve as "cages."

I like to picture slime molds as secretly enjoying their mysteries, as treasuring their unknowns in spite of man's efforts to figure them out. So far, they are the harmless, humble winners.

CANADA IN CAROLINA

A LIGHT FLASHES from the far mountain. And another.

"Somebody's up on the Blue Ridge Parkway," Tom notes as we stand on our dark porch. Headlights flash toward the cabin the instant a car rounds a certain bend on a high mountain—twenty miles away. So few people travel up there at night that lights attract attention.

"I wonder if they know they're in Canada," I comment.

He knows what I mean. We hike up there often, reveling in our visits to Canada in North Carolina. As we start our climb, we pass through forests dominated by maple and tulip tree, hickory and oak. The forest green is bright with broad-leaved trees, except for occasional darker hemlock and white pine. Sun dapples the forest floor generously. We feel the richness and lushness, the surging growth of this hardwood forest of the Southern Appalachians with its blessing of over one hundred forty species of trees.

As we plod up and up, the forest changes to mostly oak with a bit of beech, yellow birch, and mountain maple. In more open places, mountain ash and pin cherry appear. Tall, straight trees of the lower elevation give way to short, somewhat crooked trees.

Eventually we reach dark forests where Fraser fir and red spruce grow so close

*T*he range of yellow-birch growth dips into the high elevations of the
Southern Appalachians, providing a touch of the North in the South.

that walking through them without a trail is nearly impossible. Light struggles to penetrate the forest floor.

We sense change with more than legs and eyes. Aah, balsam. Smells like the north woods. It should. It *is* a north woods. Its life is similar to that of woods in the northern United States and Canada. As we rise to five thousand feet elevation and progress to over six thousand, we travel to Canada or northern New England biologically.

Trees, flowers, and ferns not seen at lower elevations surround us. A red squirrel scolds, flicking his tail vigorously. A red-breasted nuthatch voices his opinion with nasal, staccato notes. Canada mayflowers, wood sorrel, and yellow bead lilies patch the rich soil, and spruce cones dot the trail. Northern woodferns soften the rocky scene.

When we stand around six thousand feet in the highest mountains east of the Rockies, we see a different world from the lower elevations only a few miles away in the valleys. Biologists call it the Canadian Life Zone.

Range maps in tree guides, which show where a tree grows, support this striking picture. A number of trees that grow in northern United States and Canada have their range jutting southward along the Appalachian Mountain chain.

During the last ice age, northern plant and animal species thrived all over the southern mountains, though extensive ice did not cover the land. Then warmth returned, and species preferring milder temperatures replaced them, except in the cool, high elevations. There remnant northern species persisted, and we can ride or hike and find them now—red oaks, beeches, yellow birch, and mountain ash, stunted and contorted from winds and severe growth conditions—and highest up, red spruce and Fraser fir, often called balsam, the Southern Appalachian version of balsam fir.

"A veery!" Tom exclaims. We pause to listen. Its flow of rich notes stops us. "One of my favorites," I say, though he already knows that, "and a winter wren." Though calls of winter wrens have accompanied us from about four thousand feet, we listen attentively. Their rollicking notes epitomize joy and enthusiasm, yet come from a tiny drab bird of harsh terrain.

Veeries and winter wrens—symbols of the north woods—in North Carolina! Black-capped chickadees exchange two-note songs. Elevation separates this northern species from the Carolina chickadee with its four-note song. Part way down the mountain their ranges overlap.

We emerge from dark spruce-fir forest into an open heath bald or "laurel slick," where mats of three-toothed cinquefoil and mountain myrtle thrive among windswept rocks and laurel shrubs and azaleas. An occasional spruce or fir struggles in this exposed location, its limbs "flagged," all growing away from the prevailing wind direction. We might be in New Hampshire.

We scramble onto boulders and stand on an exposed point, gazing out over layers of ridges. A raven, another touch of the north, greets us with a raspy "kwok" and floats by on an updraft. Then we proceed into forest again, for the Southern Appalachians are treed to their summits.

In 1985 I wrote the following words in a journal, "Hiking isn't the only way to reach Canada in Carolina. Roads make it easy for the nonhiker, too. Accessible places like Roan Mountain, Mount Mitchell, Richland Balsam, and Clingman's Dome all rise into Canada. We're so lucky. We can visit Canada by car right here."

But by then, Canada in Carolina was changing. Dying firs and weakened spruces patched the dark green forests. Forest decline had struck the peaks of the highest southern mountains.

A biological disaster was happening, and no one knew why. A ghost forest spreads.

(See also "Ghost Forest" in August on page 187 and "A Finger on the Map" in September on page 220.)

Ghost Forest

EVERY STEP is a struggle, a decision about where to put my foot next. We six hikers have at least a mile to traverse before reaching the 6,080-foot mountain summit, a mile of plodding through jackstraws the size of telegraph poles. The tangled expanse of broken logs and limbs seems impassable, but we're determined.

I stand on a log several feet above the forest floor, but see no way to advance, so turn back to try another route. I struggle down, climb another log, and repeat my effort.

Up, down, up, down. We cannot follow a mountain trail one behind the other, a line in unison; there is no trail.

Each must determine an individual route and plan every step as we pick our way through a ghost forest.

I pause to catch my breath and look out over the devastation, sad with memories of how it looked when I first saw it in 1971. I had been overwhelmed by its cathedral beauty, its aura of reverence, a forest of red spruce and Fraser fir, dark shadowy, with rays of sun piercing onto the floor only here and there, mysterious yet quietly protective.

Back then a red squirrel broadcast our entrance into the forest, protesting with noisy chatter, joined by an equally upset black-capped chickadee. A winter wren,

*F*orest decline in the southern mountains has left vast expanses of dead trees, especially Fraser fir.

pleasantly unperturbed, sang its musical cascade. We walked a spongy trail through evergreens. Growth was dense, whole trees intermeshed. Masses of woodferns, northern clintonia, Mayflower, and oxalis greened the forest floor. They and the pungent aroma of fir needles transported me northward, and all my senses shouted, "Maine!" as I kept telling myself, "This is North Carolina."

But in a few years, much of it was gone. By the early 1980s, forests approaching 6,000-feet elevation showed signs of trouble. First twig tips on firs, then whole trees turned brown. Something awful was happening. The magnificent fir forest was dying. We began to see articles and newspaper notes about "forest decline."

By the late 1980s, great expanses of Fraser firs had lost their needles. The trees stood gray and bleak. Eventually, their fine twigs shattered in wind and rain and ice. Then bark sloughed from trunks, branches broke and fell. Trunk stalks poked into the sky; then they, too, collapsed into a tangled mess. Those, like us, who had loved and admired these northern forests in southern latitudes, lamented what we saw and wondered what was happening.

Any forest harbors an incredibly complex ecosystem, not only the plants, animals, and birds we can see, but the millions, even billions, of microorganisms that live on and in its leaves, bark, and soil. The interrelationships of these bewilder even the most competent research scientists and make pointing the finger to a single cause of forest decline a daunting task.

Blame fell first on the woolly adelgid, an imported aphid that appears white woolly. But study shows that it affects only firs, and red spruce were dying, too. Moreover, it was introduced around 1970, and scientists studying tree rings discovered that growth had slowed drastically, starting in the early 1960s.

Tests of air, rain, fog, and soil reveal high acid levels, some as high as in vinegar. Fog routinely bathes mountain peaks, some on parts of seven out of ten days, and droplets in these tested abnormally acid. Blame shifted from aphids to acid rain.

Soil shows high levels of lead and other pollutants from industry and automobiles. Blame expanded into overdoses of certain minerals and ozone, encouraged by exhaust from increased traffic in the mountains. But even these suspects cannot fill all requirements for the culprit.

Perhaps a combination kills—like acid rain affecting soil organisms and weakening trees, enabling woolly adelgids to damage them more easily.

Maybe, some scientists say, "natural causes" are influencing forests, changes not man-caused. However, such a natural phenomenon would occur over long time periods, not the relatively few years involved here. And decline is evident in forests around the world, especially in areas of heavy air pollution.

No one knows the answer, but all sense the urgency to understand. A walk through the haunting desolation of a ghost forest enforces this urgency.

Now sunlight bears down on forest floor life adapted to shade. The once-shaded neighborhood of clintonia, woodferns, and oxalis has been invaded by sun-loving mountain ash, fire cherry, blackberry, and goldenrod.

Yet among these new neighbors, left-over seeds from the old forest sprout. Evergreen seedlings struggle to remake the mountaintop spruce-fir forest. The critical question is, Will the new trees survive to maturity, producing critical seeds? Some already have brown needles on their twig tips. Is there hope for another spruce-fir forest?

(See also "Blue Ridge Haze" in August on page 177 and "Canada in Carolina" in August on page 183.)

WEBWORM IDENTITY CRISIS

WE PROBABLY would never notice those tiny webworm caterpillars except for one thing. About mid-August, in a massive cooperative effort, they construct conspicuous webs that engulf the leafy tips of tree branches.

As the hungry gang feeds on the enclosed leaves, the twig tips turn brown. Our sense of beauty for trees does not include brown twig tips in messy webs. Some person is bound to complain, "Oh, those awful tent caterpillars! Their nests are so ugly!"

This is when the little creatures inside the web should rear up and shout back, "We're not tent caterpillars! We're fall webworms."

Webworms are larvae of a small, white moth. Midsummer the female moth lays a cluster of eggs on tree leaves. She's especially likely to choose walnut, cherry, or sourwood.

In a scant week, tiny caterpillars hatch and promptly start web-building to enclose a leafy food supply. As they grow, they shed their skins six times and constantly enlarge the web to include more leaves.

In September they drop to the ground and wander in search of crevices under bark or leafy debris, where they spin cocoons. Through fall and winter and much of spring, each rests cozily inside. By midsummer, a transformation from

Webworms enclose the tip of a leafy branch in a web. They eat and grow and live within.

caterpillar to moth is completed, and moths emerge from cocoons, mate, and lay eggs.

You may wonder how to be absolutely sure these aren't tent caterpillars. Easily. If the web is built in a woody crotch of branches and encloses no leaves, tent caterpillars made it. They leave the tent when they want to feed. If the web encloses leaf tips with leaves enclosed, fall webworms built it. They stay within the web to feed. Too, tent caterpillars build in spring. Their life cycle is completed and their web is disintegrating by the time fall webworms hatch.

Tent caterpillars build a neat, tightly woven web. Webworms build loose, sloppy webs. And significantly, but less easy to observe, tent caterpillar moths lay eggs in shiny brown, crusty masses around narrow twigs, and the insect overwinters as eggs. Webworm eggs, laid on leaves and covered with white hairs from the females body, hatch quickly, and the insect overwinters as a cocoon.

So, despite the fact that both insects build conspicuous webs as home headquarters, the differences between them add up quickly.

You may want to do something about fall webworms on your trees. First, take a close look at a low-level web. It's not pretty, but visible through the web is a concentrated community of caterpillars busily eating leaves and moving about. Masses of their shed skins and droppings carpet the web's floor.

Next, realize that webworms do little significant harm to the tree. Unlike tent caterpillars which defoliate trees during the critical growth period in spring, webworms work in fall. By then a tree, even a tiny one completely engulfed by webs, has completed its annual growth and most of its food production. Losing leaves is no disaster. The easiest solution to webworms is to ignore them.

But suppose the webs look just awful. Snip off the offending branch tip and burn it. Of course, most webs hang far beyond reach, so relax. Time will take care of them.

Fall webworms are native to North America, but in 1940 some were found in Hungary, the first recorded in Europe. Since then, they have become a major tree pest throughout Europe and parts of Asia. Many insect pests in our country, like Japanese beetles and gypsy moths, are imports from other countries, but fall webworms are different—they're exports.

Next time you hear someone complain about tent caterpillars in August, you'll know you're confronted with a case of mistaken identity.

RHUS-JHUS REFRESHMENT

IF SOMEONE SUGGESTS making "sumac-ade," people are likely to react in disbelief. "From sumac? It's poisonous!"

If someone grabs a cluster of red sumac fruit, another is likely to warn, "Watch out! You can get an awful rash from that—worse than poison ivy."

Actually, most sumacs are harmless, but some species suffer undeserved rejection because one of their close relatives, poison sumac, does have an evil reputation, and rightly so. Contact with it can cause severe skin irritation.

Many a dose of skin rash has been wrongly blamed on poison sumac, however, even though few people ever contact it. This small, shrubby tree is not common and grows in swampy, boggy areas most people shun.

The true culprit of the skin rash is usually poison ivy (or poison oak), a common, frequently contacted plant. The human skin's similar response to poison sumac and poison ivy is no coincidence. Both harbor the same chemical irritant.

But people want to know how to tell which sumac is which. It's easy, especially when the fruits are showing from late July through winter.

If the plant has red fruits, it's safe. Red sumac fruits grow in dense clusters on twig tips. The clusters stand upright, though many curl over a bit at the top. They are handsome, useful, and harmless.

If the plant has whitish fruits dangling loosely and not from twig tips, avoid it.

Three common sumacs with red fruits grow in the southern mountains: staghorn, smooth, and dwarf.

Staghorn sumac (*Rhus typhina*) has toothed leaf margins, velvety branches, and velvety fruits. Its branches resemble a stag's horn when "in velvet." In the mountains, it grows mostly in higher elevations.

Smooth sumac (*Rhus glabra*) closely resembles staghorn, but lacks the soft fuzz on the branches. It is the most common sumac of the mountains.

Dwarf sumac (*Rhus copallina*) has untoothed leaf margins. The leaves are shiny with projections or "wings" along the stem between the leaflets, giving it the additional common names of shining sumac and winged sumac.

(Leaflets? All sumacs have compound leaves. Each single leaf is a stalk with many small leaflets.)

Poison sumac (*Toxicodendron vernix*) also has untoothed leaf margins, but the leaf stalk is reddish all through the growing season and has no "wings."

The three common sumacs with red fruits thrive in sunny, well-drained, relatively poor soil. They often invade disturbed soil and roadsides. Their wayward relative, poison sumac, prefers semi-shade and swampy soil.

But back to this sumac-ade business. The tiny hairs on the red fruits contain malic acid, a tart, water-soluble substance also found in unripe apples and grapes.

American Indians knew nothing about malic acid, but were fully aware that steeping crushed red sumac fruits in water produced a pink and palatable beverage. Unsweetened, it served as an astringent gargle for sore throats. Sweetened with maple syrup or honey, it became a delicious, refreshing drink.

Picture a scene of Cherokees on a hot summer day, relaxing in the shade and sipping sumac-ade chilled in the nearby branch. Or Indian youngsters begging Mother not for a bubbly soda or a powdered "fruit" drink, but for pink sumac-ade.

Indians gathered large quantities of the red fruits in their prime and stored them for winter use, when a hot drink would ease the chill of bitter days. American colonists followed suit.

The late edible-wild-foods enthusiast Euell Gibbons called the drink "Rhus-ade." One of his students dubbed it "Rhus jhus!"

If you want to try it, drop several handfuls of late summer red fruits into a pan, mash slightly, cover with boiling water, and allow to steep away from heat until the water is well colored. Strain through two thicknesses of fine cloth to remove the hairs. Sweeten, serve hot or cold, and enjoy.

And in late winter watch birds gobble the berries. Robins, mockingbirds, goldfinches, evening grosbeaks, and titmice all indulge. Even crows relish them. Berries stay on the twigs all through winter, so are available when many other wildlife foods are scarce.

Sumacs poisonous? Only one, the one with loose dangling white fruits. Avoid it, and enjoy the rest.

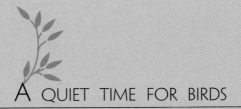

A QUIET TIME FOR BIRDS

IT'S CONTRADICTORY. Though late August boasts the year's peak of bird numbers, it's also when we're frequently asked, "Where have all the birds gone?" The surge of young has mushroomed bird population, yet we see fewer birds than before. Why?

In late summer, stores stock fall attire, parents purchase clothes for school-bound youngsters, and a chilly evening forces us to grab a sweater. It's time for a change of clothing.

Birds change clothing, too. Old feathers, tattered from the rigors of breeding and raising families, fall out, and new ones grow in, a process called molting. We can even occasionally spot a songbird with a baldish head or missing tail.

Growing new feathers requires extra energy, so nature sets molting neatly between two periods of high energy—breeding and migration. Molting birds become quiet, sometimes reclusive, often retreating into woods or shrubby areas. They seem to disappear.

An old mountain man sitting on our porch one midday explained his theory. "Hawks has ate 'em," he stated bluntly. In no way could I convince him that birds are a small part of most hawks' diet—hawks feast mostly on rodents and large insects—and that the dearth of visible birds is due to molting, not hawks.

But how can a bird that depends on flying get food, especially if it loses its long flight feathers all at once? For most birds, molting is gradual. A sequence of feather loss and replacement over a period of several weeks assures continual feathers for flight.

A few species do lose flight feathers all at once and cannot fly for a brief period, but these are mostly water birds, like ducks, geese, loons, and grebes, which feed by swimming. They escape enemies by diving or swimming beyond reach or by hiding in shoreside vegetation.

And a few species migrate before molting or lose feathers over a period of months rather than weeks.

Sometimes late August's lack of birds involves a second factor. The birds have moved. Mourning doves and robins that nested around our yards gather in country fields and open spaces. Starlings that raised young in house crevices or tree holes swirl around fields in ever-growing groups. Swallows flock and rest on telephone and electric wires like hundreds of plump clothespins on a clothesline. They haven't disappeared; they've just moved away from where we saw them frequently.

Though we notice spring's early chorus of robins, the arrival of a wood thrush, or the exuberant, endless medleys of mockingbirds, we barely notice the time of their last songs. One day in August we simply realize that most birds have stopped singing. With courting and breeding finished, song is not needed, and the energy it required now goes to making new feathers. A few straggling songsters persist—an occasional towhee, song sparrow, diligent indigo bunting, or extra-ardent dove. But most communication now is by call notes rather than song and will continue that way until early spring.

By molting, some birds unwittingly play a trick on people learning to identify them. Their fall and winter plumage differs radically from that of spring and summer. For example, the yellow of male goldfinches and red of male scarlet tanagers change to olive gray. Warblers confuse even expert birdwatchers when their bright colors change to drab olive, making some species exasperatingly similar and identification a struggle. Then, before spring breeding, a spring molt occurs, and the bright new breeding plumage grows.

To confuse the novice birdwatcher further, plumage of immature birds often differs from that of mature birds. Though most species acquire adult plumage in their first year, some require several years and have a series of intermediate plumages. Bald eagles might not get their well-known white heads and tails until ready for breeding at five years.

So, August is notoriously a quiet bird month. Birdwatchers plan other activities, content that after the molt, activity will zoom again. The flurry of migration lies just ahead.

Summer Symphony

WE'VE ALL HEARD of city folks who sleep blissfully through the din of rumbling trucks, honking cars, and shouting people, then visit the country and can't fall asleep because the night is too noisy. They complain that country nights barrage their ears with big noises from tiny sources—the unfamiliar buzzes, clicks, chirps, rasps, and trills of insects.

As spring's chorus of birds, frogs, and toads fades in midsummer, hordes of insect musicians tune up to give performances on winged instruments. Sounds of a country August and September merge into a summer symphony.

People accustomed to it love it, charmed by the thought of all those little creatures out there broadcasting their intent for romance.

Most calls are by males, hoping to attract females. But the suitors do not wander in search of their lady loves. They stay put and fiddle their music to lure the females closer and closer until mating can occur. Their call usually warns other males to keep away.

The symphony's musicians are a variety of crickets, katydids, grasshoppers, and cicadas, each species with its own instrument and music by which it can be recognized.

"I wish they'd shut up!" states a less

Rasping, noisy sounds of cicadas, usually heard at the height of summer, have earned these insects the nickname "hotbugs."

enthusiastic listener. "A katydid sits on my bedroom window screen every night. Zee-zee-zee. Zee-zee-zee. Kay-tee-did. Kat-tee-did. I find myself counting 1-2-3, 1-2-3, 1-2-3. I could fall asleep on that, maybe, but every so often it throws in kay-tee-did-not, kay-tee-did-not, 1-2-3-4, 1-2-3-4, and I'm undone!"

If we listen carefully, we can note that some have musical pitch (we can hum the note) while others are strictly mechanical—repeated clicks, buzzes, or rasps. Crickets make the sounds with pitch—high, low, steady, or broken. An assortment of grasshoppers, katydids, and cicadas makes the others—frail, strident, pleasant, or annoying.

Each has a favorite time of day or night for performing. Black field crickets chirp or "sing" intermittently day or night. Tree crickets, among the most common but least seen insect "singers," produce long, steady nighttime trills. Grasshoppers prefer to click and buzz in daylight, and the familiar serenade of cicadas sounds in daytime.

Katydids, with beautifully veined green wings astonishingly similar to leaves, tune up noisily at dusk and into night, their insistent triplets one of the most prevalent sounds of late summer. People often think their zee-zee-zees are tree frogs, but tree frogs seldom call this time of year, nor is there any Southern Appalachian frog species making triplet rasping sounds. And if you stalk the sound, approaching ever so slowly, you'll find the fiddler to be. . .an insect with beautifully veined green wings, appearing remarkably similar to a leaf with legs.

I have often marveled how we can drive through miles and miles of summer countryside, slow down anywhere and never fail to hear a din of insects. What myriads there must be!

Consider how such tiny creatures make such grand sounds. Grasshoppers that sport short antennae (short-horned grasshoppers) have projections on their hind legs that they rub across a rough spot or scraper on their wings. It's like running a fingernail across a comb.

Katydids, crickets, and the other grasshoppers, all with long antennae (long-horned), rub ridges on one forewing against a scraper on the other. The wings vibrate noisily or musically.

Cicadas use an entirely different instrument. On each side of the insect's thorax is a hole covered with a membrane, which acts like a drum head. Special muscles make the membranes vibrate, a strident sound that swells to a mighty crescendo, then fades.

One often hears that some insects sing with their wings and hear with their knees, which sounds crazy, but it's true! Most females receive the eager calls of males through a sound-sensitive organ on one segment of their front legs.

Amid this flurry, females deposit eggs into ground or twigs, depending on species. Eventually cold weather slows the adults until they perish in the frosts and freezes of winter.

But—new summer symphony players lie as dormant cells within the eggs. Though miniature, they hold the potential for a grand performance next summer.

Meanwhile, silence.

SEPTEMBER

GOLDENROD—FALSELY ACCUSED

"IT'S TAKEN OVER the whole field!" I exclaim. "Only a few years ago this all waved with grassy plumes and daisies and clover. Now it's a sea of goldenrod." My arm sweeps dramatically across the yellow field to emphasize the completeness of the takeover.

"And look at the bugs!" my walking companion adds as we peer closely at a shoulder-high flower head.

Bees of varied sizes and markings poke among the flowers for nectar and pollen. Colorful beetles and shiny wasps crawl. A yellow crab spider crouches amid yellow surroundings, almost invisible, ready to grab some unsuspecting nectar hunter as it creeps within reach. A steady hum overhangs the field in the stillness of a warm September day.

With red aphids, green aphids, butterflies, and a host of unknowns, they comprise a teeming community—all on the head of a goldenrod, multiplied countless times across this yellow field and more countless times across other yellow fields and roadsides.

Goldenrod plumes attract more insects than almost any other late summer plant. Over a thousand species have been recorded on them.

But poor goldenrod gets such bad press. If people who accuse it of being a

*Nectar in the bright flower heads of goldenrod
attracts a host of insects, assuring pollination of its tiny flowers.*

four-star cause of hay fever could hear this hum of insects, they'd realize how falsely they accuse.

To cause hay fever, pollen must float in the air, produced by plants that depend on wind to carry their pollen load to other plants of their species. They have no need to attract insects, so their flowers have no bright colors. Most of their pollen is wasted, so tremendous amounts are produced.

But many plants, like goldenrod, depend on insects for pollination. Needing to attract the insects, the plants display colorful flowers, sweet nectar, and sticky pollen. They do not waste pollen to the whims of wind, so need less of it.

The finger of blame for late summer hay fever should point to a plant that flowers with goldenrod but is barely noticeable—ragweed. Its clouds of windborne pollen from inconspicuous green flowers irritate noses mercilessly—and beautiful goldenrod gets the blame because it is conspicuous. Unfortunately, some flower books persist in perpetuating this error.

"But," wails the allergy victim (and I

am one), "when the doctor tested me for goldenrod, I reacted vigorously." (So did I.) Goldenrod often produces a reaction in medical tests but cannot be responsible for hay fever misery. Its pollen is too heavy and sticky to be air-borne.

Many people admire goldenrod. Nebraska and Kentucky have it as state flowers. Though I've seen goldenrod described as "a foul weed," I've also seen it gracing magnificent gardens in England. A New England florist told me that goldenrod is surprisingly popular for fall weddings. The yellow plumes can be enjoyed later, too. If cut in full flower and dried, they hold color well.

When seeds develop, the head becomes a mass of fluff, great for decoration, if you don't mind occasional seeds floating off. And when standing amid tall seed plumes with late afternoon sun backlighting them, you feel as if you're standing in fairyland. Later many seeds will disappear into winter birds.

A writer stated years ago, "A person is blind who does not know goldenrod, but a person is a trained botanist who can identify the kinds of goldenrod." Over seventy species grow in the United States, but identifying some confounds even trained botanists.

The Southern Appalachians host about twenty-five species, all yellow except silverrod, which has white petals and is easy to spot. It grows in the higher elevations, including along the Blue Ridge Parkway. No one species blooms throughout goldenrod season, but an overlapping succession of species produces a continual golden show from July until frost.

Have you ever tried goldenrod tea? George Washington did. American colonists and native Americans savored tea from its flowers and leaves, and praised goldenrod for its healing qualities. Its scientific name, *Solidago*, comes from a Latin word *solidare*, to heal or make whole.

Weed or wonder, goldenrod waves its gold conspicuously. And, hay fever victims, even you (we) can enjoy it.

Daddy-Longlegs, Stilt Walkers

I READ ABOUT A MAN on a crowded subway car who discovered a daddy-longlegs tiptoeing up his sleeve.

Unwilling to flick it off and cause commotion among adjacent passengers who might find the beast frightening, he casually covered it with his hat. It climbed into the protective darkness of the hat's interior, and the man set the hat upon his head and exited with the crowd.

This man understood daddy-longlegs—spidery but not a spider, ugly but harmless, frightening but without cause.

And comical! They prance around on bent stilts, eight threadlike legs that arch above their bodies and look as if, most certainly, they should get hopelessly entangled with each other. But coordination is perfect.

If human legs were as long by comparison, they'd measure forty feet or more. Imagine struggling over a landscape of tangled shrubs and fallen trees with such equipment. Yet the daddy-longlegs speeds lightly over grasses, weeds, and twigs without a trip or tumble.

I watch them silently move about in the evening. The low slung, oval bodies, barely a quarter inch long, bob up and down. Ridiculous! But as the bodies repeatedly, gently brush the ground, bush, or rock where the daddy-longlegs walk,

*A favorite activity of a daddy-longlegs is preening
its legs—running the length of leg through its mouth to clean it.*

they test for food. Aphids (plant lice) are especially delectable, but they feast on other tiny insects and scavenge decaying matter.

If I pick up a daddy-longlegs—by a leg, of course—it will struggle a moment. Then suddenly it might be scurrying away, leaving a twitching leg between my thumb and finger. When threatened by an enemy, it drops a leg, and as the enemy sidetracks to the twitching, the daddy-longlegs scurries away.

Loss of a leg or two is no problem unless it's the second, longest pair. This pair reports on food and danger through ultra-sensitive tips with a touch so light we cannot feel it on our hands, so light the creature can scamper across water and not get its feet wet.

If I put a daddy-longlegs in a margarine cup and set it in the refrigerator briefly, the chill slows the captive's activity without harming it. Then I can view it through a magnifying glass. From a black knob on its head rise two tiny lumps, the eyes. The leg joints show well, and as the captive warms, it gently grasps the base of a leg with its jaws and daintily nibbles it clean—from base to toe tip. Then it cleans another leg.

"They look like spiders to me," someone is bound to complain, obviously not feeling warmly toward spiders and shunting daddy-longlegs to the same creepy category. True, like spiders they have eight legs. Unlike spiders, they have no "neck" constriction between the head and thorax, nor do they spin threads or cover their eggs with protective silk. They do not bite a person, but do emit a hint of scent, which possibly defends them from enemies. One scientist who studies daddy-longlegs can identify various species of them by scent.

In autumn the female daddy-longlegs lays eggs in a moist crevice or under bark or a stone. By late fall most adults die. In spring, miniatures of the adult hatch, and as they grow, these young periodically pull out of their old skins. Marvelously, they can shed the outer cover of even their threadlike legs, leaving a perfect, fragile replica of their former selves.

"I've always called them harvestmen," someone comments, defending a common name for daddy-longlegs. That name is appropriate, too, for the population peaks in late summer. It has a romantic ring, too, associating the creature with the climax of the growing season.

But it ignores the animal's most striking and fascinating feature, those amazing legs. Even well before late summer's major harvest time, daddy-longlegs are easy to find as they rest during daytime around damp shrubs and gardens—and our porch, a favorite haunt.

They make good neighbors. Strike up an acquaintance with one.

Some tough characters—woodpeckers

SUPPOSE SOMEONE ordered you to bang your head against a hard wall or hammer a nail with your head. Obviously your head isn't adapted for such harsh treatment. But for woodpeckers, head banging is fine.

Repeated rat-a-tats with a beak against hard wood are necessary daily routine for woodpeckers. It's rough treatment for a head and neck, but woodpecker skulls are extra thick, unusual for birds whose light bone structure is usually top priority. Thick skulls act as shock absorbers.

People are usually unaware of a woodpecker's mighty nest-building efforts. Most of that meticulous chipping and shaping of the woody nest cavity goes on inside a tree. The entrance hole is the only part that shows.

The nest cavity of our smallest woodpecker, the sparrow-sized downy, for example, is from eight to twelve inches deep, though the circular entrance hole is only about one-and-a-half inches across, not very big when seen from the ground many feet below.

Probing for insects underneath rugged bark is no easy job either. Sound makes it possible for the woodpecker to find grubs and beetles that live completely out of sight in bark or wood. Noise from an insect's chewing or movement guides hunter to prey. With remarkable speed, the bird probes, hammers, and twists

A large woodpecker, the northern flicker, shows the sharp beak woodpeckers use for extracting insects from bark.
Photograph by J. R. Woodward

aside wood chips or drills a hole to its intended meal.

Sounds simple, but two problems arise: prey can crawl farther away, and the bore of the hole is narrow. But these won't deter a hungry woodpecker. It sticks out its tongue. And what a tongue—nearly three to five times as long as the beak. When retracted, it pulls back beyond the throat and up around the skull. The woodpecker jabs down the hole with the tongue's barbed, sensitive tip and spears its prey, quite unaware that it is helping control tree pests.

Many a joke pokes fun at a woodpecker called the yellow-bellied sapsucker, but the joke is on the jokester, for the name is highly appropriate. The belly is yellow, and the bird does sip sap. It makes horizontal rows of tiny holes on tree bark, then laps sap oozing from them and feasts on insects attracted to it. Occasionally the sap ferments, and the sapsuckers become—you guessed it—a bit tipsy! (Sappy?)

Woodpeckers are drummers as well as probers and chippers. Springtime drumming with beaks on a surface warns competitors: Stay out of my territory. The signal resounds grandly from a hollow trunk or limb. Occasionally a flicker (a woodpecker often seen feeding on the ground) will discover even more sensational effects. It hammers a metal rainspout or TV aerial, inevitably near a bedroom in early morning. Anyone experiencing this impressive eye-opener celebrates heartily the end of spring nesting, when the need to defend territories with drumming dies out.

How is a woodpecker able to hang onto a tree trunk so well during these strenuous activities? Toes and tail are adapted for extra physical stress.

Most song birds have three toes in front, one in back, the best arrangement for perching. Woodpeckers have two toes in front, two behind, permitting an extra-firm grip.

Remarkably stiff, pointed tail feathers brace the bird firmly against the tree trunk as it works. Shafts of these stabilizing feathers are almost spine-like.

Seven kinds of woodpeckers can be seen in western North Carolina. One is the size of a crow, the pileated, and another a sign of the season, the yellow-bellied sapsucker, which spends winters here.

Two look almost exactly alike except for size, the downy woodpecker and the larger hairy woodpecker, and another has a misleading name, the red-bellied woodpecker. The rusty red patch on its belly is far less obvious than the bright red cap on its head.

Still another, the flicker, laps ants from the ground. The last is rarely seen locally, though perhaps its name is the most commonly known, the red-headed. The name is often applied, in error, to the others. Its head is red to the shoulders, not just a red crest, as on the pileated, or red patches, as on others.

The best time of year for watching woodpeckers is from now until early spring. They enjoy the offerings of feeders, especially suet and peanut butter-suet combinations. Supply these—and start counting 'peckers.

Mountain Dawn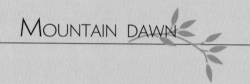

"INCREDIBLE!" I exclaimed aloud as I read that a 65-year-old woman had just seen her first sunrise. Her grandchild had talked her into looking at it. I wondered what she thought of it and whether there are hosts of others for whom sunrise is an unknown experience.

A veteran sunrise watcher, I revel in that moment when the sun first peeks above the horizon, whether it's a red ball rising out of the eastern sea or a hazy spot of brighter light over a foggy valley, whether intense shine behind a building or a golden globe through a tree or over a mountain.

It lasts only moments, rising surprisingly fast, at first an exciting glow, then a brilliant arc, then a swelling mass, finally a fiery ball. Boldly, relentlessly, it introduces day, and there is no stopping or turning back. Its shine is critical to our survival, influential in our activities, inevitable to our routine.

But dawn also includes that special time before the sun appears. A mere hint of light touches the eastern sky. One isn't sure when it starts or even if it's really happening, but gradually light increases. Literature describes it dramatically as "first light." It can be gloriously welcomed or miserably dreaded, taken for granted or viewed with awe. First light

*A mountain dawn often rewards its audience with
a lovely display of color, of both sky and mounatins.*

through the eons of man before electricity has probably affected emotions and routine even more powerfully than the appearance of the sun itself.

A mountain dawn with great hulks of high shadowy land rising against the sky can surprise with its stillness. Absolutely nothing seems to move, no blade, no sprig. A mantle of peace overlies the forest or field, valley or yard, even the street, unless the scene is truly urban with man's unceasing stir obliterating the effect.

If we stand quietly a while, however, blending into this stillness, we sense that the quiet is not complete after all—a rustle among leaves, a flutter in a shrub, a click, a chip, a scraping on bark. Despite apparent tranquillity, creatures of night are retiring as those of day awaken, a hidden, invisible world caught in daily routine.

Dampness enhances sounds, making them clearer and more resonant, but the sounds of man are few. No one mows lawns or blows snow this time of day.

Dawn tingles with freshness, colder, crisper. It exhilarates, spreading sensations of well-being and confidence. Today is under control, for sure.

And it often reveals a fairyland of dew. Stretch, stoop, or kneel to peer at myriad tiny droplets. Each has a highlight reflection of sky; each magnifies. You might discover the supreme creation of a dewy dawn. An ugly spider made it—an orb web, its geometric threads strung with diamonds, an exquisite display of curves, angles, and spheres.

Modern living with its plethora of lights diverts from dawn's beauties and moods. It lights the indoors for hosts of people so that dawn and sunrise are totally unfamiliar to them.

Tomorrow morning, stand outdoors in dawn, looking, listening, feeling. Take time to wander a bit, receptive, unpressured, enjoying the blessing of dawn.

FIERCE KILLER ON THE LOOSE

"AN EVER-HUNGRY MACHINE of destruction" is how science writers describe it. "A bloodthirsty killer," "a slave to its stomach," "a terrible tiger of the woodland." What a beast!

So ferocious it normally eats nearly twice its weight every day, this creature lives on the brink of disaster, because without food it will starve to death within twenty-four hours. Three were captured and put together. A fight started. Two killed the third and ate it. Eight hours later, one remained—quite plump.

Moreover, it's untamable.

You probably are imagining a dreadful animal, huge, dangerous, and rare. But no. It's one of our most common furred animals. In fact, some biologists claim it is the most common—and it weighs only as much as two nickels.

It goes by the name of short-tailed shrew and has a relative, the pygmy shrew, which is probably the world's smallest furred animal. It weighs the same as a dime!

The shrew's nervous, murderous ways are not because of bad temper. It's just hungry, frantically, perpetually hungry, so

Tiny ears, a pointed nose, and a voracious appetite
mark the shrew, one of our most common but least seen mammals.
Photograph by Dwight R. Kuhn

busy eating that it has little time for rest or fun. Food becomes energy almost as soon as eaten. Hard parts in it pass through the shrew's digestive tract in only two hours.

The killer hunts any time of day or night and charges full speed through all seasons with no time out to migrate or hibernate. It rushes through life so fast that by the age of sixteen months, it's an old, old shrew, quite worn out. Few live to eighteen months.

The eastern two-thirds of the United States is loaded with short-tails, but few people have heard of them and fewer still have ever seen one. They're tiny, live alone and out of sight, and don't bother people in any way.

Hearing short-tails is a lot easier than seeing them. That hasty scuffle in the leaves, that unexpected squeaking or high-pitched twitter beneath the shrub-bery—those sounds are probably shrews. They rustle about in plant debris in forests, gardens, yards, and fields and scurry in dark tunnels often borrowed from mice or voles.

Always hunting feverishly, shrews take time off only to tend a family of four to seven young several times a year. The newborns look like wrinkled pink honeybee larvae.

Daytime sightings might occur as their slate-gray forms zoom across a few feet of open space, but it's a lucky glimpse. Once I saw one drink repeatedly from a ground-level birdbath. After each sip, it dashed under the bath to hide. Though I saw it over and over, it moved so fast I could hardly tell what it looked like.

People mostly see shrews dead, caught by cats or dogs, then dropped because their musky scent smells bad. Many a shrew carcass is kicked aside as ugh! a dead mouse. But shrews often become food for hawks and owls, foxes and weasels, even snakes.

A shrew does resemble a mouse but has a longer, more pointed nose, extremely tiny eyes—one-quarter the size of a pinhead—and almost invisible ears. And a short-tail's tail is much shorter than a mouse's.

Shrews don't climb like mice or get into people's houses, food cupboards, or seed containers. They dine mainly on insects and spiders, and deserve far more credit for this helpful service to people than they get. Their menu also includes other delicious snacks—earthworms, slugs, snails, frogs, salamanders, and millipedes, picked up as the hungry beasts snuffle about with their flexible, sensitive noses. In winter, seeds and plants join the diet.

And what courage! The tiny hunters will charge prey even larger than themselves, perhaps a mouse, vole, or baby rabbit. This brave attack succeeds because the shrews have a secret weapon, venomous saliva, which paralyzes large prey and kills tiny prey. Sometimes shrews store live, paralyzed victims a short while in their runways, returning to feast a bit later.

The secret weapon makes the short-tail shrew special. It is the only venomous furred animal in North America.

But people have no reason to fear them. The venom is more irritating to humans than dangerous. How often do we hear of shrew bites?

People and shrews just don't get together, which is too bad. Each would find the other fascinating.

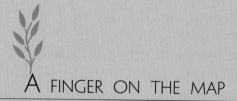

A FINGER ON THE MAP

A NEWSPAPER columnist described the event in his bird column—rather casually, I thought. A woman had called him to report that a hundred or more pomarine jaegers had flown over her mountain meadow the previous afternoon. I'd have been no more astonished had she seen a penguin waddling across her lawn—or maybe a giraffe nibbling her trees.

Seeing one pomarine jaeger in the mountains is highly unlikely. Seeing a hundred—well, think of the penguin and giraffe. Apparently neither columnist nor caller had checked a range map.

Nature guide books often include maps that show where a bird, tree, or fern lives, its range. Because birds migrate, they often have two ranges, one for breeding, one for wintering. A quick look at a penguin range map, for example, shows them living only in the Southern Hemisphere. And penguins do not fly, so no winds could whisk one north to a mountain yard.

Before moving from the Northeast to the western North Carolina mountains, I often noted a narrow finger extending into the South on range maps. I gave it little thought until I lived in the southern mountains and learned how their high elevations provide living conditions remarkably similar to those of the North. Consequently, the range of many northern birds, animals, and plants extends into southern highlands. Winter wren, veery, black-capped chickadee, red-breasted nuthatch—these and many others show that finger of range on their maps.

Excited by having range maps giving me new messages about the mountains, I checked beyond birds. Trees show the finger pattern remarkably often—eastern hemlock, yellow birch, white pine, mountain ash, pin cherry, mountain and striped maple, red spruce, and others. Canada mayflower and yellow bead lily extend a northern finger into southern regions. This was fun.

Many times I have diligently used a guide book to identify a local species. Then I checked the range map, only to see that the species name I'd chosen lives only along the South Carolina-Georgia coast—or perhaps grows only in the Canadian Rockies. Clearly I needed to try again.

Checking range maps shows not only what does live in the mountains but also what doesn't. I call these "negative maps." A long finger dips into our mountains showing where willow oak, sweet gum, eastern cottonwood, and southern red oak are *not* native. These grow in the regions around the high mountains but not in them. These species survive here when planted but do not thrive and reproduce in these forests. A map of Carolina

chickadee range shows a finger in the high elevations where that species does not live.

But getting back to those pomarine jaegers—their range map certainly does not include the Southern Appalachians. It shows nesting grounds in Canada's Arctic islands and along coasts of Greenland, with wintering at sea off our southern and western coasts. Jaegers are true sea birds. Along the Atlantic coast in winter an alert birdwatcher may spot one over the water. But to see "a hundred or so" flying over a mountain meadow?

One had to wonder what those birds were that the caller reported to the columnist. The same week the report of pomarine jaegers hit the news, we watched with delight the fall flights of nighthawks over our meadow, a spectacle of amazing aerial maneuvers as they caught insects. By the dozens, even hundreds, they flew about, a dramatic symbol of autumn as they worked their way to a winter range in South America, from Columbia to Argentina. Dark birds like the jaegers, with white patches on their wings, they could easily lure an amateur birdwatcher leafing through a bird guide into mistaking them for jaegers.

But—check those range maps.

(See also "Canada in Carolina" in August on page 183.)

Praying mantis or preying mantis

THE MANTIS made one mistake. Had it stayed motionless, its brown and leaf-green body would have blended so perfectly with surrounding honeysuckle that I'd have missed it completely. But the insect moved, reared back in a posture of defense. We were opponents.

As I extended a hand slowly toward it, the four-inch mantis held its forelegs high for the strike. Bulging green eyes on a triangular head followed every move I made. A flexible neck makes the mantis the only local insect able to move its head to direct its gaze at will.

It saw no cause to strike me, however, but how terrifying that pose and eyes must appear to potential victims of this awesome carnivore!

My finger touched its walking legs. The mantis stepped back. I inched my hand beneath and lifted her—it was a female with abdomen distended by eggs—and set her on my sleeve. Unlike most insects, she made no attempt to fly, but regarded me warily, composed and dignified, seeming as curious about me as I about her. But she held onto that attack position.

A mantis on asters poses formally for the photographer.

A question struck: Should this impressive creature be called praying or preying mantis? The oversized, folded forelegs, held high, appear convincingly prayerful, yet the pious limbs are actually tools for grabbing and gripping viselike its living prey. Either name seems appropriate.

Praying is preferred. In fact, the scientific name of the species most commonly seen is *Mantis religiosa*. Yet one reputable insect guide consistently spells it preying. I wonder if this is an error or a touch of rebellion by the author who felt the insect's victims needed more recognition than its pose.

Those legs are everything for a ravenous mantis, which waits motionless, infinitely patient amid its leafy camouflage. When its unsuspecting meal crawls or alights within striking distance, zingo! Quicker than the eye, the prey is clamped between those saw-edged, pincer-like leg segments. The diner chomps instantly, usually at the victim's neck first to immobilize it, gripping the meal as if holding an ear of corn.

European and Chinese mantises were imported because of their enthusiastic appetites for a wide variety of insects. Importers expected them to consume hosts of crop pests, and they do. But they eat beneficial insects, too, so their usefulness has been overrated.

As I examined my mantis close up, she looked me in the eye. So appealing is that face that one can barely resist associating human traits and "personality" to the odd beast. One almost expects it to state formally, "Good afternoon."

I returned her to the leaves. Soon she would deposit a frothy, cream-colored egg mass on a stalk or twig. It would harden quickly, like Styrofoam, ready to protect its precious burden through winter.

Its shape identifies her species: if round, the Chinese mantis; if mostly round but with one side flattened, the European mantis, the import we see most frequently. Cylindrical or flattened shapes indicate native species, but these are seldom seen.

People sometimes collect a mantis case and bring it indoors, thinking they've found the cocoon of some handsome moth. But come spring, the error shocks as hundreds of miniature mantises pour from a weakened seam in the case. Surroundings crawl with them.

Hungry already, they eat whatever small insect they find, even each other. Outdoors, in a curious twist of nature, hatching mantises, the scourge of other insects, are themselves devoured by many insects, birds, and toads.

Not until late summer will the survivors be fully grown and mature. Then, when mating occurs, fellows watch out! "Love" goes awry as the female often devours the male during mating. It stimulates his act. Some stimulus! The generous meal on her martyred mate apparently boosts her strength for egg laying.

Fall is when we are most likely to see a mantis, and it pleases to watch one a while. Communicating with an insect personality might even make the day. But the mantis's days are numbered. Cold and time allow no survivors. Only tiny eggs inside the tough foam cases make it through a winter.

OCTOBER

Evergreens lose leaves

"SOME PEOPLE sure are hard to convince, mighty hard." The local agriculture agent shakes his head gloomily. "'Bout this time of year folks call, all upset and saying, 'My pines 're turnin' yellow. What's wrong? Are they dyin'? Have they got some disease?' I explain how the pines 're just losing their leaves—completely normal—happens every year. Then I hear, 'But they're evergreens! Evergreens don't lose needles.'"

For many years I, too, believed that pines never dropped their needles. I can hear my fifth-grade science teacher stating, "A deciduous tree is one that loses its leaves in winter. An evergreen tree keeps its leaves in winter. The leaves stay green all year."

Mistakenly, I concluded that all evergreens had needles and the needles were there to stay—forever.

But wait a minute! A fine tamarack (larch) tree, complete with needles and cones, grew in my yard. Its needles turned a glowing yellow each fall and dropped, leaving the tree quite skeletal. Nearby grew a holly tree with no needles but broad green leaves all winter. I was confused. The teacher's oversimplified description omitted important facts.

Experience eventually filled the information gap when I later lived under pines and became pleasantly familiar with the soft tan layer of needles that carpeted our premises each October. I watched tiny needle bundles drop from boughs above

Needles of white pine, having lived on the tree for several years, turn yellow, then light brown before dropping in autumn.

and lance downward, piercing the air. Sun and a slight puff of breeze often made the air glitter with hundreds of these miniature, plummeting spears.

A tree and shrub book explained that first, not every evergreen has needles. Many have broad leaves, like holly, southern magnolia, laurel, and rhododendron.

Second, it explained that not every deciduous tree has broad leaves. The needled tamarack of the north and bald cypress of the south shed annually.

Third, all leaves, whether deciduous or evergreen, are only temporary. They work hard producing food for the plant, and they wear out. They need replacement. Deciduous plants replace all leaves each year. Evergreens replace only the oldest leaves, the ones farthest back from the growing tips.

These oldest leaves fall, not in the year they burst from a bud, maybe not even in their second year. Some can last three or four years. But fall they must, and they change color first.

Behind the rich green leaves of autumn rhododendron cling leaves that are yellow or splotched with brown, or, if the shrub gets lots of sun, even orangy red. Laurel shows quantities of bright yellow leaves. Pines, hemlocks, spruce, and fir feature colored foliage, too—that of white pines especially lovely in its brief, two-toned (yellow and green) stage. Touching a bough of spruce or hemlock

at the right stage often loosens a tickly shower of yellow-brown needles.

Holly sheds in the spring, presenting a temporarily straggly, sickly appearance as old leaves die and new ones emerge from buds.

Tender deciduous leaves cannot withstand freezing. The plant sheds them and stands safely dormant through freezing weather. Evergreen leaves are more leathery. When needled or scaled (like juniper), they offer less surface to cold, drying winds. Their chemistry keeps ice crystals small within the cells. Large crystals rupture cells and kill the leaf. Cell membranes are more flexible in evergreens so less likely to have freeze damage.

So, evergreen leaves are cold-tolerant. On sunny days, if the temperature rises above freezing, they can even manufacture a small amount of food.

Each fall the patient agriculture agent explains how yes, pines are evergreen and do stay green in winter, and no, the yellowing trees are not sick. They're absolutely normal. They're just shedding their oldest leaves and next spring will grow lots of new ones.

"Maybe I can convince people this year," he adds, grinning.

(See also "Golden Dust Rides the Air" in May on page 122 and "Conifers for Christmas" in December on page 271.)

SEVEN WONDERS IN MY YARD

REMEMBER the seven wonders of the ancient world? A few people might recall the Pyramids of Egypt, the Hanging Gardens of Babylon, or even the Colossus of Rhodes. But the rest?

Ever since the list was created in the several 100's B.C., people have amused themselves with making other lists of seven wonders: of the modern world, of North America, of science, of literature, and so on. On a bright afternoon, I set out to choose seven wonders in my yard and found too many. But I winnowed it down to these seven:

1. A monarch butterfly. It drifts in the air as if suspended from an invisible filament, riding an updraft. Then wings flutter, and the monarch, one of the hundreds passing through our mountains each day recently, continues its inexorable migration south. Its destination is a remote mountain region in Mexico where it will winter with millions of its kind. It has never made the trip before, so how does it know where to go?

2. A spider web. The undisputed beauty of an early morning in autumn is a spider web. Filmy strands, laden with dew, festoon stalks, sprigs, and blades in my meadow. The droplets, each perfectly

spaced from its neighbor, cling and glitter in misty light. Each webbed masterpiece is created precisely—a filmy sheet, dome, orb, funnel, bowl, or hammock—revealing the species of its maker. Then in daytime's warmth, the jewels disappear, and the web they adorned hides waiting, an invisible trap.

3. A seed. Hard and dry, a seed needs only a bit of moisture and a touch of warmth to transform it. Tiny cells swell and divide, then these new cells swell and divide, and we name this growth. A root sprout emerges, always growing downward, and a stem, always growing upward. What seemed lifeless becomes a growing, producing plant. I wonder not how it happens—that's beyond my comprehension—but at the astonishing fact that it does happen.

4. An earthworm. The fertility of natural soil can often be measured by the number of earthworms in it. As these hidden creatures eat their way through soil, they not only loosen and aerate it, they release waste into it, thus adding organic nutrients. The lowly worm may not charm with the beauty of a butterfly or delight with the song of a thrush; it may not please with a bunny's cuddliness or amuse with a fox pup's antics. But it tops them all for economic importance.

5. A root hair. Beneath each plant lie branching roots, probing and pushing through the soil. It's easy to picture this entire network of roots as actively absorbing water. But most of a root's length serves only to anchor the plant. Absorption occurs only in the wondrously thin, almost microscopic root hairs that grow just behind the remote root tips—millions, even billions of hairs in intimate contact with the watery film between soil particles. Watering a tree near its trunk merely gives it a bath. The absorbing root hairs are away from the trunk, out below the drip line of the twigs and beyond.

6. A leaf cutter bee. Perfect round and oval holes in a redbud leaf reveal the presence of leaf cutter bees in the yard. The female bee chooses a cranny for her nest and cuts a round piece of leaf to line its far end. Then she cuts oval pieces to line its sides. In this cozy cell she lays an egg and places pollen-nectar paste as food for the larva that will hatch. A second round piece of leaf closes the cell. How does she know to cut some pieces round, some oval?

7. A bud. The bud, a compact masterpiece of potential, each formed uniquely for its species, joins the list only because it houses and protects the real wonder, a leaf. Flat, green, commonplace, a leaf

carries out one of the world's most remarkable chemical reactions. Using water absorbed through roots and carbon dioxide taken from the air through its pores, it creates the sugars that feed the world. Sunlight provides energy for the reaction; green chlorophyll controls it. From those sugars, the plant makes leaves, stems, roots, seeds, and fruits—foods. All from just air and water plus a salting of minerals from the soil. If there were no leaf, we could not exist.

My list of wonders could go on and on, each addition a humbling experience

(See also "Spring's Year-old Buds" in March on page 55, "Earthworms, Lowly Plowmen" in May on page 101, "Mystery of the Monarchs" in July on page 160, and "The Next-to-last Leaf" in October on page 233.)

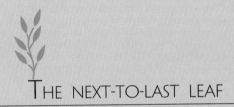

THE NEXT-TO-LAST LEAF

ITS FRANTIC RATTLING diverted me from reading. I leaned back in the old porch rocker and looked up.

A tulip tree leaf, partly gold, mostly brown, struggled vigorously on its twig as if flagging my attention. It was not the proverbial last leaf but an actual next-to-last leaf.

Odd, I thought. There is no breeze, yet the leaf flails about. Then the slightest touch of moving air reached me.

The struggle was brief. The leaf lifted against October-blue and floated upward effortlessly. It danced and dipped and cavorted, then swirled high on a sudden updraft, fluttering wildly, as if trying to indulge in every last chance of freedom before it drifted to earth.

But the breeze died. The leaf tumbled, a wobbling, erratic fall, and settled gently between a clump of field grass and a ragweed stalk. Nudged by another breeze, it adjusted deeper into the grass, against the earth at last.

Six months earlier the leaf had emerged from a bud, tiny and tightly folded. As its cells expanded, its green blade spread wide, exposing a broad surface to the sun. Throughout spring and summer the leaf worked to combine air and moisture into food for the growing tree, using the sun's glowing energy and it's own green chlorophyll to perform this complex chemistry.

The leaf's broad blade shaded a fraction of earth below, a wee spot that crept across its private patch of forest floor each day as the sun crossed the sky.

The leaf sheltered and fed hosts of miniature creatures on its surfaces and within its tissues. One day, briefly, its stalk even held a singing hooded warbler.

As the calendar progressed, the leaf sensed changes—cooler temperatures, shorter periods of daylight. These triggered hormones which in turn stimulated a thin layer of cells at the base of its stalk to divide, some new cells added toward the leaf, some toward the twig.

Those on the leaf side of this layer began to disintegrate, causing an abscission, a cut-off, of food and water to and from the leaf. The leaf was being separated from its twig. Cells on the twig side became corky scar tissue over the wound where the leaf was separating.

With nutrients cut off, the blade could no longer replace its chlorophyll. Its green faded and revealed the leaf's yellow pigments. Yellow brightened daily as chlorophyll disappeared.

Thousands of vibrant yellow tulip tree flags flapped with every breeze, and thousands of tulip trees decorated mountainsides with cone-shaped crowns of yellow. Mixed with maple reds and pine greens, they contributed grandly to the autumn mountain spectacle. My leaf was one of these thousands. Then it began to brown. It dried and curled.

One day the impact of raindrops hastened the fall of some of its neighbors, and a stiff wind swept away others. A week of sunny weather dried separation cells in still others. The leaves dropped quickly.

But the dried leaf and its neighbor clung to the tulip tree, their separation layers not yet complete.

That I should be alerted by its papery rattling and happen to be watching as it left the tree and danced in the sky before meeting earth was nothing momentous, a remarkably obscure incident in the grand scope of nature.

But witnessing it was quietly satisfying, and I returned to my reading a tiny bit richer.

(See also "Seven Wonders in My Yard" in October on page 230.)

CATERPILLAR IN A HURRY

AS THE WOOLLY BEAR caterpillar rushes across my path, I can't resist asking, "What's the hurry?" The woolly bear and I both know the answer.

The caterpillar charges across my path and into the weedy field, exploring, investigating, seeking something special, but more on that later.

People enjoy the harmless woolly bear. Its dense blanket of woolly tufts makes it far more appealing than caterpillars that run about naked. Black on both its front and rear ends, with a rusty band between, it marches from September through November so intent it seems a true but humble symbol of determination.

For generations people have insisted on attaching significance to the size of the woolly bear's central band of rust. They claim if the band is wide, the coming winter will be milder than usual; if narrow, the winter will be more severe. But studies have never been conclusive.

Young woolly bears have more black than older ones. If a cold spell hits early, the caterpillars start hunting winter quarters early, while still showing more black. Perhaps this influences people's thoughts, but it results from existing conditions, not coming ones.

Did you ever try to pick up a woolly bear? Grins inevitably spread across faces of kids of all ages as they try this challenge. You think you have the woolly bear

Wooly bear caterpillars wander widely on the ground in late summer and fall, always seeming to be in a rush.

safely in your fingers or on your palm, and suddenly it's rolled in a tight ball and back on the ground. Because its hairs are not only stiff but elastic, the almost weightless ball just will not stay where you expect it to. Pity the perplexed and frustrated bird that tries to gobble one!

But skunks have woolly bears figured out. They roll and roll the ball until the hairs wear off, then consume the naked morsel.

To country folk who know this, "to caterpillar" is to silently yield to the unavoidable.

That "something special" woolly bears hurry to find is serious, a matter of life or death. The caterpillar must locate a protected place to spend the cold winter months or it will die. So it charges along, a naturally fast walker, looking for a crack or crevice, a leaf or log to hide in or under. Through winter it hibernates snugly.

In early spring, the rugged caterpillar charges into the world and eagerly chomps on grasses and clover and especially plantain leaves. Unlike many caterpillars, which are superbly picky about what plants they eat, woolly bears eat many kinds.

But eating lasts only a few days. It's time for change. The caterpillar spins silk threads as it makes its cocoon, and it weaves in hairs from its "fur coat," mak-ing the cocoon felt-like. Then, for about two weeks, all appears still.

Inside the cocoon marvelous changes turn caterpillar into moth, an Isabella Tiger Moth, *Pyrrharctia isabella* (formerly *Isea isabella*), small and dull yellow, with three bands of dark spots on its golden abdomen. The moth emerges from the cocoon in early summer, mates, and lays clusters of eggs on a variety of plants.

The new caterpillars hatch, feed, grow, and spin cocoons, and new adults emerge and lay eggs, a busy schedule! Caterpillars from this second summer brood are the ones we see in the fall hurrying around, seeking, investigating, the ones that will overwinter in cracks and crevices, logs and leaves.

I reverse the direction of several wandering caterpillars, and they turn right back again, determined to pursue their previously intended direction. This is great! I've discovered something new to me. But the next several caterpillars I reverse hurry off eagerly in the direction they'd just come from. My discovery is undone.

The more familiar I become with the ways of woolly bears, the more I enjoy our frequent autumn greetings to which we both know the answer, "Where are you headed in such a hurry, woolly bear?"

THE RARE TREASURE OF FALL COLOR

THEY COULDN'T BELIEVE IT. "Those photographs have been painted," insisted my cousins' hosts in India. "Trees can't possibly look like that!"

My cousins, visiting India in the 1930s, had shown their hosts some of those amazing new photographs called color slides. The slides displayed images of home in the northeastern United States, including brightly colored autumn trees.

"Did we ever have a time convincing them that trees do turn red and orange and yellow and that our photos weren't hand-painted fakes," recalled my cousins. "When they finally believed us, they exclaimed, 'We'd sure like to see trees so beautiful!'"

People who live where autumn means color tend to take foliage changes for granted, a beautiful but routine annual occurrence.

But leaf colors brighten the land in relatively few places in the world. Major sites in the Western Hemisphere include the Northeast and North Central United States (extending into southern Canada in the north and into the southern mountains), western mountains where yellow predominates, small parts of Alaska, and patches of southern South America. Parts of east Asia have autumn color—northern Japan is especially brilliant—and small bits of southwest Europe.

Marking these locations on a world

The attraction of colorful foliage makes autumn tourism big business in the southern mountains.

map helps you realize that a vast area of the world is left out. Forests with brilliant fall leaves are an obvious minority. Only a small proportion of the world's people can routinely experience fall color, and folks in the Southern Appalachians are among the fortunate. We host one of the top-rated shows.

One mid-October day during her first year in college in the North Carolina Piedmont, our daughter telephoned. "I need color!" she lamented. "Everything here is dingy yellow and brown. It doesn't seem like fall at all. May I come home this weekend?"

We took her along roads which wind

through western North Carolina hills and up to the Blue Ridge Parkway, where then, as now, mountain ash, sourwood, pin cherry, maple, blueberry, hickory, and birch painted the landscape. Oaks were starting to join the color splash with their magnificently rich hues.

Precedent had been set. An October color visit to the mountains became an annual event for our daughter. Then graduation and a job took her to other regions—colorful ones.

A Michigan man living in a non-color part of the country felt so strongly about autumn that he poured his woes into a magazine article. He complained of the severe affliction of "autumn doldrums"— a yearning to see a blazing maple or a sunny birch, to scuffle through gaudy leaves or look up into scarlet branches against blue sky. He had never fully appreciated what fall colors meant until they were missing.

We get impatient when carloads of "leaf watchers" clog our mountain roads, but we who live with color can sense their need for a few hours or days in these splendidly chromatic hills.

Much is written each year about whether the colors will be "good" because it's been wet or dry or frosty or balmy or some combination of these. Influenced mostly by diminishing daylight hours, leaves change despite weather, although it does affect the intensity of color change.

Red pigments develop most brilliantly when days are warm, causing leaves to manufacture much sugar, and nights are cold, preventing movement of the sugar to other parts of the tree. The spectacle of red—maple, black gum, sourwood, scarlet oak, dogwood, sumac—keeps mountain motels, hotels, and tourist homes filled to capacity each October.

Yellows are present in the leaves all season, but heavy green pigment in the leaves masks them. As shorter daylight hours and lower temperatures slow, food-making stops, and yellows show.

And such cheerful yellows! Light falling on an amber hickory outside a window can brighten a room as if glowing sunlight were pouring in. Who can feel gloomy when a bank of golden tulip trees gladdens a hillside or the clear yellows of birch burst out among green pines and spruce?

What a privilege to have autumn's annual spectacle so convenient and easy— and free!

Ragweed—Friend and Enemy

WRITERS use the adjectives "despised," "abhorrent," "obnoxious," and "pernicious" to describe a common plant. One even recommends its complete annihilation! Yet its scientific name, *Ambrosia*, means "food of the gods," a throwback to Greek and Roman mythology.

Perhaps the botanist who gave ragweed its scientific name was jesting, displaying a whimsical touch of humor, creating a name to puzzle and amuse plant enthusiasts for generations.

A more scholarly supposition states that our New World ragweed species merely tagged along on the name of a closely related European plant. Early scientists had already named that relative Ambrosia because of its delightful aroma, like the mythical ambrosia; but what a misnomer for our species.

Our Ambrosia's notoriety comes from its miserable effect on humans. Masses of airborne pollen from its flowers are a prime cause of hay fever. Only victims who have suffered this affliction can fully appreciate how genuinely the plant is hated, how gratefully the first killing frost is welcomed.

Why do I choose to write about this contemptible reject, this plant we call ragweed? And, why write of it in late October when it is dead?

Though condemned in early fall while it loads the air with pollen, ragweed redeems itself through other seasons. I discovered its positive qualities when I noted that white-throated sparrows feast on ragweed seeds. Curious what other wildlife dines on this generous seed supply, I researched a bit and tallied a list of over sixty birds and eight mammals that use the six or more species of ragweed in the United States, especially our common ragweed, *Ambrosia artimesifolia*.

White-throats have a fall-winter diet consisting of between 25 and 50 percent ragweed seeds. So does our local bobwhite. Many well-loved songbirds—goldfinches, juncos, towhees, and song sparrows—include ragweed seeds in up to 25 percent of their diet.

Ragweed leaped from my "Unloved Species" list onto my "Attracts Wildlife" list, and that fact lured me into pulling books from the shelf to learn more about this common weed. I'd always thought its lobed leaves quite lovely, but those green flower spikes, spewing out their pollen, conjured only evil wishes for the plant.

One day recently I stooped beside a miserably dried up, frost-killed ragweed at the edge of the vegetable garden. I'd read that it has two kinds of flowers—male flowers on the finger-like spikes that point upward rather artistically at its branch tips, and female flowers at the points where leaves join stems, the leaf axils.

Of course, the male flowers, having finished their job of producing clouds of pollen, are only remnants in this season, mere miniature inverted cups on a shriveled stalk, but female flowers have become seeds, important seeds for wildlife. They merited a closer look.

When I peered at one through a 10X hand lens, my instant reaction was WOW! I'd hate to swallow one of those! Sharp projections jutted from the exposed end of the top-shaped seeds. But wildlife apparently finds this no problem and gobbles them freely.

Ragweed has other benefits to boast. When bulldozers and scrapers denude the land, ragweed seedlings appear quickly and grow fast, greening the brown. Their ability to thrive in heavily disturbed soils and "waste places" is admirable. Ragweed holds the soil and starts enriching it.

But this eagerness to take over bare soil has earned the enmity of farmers, for ragweed cannot distinguish between bare, despoiled land and a newly plowed and seeded field. It charges in gallantly to take over. If plowed under before it sets seeds, however, it provides excellent "green manure," providing both organic matter and chemical enrichment for the soil.

My qualifications as a ragweed puller-outer once rated A+. I ripped it eagerly from my garden, severely condemning its presence. Now I tolerate it patiently, within reason, knowing that wildlife savors its seed supply, that soil improves and erosion diminishes where it grows.

Understood now, my old enemy inches its way into friendship.

Wind disperses ragweed's pollen, so its flowers have no need to attract insects by being showy or colorful.

The hognose snake's big bluff

THE PICTURES in animal books have always been impressive, showing the frantic creature making every effort to frighten its enemy. First, it flattens its head and neck grotesquely and blows ominously. If this fails, it rolls onto its back and opens its mouth, gaping horridly with tongue dangling limp. Certainly no enemy would be interested in a snake so obviously dead.

Beneath the pictures, vividly worded captions describe the hognose snake as ugly, yes, but fascinating. I've always felt unabashed admiration for its splendid bravado, the sheer pluckiness of a defenseless creature that bluffs so convincingly when faced with overwhelming odds that would make most animal enemies retreat.

Considering the bad name the hognose snake has among people, it works on us, too. The drama convinces many that this fearsome actor is dangerous, and to show our contempt, we give the snake an impressive array of derogatory names—puff adder, puff viper, and sand viper. The hognose snake is neither viper nor adder. It is absolutely harmless, but inevitably most people, steeped in misinformation, kill it.

Through many decades I yearned to witness this defense drama, but any hognose snake I chanced to see fled into weeds and brush.

Then one warm October afternoon,

A hognose snake lies on its back, pretending to be dead.

while wandering a mountain roadside with friends, a sudden ground movement near my foot froze us all. I signaled the others to approach, slowly, quietly, and we watched, engrossed. The wonderful creature had a short, thick body—for a snake. Its upturned snout gave away its identity. That hog-like nose helps root out worms which, along with toads and insects, are the snake's only diet.

It paused, undecided, then darted for the road bank. I brushed it quickly with a sheet of paper to discourage escape. Surrounded by people and unequipped for fighting, the terrified animal did the only thing it could—it bluffed. It coiled and reared, puffed to make itself look big, and blew. The first several inches of its head and body flattened and spread like a cobra. The mouth gaped formidably, showing pink and blue lining. It looked thoroughly dreadful and strived gallantly to scare us away.

"Leave me alone!" its actions screamed, almost begged.

But this was our first experience with a hognose bluff, and we had no intention of ignoring the opportunity. We knew the snake was not poisonous, so drew closer, fascinated. Suddenly its courage faltered. It made a dash toward the bank, but again my piece of paper blocked the way.

A hasty repeat of the blowing-flattening act failed to disperse our ominous though quiet circle of giants, so the frantic actor made a desperate move. With mouth still open, it writhed on the ground in apparent agony, thrashed, and convulsed. Then quietly it rolled onto its back, quivered dramatically, and "died"—absolutely motionless, tongue lolling, unresponsive even to nudges, a true life replica of the pictures in books.

Several times the snake's gentle persecutors righted it, amused how each time it instantly flipped onto its back, insisting on its lifeless pose, unaware that dead snakes do not change position. To it, a dead snake should be bottom side up!

We backed away—the bluffer deserved relief from its "enemies"—but watched from a distance, quietly excited by what we had witnessed.

For several minutes the snake lay still, then lifted its head and looked around. The world seemed benign enough, for it suddenly "came alive," righted itself, and glided off on its intended way, quietly victorious.

As the old adage goes, a picture is worth a thousand words—but the real thing is worth a thousand pictures!

(See also "Understanding Snakes" in July on page 169 and "Snakebite" in July on page 172.)

NOVEMBER

The Buzzing Board

DID YOU EVER hear a board buzz? Over a year ago we removed a narrow, eight-foot batten board from the house siding for a repair job. We set it in the porch corner and promptly forgot it.

One day I tossed it from porch to lawn.

"Today that batten gets nailed back on the wall," I announced, inspired to great accomplishments by superb weather, a perfect mountain day when spicules of ice needle across the birdbath at breakfast, but we shed sweaters by eleven o'clock.

When the batten hit the ground, it buzzed—noisily! Astonished, I hopped from the porch and approached it. Maybe I hadn't heard right. After all, boards don't customarily buzz. It said nothing.

With hammer in hand, I knelt over the batten to knock several nails back into position for renailing to the wall. On the first bang the batten buzzed vigorously. Then silence.

I tried tapping the wood lightly, and it buzzed just as wonderfully. This was fun! I lowered my head to listen more carefully, tapping intermittently. The puzzling sounds issued from about three feet of the strip's length.

I flipped the wood and spotted two perfectly round holes a bit greater than a quarter inch in diameter and several feet apart. Aha! I thought. Carpenter bees! They verified my suspicion promptly as, one by one, big, black bees spilled groggily from the holes, fourteen of them. Each crawled a moment as if shocked by emergence, then took off into space.

Why would adult carpenter bees be in a board in late fall, I wondered. I thought they overwintered as pupae.

When the exodus had stopped and all was quiet again, I tapped the batten to test for stragglers. It buzzed. More bees were in there, but no more emerged. I nailed the strip in place on the wall, holes to the outside, of course.

This seemed to be the end of the incident, but actually it was a beginning, for curiosity led me to investigate carpenter bees. The first delight was a new word— *xylophagous*, which derives from two Greek words for "wood" and "eat" and logically means "wood eating." Carpenter bees are classed as xylophagous insects, but they do not actually consume and digest the wood. They merely excavate it to make nests for their young.

They chew a hole, a perfect circle, into dead wood, either a tree, post, or unpainted building. We had watched them many times as they buzzed about our porch, intent on finding just the right spot to do their chewing. They found our unpainted door especially attractive and polka-dotted it with their work, much to our dismay.

The channel they excavate extends inward less than an inch, then turns abruptly down at a right angle, extend-ing from a few inches to a foot. The bee, a female, packs honey-pollen paste in the bottom, lays an egg on it, leaves a roomy space for the larva to grow, and seals the cell with tiny wood chips cemented with saliva. She repeats this up the excavation, making up to ten cells.

When the grubs hatch, they dine on the paste, and by the time the supply runs out, they are full size, ready to pupate, that resting stage during which they change into an adult. The literature I read stated that the bees overwinter within the pupal skin.

But I wondered if they overwinter within that skin as pupae or develop into adult bees but just do not emerge from the skin. No books gave the answer, no expert could say for sure. So we speculated.

Perhaps the warmth of a sun-filled corner of the porch encouraged premature development into adulthood, or perhaps it's not uncommon for carpenter bees to overwinter in their pupa cases after a change to adulthood.

An answer was not that important. The delight was in what happened. On a glorious November day, a board buzzed and bees poured out.

(See also "Bees and Wasps: A Matter of Waistlines" in January on page 17.)

MIGRATION MYSTERIES

"I ACQUIESCE entirely to your opinion that though most of the swallow kind may migrate, yet that some do stay behind and hide with us during the winter. But no man pretends to have found them in a torpid state in the winter." Gilbert White, noted naturalist of Selborne, England, wrote these rather stilted words to a fellow naturalist over two hundred years ago.

Other naturalists of his time firmly believed that swallows retreated under water in September. Even the noted Linnaeus was sure they hibernated in mud. White observed how "myriads of the swallow kind" gather in shrubs near the river. "This resorting toward that ele-ment at that season seems to give some countenance to the opinion of their re-tiring under water."

Throughout history the seasonal ap-pearance and disappearance of birds have perplexed and fascinated people. Hiber-nation in burrows, shrubs, or mud were all suspect as well as migration. Knowledge was scant and scattered, observations sel-dom recorded, and communications slow and infrequent.

Even Gilbert White questioned, "Is it likely that these poor little birds, hatched but a few weeks, should at that late season attempt a voyage almost to the equator?" He added later, "In regard to migration, what difficulties attend that supposition,

Brown thrashers leave the mountains in autumn,
migrating to southern United States for the cold months.
Photograph by J. R. Woodward

that such feeble fliers who never flit but from hedge to hedge should be able to traverse vast seas and continents!"

Now we know they do, but we still marvel.

If we lived in these mountains two hundred years ago, think how mystified we'd be at the spring appearance and fall disappearance of catbirds, thrushes, and swallows. Yet juncos and white-throated sparrows would vanish in spring and show up in fall. And some birds would stay around all year. Perhaps if we had a friend living in New Hampshire who wrote telling of juncos and white throats appearing in spring, we'd begin to see the picture.

Clues accumulated as communication improved. Seafarers reported familiar northern birds landing on their ships in southern seas. Heavy concentrations of birds gathered seasonally at narrow water crossings like Gibraltar. More and more naturalists visited tropical areas and found northern birds present in great numbers during seasons when they were absent in the North. Gradually they pieced together the puzzle of migration.

Modern communication and research have heaped us with knowledge on migration. We know that tiny hummingbirds fly across the vast Gulf of Mexico, that many warblers fly over water nonstop for up to three days en route to South America, that Arctic terns travel 22,000 miles to and from the Antarctic. Mountain quail in the western United States nest at 9,000 feet and walk down, often single file, to winter at 5,000 feet—then walk back in spring. Some tiny warblers as well as huge geese can fly as much as four miles high.

Most small birds travel by night. In still, autumn darkness their calls can often be heard. But what guides them? How do they know where to go? Experiments in planetariums show that indigo buntings orient by stars, starlings by sun. (European starlings migrate.) Yet radar studies reveal that birds can migrate under cloudy conditions. Ground features, wind directions, sounds, and magnetic fields may be guides. But consider young birds that fly south before their parents. How do these birds know where to go? No one knows for sure.

We might expect that insect-eating birds would fly southward when cold weather depletes the northern insect supply. But what urges them northward again, away from warm climes where insects continue to be plentiful?

Scientists explain some behavior in terms of hormones stimulated by the hours of daylight reaching the eye and with complex tomes on genetic codes. Yet even as more is learned, major mysteries persist.

As we fly across oceans like birds, mark birds with bands, colors, and radio transmitters, and consider the mush-rooming data on migration, we can still look at these feathery marvels as they hop or fly about our yards and wonder where they have been and how they got here. I want to ask each one, How do you hap-pen to be in this yard at this time?

(See also "Birds that Fly South—To Here" in February on page 25 and "The Challenge of Warblers" in April on page 96.)

WILDLIFE NEEDS COVER

MANY YEARS AGO we set a platform feeder about fifteen feet outside our window and supplied it with an inviting variety of grains and seeds. Surely birds in the woods and field around our new home would find it irresistible.

But though many birds eyed our feeder eagerly, only one titmouse braved the fifty-foot expanse between trees and feeder. It grabbed a seed nervously, dashed away, and did not return.

After several days of inactivity, Tom said, "We need cover."

"Is it that important?" I asked.

Within days we watched workers dig holes in a semicircle around the feeder, starting about eight feet from its pole. They planted a clump of birch and a variety of native shrubs, then collected their tools and drove away.

But we weren't the only watchers. Birds had found the project interesting, too. Even before the truck had pulled from the drive, a chickadee flitted into the birch and a song sparrow into a shrub. Others joined them quickly. Our restaurant was in business!

Is cover that important? It sure is. It's one of the three basic "musts" for attracting wildlife—food, cover, and water. A birdbath soon provided the last, and our feeder area thrived.

What precisely is cover? Simply stated, a safe place. Whether called shelter, refuge, or haven, it provides protection. Cover for birds can be trees, shrubs, wild weeds, a high hole, or a lake for waterfowl. Cover does not mean that the bird

Cover attracts birds. As they approach food and water, they need a place to perch for checking safety, and a place to escape to when danger threatens.

is actually hidden, only that it is safe.

Wildlife is shy. The farther it must wander from cover, the more vulnerable it is. It ventures into dangerous territory only if quick cover is nearby.

Someone is sure to mention that they get plenty of birds, particularly bluebirds, at their feeder without having any cover nearby. Such a feeder can have partial success, but only with a few species that relish open spaces, such as bluebirds, and even they prefer a tree or shrub to land in first.

Watch birds approach a feeder. They usually fly to some peripheral perch and check out the scene, then hop to a closer twig or sprig, always alert, keeping secure. To fly direct to the feeder requires courage, and if the gap of insecurity is too great, fear overcomes hunger. The bird refuses to visit.

Cover should not be so close that squirrels can climb it and leap to the feeder—unless you want to feed them, too. And dense shrubs too close—less than eight feet—allow cover for cats to crouch, awaiting an approaching ground-feeding bird.

We once knew an army colonel who led a Boy Scout troop. He guided them through many worthwhile projects, but despite our pleas, seemed dedicated to one misdirected pursuit. As a "conservation" project for the boys, he led them to "improve" several precious community woodlots by chopping out the shrubs and tall weeds.

His well-intended project, aimed at attracting wildlife, had the exact opposite effect. Wildlife stayed away. To him shrubs and weeds (cover) were "straggly, messy stuff." To wildlife they were room, board, and safety.

Natural growth offers the best plant diversity and should be preserved, if possible. The best cover is an over-grown thicket, a tangle of shrubs, vines, small trees, and weeds—including briers! It provides berries and seeds as well.

But maybe a tangled thicket does not fit your landscaping dreams. A mixed, well-chosen shrub border from a nursery, set around the edge of a yard, can provide good cover, though perhaps not with as much protection as a natural, thorny thicket. Allowing low shrub and tree limbs provides easy escape.

Much to the perplexity of a realtor, we once rejected a fine house because its trees and shrubs had been trimmed several feet above ground and all beneath was tidily mowed. We called it "that sterile place."

Overly eager trimmers often create yards the birds avoid. The trimmer forgot the critical trio for attracting wildlife: food, water—and cover!

(See also "Bird Feeder Etiquette" in December on page 277.)

Redwings and Thanksgiving

As we wound along a dirt mountain road in mid-November, Tom turned the car abruptly into roadside weeds beside a garden patch and stopped. A lone pick-up truck stood parked a short distance ahead, but when Tom hastily rolled down his window, he did not look toward the truck as I expected. He looked up.

The top branches of a tall tulip tree teemed with birds, hundreds of red-winged blackbirds chatting noisily. Every few moments they exploded into the air, circled the tree several times, then settled back onto its branches, boisterously.

I couldn't understand why Tom had stopped to watch this common behavior of these common birds.

Then I saw it. With each takeoff and landing, thousands of pale tulip tree seeds shook loose. Tiny blades pinwheeled earthward, a whirling shower. Orange glow from late afternoon sun turned them gold and glittering against a shadowed background. The air came alive.

When the last seeds of each shower struck the ground, the air seemed remarkably still, but only until the next mass uplift of redwings loosened another golden cascade.

"I wonder which bird decides it's time to take off?" I asked, not expecting an answer.

"And why? For exercise? For fun?"

"I'll bet the road feels like crunchy corn

Red-winged blackbirds collect in great flocks in late summer and fall,
often joined by mixed flocks of other "blackbirds."
Photograph by Arthur Morris/VIREO

flakes with those seeds all over it."

An old man diverted our attention. He stepped from the roadside garden patch and carried several late season broccoli heads to the parked truck. Before opening the door, he stared at us with open curiosity, looked up in the direction of our repeated watchfulness, then stared at us some more. His expression silently asked, "What are you folks watching?"

"Let's satisfy his curiosity," I suggested. Tom started the car, and we crept slowly toward the man.

"Afternoon!" he greeted us cheerfully.

"Hi! Nice broccoli you've got there," said Tom.

"'Tis, ain't it! Got some nice greens, too, and even a couple of 'maters still. It's been good for growin'."

"Guess you're wondering what we've been watching."

"Sure am."

"Those blackbirds up there, those red-wings." Tom described what we were enjoying, and as if rehearsed and presented just for the man, the birds repeated their performance, grandly. Seeds spun and glittered all around us.

"How 'bout that! Never saw that before. Sure is a mess of 'em. I hear tell them blackbirds'll do lots of damage. Guess they'll do it 'specially in a grain field."

He paused, looked at the road a moment, then up at the birds. "But y'know,

them birds belong here, too. They was put here for a reason. Problem is, we don't always understand what the reason is."

We stood with a man who probably had never sat through a course in biology or ecology, but he understood that each living thing has its role in the complex interaction of plants and animals in the natural world.

He knew that the things we call "bad" because we find them unpleasant and destructive—like ticks or poison ivy or cold viruses or corn worms—are not bad in the overall scheme. They are "good" or "bad" or "useful" or "harmful" only as they affect people. We categorize them only on the basis of our subjective point of view, overlooking their relationship with other living things. The old mountain man with broccoli in his hands understood a concept that eludes many more highly educated people.

As we approach Thanksgiving, feeling grateful for blessings, we feel special gratitude for a mountain man with broccoli—and for the troops of unsung people who, like him, understand our natural world.

And incidentally, I did get out of the car, and the road did feel like crunchy corn flakes!

More than "just a tree"

NOVEMBER has ended, and we complain. Summer greens are gone, fall colors are gone. Nothing's left but bare trees, gloomy, lifeless, dull. But wait.

Now's the time to admire the heart of a tree—not one pastel with new leaves, festooned with blossoms, or resplendent in red and gold, but a bare tree, stark with winter.

A bare tree is a basic tree, exposing fully its twiggy outline, its arching and angling, its patterns against winter sky— and its beauty. It no longer hides in its clothing; its true self is revealed.

To some people a bare tree is, well, just a tree, a thing with branches, trunk, and unseen roots, worth considering only as board feet or cord wood. They lump all tree species as one—tree.

But to others, each species has its own identity, its own special qualities and traits. Who could possibly think similar the oak and dogwood, the beech and sourwood?

Knowing a tree involves more than its visible parts, more than its chemistry or productivity. It includes sensing the spirit of its species. To inject a bit of fun into it, I play around lightly by giving each tree species a "personality."

Dogwoods, for example, seem comfortable and friendly, aiming to please in all seasons. Their winter twigs, artistic and simple, will be transformed by snowy blossoms in spring. Later, their fine summer foliage will turn rich red. Dogwoods in the tree world are like chickadees in the bird world—small, pert, and well behaved, busily spreading charm. Everyone loves a dogwood.

The oak is strength. One need only look up into the spread of an oak to sense its power. The old cliché, "the mighty oak," didn't just happen; might is synonymous with oak. And if a tree could be wise, what better candidate for wisdom than the oak. A tree of the mature forest, oak represents long life, experience, dependability. It is solid.

Oak keeps company with beech, but any other similarity ends there. Beech's smooth bark and tidy twigs with streamlined buds separate it from its rough and rugged neighbor. So neat, so classic and classy, the beech seems a tree refined, composed, well organized.

Some trees are stand-outs. Sycamore's bark sports a patchwork of grays and browns pieced in with creamy white that is strikingly visible from far away. "Notice me," it shouts with white arms reaching high. Sycamores enjoy the company of streams, lining their banks, revealing themselves from a distance.

The happy-go-lucky sourwood, a disorganized youth of haphazard style, presents an awkward silhouette that rarely merits admiration. Its red winter twigs sport ridiculous, shapeless lumps, supposedly buds. But when plumed with white summer blossoms or scarlet autumn foliage, the sourwood, irrepressibly handsome, becomes a prince and claims a special niche in any tree-lover's heart.

If trees have a messenger, surely swamp maple qualifies. A few spells of warmth signal its buds to burst early, announcing spring with crimson blossoms and seeds, often even before snows have vanished. Swamp maple is color, excitement, anticipation.

Stand beneath an arch of oak limbs—or dogwood, beech, sycamore, sourwood, or maple—or one of many other species—and sense their differences.

A tree is so much more than "just a tree."

(See also "Dogwood, A Special Mountain Beauty" in April on page 87.)

DECEMBER

Decorations on Rocks and Trees

THEY'RE ASTONISHING! They can live in temperatures hotter than 100 degrees above water's boiling point or colder than 100 degrees below zero.

They're the most northern plants in the Arctic, the most southern in the Antarctic, and the highest in the mountains at 18,000 feet in the Himalayas, yet they thrive in the tropics, too.

They can grow on bare rock or on soil so poor it supports no other plant life. Some are older than redwoods, others take a thousand years to grow an inch.

Great European and Asian dye industries once depended on them, and the famous soft colors of Harris's tweeds came from them. Wools dyed in them repel moths.

From early history they have been a basic ingredient in many cosmetics, and white wigs powdered with them were high fashion in colonial times.

Caribou and reindeer depend on them for food, and Arctic explorers survived near-starvation because of them.

As if all that weren't enough, they also decorate our trees and rocks.

What are these remarkably versatile plants? Surely they must be spectacular. Well, yes—if you have a magnifying glass in hand, for they are tiny, the lowly lichens (pronounced like'ens in United States, lich'ens in the British Isles).

Gray-green is their prime color, but some are fire-engine red or pumpkin orange. Some are brilliant yellow or creamy white—or blue or black or rust. A few of them have common names, ones that

Fruiting tips of British soldier lichen look as if they were dabbed in red. They reminded colonists of the British "red-coats."

reveal certain resemblances: goblet, coin, shell, fan, beard, pixie cup, map, script, toad skin, lung, spoon, ladder, British soldiers. Most have scientific names only.

Many people trying to identify lichens find it challenge enough just to group them into one of their three basic forms:

Crustose lichens often resemble smears of paint on rocks and tree trunks. Close inspection, however, reveals beautiful designs and colors. Flat and crusty, they cannot be pulled off.

Foliose lichens are attached only in spots, with loose, sometimes curly margins giving a leafy effect, like foliage. Some form decorative circular patches on rocks and tree trunks.

Fruticose lichens branch like miniature shrubs. They grow either upright, such as reindeer lichen and British soldiers, or hanging, such as old man's beard, which festoons trees.

It's fun to try to find all three forms growing on a single rock or branch.

The list of wonders about these strange plants goes on and on. For example, each lichen is actually a combination of two kinds of plants. Strands of certain fungi (relatives of mushrooms and molds) imprison microscopic cells of algae. The algae contain green chlorophyll that enables them to manufacture food, which they do for the fungi as well as themselves.

The superbly absorptive fungi, not to be outdone in good neighborliness, return the favor by keeping their captives supplied with water and minerals and safe housing. It's a handy, highly successful arrangement that benefits both algae and fungi—that is, lichen!

And lichens can create soil from hard rock and better soil from terrible soil. They secrete acids that break apart the rock, particle by particle, an effect particularly noticeable in old graveyards. Old tombstones' surfaces are often etched away by lichens until letters and numbers are barely readable or even obliterated.

When lichen debris mixes with rock particles, presto, new soil! Watch any scraped bank where subsoil cannot support most plants. Within a few years an inconspicuous film of lichen will color the soil surface, actively building soil until other plants can take over.

As if all these accomplishments weren't enough, science has found a new use for these lowly plants—as indicators of pollution. Many lichens cannot survive certain industrial fumes or excess auto exhaust. If they begin to die out in places where normally they thrive, the message is clear.

Lichens flourish at all elevations of the Southern Appalachians and in winter show up especially well.

Now when you find some lichens, you can have fun deciding whether they are crustose, foliose, or fruticose.

THE SURPRISE OF MOUNTAIN BALDS

"THIS IS A BALD?" our hiking companion asked in perplexity and surprise. He expected a bald to be bare—bare dirt or bare rocks, a natural reaction by someone who has heard the name but never experienced a Southern Appalachian mountain bald.

Hikers meet a bald unexpectedly. They walk through shaded forest as they climb the mountain, then suddenly emerge from forest into a broad, open space, often chilly and wet with fog—and lush with vegetation, but not trees. The sky arches uninterrupted; the view is often breathtaking. Surely this is timberline, that range above which trees cannot grow because of climate. Yet hikers can look farther up the mountain and see trees growing to the summit.

The southern mountains have no timberline. Even the highest North American mountain east of the Mississippi, Mount Mitchell in western North Carolina, would have to be more than one thousand feet higher to qualify for climatic timberline.

Early explorers in the Southern Appalachians described these strange, treeless, high elevation patches. Early settlers wondered about them but were too busy with wilderness survival to give much thought to why they were there. They called them "balds" because the shape was somewhat rounded and no trees grew.

They noted that some grew lush pasture grass, "grassy balds"; others were tangles of laurel, rhododendron, blueberry, and sand myrtle, "heath balds."

Settlers fortunate enough to live near a grassy bald developed a "cove-bald" way of life. They called their low elevation valleys "coves." During summer, farmers herded animals up to grassy balds for nature's free pasturage, meanwhile growing cove hay to be dried and stored for winter. The life was rugged but good.

Nature writer Maurice Brooks describes mountain balds as "islands in a sea of forest," emphasizing their uniqueness, their existence only in the Southern Appalachians from Virginia to Georgia, where there are about eighty of them. One might expect these treeless patches to be perched on the highest peaks, but they tend to be more often in the saddles between peaks.

From Newfoundland to New England, treeless areas in the mountains stay that way because of climate. But from Virginia to Georgia, treeless balds persist because of—well, no one knows.

From explorers to modern times, descriptions of balds abound with terms like baffling, perplexing, remarkable, and mysterious, words that express man's inability to explain the presence of these strange places.

Why are they there? If something destroyed the trees long ago, why, in a region suited for trees, has the normal succession from bare land to forest not progressed on balds?

Scientists as well as laymen have struggled with these questions for generations. Many factors, some tangled with each other, appear to be at work.

Perhaps fires started by Indians or lightning destroyed the humus, causing soil conditions incompatible with tree growth. Thick turf on balds reveals that the changes happened long ago, before the early settlers. Perhaps intense grazing by animals of early settlers kept forests from regenerating even in healed land. Maybe insect attacks played a role. No one knows.

Some of the finest balds lie in or near the Great Smoky Mountains of western North Carolina and eastern Tennessee. The names Andrews Bald, Grassy Bald, and Gregory Bald stir emotions in people lured to high places by balds. A hike to Andrews Bald from Clingman's Dome reveals a grassy bald once used as grazing ground—and a fine view. Grassy Bald on Roan Mountain, Tennessee, can be reached easily by car, where plant enthusiasts feast eyes on its varied flora— mountain alder, Gray's lilies, three-leafed cinquefoil, sand myrtle, lady and hay-scented ferns galore.

When we hiked up to Gregory Bald one spring, we emerged into a sea of red. Flame azaleas burst like bonfires in every direction. Our cameras worked and overworked in an inevitably disappointing attempt to capture the beauty. One cannot possibly print the beauty of a blooming heath bald on flat photographic paper or transparency film. One has to view the bald in three dimensions, with sky to add depth and brisk mountain air to supply atmosphere. Even the most superb photo of the scene cannot touch this.

To visit any bald impresses, but to visit Gregory Bald at flame azalea time is unforgettable.

CONIFERS FOR CHRISTMAS

FEW PEOPLE would thrill at the prospect of buying a conifer. But change conifer to Christmas tree, and everyone bursts with excitement.

A Christmas tree! The name is magic. A tree seems the very heart of Christmas—a gathering place for family and friends, a festive decoration, an evergreen symbol of life, hope, and love. Bringing home the Christmas tree truly starts the holiday season.

And all the while, a Christmas tree is simply a conifer, which means, literally, a cone-bearer.

Most cone-bearing trees have two kinds of cones—male and female. The male cones grow small and fragile, lasting only a few weeks before dropping off. Their mission—to dispense clouds of springtime pollen. It coats cars and porches with yellow dust and tickles noses; but most important, it settles on female cones and fertilizes tiny egg cells within.

When female cones receive pollen in spring, they are tiny and inconspicuous. Few people see them. Then growth begins, and eventually the cones stand out prominently. Their hard, woody scales clasp the winged seeds tightly, but when seeds ripen, the scales flare, spilling them generously.

In some conifers, young female cones stand upright on the twigs. Then nature performs a startling maneuver. As the

Nature loads a Christmas spruce with a magnificent mantle of rime.

seeds ripen, the cones slowly turn on the twig until they head downward. Now, when scales dry and flare, seeds beneath spill out easily, pinwheeling groundward.

People who teach about trees of the eastern United States enjoy using a trick question: "When you pick up a fir cone from the ground, what is its shape?"

Students familiar with fir cones eagerly describe their characteristic oval shape. Twinkle in eye, the teacher persists. "What time of year did you pick up your cone?"

No one can answer—and for good reason. You can't pick up a fir cone. Balsam firs of the Northeast and Fraser firs, the "balsam" of the Southern Appalachians, do not drop their cones. The cones ripen and disintegrate while still clinging upright on the top branches of the tree. The protective scales drop off, a few at a time, releasing their seeds. All that remains on the tree is the spindly stalk on which the scales grew.

Many people who live in the mountains have the pleasure of cutting a Christmas tree on their own land, the best way to acquire one. To bundle up, tramp in woods and fields, select that special tree, and return rosy-cheeked builds a host of glowing memories.

Next best is cutting one on a relative's or friend's land—with permission—or at a "Cut your own tree" place. Most people purchase a pre-cut tree at a commercial stand, but selecting it still brims with excitement and cheer.

Nearly fifty kinds of conifers are sold as Christmas trees in the United States, though any one area offers only about five or six species. Of the five native western North Carolina pines—white, Virginia, pitch, short leaf, and mountain—white pine is the favorite for Christmas.

Hemlock, with gracefully drooping branches and tip, looks lovely, but its short, flat needles drop quickly and its flimsy boughs do not hold ornaments well. Two native hemlocks grow here—eastern and the less common Carolina.

Spruce trees display classic Christmas tree shape. Our native species, red spruce, grows in high elevations and is a popular Christmas tree, but its needles dry quickly—and they prick!

I'm saving my favorite till last—the fir tree, the ultimate Christmas tree for me—lovely shape, glorious fragrance, and blunt needles that cling. My feelings run high. If it isn't a fir, it isn't a "real" Christmas tree. Two native firs grow in eastern United States—the balsam fir of the Northeast and the Fraser fir of the Southern Appalachians.

Sentiment, tradition, looks, practicality, and whim all influence the choice of a tree, and everyone's favorite is right. A Christmas tree of any kind warms the heart and bursts with festivity and spreads excitement. Take your pick!

DOVES AND CHRISTMAS

A dove with outstretched wings decorates a Christmas card on our table. Nearby lies a December magazine with a dove flying across its cover. Both doves are white and carry green sprigs in their beaks.

Christmas and doves go together. These birds symbolize peace, gentleness, and brotherhood—what Christmas is all about.

Just when doves acquired this symbolic association is hard to pinpoint. "Since ancient times" was one answer I culled from a fascinating assortment of literature. Because of a dove's harmless, affectionate ways and soft sounds, it is on record as a symbol of peace since early Bible times—six thousand years of service!

You may wonder how that green sprig got in there. During ancient wars, an invading army invariably hacked down economically important olive trees to weaken the enemy's resources for years to come. Therefore, the presence of flourishing olive trees, commonly represented by a sprig of olive branch, indicated a long period of peace. The combination of a dove carrying an olive branch, especially a white dove connoting purity, produced the ultimate symbol for peace.

Nowadays, Christmas card artists practice a bit of license, often modifying the olive branch into a sprig of needled ev-

*Since ancient times, the gentle calls and affectionate behavior of doves
of many kinds have imspired their use as symbols of peace.*
Photograph by J. R. Woodward

ergreen, itself a symbol of everlasting life that finds wide use in the Christmas season.

Religious interpretation of the dove and olive branch goes even deeper. The first significant mention of doves in the Bible is found in the story of Noah in Genesis. The dove flew from the ark, seeking dry land. When it returned with an olive sprig, the message was significant. Olive trees grow only at the lower elevations; the waters had receded.

In the New Testament, the dove once again becomes an important symbol. After Jesus' birth, Mary offered two sacrifices, according to the law. Had she been wealthy, she would have presented a lamb and a dove; but her offer was humble, as befit her means—two doves.

When Jesus was baptized by John, gospel writers describe the Holy Spirit descending upon him "as a dove." Hence, in Christian art, the dove became a symbol of the Holy Spirit, giving the bird even greater significance.

Four species of doves or pigeons were common in Biblical times in Palestine, and all still live in that region. The Southern Appalachians have only two species, both common—the mourning dove, so-called because of its mournful call, and the domestic pigeon. They belong to a worldwide family of birds the larger members of which we call pigeons, the smaller members doves. In an interesting twist, people usually call white pigeons doves.

Man bred domestic pigeons from the rock doves of Europe, which nest on rocky ledges. Therefore, pigeons take readily to the ledges of man's city buildings, country barns, and bridges. When we visited the windy, foggy coastal cliffs of Scotland to watch sea birds, we found pigeons living among puffins, murres, and kittiwakes. They seemed ridiculously out of place. We even laughed. Pigeons on wild sea cliffs, of all places. Pigeons with puffins!

But on second thought, these rock cliffs are the natural home of rock doves or pigeons. Those we see on city "cliffs" are out of place.

Breeders have produced domestic pigeons with a wild assortment of color combinations, browns, blacks, grays, white, even touches of green, but mourning doves are more subdued, feathered in soft, grayish brown. Like all their family, both have compact bodies, short necks, and small heads, and do not sip water and tip their heads back to swallow as most birds do. They poke beaks deep into water and suck it down.

Though the dove has symbolized peace for more than six thousand years, by the early 1800s human greed caused the slaughter and extermination of a third species that once lived in the Southern Appalachians, the passenger pigeon. Pioneers saw these not in millions but billions and caused the annihilation of every one.

The mourning dove is in no such danger. It frequents roadsides and forest edges, fields and backyard feeders, even open lawns—just about anywhere except in the hearts of towns or in deep forests. Being common and good to eat, it stays on the hunter's list in many states, considered a "game" bird.

All is not easy for doves, nor is it for peace. Yet the symbolism persists, and it is happy and heartening each year to have Christmas reemphasize the beautiful message of gentleness and peace and the greatest of all—love.

Bird feeder etiquette

STAND BACK at a cocktail party and watch people's behavior. When food appears, they work their chatting position closer and closer to it. Then one person will nibble a nut here, an olive there, while another, in quiet concentration, pokes carrots in a cheese dip. An impulsive guest grabs a handful of crackers and hastens away to sit down and munch on them. A few folks wait patiently until the table is free of guests, while others garrulously push in, intimidating less aggressive sorts. Some folks arrive singly, others in friendly groups, driving and arriving together. If you know the people, you can anticipate who will do what.

Birds at feeders bear a startling resemblance to people at parties. Certain ones arrive together. Some wait to eat, some grab food and run (fly). Some eat at the source, some eat it elsewhere. Each guest species has characteristic behavior patterns that can be anticipated.

Consider sunflower seeds, those year-round favorites. Cardinals and evening grosbeaks settle on the feeder and work on seed after seed, capably cracking and shelling hulls from kernels with strong, crushing beaks. Gold finches, purple finches, and siskins, with far less powerful beaks, patiently mouth the seed until the hull crumbles away and the kernel is free to eat. Chickadees and titmice hammer the hulls apart. Nuthatches fly off with a single seed and poke it into a crevice for later dining. Blue jays grab eight or ten seeds in a mouthful and fly off with them.

Some birds enjoy finely cracked corn, best scattered on the ground. Doves pick it with rapid jabs until they're full, then fly off to perch for a quiet period of digestion. Sparrows feed on the corn erratically. Blue jays try to scoop up a mouthful and fly off.

The delight of the birdwatcher intensifies as these behavioral differences among species become familiar and anticipated.

Even the positions of feeding are distinctive. Chickadees and titmice have nervous movement with frequent acrobatics. Nuthatches often feed head downward, swallowing upside down. Woodpeckers prefer a vertical position, sparrows more horizontal. Towhees flick outer white tail feathers as they feed. Bluebirds perch calmly, quietly.

Sparrows and towhees enter the feeding area from low shrubs, grosbeaks, goldfinches, and jays from higher branches, and the peck order is a never-ending source of entertainment—or often exasperation. Which species is more likely to peck its neighbor to drive it away? No absolute rules of belligerence exist; aggressiveness varies with season and individual bird "personality" as well as species.

Size has nothing to do with peck order. Large woodpeckers are notoriously timid, while a lone male hummingbird can be lord of the feeder, driving all others away. We once watched a yellow-rumped warbler dominate a feeder for over a week, though it never ate a morsel, and a normally peaceful bluebird became downright mean while his mate brooded eggs in a box nearby.

But usually, jays and evening grosbeaks top the peck order, though a feisty mockingbird can clear even them away, and tiny but belligerent siskins can make a jay reconsider.

Having a variety of feeders permits timid species to have a place to feed while aggressive diners flap and scrap boisterously.

Watching a feeder at daylight and dusk for several days and jotting down the order of arrivals and departures reveal that each species has a regular pattern of timing. Cardinals and song sparrows are the earliest and latest at our feeders.

Hasty glances to chalk up species lists are only a fraction of the pleasure of birds. Behavior watching offers the biggest—and most enlightening—proportion of the fun. But watch out! It's habit-forming.

(See also "Wildlife Needs Cover" in November on page 255.)

A GATHERING OF SNOWFLAKES

IT HAPPENED years ago, before we moved to the mountains, but each December the picture returns.

The white New England-style church with its graceful steeple stood on a hill in New Jersey. All year, lights flooded it at night so that for miles around it stood as a conspicuous and beautiful beacon of hope in an often confusing world. It could even be seen from out on the ocean.

One Christmas Eve our family joined others there for the candlelight service. At the end of the service, each person held a lit candle, joined in a Christmas hymn, and walked from the church— into a deluge of falling snow.

Already several inches blanketed the ground, and the fine spruce tree beside the church, festooned with multicolored lights, was heaped with soft mounds. Flakes floated from blackness above into floodlit brilliance.

People gathered around the tree, drawn by its white beauty and by the floodlit steeple that disappeared into snowflakes and night. They heard the organ inside exhilarating in "Joy to the World." The warmth of hope and love engulfed us.

"How gloriously Christmasy!" someone exclaimed.

Each year Christmas cards show snowy scenes of deer, rabbits, and birds, of

A narrow road winds through snowy mountains
and leads to higher elevations where superb winter vistas reward a traveler.

lanterned villages, old-fashioned sleighs, steepled churches, and laden evergreens. We sing of white Christmas and jingle bells and let it snow.

But what is snow, this stuff that thrills the kids and exasperates commuters, that dresses tired buildings and obliterates roadside trash, that outlines trees and cancels meetings?

Little was known about how snow formed until this century. In the late 1800s an eccentric dairy farmer in Vermont, Wilbur A. Bentley, paved the way, though his preoccupation with snowflakes was more as art than science. Famous as "Snowflake" Bentley, he took superb snowflake photographs over a period of fifty years. More than five thousand photographic negatives, taken in frigid air through microscope and primitive camera, survive as his unique, enduring monument.

In the 1930s and 1940s a Japanese physicist, Ukichiro Nakaya, found that snow crystals form around minute dust specks in the atmosphere. Vaporous water—in droplets so tiny ten thousand could fit in a line across the head of a pin—is attracted to this speck and freezes, building into a crystal, a "flower of the air."

Temperature and humidity in the upper atmosphere determine the crystal's shape. Though all are six-sided, none are exactly alike. The classic "star" snowflakes are less common than plate-like, needle-like, or columnar crystals.

And snowflakes are gray! With so many reflective surfaces (85 percent of their sunlight is reflected) and with so much air between them, amassed flakes appear dazzling white—or blue or lavender or pink, depending on lighting and time of day.

Dry, new-fallen snow is ten to twelve parts air to one part water; nearly a foot of snow melts into one inch of water! Even old snow is half air. Since air is one of the best insulators against heat and cold, snow serves as a blanket, protecting whatever it covers from bitterly cold temperatures. If a person is stranded outdoors in severe cold, insulating snow can save his life.

Most North Carolina mountain snows, however, are wet and heavy. Crystals clump together into oversize flakes. Folks familiar with dry snow miss the squeaky, crunching sounds as tips of crystals break when boots plod through the powder, but people do enjoy the infrequency of snow-storms in these southern mountains.

Snow falls on only one-third of the earth's surface. Many millions of people have never seen the soft beauty of falling snow nor charged downhill on a sled. They've never sat in a schoolroom and thrilled to see those first flakes nor packed a proper snowball. They've never spun their car wheels on ice, nor poured maple syrup over new snow for lip-smacking sweetness, nor rolled giant balls to make a snowman.

The all-time United States record for annual snowfall was set on Mount Ranier in Washington state in the winter of 1955/1956, an astonishing eighty-five feet! Our mountain county's record 1968/1969 winter added to a mere three and a half feet. Back in 1921, Colorado set the record for the most snowfall in twenty-four hours—seventy-six inches!

Our mountain county has had only four snowy Christmases since 1898, so the probability for a white Christmas is always low. But when snow blankets our surroundings, whatever the date, we can walk out into it to absorb its silence and beauty, its sense of peace on earth—and then, with a sigh, start shoveling.

(See also "Rime, Snow, or Hoar Frost?" in February on page 36.)

As snow lies about, rhododendron leaves curl,
signifying temperatures dipping into the teens.
The calendar is poised to slip into January,
seeming to end one mountain year and start
another. But the natural world does not determine
starts and finishes by a calendar. Each day blends
into the next regardless of dates, making changes
not always discernible even to the most meticulous
human observer. The sun controls, the natural
world responds, and its year proceeds
in a superb cycle—on and on and on.

REFERENCES

Appalachian Mountains

Blackmun, Ora. *Western North Carolina: Its Mountains and Its People to 1880*. Boone, NC: Appalachian Consortium Press, 1977.

Brooks, Maurice. *The Appalachians*. Grantsville, WV: Seneca Books, Inc., 1965.

Constanz, George. *Hollows, Peepers, and Highlanders*. Missoula, MT: Mountain Press Publishing Company, 1994.

Farb, Peter. *Face of North America*. New York, NY: Harper and Row, Publishers, 1963.

Frome, Michael. *Strangers in High Places*. Garden City, NY: Doubleday and Company, Inc., 1966.

Jolley, Harley E. *The Blue Ridge Parkway*. Knoxville, TN: The University of Tennessee Press, 1969.

Ogburn, Charlton. *The Southern Appalachians: A Wilderness Quest*. New York, NY: William Morrow and Company, Inc., 1975.

Birds

Bent, Arthur Cleveland. *Life Histories of North American Birds, 22 vols., 1919-1968*. Reprint, New York, NY: Dover Publications, 1962-1968.

Cruickshank, Allan D. and Helen G. Cruickshank. *1001 Questions Answered about Birds*. New York, NY: Dodd Mead and Company, 1958.

Griggs, Jack L. and the American Bird Conservancy. *All the Birds of North America*. New York, NY: HarperCollins Publishers, 1997.

National Geographic Society. *Field Guide to the Birds of North America*. Washington, DC: National Geographic Society, 1983.

Pasquier, Roger F. *Watching Birds: An Introduction to Ornithology*. Boston, MA: Houghton Mifflin and Company, 1977.

Peterson, Roger Tory. *A Field Guide to the Birds East of the Rockies*. Boston, MA: Houghton Mifflin Company, 1980.

Potter, Eloise F., James F. Parnell, and Robert P. Teulings. *Birds of the Carolinas*. Chapel Hill, NC: The University of North Carolina Press, 1980.

Simpson, Marcus B., Jr. *Birds of the Blue Ridge Mountains*. Chapel Hill, NC: University of North Carolina Press, 1992.

Welty, Joel Carl. *The Life of Birds*. Philadelphia, PA: W.B. Saunders Company, 1975.

Edible Wild Plants

Ipswich River Wildlife Sanctuary, Edible Wild Foods Committee. *Eating Wild*. Ipswich, MA: Massachusetts Audubon Society, 1971.

Harris, Ben Charles. *Eat the Weeds*. Barre, MA: Barre Publishers, 1968.

Ferns

Hallowell, Anne C., and Barbara G. Hallowell. *Fern Finder*. Berkeley, CA: Nature Study Guild, 1981.

Lellinger, David B. *A Field Manual of the Ferns and Fern Allies of the United States and Canada*. Washington, DC: Smithsonian Institution Press, 1985.

Mickel, John T. *How to Know the Ferns and Fern Allies*. DuBuque, IA: Wm. C. Brown Company Publishers, 1979.

———. *Ferns for American Gardens*. New York, NY: Macmillan Publishing Company, 1994.

Montgomery, James D., and David E. Fairbrothers. *New Jersey Ferns*. New Brunswick, NJ: Rutgers University Press, 1992.

Flowers

Brown, Lauren. *Weeds in Winter*. New York, NY: W.W. Norton and Company, 1976.

Fernald, Merritt Lyndon. *Gray's Manual of Botany*.

New York, NY: D. Van Nostrand Company, 1970.

Newcomb, Lawrence. *Newcomb's Wildflower Guide*. Boston, MA: Little Brown and Company, 1977.

Peterson, Roger Tory, and Margaret McKenny. *A Field Guide to Wildflowers*. Boston, MA: Houghton Mifflin Company, 1968.

Radford, Albert E., Harry E. Ahles, and C. Ritchie Bell. *Manual of the Vascular Flora of the Carolinas*. Chapel Hill, NC: The University of North Carolina Press, 1968.

Smith, Richard M. *Wild Plants of America*. New York, NY: John Wiley and Sons, 1989.

Stokes, Donald and Lillian Stokes. *A Guide to Enjoying Wildflowers*. Boston, MA: Little Brown and Company, 1984.

Stokes, Donald W. *A Guide to Nature in Winter*. Boston, MA: Little Brown and Company, 1976.

Frogs, Toads, Salamanders, and Snakes

Conant, Roger. *Field Guide to Reptiles and Amphibians*. Boston, MA: Houghton Mifflin Company, 1958.

Dickerson, Mary C. *The Frog Book*. New York, NY: Dover Publications, Inc., 1969.

Ellis, Harry. "A World of Salamanders," *Wildlife in North Carolina* (April 1979): 2-7.

Huheey, James E., and Arthur Stupka. *Amphibians and Reptiles of the Great Smoky Mountains National Park*. Knoxville, TN: The University of Tennessee Press, 1967.

Morris, Percy A. *An Introduction to the Reptiles and Amphibians of the United States*. New York, NY: Dover Publications, Inc., 1974.

Palmer, William M. *Poisonous Snakes of North Carolina*. Raleigh, NC: NC Department of Agriculture, 1974.

Petranka, J.W., M.E. Eldridge, and K.E. Haley. "Effects of Timber Harvesting on Southern Appalachian Salamanders." *Conservation* Biology (June 1993): 363-370.

General

Comstock, Anna Botsford. *Handbook of Nature Study*. Ithaca, NY: Comstock Publishing Company, 1931.

Howes, Paul Griswold. *Hand Book for the Curious*. New York, NY: G. P. Putnams's Sons, 1936.

Martin, Alexander C., Herbert S. Zim, and Arnold L. Nelson. *American Wildlife and Plants: A Guide to Wildlife Food Habits*. Reprint, New York, NY: Dover Publications, 1961.

Palmer, E. Laurence and H. Seymour Fowler. *Fieldbook of Natural History*. New York, NY: McGraw-Hill Book Company, 1975.

Snediger, Robert. *Our Small Native Animals: Their Habits and Care*. Reprint, revised and enlarged, New York, NY: Dover Publications, 1963.

Insects

Borror, Donald J., and Richard E. White. *A Field Guide to the Insects of America North of Mexico*. Boston: Houghton Mifflin, 1970.

Dethier, Vincent G. *Crickets and Katydids, Concerts and Solos*. Cambridge, MA: Harvard University Press, 1992.

Frost, S.W. *Insect Life and Insect Natural History*. Reprint, New York, NY: Dover Publications, 1959.

Hubbell, Sue. *Broadsides from the Other Orders: A Book of Bugs*. New York, NY: Random House, 1993.

Johnson, Warren T., and Howard H. Lyon. *Insects That Feed on Trees and Shrubs*. Ithaca, NY: Comstock Publishing Associates, 1976.

Klots, Alexander B. and Elsie B. Klots. *1001 Questions Answered about Insects*. New York, NY: Dodd Mead and Company, 1961.

Stokes, Donald W. *A Guide to Observing Insect Lives*. Boston, MA: Little Brown and Company, 1983.

Von Frisch, Karl. *Animal Architecture*. New York, NY: Harcourt Brace Jovanovich, 1974.

Invertebrates
(not insects)

Charnow, Jody Allen. "Millipedes Don't Really Have A Thousand Legs," *The Conservationist* (May-June 1982): 38-41.

Farb, Peter. *Living Earth*. New York, NY: Harper and Row, Publishers, 1959.

Mammals

Burt, William Henry. *A Field Guide to the Mammals*. Boston, MA: Houghton Mifflin Company, 1952.

National Geographic Society. *Wild Animals of North America*. Washington, DC: National Geographic Society, 1987.

Reader's Digest. *North American Wildlife*. Pleasantville, NY: The Reader's Digest, 1982.

Plants Miscellaneous

Bland, John. *Forests of Lilliput: The Realm of Mosses and Lichens*. Englewood Cliffs, NJ: Prentice-Hall, 1971.

Ellis, Harry. "Life on the Rocks," *Wildlife in North Carolina* (1989): 20-25.

Steward, F.C. *Plants at Work*. Reading, MA: Addison-Wesley Publishing Company, 1964.

Slime Molds

Barron, George. "Protoplasm in Motion," *Seasons* (Summer 1991): 20-25.

Sharnoff, Sylvia Duran. "Beauties from a Beast: Woodland Jekyll and Hydes," *Smithsonian* (July 1991): 98-103.

Trees, Shrubs, and Forests

Elias, Thomas S. *The Complete Trees of North America*. New York, NY: Van Nostrand Reinhold Company, 1980.

Jackson, James P. *Pulse of the Forest*. Washington, DC: The American Forestry Association, 1980.

Petrides, George A. *A Field Guide to Trees and Shrubs*. Boston, MA: Houghton Mifflin Company, 1958.

Platt, Rutherford. *1001 Answers to Questions about Trees*. New York, NY: Grosset and Dunlap, 1959.

———. *This Green World*. New York, NY: Dodd Mead and Company, 1947.

Symonds, George W.D. *The Tree Identification Book*. New York, NY: William Morrow and Company, Inc., 1958.

———. *The Shrub Identification Book*. New York, NY: William Morrow and Company, Inc., 1963.

Rogers, Walter E. *Tree Flowers of Forest, Park, and Street*. Reprinted New York, NY: Dover Publications, 1965.

Weather

Bentley, W.A. and W. J. Humphreys. *Snow Crystals*. Reprint, New York, NY: Dover Publications, Inc., 1962.

INDEX